SECOND EDITION

Legal Fundamentals

for Canadian Business

RICHARD A. YATES Simon Fraser University

Pearson Canada
Toronto

Library and Archives Canada Cataloguing in Publication

Yates, Richard

    Legal fundamentals for Canadian business / Richard A. Yates. — 2nd ed.

Includes bibliographical references and index.
ISBN 978-0-13-814042-7

    1. Commercial law—Canada—Textbooks. I. Title.

KE919.Y38 2010   346.7107   C2009-905166-4   KF889.Y38 2010

Copyright © 2010, 2006 Pearson Education Canada, a division of Pearson Canada Inc., Toronto, Ontario.

Pearson Prentice Hall. All rights reserved. This publication is protected by copyright and permission should be obtained from the publisher prior to any prohibited reproduction, storage in a retrieval system, or transmission in any form or by any means, electronic, mechanical, photocopying, recording, or likewise. For information regarding permission, write to the Permissions Department.

ISBN: 978-0-13-814042-7

Vice-President, Editorial Director: Gary Bennett
Sponsoring Editor: Alexandra Dyer
Marketing Manager: Leigh-Anne Graham
Associate Editor: Ben Zaporozan
Developmental Editor: Victoria Naik
Production Editor: Cheryl Jackson
Copy Editor: Catharine Haggert
Proofreader: Susan Bindernagel
Production Coordinator: Lynn O'Rourke
Compositor: Aptara® Inc.
Art Director: Julia Hall
Cover and Interior Designer: Miriam Blier
Cover Image: Randy Faris/Corbis

The information in this text is intended to be current and accurate. It is not, however, intended to be comprehensive or complete, and therefore should not be relied upon in making decisions on particular legal problems. In such cases, the services of a competent professional should be sought. The authors and publishers expressly disclaim any responsibility for any liability, loss, or risk, personal or otherwise, that is incurred as a consequence, directly or indirectly, of the use and application of any of the contents of this book.

1 2 3 4 5   13 12 11 10 09

Printed and bound in the United States of America.

This edition of *Legal Fundamentals* is dedicated to the 10 grandchildren
(all girls except for 9 of them) that have been born since I
envisioned the book. These future
scholars and authors are

Milo, Connor, Ryan, Rowan, Euan, Aidan, Rhys, Oliver , Lukas, and Katie.

BRIEF CONTENTS

CONTENTS

PREFACE

This, the second edition of *Legal Fundamentals for Canadian Business*, provided an opportunity for "sober second thought," as I responded to helpful reviewers and student reactions to the first edition of the text. The chance to re-evaluate, revise, and update is welcome, and in law especially timely as social, political, and judicial changes continue to develop and amend the law. It was still important to maintain the original purpose of the text, which was to be a somewhat restrained approach to business law so that instructors in colleges and universities who wanted a solid introduction to the law could also have the time to focus on special areas of the law or tailor the material to fit their needs. Thus I have retained the original introductory material, and carefully updated the law where necessary, clarifying some discussions and substituting new cases to illustrate the content. At the request of reviewers I have switched some of the content around in the latter chapters by reducing and moving the contents of the former Chapter 10. An introductory discussion of administrative law can now be found in Chapter 1 after the section on litigation and alternate dispute resolution. Environmental law is now covered in Chapter 8 with property law. A discussion of competition law seemed to fit nicely in Chapter 5 with legislation in the marketplace. With the opportunity to write a new concluding chapter, I have followed the counsel of many instructors to include new discussions on ecommerce and Internet law along with global commerce. It was an interesting challenge to tackle both of these subjects and restrain myself from devoting an entire book to each of them.

The search for new, interesting, and appropriate cases is one of the most challenging tasks in revising a law text. This edition is no exception. I am indebted to the editors of the *Lawyers Weekly*, which provides regular digital updates of what is happening in Canadian courts with sometimes amusing and always stimulating reviews of the law. That I can quickly scan the indexes of this publication and other online services using their links to the official court reports is a tremendous boon. I hope that this transfer of information to the student reader proves as beneficial.

An aid for students has been added to Chapter 1: a standard method has been developed to analyze legal cases and Table 1.1 sets out one variation of that approach to help students find the essential elements of a case. I have added **learning objectives** at the beginning of each chapter to help students grasp what they will encounter in the chapter and key terms at the end to assist them to remember essential content.

PREFACE TO THE FIRST EDITION
Approach

Although some may raise their eyebrows at yet another business law text in an already crowded field, I have observed that most of the texts currently used are too extensive or detailed for some courses. I have attempted in this text to create a shorter book (only 10 chapters) without sacrificing essential content. I have found that the text usually drives the course, and many instructors complain that they don't have enough time in a 14-week term to deal with all of the subjects they would like to cover. Sometimes instructors teach a course that must be delivered in an even more condensed time frame. Some teach specialized courses in marketing, computers, finance, and the like and find that they have to spend so much time on a general introduction to business law that they don't have time to focus on the law that affects the specialized topic that is the primary objective of the course. This text gives business law instructors the flexibility to deal with all of the topics, to customize their course by supplementing it with additional material, and/or to concentrate on an area of specialization.

Many instructors feel a pressing need to deliver the introductory and foundation material efficiently so that there is enough time left to cover more advanced material. Hence, in this text there is only one introductory chapter setting out the history, institutions, and litigation processes used in Canada, only one chapter on torts, and three chapters on contracts. A great deal of effort has gone into making these chapters as efficient as possible, while still covering the essential concepts and rules. The remaining five chapters deal with more advanced and technical information—everything from the legal issues regarding agency and employment to the timely issues of intellectual property—and have not been simplified to the same extent as the first five. Although somewhat condensed here, these topics don't really lend themselves to abbreviation.

Features

I've incorporated several features in the text to engage students. Visuals are used to help students grasp concepts quickly.

Throughout the text there are **Case Summaries** designed to illustrate the legal concepts being discussed. Such case studies are the heart of any business law course and create a dynamic practical environment for a subject that, without them, would be dry and uninspiring at best.

For some I have also included **diagrams** that illustrate the legal relationships in the case. There are also a number of **figures** and **tables** included throughout the text; these are designed to clarify and summarize information so that it's easily accessible to students.

The **Cases for Discussion** at the end of each chapter are based on actual court reports. I have not included the decisions so that the cases can be used in assignments or for classroom discussions. Instructors have access to the actual outcomes in the Instructor's Manual, or students can follow the reference to discover the outcome for themselves.

Also at the end of each chapter, **Questions for Further Discussion** can be used in class or group discussions. They raise issues with respect to the topics discussed. There are no solutions provided as they are intended to point out the dilemmas often faced by those who make or enforce these legal principles.

54 Legal Fundamentals for Canadian Business

Cases for Discussion

1. *Lewvest v. Scotia Towers Ltd.* (1981), 126 D.L.R. (3d) 239 (Nfld. T.D.).

    Scotia Towers Ltd. was constructing a building in St. John's, Newfoundland, and in the process a crane they were operating often swung over the adjoining property owned by Lewvest. Lewvest had not given permission for such an intrusion and sued. Explain the nature of Lewvest's complaint, the arguments on both sides, and the appropriate remedy if the action is successful.

2. *Malette v. Shulman* (1990), 67 D.L.R. (4th) 321 (Ont. C.A.).

    Mrs. Malette was seriously injured in an automobile accident, and at the hospital Dr. Shulman determined she was in need of a blood transfusion to save her life. The nurse, however, discovered a card in the patient's purse indicating she was a Jehovah's Witness.

Questions for Further Discussion

1. Individuals are sometimes convicted of a crime and then sued in tort for the same conduct. Is it fair or just for one person to face trial twice for the same thing?

2. Is the reasonable person test appropriate for determining what standard of behaviour should be imposed in a negligence action? Would it be more appropriate to determine negligent conduct on the basis of the average person or some other test?

3. In Canada when someone produces a defective product or performs an imperfect service he or she must be shown to have been careless—to have fallen below a community-established standard of behaviour (the reasonable person test)—before he or she can be found liable for negligence. When a person is suing for breach of contract, it is unnecessary to establish fault; the breach is enough. Consider whether the requirement to establish fault where someone's conduct causes another injury ought to be abandoned in a tort action. In other words, should it be enough to show that one person caused the injury for him or her to be liable?

4. Freedom of expression has been guaranteed in our constitution. Yet when people criticize public officials and other public figures, they can be sued for defamation, even if they believe what they say is true. Do you think we should adopt an approach similar to that

Questions for Student Review

1. What is a tort? Distinguish between a tort and a crime, and explain when a tort can also constitute a crime.

2. Explain vicarious liability and any limitation on its availability.

3. Distinguish between intentional and inadvertent torts.

4. Explain what is meant by a reasonable person and the reasonable person test.

5. Distinguish between assault and battery, and explain how this distinction might be affected by self-defence.

6. Explain what is required to establish a false imprisonment.

7. Why is trespass to land considered an intentional tort? Under what conditions does a trespass occur? What is a continuing trespass?

8. Explain the obligation of an owner or occupier of land for injuries suffered by a trespasser.

9. Under what circumstances might one neighbour sue another for nuisance?

10. What is meant by defamation? What is an innuendo?

11. Distinguish between libel and slander. Why is the distinction important?

Finally, the **Questions for Student Review** are designed to help students review the chapter material. As they respond to the questions, referring back to the content of the chapter, students should develop a good grasp of the concepts and principles contained in the chapter.

Supplements

Legal Fundamentals for Canadian Business is accompanied by a comprehensive supplements package.

Instructor's Manual   This manual includes a number of aids, including outlines of how lectures might be developed, chapter summaries, answers to review questions, and suggestions for conducting classroom discussions. The court decisions for the end-of-chapter cases are also provided, and sample examination questions are included for each chapter.

TestGen   This supplement contains a comprehensive selection of multiple-choice, true/false, and short essay questions with answers. Each question has been checked for accuracy and is available in TestGen format. This testing software permits instructors to view and edit the existing questions, add questions, generate tests, and distribute the tests in a variety of formats. Powerful search and sort functions make it easy to locate questions and arrange them in any order desired. TestGen also enables instructors to administer tests on a local area network, have the tests graded electronically, and have the results prepared in electronic or printed reports. TestGen is compatible with Windows and Macintosh operating systems.

PowerPoint® Presentations   This supplement provides a comprehensive selection of slides highlighting key concepts featured in the text to assist instructors and students.

Instructor's Resource CD-ROM   This supplement includes electronic files for the complete Instructor's Manual; the TestGen testbank; and the PowerPoint Presentations. These instructor supplements are also available for download from a password protected section of Pearson Canada's online catalogue (at vig.pearsoned.ca). See your Pearson Canada sales representative for details and access.

Companion Website   To supplement the book, we have prepared a Companion Website (www.pearsoned.ca/yates) for instructors and students. This comprehensive resource includes Provincial Supplements for British Columbia, Alberta, Saskatchewan, Manitoba, and Ontario, covering special topics for each of these areas. These topics include a brief overview of business legislation specific to the province, along with links to relevant cases, legislation, and additional resources. The Companion Website also features Chapter Summaries, Quizzes, a Glossary, and

Weblinks. Students can also use the Companion Website's Grade Tracker function to record and review their own progress on the self-regulated quizzes.

Technology Specialists Pearson's Technology Specialists work with faculty and campus course designers to ensure that Pearson technology products, assessment tools, and online course materials are tailored to meet your specific needs. This highly qualified team is dedicated to helping schools take full advantage of a wide range of educational resources, by assisting in the integration of a variety of instructional materials and media formats. Your local Pearson Education sales representative can provide you with more details on this service program.

CourseSmart for Instructors CourseSmart goes beyond traditional expectations–providing instant, online access to the textbooks and course materials you need at a lower cost for students. And even as students save money, you can save time and hassle with a digital eTextbook that allows you to search for the most relevant content at the very moment you need it. Whether it's evaluating textbooks or creating lecture notes to help students with difficult concepts, CourseSmart can make life a little easier. See how when you visit www.coursesmart.com/instructors.

CourseSmart for Students CourseSmart goes beyond traditional expectations–providing instant, online access to the textbooks and course materials you need at an average savings of 50%. With instant access from any computer and the ability to search your text, you'll find the content you need quickly, no matter where you are. And with online tools like highlighting and note-taking, you can save time and study efficiently. See all the benefits at www.coursesmart.com/students.

Navigate to the book's catalogue page to view a list of available supplements. See your local sales representative for details and access.

ACKNOWLEDGMENTS

I would like to acknowledge the help of all those who have assisted in making the production of this work possible. My wife, Ruth, has helped, encouraged, and supported me in more ways than I can list. I wish to thank as well the reviewers whose suggestions and criticisms were invaluable as the text was honed and shaped into its final form, including:

Michael Bozzo, Mohawk College
John Cavaliere, Sault College
Odette Coccola, Camosun College
Julia Dotson, Confederation College
Brian Furzecott, Georgian College
Brian Murray, Holland College
David L. Orr, Lethbridge College
Fran Smyth, Seneca College
Craig Stephenson, Mohawk College

Also, my thanks to the firm, guiding hands of all those at Pearson, who supported me throughout the long gestation period of this text, including Gary Bennett, Vice-President, Editorial Director, Business and Economics; Alexandra Dyer, Sponsoring Editor; Ben Zaporozan, Associate Editor; Victoria Naik, Developmental Editor; Cheryl Jackson, Production Editor; and Lynn O'Rourke, Production Coordinator.

A Great Way to Learn and Instruct Online

The Pearson Canada Companion Website is easy to navigate and is organized to correspond to the chapters in this textbook. Whether you are a student in the classroom or a distance learner you will discover helpful resources for in-depth study and research that empower you in your quest for greater knowledge and maximize your potential for success in the course.

[www.pearsoned.ca/yates]

Jump to... http://www.pearsoned.ca/yates ⇕ Home | Search | Help | Profile

Home >

Companion Website

Legal Fundamentals for Canadian Business, Second Edition, by Richard A. Yates

Student Resources

The modules in this section provide students with tools for learning course material. These modules include:

- Chapter Summaries
- Multiple Choice Questions
- True/False Questions
- Weblinks
- Glossary

In the quiz modules, students can send answers to the grader and receive instant feedback on their progress through the Results Reporter. Coaching comments and references to the textbook may be available to ensure that students take advantage of all available resources to enhance their learning experience.

In addition to the self-study material, students will also find comprehensive Provincial Resource Supplements for British Columbia, Alberta, Saskatchewan, Manitoba, and Ontario. These modules highlight information, case material, and weblinks relating to the specific business legislation found in each featured province.

Instructor Resources

A link to this book on the Pearson Education Canada online catalogue (www.pearsoned.ca) provides instructors with additional teaching tools. Downloadable PowerPoint® Presentations and an Instructor's Manual are just some of the materials that may be available in this section. Where appropriate, this section will be password protected. To get a password, simply contact your Pearson Canada Representative or call Faculty Sales and Services at 1-800-850-5813,

Chapter 1
The Canadian Legal System

Learning Objectives

- Define what law is

- Identify where Canadian laws come from

- Distinguish the components of Canadian law

- Explain the nature and role of the *Charter of Rights and Freedoms*

- Describe the structure of the courts in Canada

- Illustrate the litigation process

- Outline the processes of trial and judgment

- Explain the function and use of alternative methods for resolving disputes

- Define administrative law and explain when and how it is used

- Describe the aspects of criminal law that should be of concern to a business person

An understanding of law and the legal system in Canada is essential for the business person. Business activities, like other forms of human endeavour, involve significant human interaction. Whether you are a manager, a consultant, a professional, or a consumer, you must deal with suppliers, employees, creditors, lawyers, insurance agents, landlords, accountants, shareholders, senior managers, as well as government agencies. All of these relationships carry with them important rights, responsibilities, and obligations. These rights and obligations take the form of legal rules and to participate in business it is important to understand them. As with other aspects of business, it is not good enough to simply leave legal matters in the hands of the professionals. A basic understanding of the law is necessary to manage the legal affairs of a business and to be a knowledgeable client. This text reviews both the structure of the Canadian legal system and the principles that most affect people in their business dealings. The first chapter examines the underpinnings of the legal system and some basic Canadian institutions upon which the commercial legal environment is built.

Knowledge of law is vital for business

WHAT IS LAW?

Most people think they understand what law is, but, in fact, an accurate definition is difficult to come by. For the purposes of this text, **law** is defined as the body of rules that can be enforced by the courts or by other government agencies. There are serious problems even with this simple definition, but from a practical standpoint and for the purposes of this book,

Law consists of rules enforceable in court or by other government agencies

which is primarily about business law, law consists of rules with penalties that are likely to be enforced either by the courts or other agents of government. A business person should keep in mind that having their problems resolved by the courts or regulatory enforcement agencies is rarely an indication of success and every effort should be made to avoid litigation and settle disputes without resorting to these institutions. It is hoped that understanding the rules discussed in this text will help you to prevent and resolve legal problems.

It is especially important for business people not to confuse law and morality. The impetus for any given legal rule can vary from economic efficiency to political expediency. It may well be that the only justification for a law is historical, as in "it has always been that way." Hopefully, legal rules express some moral content, but no one should assume that because they are obeying the law, they are acting morally. Ethics has become an important aspect of any business education and with recent, high-profile incidents of corporate abuses such as the Enron and WorldCom scandals, as well as the corrupt practices that led to the recent worldwide financial crisis, the topic of ethics has become a major area of discussion both at the academic and the practical levels. The law is an important consideration in this discussion, if only to understand that law does not define ethical behaviour, and that business people should rise above the minimal requirements of the law. This text will not normally deal directly with such moral issues, but they will be raised in the Questions for Further Discussion at the end of each chapter.

While this text is most concerned with **substantive law** (the rules determining behaviour), we must also be aware of the other great body of law that is concerned with how legal institutions work (**procedural law**). While there will be some examination of **public law**, where the dispute involves the government (including criminal law and government regulation), the main objective of this text is to examine the rules governing business interactions. **Private** or **civil law** is comprised of the rules that enable an individual to sue a person who has injured them. While only a small proportion of such disputes ever get to court, legal rules are developed in the cases that do. Knowing that the principles established in court decisions will be enforced in subsequent judicial cases helps parties to resolve their disputes without actually going to trial.

SOURCES OF LAW

Each province was given the right to determine its own law with respect to matters falling under its jurisdiction. Since private law is a provincial matter, it is not surprising that the English-speaking provinces adopted the law used in England while Quebec adopted the French legal system based on the Napoleonic Code. In fact, the French **Civil Code** traces its origins to the Romans and a unique characteristic is that it is a codified body of rules stating general principles that are applied by the courts to the problem before them. In this system the judge is not bound by precedent (following prior decided cases), but must apply the provisions of the Code. For example, when faced with the problem of determining liability in a personal injury case, the judge would apply section 1457 of the Quebec *Civil Code*, which states:

> Every person has a duty to abide by the rules of conduct which lie upon him, according to the circumstances, usage or law, so as not to cause injury to another. Where he is endowed with reason and fails in this duty, he is responsible for any injury he causes to another person and is liable to reparation for the injury, whether it be bodily, moral or material in nature.

Law and morality should not be confused

Quebec uses the **Civil Code**

When a person drives carelessly and injures another in Quebec, the judge would apply this provision and order that the driver pay compensation. The decisions of other judges may be persuasive, but the duty of a judge in Quebec is primarily to apply the Code. Most other countries in the world use a variant of this codified approach to law, and it is this codification that makes the law predictable in those countries.

The other Canadian provinces and the territories adopted a system of law derived from England, referred to as the **common law**. The unique aspect of the common law system is that instead of following a written code, the judge looks to prior case law. When faced with a particular problem, such as the personal injury situation described above, a common law judge would look at prior cases (normally brought to the judge's attention by the lawyers arguing the case), and choose the particular case that most closely resembles the one at hand. The judge will determine the obligations of the parties on the basis of that **precedent**. Of course, there is a complex body of rules to determine which precedent the judge must follow. Essentially, a case involving the same issue decided in a court higher in the judicial hierarchy is a binding precedent and must be followed. Thus a judge in the Provincial Court of Saskatchewan is bound to follow the decision of the Court of Appeal of that province, but not the decision of a Court of Appeal in New Brunswick, which is in a different judicial hierarchy. That decision may be persuasive but is not binding. When the judge prepares a report of the case, a considerable portion of the decision is usually an explanation of why the judge chose to follow one precedent rather than another. This process is referred to as **distinguishing cases**. The system of determining law through following precedent in our legal system is referred to as *stare decisis*. Following prior decisions requires that judges and lawyers know and understand the implications of many cases that have been heard in the courts.

Other provinces use common law

Common law is based on cases

Judges are bound to follow prior cases

Reports of cases are normally long and complex documents. To recall the significant aspects of the case quickly, students of the law use case briefs to summarize these reports. The following table describes the important elements of a case brief. Most of the cases summarized in this text will include these components, although because the cases are used to explain a principle we may not specify each of them. When you read the case summaries try to extract the information using the following elements.

Case Summary 1.1 *R. v. Clough*[1]

Provincial Supreme Court Judge Must Follow Appeal Court Decision

Ms. Clough was sentenced by a British Columbia Supreme Court judge to a nine-month jail term for possession of cocaine for the purposes of trafficking. That trial judge refused to follow a Court of Appeal case in a similar matter where a conditional sentence had been imposed (no prison time), claiming that case had been "wrongly decided." The British Columbia Court of Appeal overturned his decision and imposed a conditional sentence stating that the trial judge ". . . was bound by the rule of stare decisis to accept the decisions of this court to the extent that they may apply to the case before him."

Judges who are lower in the hierarchy are bound to follow the decisions of the courts above them, even when they think those above them are wrong. Although this is a criminal case, not a business one, it illustrates how a lower court must follow the decision of a higher court, a reminder to business people involved in a legal dispute that a previous decision in a similar case will require the judge to make the same decision when he or she hears the matter.

---

[1] 2001 BCCA 613, [2001] B.C.J. 2336 (B.C.C.A.).

Table 1.1 Elements of a Case Brief

Parties This identifies the parties to the action and distinguishes the plaintiff and the defendant (**appellant** or **respondent** at the appeal level). When the letter R is used to signify one of the parties it refers to Rex or Regina, the king or queen, who symbolize the state or government, meaning this is a public law case in which the Crown or state is prosecuting the defendant. When both parties are named as individuals or companies it is a private law case where the plaintiff is suing the defendant.

History of the Action This lists the various courts that have dealt with the matter and the decisions at each hearing, that is at the trial level, appeal level, and Supreme Court of Canada.

Facts This is a brief description of what happened to give rise to the dispute between the parties. Only the facts necessary to support the decision are usually included in a brief.

Issues These are the legal questions that the court must consider to decide the case.

Decision This is the court's decision, either in favour of or against the plaintiff or appellant.

Reasons This is a summary of the reasons for the decision, and is usually a response to the issues raised. In this text this is the most important part of the judgment because the case will normally be used as an example illustrating the principle of law.

Ratio This is the legal principle established by the case and is usually only included when it will be binding on other courts.

Common law developed by common law courts

    The common law evolved from case decisions made in three common law courts set up under the king's authority during the Middle Ages in England. This body of judges' decisions continued to develop in England and then in Canada. English-speaking provinces adopted the common law at different times in their history. British Columbia declared that the law of England would become the law of that province as of 1857 and Manitoba did the same in 1870. Since adopting the common law of England, the courts of each province have added their own decisions, creating a unique body of case law particular to each province (see Figure 1.1).

Equity developed by Court of Chancery

    A complicating factor in the development of the common law in England was the creation of the **law of equity** by the **Courts of Chancery**. For both political and institutional reasons, the common law courts of England became harsh and inflexible, often failing to provide either a right to sue or remedies adequate to satisfy the basic demands of justice. To provide relief, the practice developed of petitioning the king to overcome these problems. Since, in theory, the king was the source of power for these courts, he also had the power to make orders overcoming individual injustices caused by their shortcomings. This task was soon assigned to others and eventually developed into the Court of Chancery. The common law courts and the Courts of Chancery were often in conflict and were eventually merged in the 19th century, but the body of rules developed by the Courts of Chancery (known as the Law of Equity) remained separate. Today, when we talk about judge-made law in our legal system, we must differentiate

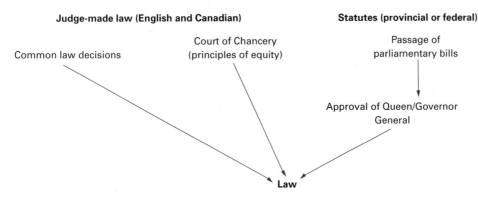

Figure 1.1 Sources of Law

Law applied in courts today is derived from judge-made law (common law and equity) and from statutes including regulations at both federal and provincial levels.

between common law and the law of equity. For example, if someone erected a sign that encroached on your property, you could claim trespass and ask a court to have it removed. Monetary compensation is the normal common law remedy to trespass, but that would not solve this problem. An order to remove the sign would require an injunction, which is an equitable remedy developed by the Courts of Chancery. Equity, then, is a list of rules or principles from which a judge can draw to supplement the more restrictive provisions of the common law.

The third body of law used in our courts is derived from government **statutes**. As a result of the English Civil War, the principle of **parliamentary supremacy** was firmly established with the consequence that any legislation passed by Parliament overrides judge-made law, whether in the form of common law or equity. Today in Canada most new law takes the form of statutes enacted by either the federal parliament or the provincial legislatures. Since statutes override prior judge-made law, the judges will only follow them when the wording is very clear and specific, which goes some way toward explaining their complicated legalistic form. In any given case today, a judge may be required to follow statutes, equity, or common law, and in that order, when reaching a decision.

Statutes are passed by Parliament or legislatures

Our law is based on statutes, common law, and equity

THE LAW IN CANADA

Canada was created with the passage of the *British North America Act* (*BNA Act*), which, in 1867, united several English colonies into one confederation. The *BNA Act* declared that Canada would have a constitution "similar in principle to that of the United Kingdom." In contrast to the United States, which has one constitutional instrument, England has an unwritten constitution in the sense that it is found in various proclamations, statutes, traditions, and judicially proclaimed principles. Thus the **rule of law** (the principle that all are subject to the law and legal process), the *Magna Carta* (the first proclamation of basic human rights), and parliamentary supremacy (the principle that everyone, even the king, is subject to laws made by parliament) are all part of the constitutional tradition inherited by Canada. The *BNA Act* itself—now called the *Constitution Act* (1867)—has constitutional status in Canada. This means

BNA Act creates Canada with constitution like Britain's

its provisions cannot be changed through a simple parliamentary enactment; they can only be altered through the more involved and onerous process of constitutional amendment.

Constitution Act (1867) (BNA Act) divides powers between federal and provincial governments

Today the main function of the *Constitution Act (1867)* is to divide powers between the federal and provincial governments. Parliament is the supreme law-making body in Canada (parliamentary supremacy). But this constitutional principle, inherited from England, presented our founding fathers with a problem. In Canada there are 11 sovereign governing bodies (10 provincial legislative assemblies and one federal Parliament). Which of these bodies is supreme? The answer is that each governs in its assigned area. Thus the *Constitution Act (1867)*, primarily in sections 91 and 92, assigns powers to the federal and the provincial governments. Section 91 gives the federal government the power to make laws with respect to such areas as money and banking, the military, criminal law, and weights and measures, whereas other areas such as health, education, and matters of local commerce are assigned to the provinces under section 92. Because these are sources of power rather than watertight compartments there can be occasional overlap. When that happens and there is a true conflict (where it is not possible to obey both) the federal legislation takes precedence over the provincial. Sections 91 and 92 of The *Constitution Act (1867)* appear in Appendix A on page 283 of this text. You can also access the Act at www.canlii.org.

Federal law followed where provincial and federal laws conflict

Case Summary 1.2 *British Columbia (Attorney General) v. Lafarge Canada Inc.*[2]
Federal Law Supersedes City Bylaws

Lafarge is a cement company that wanted to build a plant on the Vancouver waterfront. A group of ratepayers brought an application before the Supreme Court of British Columbia to require Lafarge to obtain a development permit from the City of Vancouver.

Lafarge felt that it was under the jurisdiction of the Vancouver Port Authority (a federal entity created under the *Canada Marine Act*) and it didn't have to comply with provincial or municipal regulations. The Court had to decide whether city zoning rules applied to this project and how the federal and provincial laws interrelate.

The British Columbia Supreme Court decided in favour of the ratepayers and the province. Lafarge went to the British Columbia Court of Appeal, which found for Lafarge and the matter was then appealed to the Supreme Court of Canada.

The Supreme Court first looked at the power granted to the province and thus to the city under the *Constitution Act (1867)* and decided that the municipal by-laws and zoning rules did apply to the Lafarge project. It is clear that under section 92(8), 92(13) and 92(26) of the Act that the City of Vancouver's bylaws were constitutionally valid.

The court also found that the project was necessarily incidental to the exercise of federal power with respect to "debt and property" and "navigation and shipping" under section 91(1a) and section 92(10) of the Act. The Vancouver Port Authority was properly created under the *Canada Marine Act* and the Lafarge project fell within its mandate and only its approval was required. There was a clear conflict between valid federal and valid provincial law and under the principle of paramountcy only the federal law applied.

This case illustrates not only how the powers to government are divided between the federal and provincial government under sections 91 and 92 of the *Constitution Act (1867)*, but also what happens when the provincial law and federal law are in conflict. When both cannot be obeyed the principal of paramountcy requires that the federal laws prevail and be followed.

---

[2] [2007] 2 S.C.R. 86; (2007), 281 D.L.R. (4th) 54 (S.C.C.).

Both the federal and provincial governments make law by enacting **legislation** (see Figure 1.2). Elected representatives form the House of Commons while appointed members make up the Senate. Together those bodies constitute the Parliament of Canada. The provinces have only one level consisting of elected members referred to as the Legislative Assembly of the Province. The Prime Minister or Premier and cabinet are chosen from these members and form the federal or provincial government. The governments of the territories function in the same way, but they don't have the same status as the provinces; they are subject to federal control. Legislative bodies begin the law-making process when an elected member—usually a cabinet minister—presents a **bill** for the consideration of the House of Commons. This bill goes through a process of introduction, debate, amendment, and approval, known as first, second, and third readings. Eventually the approved bill is presented to the Governor General at the federal level or the Lieutenant Governor at the provincial level to receive royal assent. With that assent the bill becomes law, and is then referred to as an **act** or **statute**. At the federal level the bill must also go through the same process in the Senate before receiving royal assent. Government enactments are published each year and are made available to the public in volumes referred to as the Statutes of Canada (S.C.), Statutes of Alberta (S.A.), Statutes of Ontario (S.O.), and so on. Every few years the statutes are summarized and are referred to as the Revised Statutes of Canada [R.S.C. 1985], Revised Statutes of B.C. [R.S.B.C. 1996], etc. Today most jurisdictions have made unofficial versions of their current consolidated legislation available on the internet or on CD. You can access these statutes at www.canlii.org.

Statutes often authorize a cabinet minister or other official to create sub-legislation or **regulations** to accomplish the objectives of the statute. These regulations are published and also made available to the public. If the regulations have been properly passed within the authority as specified in the statute, they have the same legal standing as the statute. Thus, a motor vehicle act in a particular province might set out the requirement to register a vehicle, list particular offences, or stipulate the right to appeal. The regulations would be more concerned with setting out specific penalties for violations or the fees to be charged for different services. Both aspects of the statute have the force of law and can be enforced by the government department that created them.

Federal law followed where provincial and federal laws conflict

Statute created by first, second, and third reading, and royal assent

Statutes published in print, on CD, and online

Regulations have status as law

Figure 1.2 The Making of Statutory Law

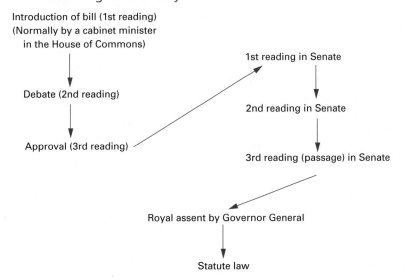

THE *CONSTITUTION ACT (1982)* AND *THE CHARTER OF RIGHTS AND FREEDOMS*

Constitution Act (1982) gives Canada independence

Canada cut its last ties to England with the simultaneous passage of the *Canada Act* in England and the *Constitution Act (1982)* in Canada. The English Parliament can no longer pass legislation that affects Canada. Although our ties with the English government have been severed, our ties to the monarchy remain intact, and Queen Elizabeth II remains the Queen of Canada. The *Constitution Act (1982)* also included the *Canadian Charter of Rights and Freedoms*.

Federal and provincial statutes guarantee human rights

The beginning of the latter half of the 20th century saw an upsurge of interest in basic human rights. Most jurisdictions enacted legislation prohibiting discrimination on the basis of race, religion, ethnic origin, gender, and disability in areas such as accommodation, public services, and employment. All Canadian provinces and the federal government enacted statutes and established regulatory bodies to ensure that these basic human rights were protected.

Case Summary 1.3 *Council of Canadians with Disabilities v. Via Rail Canada Inc.*[3]

Public Transportation Must Accommodate People with Disabilities

Via Rail purchased 139 used rail cars that were not wheelchair accessible. The Canadian Transportation Agency ordered Via to convert 13 economy coach cars and 17 service coaches for wheelchair use. Via argued that this would place undue hardship and expense on the company. They said that they would transfer disabled customers to modified wheelchairs that would fit on the trains and that assistance would be provided when they needed to use the restrooms. At this stage Via provided scant evidence of the costs that would be incurred in making the substantial modifications. This was unacceptable to the Agency, which continued to insist that Via Rail make the modifications. Via appealed to the Federal Court of Appeal, which decided in their favour, finding that there was a failure with respect to procedural fairness since the decision had been made without adequate information with respect to the hardship and costs to be incurred. At the time of the appeal the Federal Court had the advantage of a further report from Via that the costs of making the modifications would be around $48 million.

The Agency then appealed the matter to the Supreme Court of Canada, which overturned the Federal Court's decision, reinstating the order of the Canadian Transportation Agency to Via Rail to make the modifications. The Court found that the Agency had been specifically mandated to make transportation facilities more accessible to people with disabilities. When the Agency found a problem it was to see that it was resolved unless it imposed an undue hardship on the service provider. Via had failed to show that the requirement to modify the cars would place an undue hardship on them. What constitutes reasonable wheelchair accessibility is widely and internationally established and Via's concession did not comply. They found that the actual costs to make the cars wheelchair accessible would be nowhere near what Via estimated.

This case illustrates the importance the Supreme Court of Canada places on the human rights of people with disabilities, and the requirement that government agencies in addition to human rights tribunals were required to respect and enforce those rights. It also illustrates the court's willingness to review the decisions made by government agencies. The area of law that deals with government agencies at both the federal and provincial level is called administrative law and will be briefly summarized at the end of this chapter.

---

[3] [2007] S.C.J. No. 15.

The problem was that none of these statutes had the power to remedy discrimination when it took place at the hands of government. The doctrine of parliamentary supremacy provides that, in Canada, the supreme law-making body is Parliament. Thus Parliament or the legislative assemblies in the provinces could simply pass legislation overriding the rights protected in these human rights statutes.

The *Charter of Rights and Freedoms*, which is part of the constitution of Canada, over-comes this problem. All constitutional provisions, including the Charter, are declared to be the "supreme law of Canada." Neither the federal nor the provincial governments can change the provisions of the *Charter of Rights and Freedoms* without going through the constitution amending process. Any statute enacted by any level of government that is inconsistent with the provisions of the Charter is void, and any action by a government official violating the provisions of the Charter is actionable under the Charter.

Charter protects from rights abuses by government

We have to be careful here, because there are limitations built into the Charter that give back to government some of the power that the Charter takes away. Section 1 allows for reasonable exceptions to the rights and freedoms set out in the Charter. This is only common sense and prevents prisoners in jail from claiming their mobility rights, or allows a person to be held liable for his or her fraud or defamation despite the guarantee of free speech. These are simple examples, but the problems can be quite complex, and when dealing with Charter questions today, much of the effort of the courts is directed at deter-mining the reasonable extent of these exceptions.

Section 1 limitation allows for reasonable exceptions

Another limitation is found in section 33; it is known as the "notwithstanding clause." This provision allows both provincial and federal governments to pass legislation directly in contravention of specified sections of the Charter (section 2 and sections 7–15). While this clause seems to undo much that the Charter sets out to accomplish, a government choosing to exercise this overriding power must do so clearly, by declaring that a particu-lar provision will be in force "notwithstanding" the offended section of the Charter. Those advocating for the inclusion of the clause knew that its use would come at a high political cost, and as a result section 33 would rarely be used. In fact, this has proven to be the case, and very few legislators have had the political will to use the notwithstand-ing provision of the Charter. The Quebec law requiring business signs to be in French only is one notable example of its use. The political consequence of that action was the defeat of the Meech Lake and Charlottetown Accords, which in turn led to an upsurge in the separatist feelings in Quebec and a referendum that almost led to the breakup of Canada. Excerpts from *The Constitution Act (1982)* appear in Appendix B on page 286 of this text. You can also access the Act at www.canlii.org. The third limitation on the power of the Charter, set out in Section 32, is that it only applies to government and cannot be relied on to challenge other infringements on fundamental rights such as discrimination faced in normal non-governmental situations.

Section 33 limitation allows opting out

The provisions of the Charter protect basic or **fundamental freedoms** (section 2) such as freedoms of speech, religion, the press, and association. It also protects **democratic rights** (sections 3–5) at both the federal and provincial levels such as the right to vote, to run in an election, the requirement that an election will be held at least every five years, and that the elected government will sit every year. **Mobility rights** (section 6) include the rights to live and work in any part of Canada, as well as to enter and leave Canada. The most extensive provisions relate to **legal rights** (sections 7–14), which include the right to life, liberty, and the security of person; the right to be told why you are being arrested and to have a lawyer; the right not to incriminate yourself; the right to be tried

Charter protects:
- Fundamental freedoms
- Democratic rights
- Mobility rights
- Legal rights
- Equality rights
- Language rights

within a reasonable time; the right to a jury trial; and the right not to be exposed to any unreasonable search and seizure or cruel or unusual treatment. Perhaps the best known provisions of the Charter relate to **equality rights** (section 15), where it states that everyone is equal under the law and, "in particular," discrimination based on race, national or ethnic origin, colour, religion, sex, age, or mental or physical disability is prohibited. Note that this list does not exhaust equality rights. It only lists some of them. Others are protected through the general provision prohibiting discrimination in the first part of section 15. For example, there is no specific protection of "sexual orientation" rights, but the Supreme Court of Canada has found that they are protected under this general prohibition. Finally, **minority language education rights** (section 23) are protected. Both the Charter and a separate part of the *Constitution Act (1982)* make it clear that **aboriginal rights** inconsistent with Charter provisions are not affected by it and are preserved. These treaty rights predate the Charter, and in many cases, predate Confederation itself. They include rights yet to be determined in the native land claims process.

Case Summary 1.4 *Whatcott v. Saskatchewan Assn. of Licensed Practical Nurses*[4]

Freedom of Expression Includes Right to Protest

Mr. Whatcott was a member of the Saskatchewan Association of Licensed Practical Nurses when he picketed the Regina office of Planned Parenthood graphically and forcefully denouncing the practice of abortion. For this, he was disciplined by the Nurses Association for professional misconduct, fined, and had his membership suspended until the fine was paid. The Association took the position that his conduct negatively affected the reputation of practical nurses and therefore it was within their right to discipline him. He appealed the decision to the Saskatchewan Court of Queens Bench, which held in favour of the Association. Whatcott took the matter to the Saskatchewan Court of Appeal, claiming that his Charter right to freedom of expression (section 2b) had been breached. The Court of Appeal agreed with Whatcott, and disagreed with the Association's claim that its action was a reasonable limit on his free

speech (Charter section 1). This happened on Whatcott's time off and the Court felt it was much more likely that public perception of nurses would be based on what they did on the job rather what was done in their off-duty hours. The action of the Association went too far and their action was not justified as a reasonable exception to his right to freedom of expression.

This case illustrates the importance that is put on freedom of expression, but should be contrasted with a case where a teacher in British Columbia published negative comments about homosexuality in the local newspaper and his teaching certificate was suspended. In this case the Court of Appeal held that although his freedom of expression rights were infringed, this was a reasonable exception under section 1 of the Charter.[5]

Charter limited to government actions

It must be emphasized that the Charter and its provisions only apply to our relations with government. Thus, legislation passed by all levels of government and the conduct of government officials must comply with the provisions of the Charter. In other situations where discrimination is experienced, for example in employment, housing, or public services such as hotels, restaurants, and places of entertainment, individuals can make a claim to a human rights tribunal rather than the courts. Such tribunals act under separate provincial or federal human rights legislation.

---

[4] [2006] S.J. No. 449.

[5] *Kempling v. British Columbia College of Teachers*, (2005) 255 D.L.R. (4th) 169, (B.C.C.A.).

THE COURTS

The traditional means of resolving disputes in our culture is in a court of law. Under the *Constitution Act (1867)*, the actual structure of the courts is left to the provinces, resulting in some variety from province to province, although they are generally similar in nature and function. The lower-level courts (provincial courts) are divided into various functions. The small claims court deals with civil actions where one person sues another for relatively small amounts of money (up to $50 000 depending on the province). Other specialized divisions of the lower-level provincial courts include family courts that deal with family law matters, including the division of assets, awarding maintenance and custody of children, but not the divorce itself, which must be handled by the superior trial court of the province; youth courts dealing with juveniles; and criminal courts dealing with the less serious criminal offences. Note that Ontario's small claims courts and family courts are a division of the Superior Court of Justice, leaving the Ontario Court of Justice to deal primarily with criminal matters. Since 2002 the provinces of British Columbia, Alberta, Ontario, and Quebec have established specialized courts that deal with such matters as drug-related offences, domestic violence, and mental health-related problems. Other provinces, including Saskatchewan, Manitoba, and New Brunswick have also considered establishing specialized courts for these types of cases. British Columbia created a Community Court in 2008, which deals with certain offenders who plead guilty and agree to terms of community service and/or rehabilitation in specified substance abuse recovery programs. The goal is to reduce recidivism and increase opportunities to improve the health and well-being of repeat offenders.

Court structure varies between provinces
- Provincial court
- Small claims
- Family
- Criminal

The superior trial courts of the province are variously referred to as the Supreme Court, Court of Queens Bench—or in Ontario, Superior Court of Justice. They are the highest-level trial courts of the province and deal with all serious civil and criminal matters. In the case of Ontario, the Superior Court of Justice is divided into a Divisional Court and the Superior Court, which in turn is divided into Small Claims and Family branches. The divisional court deals mostly with provincial statutory offences and has a limited civil jurisdiction. Note that some jurisdictions still retain a separate probate or surrogate court to handle estate matters.

Superior court highest trial court

In all provinces the highest court is a Court of Appeal. This court only deals with appeals from lower courts and some government regulatory bodies, such as human rights tribunals, labour relations boards, and worker's compensation boards. A matter tried in any of the lower courts can be taken to the appeal court of that province, which may be the final appeal for the case. Whereas at the trial level there is a single judge who is sometimes assisted by a jury, at the appeal level usually three judges hear the case. Juries are limited to the trial level and are rare in civil cases, with the exception being personal injury cases under tort law. But in criminal matters, where the potential penalty is over five years, trial by jury is guaranteed under the *Charter of Rights and Freedoms*. Where a jury is involved, its function is to hear the evidence and decide issues of fact (what happened and who did what?), whereas the questions of law (what are the legal obligations of the parties?) are left to the judge, who gives instructions to the jury on such matters before they retire to make their decision.

Superior appeal court.

*Jury guaranteed by **Charter***

The federal government has established the Supreme Court of Canada, located in Ottawa, as a court of last resort for Canadians. Nine judges, appointed by the prime minister and cabinet, are chosen from the various regions of the country. The Supreme Court hears appeals from all of the provincial appeal courts, including Quebec's. There is no

Supreme Court of Canada highest court

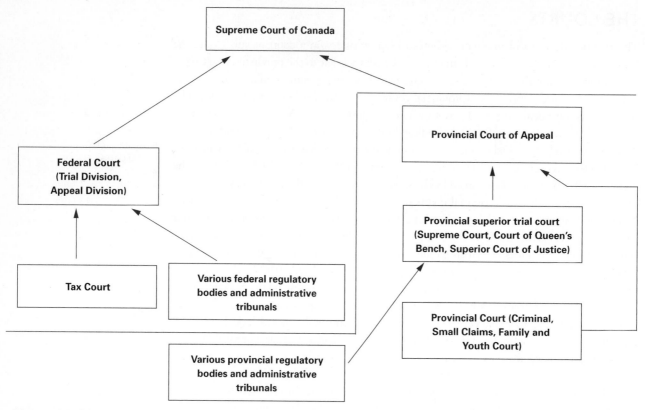

Figure 1.3 Court
Structure*

*Provincial structure will vary

Federal Court deals with disputes
in federal arena

longer a right to appeal to the Supreme Court of Canada. The court selects the cases to hear on the basis of what it thinks is most important for the country. If it refuses to hear a particular case, it is not a comment on the validity of the arguments or the lower court decision. It means only that it has other more important cases to deal with. Usually seven or nine judges will sit to hear a case. The Supreme Court of Canada will also on rare occasions hear **references** (questions involving serious legal issues normally involving some urgency), directed to the court by the Prime Minister. A significant example was put to the court in 2004 on the question of same-sex marriage, which led to such unions being legalized in all provinces.[6] The federal government has also established a Federal Court with a Trial Division and an Appeal Division. These courts handle matters that fall within the federal jurisdiction, such as copyrights, patents, and trademarks as well as matters brought from the federal Tax Court, Military Courts, and other federal government regulatory bodies such as the Immigration and Refugee Board and the Competition Tribunal.

THE LITIGATION PROCESS

A civil action involves one person (called the **plaintiff**) suing another (the **defendant**). The process is complex and time consuming, but each step is designed to uncover more information, so that the parties will be encouraged to settle without going to trial. In fact the vast

---

[6] Reference re Same-Sex Marriage, [2004] 3 S.C.R. 698; (2004), 246 D.L.R. (4th) 193; (S.C.C.).

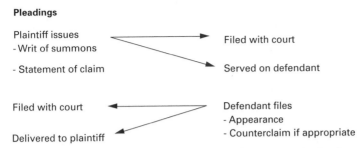

Figure 1.4 Pre-Trial Litigation Process (Usually After Negotiation)

majority of cases never make it to trial. But if a trial cannot be avoided, this pre-trial process also ensures that the actual issues to be decided on by the court are narrowed and refined. The following describes the process in place in a civil action in a superior court. It should be noted that in small claims court many of these steps have been eliminated altogether. There is also considerable provincial variation and many provinces have introduced changes to increase efficiency and reduce delay. See Figure 1.4 for an outline of the initial stages of the litigation process. Provincial trial courts normally only hear matters that have taken place in or are closely connected to their area of jurisdiction. The matter of jurisdiction and particularly the exceptions to this policy will be addressed more specifically in other chapters.

In all provinces where a civil action is involved, that action must be commenced within a time limit, known as a limitation period, specified in statute. The limitation period traditionally varies with the type of action being brought. For example, in most jurisdictions where personal injury is involved the action must be started within two years of the accident. A failure to start the action within that period ends the plaintiff's right to sue. There is a movement in many provinces to rationalize these various limitation periods. For example, Ontario has imposed a two-year limitation period for most proceedings.[7]

Case Summary 1.5 *Castillo v. Castillo*[8]
Expiration of Limitation Period Causes Loss of Right to Sue

Mr. and Mrs. Castillo were in the process of moving their residence from British Columbia to Alberta when they were in a single car accident in California. Mrs. Castillo waited until she returned to Calgary before getting medical treatment for her injuries. In this action brought in Alberta she is seeking compensation from her husband, the owner and driver of the vehicle, for her injuries. The problem was that she waited almost two years before bringing the action. The Alberta limitation period (the period within which an action must be brought) is two years, but the California limitation period is only one year. The question for the Court was which limitation period applied.

The decision went against her in the Court of Queens Bench and she appealed. The Alberta Court of Appeal, after examining their limitation statute, found in effect that both limitation periods applied and she had to comply with both. Since the California period was shorter and she had failed to comply with it the action was statute barred in Alberta as well. The court found that since the limitation period of one year had expired, "there is no basis upon which to sue. Thus, there is no actionable tort in California. Without an actionable tort, no action can be commenced in Alberta regardless of any longer limitation period . . . .".

>

---
[7] *Limitations Act*, 2002, S.O. 2002 c. 24, (2004).

[8] [2005] 357 A.R. 288; (2004), 244 D.L.R. (4th) 603; [2004] 9 W.W.R. 609; (2004), 30 Alta. L.R. (4th) 67.

For our purposes the case is important for two reasons. It illustrates the operation of limitation periods and the importance of being aware of what limitation applies and complying with it. Failure to do so will end any right to sue before you start. It also illustrates that an action that takes place in one jurisdiction can be pursued in another. Although the court didn't deal with which jurisdiction was appropriate to bring the action, having disposed of the matter on the basis of the missed limitation period, it is important to understand that a court will have jurisdiction if it considers that the matter is more closely connected with that jurisdiction. Here, because the person being sued (the husband) also resides in Alberta, the court would likely not hesitate in assuming jurisdiction to try the matter had that been appropriate.

Service of writ of summons commences process

Once questions of jurisdiction and time limits have been decided the plaintiff initiates the action by issuing a **writ of summons**, registering it with the court and serving it on the defendant. The writ contains a brief description of the nature of the complaint and the address where future documents related to the case can be served. The defendant responds by filing an **appearance** at that same court registry. This is simply an indication that the matter will be disputed. It is unwise to ignore a writ of summons. If the defendant fails to file an appearance, the plaintiff can normally proceed to judgment without any further notification to the defendant.

Statement of claim identifies issues

The plaintiff then issues a **statement of claim**, which contains a summary of the allegations that support the **cause of action** (that is, what the plaintiff is suing for), such as a claim of negligence or breach of contract. It also contains an indication as to the remedy requested, and, where damages are claimed, the specific amount sought. Often the statement of claim is included with the writ of summons. In Ontario, the action is commenced with the issuance of a **notice of action**, including the statement of claim.

Statement of defence defines area of contention

Upon receiving the statement of claim, the defendant must respond with a **statement of defence**, stating what is agreed and what is disputed in the statement of claim. The defendant can also issue a **counterclaim** that, in effect, initiates a counter action on the defendant's behalf. It is similar to the plaintiff's statement of claim. These documents are referred to as the **pleadings**, and there may be further communications between the plaintiff and defendant to clarify any uncertainty arising from them.

Discovery: Discloses documents

Next comes the two-stage discovery process (see Table 1.2). First, each party has the right to look at and copy documents held by the other side, such as receipts and reports from experts that might later be used as evidence in the trial. The second stage involves

Table 1.2 Litigation Process Continued

Discovery Process
- Plaintiff inspects documents in possession of defendant.
- Defendant inspects documents in possession of plaintiff.
- Plaintiff examines defendant under oath.
- Defendant examines plaintiff under oath.

Payment into Court
- Defendant may pay money to the court.
- Defendant informs plaintiff, who may then accept payment.
- Plaintiff may make an offer to settle.
- Offer to settle is filed with the court. Defendant is informed of the offer and may or may not accept.

the examination under oath of each party by the other side's lawyer. Where companies are involved, an officer or other employee who has direct knowledge of the matter must be made available to answer these questions. This is done before a court reporter who puts the party to be examined under oath and records the process, making a transcript available to the parties for a fee. Transcripts can later be used as evidence at the trial. It should be noted that, in an attempt to increase efficiency, many jurisdictions have reduced or eliminated this discovery process, at least in matters involving smaller claims.

Discovery: Produces statements under oath

To further encourage the parties to settle, either party can make formal offers before trial, which are recorded. If the offer is not accepted and the judgment turns out to be less favourable than the offer, the party refusing the offer will pay a penalty in the form of higher costs.

Payment into court and offers to settle encourage settlement

Although pre-trial proceedings ease the burden on the court and encourage settlement, they also cause considerable delays and become frustrating for the parties. In most provinces steps have been taken to simplify or reduce the process. Some innovations include summary trials, increased use of **affidavits** instead of direct testimony by witnesses, elimination of discovery, mandatory mediation before trial, and case management by a judge. That is when the assigned judge examines the pleadings and discovery documents, and during the pre-trial proceedings advises the parties what will be the likely outcome if the case does proceed to trial.

Case Summary 1.6 *Lawton's Drug Stores Ltd. v. Mifflin*[9]

Discovery Requires the Production of Customer Lists

When Mifflin sold their business to Lawton's Drug store, the contract included a clause restricting them from opening a similar business in competition. Lawton's had paid extra for customer goodwill which would be lost if Mifflin were to start up a business in competition and recapture that customer loyalty. Six months later Mifflin did open up a business in competition and Lawton's sued for breach of contract. As part of the pre-trial discovery process, Lawton's demanded a copy of Mifflin's customer list. Such lists are extremely confidential and must be kept out of the hands of competitors at all costs, and so Mifflin refused. Upon application to the court, the judge ordered that the customer list be produced. It was relevant to the proceeding in that it could disclose information about whether the restrictive covenant was breached and to what extent. To prevent its misuse by Lawton's, the judge ordered that the list be kept in the possession of Lawton's lawyer, not be shown to Lawton, and only be used for trial purposes. This case shows us just how extensive the discovery process is in requiring the disclosure of all information that has potential relevance.

In some situations, instead of just one plaintiff there are many. These are called **class action suits**, where a number of individuals have suffered the same loss as a result of the conduct of a particular defendant. It makes no sense for each injured party to bring a separate action; consequently, many jurisdictions have enacted statutes allowing the actions to be brought all at the same time. The result is that one action and decision will be applicable to all those represented in the class. The process is essentially the same, with the exception that an application must first be made to the court to have the matter certified as a class action. The court may also be asked to decide whether a given individual is

Class actions involve many plaintiffs represented by one procedure

---

[9] (1995), 402 A.P.R. 33, 38 C.P.C. (3d) 135, 129 Nfld. & P.E.I. R. 33 (Nfld. T.D.).

entitled to be a member of that class or whether his or her particular situation is different enough to merit a separate action. Class actions are becoming much more common. Some examples include product liability cases and disputes involving complaints against moneylenders, franchisers, financial advisers, and employee benefit and pension plans. Class actions have even included claims against government by veterans for improper compensation, female public services employees who claimed gender-based wage disparity, and a claim of systemic negligence leading to sexual abuse experienced by military cadets. A classic example involved Air Transat flight 236 flying from Toronto to Lisbon. Due to human error the plane ran out of fuel in the mid Atlantic and had to glide for 19 minutes before making a safe but perilous landing in the Azores. The passengers suffered some minor injuries, but great stress, and brought a successful class action against the airline, which was settled before going to trial. Note that it was also necessary to bring the agreed-upon settlement to the court for approval.[10]

THE TRIAL AND JUDGMENT

At trial, the plaintiff goes first . . .
Then the defendant

The trial usually begins with an opening statement by the lawyer for the plaintiff, followed by witnesses called by the plaintiff who respond to questions from the plaintiff's lawyer. This is called **direct examination**. As each witness testifies, the defendant's lawyer is given an opportunity to cross-examine. The types of questions that can be asked are broader on **cross-examination** than on direct examination. For instance, leading questions, where the answer is suggested in the question, are permitted on cross-examination but not on direct examination. After the plaintiff has presented his or her evidence through the testimony of witnesses, the defendant responds by calling his or her witnesses. The defendant's lawyer questions them and the plaintiff's lawyer cross-examines. Finally, the lawyers for both the plaintiff and defendant have an opportunity to summarize their cases and make their arguments.

The case must be proved "upon
balance of probabilities"

In civil actions plaintiffs must establish their claim on the "balance of probabilities." This means that the judge need only be satisfied that the plaintiff's position is more correct than that of the defendant's. In a criminal matter the standard is much higher, where the prosecution must establish to the satisfaction of the decision-makers that the accused is guilty "beyond a reasonable doubt." That is, even if the judge thinks the accused is guilty, if there is another reasonable theory that could explain what happened there must be a verdict of not guilty.

Judge instructs the jury in law, but
the jury decides facts

If the matter is heard before a judge alone, he or she will determine both questions of law and questions of fact and render a decision. If a jury is involved it must determine the facts or exactly what happened. These are called **questions of fact**. The judge instructs the jury, setting out the law to be applied to the matter before them. These are called **questions of law**. Then the jury retires to consider the matter and renders a decision. Criminal juries consist of 12 people and all must be in agreement with respect to the verdict. In civil cases juries are much less common, but when used, they typically consist of a lesser number (seven in Nova Scotia), and the decision does not have to be unanimous.

Once a judgment for **liability** is obtained in a civil action, the standard remedy is a monetary award called **damages** that the defendant must pay the plaintiff. Damages are

---

[10] *Nunes v. Air Transat A.T. Inc.*, 2005 CanLII 21681 (ON S.C.).

usually designed to compensate the victim for his or her loss. **Special damages** are those that can be accurately calculated such as medical expenses or lost wages. **General damages** are estimates of losses that aren't capable of direct calculation, such as lost future wages or pain and suffering. Note that significant limitations have been placed on the availability of damages for pain and suffering by the Supreme Court of Canada.[11] This restriction on damages is just one of the reasons judgments in Canadian courts in civil matters are often considerably lower than in the United States. In rare circumstances where the conduct complained of was deliberate, **punitive damages** may also be granted where the object is to punish the wrongdoer rather than simply to compensate the victim.

Damages and other remedies awarded

Where a monetary award will not appropriately compensate the victim, the court may order one of the following equitable remedies: an **injunction** (an order to stop the offending conduct); **specific performance** (an order that one contracting party actually fulfill the terms of an agreement, for example, transfer title to his or her house); an **accounting**, where the defendant must pay over any profits he or she has made because of his or her misdeed (as opposed to compensating the victim for any loss); or other unique remedies associated with particular kinds of action.

Payment of damages cannot be guaranteed by the court. Where damages are awarded and the defendant, now referred to as the **judgment debtor**, fails to pay, the **judgment creditor** (plaintiff) must take extra steps to collect that money (see Figure 1.5). This may include a post-trial hearing to identify the judgment debtor's assets and what steps can be taken to execute against those assets. Bank accounts or wages may be taken (garnisheed) by court order. Assets such as cars, boats, and other types of valuable equipment can be seized, pursuant to the court order, and sold to satisfy the judgment. Similarly, real property in the form of land and buildings can be required to be sold, and title transferred to satisfy the judgment. Of course, if the judgment debtor has no assets, or is bankrupt, trying to collect may be a fruitless exercise. This risk must be taken into consideration when deciding to sue in the first place. Where specific conduct has been ordered under an injunction or specific performance, for example, and the defendant fails to comply, his or her conduct may amount to **contempt of court** and the defendant can face stiff fines and even imprisonment as a result.

The plaintiff (now judgment creditor) must enforce judgment

The question must be asked whether the litigation is worth the trouble it creates. The fees charged for court services, discovery transcriptions, and document reproduction can be

Figure 1.5 Enforcing Judgment

---

[11] *Thornton v. Prince George School District* No. 57 [1978] 2 S.C.R. 267.

high, but nothing compared to the cost of expert witnesses and lawyers whose fees can range from a few hundred to thousands of dollars per hour. It has been reported that a single day in court in Toronto can cost up to $10 000. Since many trials last much longer than that, a plaintiff must be very certain of some return before risking litigation. It may be possible to reduce some of these costs by checking out student-run legal clinics for assistance. This can be an invaluable service for those who are hesitant to take their problems to a practicing lawyer. And for those that haven't already established a relationship with a lawyer, provincial branches of the Canadian Bar Association offer a lawyer referral service.

ALTERNATE DISPUTE RESOLUTION

Alternatives to litigation provide advantages

Before taking a matter to court, it is vital to consider some alternatives to the litigation process—referred to as alternate dispute resolution or ADR. Some professionals have suggested that this acronym should be Appropriate Dispute Resolution so that injured parties will participate in the most efficient form of resolution for their particular problem.[12] The object of turning to alternative methods is to avoid the delay, expense, lost productivity, and publicity normally associated with the litigation process. The first option and one that results in a quick and cheap resolution is for the parties in dispute to simply negotiate with each other, either directly, or indirectly through their lawyers, until they reach a settlement. Where there is some degree of goodwill and the parties are willing to cooperate and compromise, **negotiation** should be the method of choice for resolving disputes. Sometimes, however, it is necessary to turn to the more structured methods of ADR that have been gaining prominence in recent times (see Figure 1.6).

Negotiation avoids conflict

Figure 1.6 Alternate Dispute Resolution (ADR) Methods

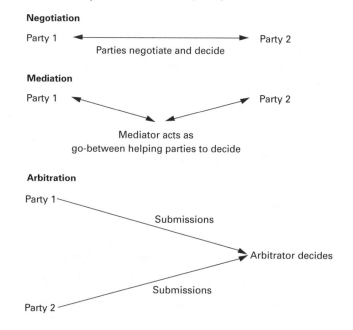

Negotiation

Party 1 ←——————————————→ Party 2

Parties negotiate and decide

Mediation

Party 1 ↘   ↙ Party 2

Mediator acts as
go-between helping parties to decide

Arbitration

Party 1 ⟍
            Submissions
                        ⟶ Arbitrator decides
            Submissions
Party 2 ⟋

---

[12] Ken Acton, "ADR Director Reflects on Changing Attitudes to Mediation in Saskatchewan," (June 2006) *Lawyer's Weekly*.

Mediation is the process whereby some trusted third party acts as a go-between or facilitator and assists the parties to resolve their dispute. The job of the mediator is to communicate with both parties and try to find some area of common ground between them. This may include making suggestions to the parties, but it is still up to the parties themselves to make the final decision, not the mediator. When both parties agree to the settlement, it is more likely that they will live up to the obligations they have assumed. But if they fail to do so, the terms of the settlement will be influential in a court hearing or may even form the basis of the court-imposed decision. Where a settlement is not reached what happened in the mediation is normally kept confidential. Thus a willingness to compromise will not weaken a party's position in subsequent proceedings. Mediation is required in some situations, such as collective bargaining, before any action, for instance, a strike or lockout, can be taken. Mandatory mediation is also now required in many jurisdictions as part of the pre-trial proceedings in civil disputes. A mediated settlement is convenient, inexpensive, private, and allows parties to resume their business relationship.

Mediator helps parties to reach a decision

Arbitration is where the decision-making is surrendered to an arbitrator who is selected by both parties, or they may choose to have the matter heard by a panel of three. Each side chooses a panel member and those two recommend a third neutral person. The parties must agree in advance to be bound by the decision, but can place limitations on the scope of the decision and what remedies can be imposed. Arbitrators usually have expertise in the area under dispute and this, along with the power to make a binding decision, makes them particularly effective. Arbitration is mandated in some areas, such as collective bargaining. Once a collective agreement is in place, it must include some mechanism where any dispute arising under the contract will ultimately be arbitrated rather than made the subject of litigation in the courts. Another good example is the Canadian Motor Vehicle Arbitration Plan (CAMVAP). Contracts between customers and dealers require disputes arising in that industry to be arbitrated before that body, rather than through litigation. It is now a much more common practice to include contract provisions requiring arbitration of disputes in all sorts of business and consumer transactions.

Arbitrators make binding decisions

There is a growing practice to merge mediation and arbitration (called Med-Arb). This involves a two-stage process, with an attempt at mediation first, and if that fails, to empower the mediator to then arbitrate the dispute imposing a binding solution.

There are many variations of negotiation, mediation, and arbitration, making flexibility one of the most attractive features of ADR (see Table 1.3). The parties are free, either at the beginning of their relationship or after the dispute arises, to individually tailor a dispute resolution process to best suit their particular business needs. Although litigation is central to our legal system, a business person should turn to the litigation process

ADR provides flexibility

Table **1.3** Pros and Cons of Alternate Dispute Resolution (ADR)

Advantages	Disadvantages
Lower cost	Does not deal with legal complexities
Flexible	Not appropriate when power imbalance
Less time-consuming	No precedent set
Private	No pressure to satisfy public demands
Win-win resolution	Limited powers of enforcement

only as a last resort. But keep in mind that court cases that have been decided determine the law. If we understand that law, we should be able to use those standards to help us as we negotiate, mediate, or arbitrate disputes.

ADMINISTRATIVE LAW

Dealing with regulatory bodies

Government regulation of business is an ever-increasing reality. Federal and provincial statutes control everything from providing permits to build to enforcing environmental protection codes. The power to administer its terms is provided in the statute and the government department will appoint officers to educate, enforce, investigate, conduct inquiries, and penalize offenders. Since the officials, boards, and tribunals are employees of the government, their extensive powers are used in the interests of the department that employs them. If, when they exercise those powers, they overstep their authority or act unfairly, the court may be asked to review the process and the decision. An account of the procedural requirements for an administrative hearing follows.

Requirement of Authority

Administrative decisions must be within jurisdiction and compliant with the **Charter**

The statute itself, or regulations passed under it, must deal with matters within its constitutionally mandated area and must not infringe on the rights set out in the Charter. Thus where a provincial statute is not authorized under the *Constitution Act (1867)*, encroaches on a federal area, or violates the Charter provisions, decisions made under it will be void. Similarly, the appointed decision-maker must not overstep the powers authorized by the legislation, nor act outside of his or her jurisdiction. Thus where a statute requires a decision in writing, the failure to provide one would be fatal to that decision. The courts will not tolerate an error of law associated with the documentation of the tribunal process, and will overturn the decision if the error is serious enough. For example, if the written decision of a tribunal made it clear that they assumed that the right of freedom of assembly under the Charter did not include the right to belong to a trade union, that error if vital would make the decision void.

Procedural Fairness

Procedural fairness required in administrative hearing

The decision-making process must comply with the principles of procedural fairness, the first of which is a **fair hearing**. This means that a person appearing before the board or tribunal must have received reasonable notice of the hearing and be made aware of exactly what the hearing is about so that he or she can prepare an appropriate response. The person must be given the opportunity to speak before the decision is made. In some situations the right to submit his or her position in writing may be sufficient. The persons making the decision must be present to hear all of the evidence. The decision-maker must not be biased or have a personal interest in the decision. A fair hearing does not necessarily mean that a person has a right to legal representation or to cross-examine witnesses, or that the rules of evidence, common in a judicial hearing, will apply.

If any of the questions posed in Table 1.4 are answered negatively, suggesting that the tribunal may have made an error of law, acted beyond its jurisdiction, or failed to meet the requirements of procedural fairness, the decision of that tribunal can be challenged or reviewed by the courts. The courts will review when the decision is clearly unreasonable

Case Summary 1.7 *Agostini v. Parkland (County)*[13]

Brief Absence Denies Procedural Fairness

Burnco applied to Parkland County for a permit to take gravel from a particular location. A hearing was held before the Subdivision and Development Appeal Board of Parkland County where residents who were opposed could be heard. The Board consisted of six panel members and presenters were allowed 10 minutes each to present their position. During one of these presentations one of the six panel members took a break coming back two minutes later. After the hearing the board granted the permits and one of the opposing residents, Mr. Agostini, brought this application to overturn the decision. He claimed that the absence of that one member violated the requirement of procedural fairness that the decision had to be made by those who heard the evidence.

This case actually deals with an application to the Alberta Court of Appeal for leave to appeal and the Court had to decide whether there were grounds for appeal that had a reasonable chance of succeeding. The board argued that this was frivolous and that the absence for two minutes of one of the members was insignificant and made no difference to the outcome. The judge in granting leave to appeal, however, applied the principle that "the general rule is that he who hears must decide ... Implicit in this rule is the notion that adjudicators must hear the case made by all parties to a dispute." Since the hearing continued during the member's absence that member had not heard all of the evidence when he participated in the decision. Therefore, there were arguable grounds for appeal and a reasonable likelihood of success. Leave to appeal was granted. This case graphically illustrates just how seriously the requirement of procedural fairness is treated by the courts.

or unauthorized. Even then it is important to remember that a review is not an appeal. The Courts will normally not question the decision, only whether it was appropriately made. If they find an error they may order the matter to be reheard by a tribunal exercising proper authority and following the requirements of fair process. Of course the challenge will be a waste of time and resources if the tribunal, this time being more careful, reaches the same decision. This fact and the great expense usually associated with such challenges gives validation to the old saying that "you can't fight City Hall." The court exercises its review power with the option to apply the remedies listed in Table 1.5.

Naturally, the goal of the statute is to avoid having its terms and processes challenged, and so usually included in the statute are **privitive clauses** designed to insulate tribunal decisions from judicial review. Courts often find ways to ignore or avoid such

Table 1.4 Checklist for Action

Ask the following questions to determine if a complaint should be made:

- Is the decision authorized by properly enacted statutes and regulations?
- Has the decision-maker acted within his power?
- Have the statutory procedures been followed?
- Have the rules of natural justice or procedural fairness been complied with?
- Is there any benefit in seeking a court to review the decision?
- What is the appropriate remedy to ask for?

---

[13] 2006 AB C.A. 127 (CanLII).

Court may review process

Table 1.5 List of Available Remedies

- Court may order prohibition. Decision-maker will be ordered not to proceed.
- Court may order certiorari. Decision will be overturned.
- Court may order mandamus. Decision-maker will be ordered to decide.
- Court may declare the law. Court will state the correct law applicable.
- Court may issue injunction. Court will order offending conduct to stop.
- Court may award damages. Court will award monetary compensation.
- Court may make another order under section 24 of the Charter, where appropriate.

restrictions on their authority, although today considerable deference is given to such tribunals, especially where special expertise and complex matters are involved. It is important to keep in mind the benefits of having these matters decided outside of the courts. We have already discussed the challenges of court processes. Tribunals are more efficient, are usually made up of experts in the field under dispute, and can render decisions more quickly and cost-effectively than can the courts. They play an important role enforcing the law and business people need to be aware of their powers and how they are exercised.

CRIMINAL LAW

Although this text focuses primarily on civil law, the topic of criminal law has become much more important for businesses in recent years. Corporations are commonly the victims of criminal activities such as shoplifting, employee theft, and fraud in its various forms. Increasingly, senior employees, directors, and executives run afoul of criminal law. Conrad Black and Martha Stewart are just two examples of well-known business executives who have found themselves behind bars. It is, therefore, important to make some reference to the criminal process.

In a criminal action the state prosecutes the accused

First, we should define criminal law and distinguish it from civil law. In a civil action one individual, the injured party, sues the party causing the injury, usually seeking compensation or other remedy. In a criminal matter the state prosecutes the accused. The victim has the status of a witness only in this process. The accused may be a corporation, which can be held criminally liable for offences committed by senior executives or those acting under their direction. Sometimes the senior executives can be charged. It is not uncommon for both criminal charges and a civil action to arise from the same incident. For example, where insider trading causes losses to investors, a criminal offence has taken place and those involved can be prosecuted. In addition, the shareholders who have been injured by such insider trading can also sue civilly for compensation.

Power to make criminal law resides exclusively with federal government

Regulatory offences and criminal law very similar

Although the power to make criminal law is given exclusively to the federal government under the *Constitution Act (1867)*, provinces also have power to create and enforce statutes, the violation of which can result in serious penalties including significant jail terms. From a business point of view there is little difference between these regulatory offences and criminal law, since both impose fines and/or imprisonment. In this text these regulatory offences will be treated as another form of criminal law.

Federal criminal law found in *Criminal Code* and other federal statutes

Federally, the criminal law is found mainly in the Canadian *Criminal Code*, but other federal statutes such as the *Competition Act*, the *Controlled Drugs and Substances Act*, and the *Copyright and Patents Acts* also contain true criminal provisions. In this chapter a few important criminal law principles will be set out, and in subsequent chapters other criminal rules and principles will be discussed as they relate to chapter topics.

In a criminal case the prosecutor must establish "beyond a reasonable doubt" that the accused is guilty of the offence. It is not enough to show that the offensive conduct has taken place; it is also necessary to prove that there was an intention to do the act. This intention is usually presumed once a person has been shown to have committed the offensive conduct, and so it is the defence that usually must try to show there was no intention present. Insanity is an example of a defence that may rebut that presumption. It must be noted, however, that intoxication is not a defence for most criminal charges. Nor is ignorance of the law normally an excuse.

Standards of proof and the rights set out in the *Charter of Rights and Freedoms* (primarily sections 7–14) are imposed whenever imprisonment is the potential outcome. Where only fines can be levied, it may be sufficient to prove that the offensive conduct took place. These are called **strict liability offences** and the only defence normally available is that the accused acted with **due diligence**. Essentially, due diligence can be established where the manager or executive involved is shown to have taken reasonable steps to ensure that the offensive conduct would not take place, including proper training of the employees involved as well as the establishment of adequate procedures and safeguards that would reasonably be expected to prevent its occurrence.

Criminal standard beyond a reasonable doubt

Prosecution must prove intent as well as the act

Note **Charter of Rights** *protections*

Due diligence is the only defence to strict liability offence

Case Summary 1.8 *R. v. MacMillan Bloedel Ltd.*[14]
Due Diligence Not Established

MacMillan Bloedel's underground pipeline located in the Queen Charlotte Islands leaked into a watercourse, and the company was charged under the federal *Fisheries Act* with allowing a deleterious substance to escape, contaminating water frequented by fish. This is a strict liability offence in that it is sufficient to prove the offensive conduct took place to obtain a conviction. The only defence available is that of due diligence. Due diligence is established in two ways. First, that the event that constituted the offence was not reasonably foreseeable and so could not have been anticipated. Second, that the company had taken reasonable steps to make sure that the offensive conduct would not occur. Although the pipes in question were old, the company and a government inspector had recently inspected the pipeline and found them to be sound with no indication of trouble. It was discovered that the leak was caused by microbiological corrosion, something no one could have anticipated. At trial in the Provincial Court the company's due diligence defence was rejected. It was then appealed to a summary conviction appeal judge (in the Supreme Court of British Columbia) who decided in favour of the company.

The Crown in turn appealed to the British Columbia Court of Appeal. That court allowed the appeal and reinstated the conviction rejecting the company's due diligence defence. It was true that the company could not have reasonably anticipated leakage caused in this particular way, but they could anticipate that the aging pipes could fail and so leakage in general was reasonably foreseeable. Secondly, while the company did have a good inspection process in place and their conclusion that the pipes were in good shape was reasonable, they had no plan in place to deal with the leakage when it did occur.

Although the company was convicted and their due diligence defence was rejected, the case nicely illustrates the two branches of the due diligence defence and what is necessary for it to succeed. First due diligence can be established where the conduct that incorporated the offence could not have been reasonably foreseen, and second, where all reasonable steps have been taken to ensure that the offensive conduct does not take place.

---

[14] (2002), 220 D.L.R. (4th) 173 (B.C.C.A.).

Police can arrest or issue an appearance notice

While a security guard or other employee of a business has the power to arrest when they see a crime being committed, the police have broader powers to arrest and only the police have the right to make a search. Often, however, the decision to arrest follows an investigation and then the police file a complaint setting out the allegations and obtain an arrest warrant from a justice of the peace or judge. Alternatively, the judge may issue a **summons to appear**, which is served on the accused, requiring that they present themselves before a judge at a specified time. An arrested person must be brought before a judge within 24 hours. The judge decides whether to keep the person in jail, release the accused with a promise to appear later, or require the posting of bail or a surety.

Justice can issue a search warrant, arrest warrant, and summons to appear

Accused must be brought to judge within 24 hours of arrest

Summary conviction for minor offences

Indictment for serious offences

Summary conviction offences are minor offences and usually involve lesser penalties with a jail term limited to two years. An **indictable offence** is more serious, with penalties involving heavy fines and up to life in prison, depending on the offence. These terms refer to the judicial process that is undertaken with each type of offence. A summary conviction involves little more than the exchange of information and negotiation by the prosecutor and the defence between the appearance and the trial. An indictment is a more involved and lengthy process, which normally includes a preliminary hearing before a provincial court judge to determine whether there is enough evidence to proceed to trial. Some offences give the prosecutor the choice of proceeding by indictment or by summary conviction. Usually the choice is based on how serious the offending conduct was. For example, where a drunk driver injures or kills someone, it is much more likely that the prosecutor will choose to proceed by way of indictment. The accused can then choose the simpler summary trial before a provincial court judge, but with the more serious penalties, or trial before a superior court judge with or without a jury. For example, where a business person has been accused of false and misleading advertising under the federal *Competition Act*, the prosecutor can choose to proceed by way of summary conviction or indictment. If the choice is for the summary process the penalties are limited to a maximum fine of $200 000 or up to one year in jail or where indictment is chosen the maximum penalty is 5 years in prison and/or a fine left up to the discretion of the court.[15]

Prosecutor has choice with hybrid offences

Accused can choose trial before provincial court judge, superior court judge, or judge and jury

Plea-bargaining can avoid trial

Plea-bargaining is also a common aspect of the criminal process. This involves giving the accused the opportunity to plead guilty to a lesser offence. This process offends some people, but it has advantages from the point of view of serving justice, ensuring a conviction, and avoiding the costs and uncertainty of a trial.

A criminal trial is similar to a civil trial, with a prosecutor presenting evidence against an accused, who then presents his defence. When there is a jury it will hear the evidence and then receive instructions from the judge as to the law. The jury then decides whether or not the defendant is guilty. If the jury can't agree on a verdict, a new trial may be ordered. If the trial is before a judge alone he or she will decide on the guilt or innocence of the accused, and impose a sentence within the sanctions set out in the *Criminal Code* for the offence. The length of sentence will vary with the seriousness of the criminal conduct. For example, when an Alberta lawyer misappropriated trust funds in his care, he was convicted of criminal breach of trust and sentenced to three and one-half years' imprisonment. He was also required to repay the Alberta Law Society the amount misappropriated.[16] In another example of criminal breach of trust, a travel agent was sentenced

Criminal trial similar to civil trial

---

[15] *Competition Act*, R.S.C. (1985) c. 19 s 52 (5).

[16] *R. v. Manolescu*, Alta. Provo Ct., as reported in *Lawyers Weekly*, Vol. 17 No. 17 (September 12, 1997).

to two years less a day and fined $200 000 for cheating the government out of $750 000 in GST payments.[17] A judge may also have the discretion to impose a suspended sentence. This is still a conviction but with no penalty. Sometimes conditions are attached, such as community service or probation, rather than a fine or imprisonment. The judge also may order an absolute discharge, which does not involve a conviction.

Alternative sentences

Finally, it should be noted that there are a number of offences that don't involve the direct commission of the actual crime. For example, it is an offence for someone to aid or abet another in the commission of a crime, to be an accessory before or after a crime, or to counsel the commission of a crime. A particular danger from a business point of view is conspiracy. Where several people together plan the commission of a crime, this constitutes a conspiracy and all are guilty even though they may not have directly participated in the offence.

Key Terms

aboriginal rights (p. 10)

accounting (p. 17)

act (p. 7)

affidavits (p. 15)

appearance (p. 14)

appellant (p. 4)

arbitration (p. 19)

bill (p. 7)

cause of action (p. 14)

Civil Code (p. 2)

civil law (p. 2)

class action suit (p. 15)

common law (p. 3)

contempt of court (p. 17)

counterclaim (p. 14)

Courts of Chancery (p. 4)

cross-examination (p. 16)

damages (p. 16)

defendant (p. 12)

democratic rights (p. 9)

direct examination (p. 16)

distinguishing cases (p. 3)

due diligence (p. 23)

equality rights (p. 10)

fair hearing (p. 20)

fundamental freedoms (p. 9)

general damages (p. 17)

indictable offence (p. 24)

injunction (p. 17)

judgment creditor (p. 17)

judgment debtor (p. 17)

law (p. 1)

law of equity (p. 4)

legal rights (p. 9)

legislation (p. 7)

liability (p. 16)

mediation (p. 19)

minority language education rights (p. 10)

mobility rights (p. 9)

negotiation (p. 18)

notice of action (p. 14)

parliamentary supremacy (p. 5)

plaintiff (p. 12)

plea-bargaining (p. 24)

pleadings (p. 14)

precedent (p. 3)

private law (p. 2)

privitive clauses (p. 21)

procedural law (p. 2)

public law (p. 2)

punitive damages (p. 17)

---

[17] *R. v. Onkar Travels Inc.*, [2003] OJ. No. 2939, as reported in *Lawyers Weekly*, Vol. 23 No. 20 (September 26, 2003).

questions of fact (p. 16)

questions of law (p. 16)

references (p. 12)

regulations (p. 7)

respondent (p. 4)

rule of law (p. 5)

special damages (p. 17)

specific performance (p. 17)

stare decisis (p. 3)

statement of claim (p. 14)

statement of defence (p. 14)

statute (p. 5)

strict liability offences (p. 23)

substantive law (p. 2)

summary conviction offences (p. 24)

summons to appear (p. 24)

writ of summons (p. 14)

Questions for Student Review

1. Why is it important for a business student to understand the law?

2. Define law and distinguish between substantive and procedural law.

3. Explain the origin and function of the *Constitution Act (1867)*, formerly the *British North America Act*, and its importance with respect to how Canada is governed.

4. Explain parliamentary supremacy and its place in our legal system.

5. Indicate the importance of the *Constitution Act (1982)*, and explain why it was important to the development of Canada.

6. How are individual human rights protected in Canada?

7. Explain the significance of the *Charter of Rights and Freedoms* and identify three limitations on its application.

8. Describe the basic rights and freedoms protected in the Charter.

9. Describe the court structure in place in your province.

10. Contrast the nature and function of the provincial court and superior trial court in your province and distinguish between the roles of trial courts and courts of appeal including the Supreme Court of Canada.

11. Explain the purpose of the Federal Court, and the role it plays in the Canadian judicial process.

12. How is a civil action commenced?

13. Explain the nature and role of a statement of defence, a counterclaim, and the discovery process.

14. Contrast the process and the requirements of proof required in a civil as opposed to a criminal action.

15. Compare the roles played by a judge and a jury in a trial.

16. Explain how a judgment can be enforced.

17. Distinguish between negotiation, mediation, and arbitration, and indicate the advantages and disadvantages of alternate dispute resolution over litigation.

18. Explain the nature of regulations and their legal status.

19. Explain the nature of administrative tribunals and their relationship to our legal system.

20. Distinguish between criminal and regulatory offences.

21. Explain the difference between a criminal and a strict liability offence.

22. Distinguish between summary conviction and indictable offences and explain the various options of the parties involved.

Questions for Further Discussion

1. Discuss the relationship between law, morality, and ethics. How does one determine what is ethical behaviour and what is not if you can't use the law as the test? What would be the outcome if the courts tried to set a social or personal moral standard?

2. Canada has a tradition of parliamentary supremacy inherited from Great Britain. However, that has been modified somewhat by the passage of the *Charter of Rights and Freedoms*. Explain how parliamentary supremacy has been limited by the Charter, how that affects the role of the courts, and whether these changes enhance or are detrimental to Canada as a democracy.

3. The process leading to trial is long, involved, and costly. Most jurisdictions are trying to change the procedures to alleviate delays and costs. How successful are they and what other changes would be appropriate? Keep in mind the benefits of the current system; do they outweigh the disadvantages? In your discussion consider the advantages and disadvantages of alternate dispute resolution methods.

4. Government boards and tribunals may be considered an appropriate form of dispute resolution. Is it appropriate for the courts to be able to exercise review powers over their decisions? Are there enough safeguards in place to protect the rights of people who are affected by administrative decisions?

5. Describe the essential difference between a criminal prosecution and a civil action, and discuss the advantages and challenges associated with each process. Consider when a business person might have to choose between them and what factors would affect that decision.

Cases for Discussion

1. *Shirley v. Eecol Electric (Sask.) Ltd.* (Sask. Human Rights Board of Inquiry), February 16, 2001, as reported in *Lawyers Weekly Consolidated Digest*, Vol. 21. [1993] 2 S.C.R. 1094, 106 D.L.R. (4th).

   Mrs. Shirley had a good work record until she suffered a serious whiplash injury in an automobile accident. As she recovered, she wanted to take advantage of a government-funded graduated work program where she would work an increasing number of hours each week until she was able to resume her full-time employment. Her employer, however, insisted on a firm date when she would return to full-time employment, and when she couldn't give such a commitment, her employment was terminated. Indicate what grounds she has to complain, where she would take that complaint, and her likeli-hood of success. In your answer consider the impact of such a decision on the business.

2. *Ramsden v. Peterborough (City)*, [1993] 2 S.C.R. 1094, 106 D.L.R. (4th) 233 (SCC).

   This is a classic case dealing with freedom of expression. The City of Peterborough had passed a bylaw prohibiting the posting of any material on city property. The bylaw prohibited the posting of "any bill, poster or other advertisement of any nature," on any "tree . . . pole, post, stanchion or other object . . ." within the city limits. Ramsden put up advertising posters on several hydro poles to advertise an upcoming concert for his band. He was charged with committing an offence under the bylaw. It is not disputed that he posted the bills on the hydro pole. Indicate what other defence he might have to the charge and the arguments for both sides and likely outcome.

3. *British Columbia Government and Service Employees' Union v. British Columbia (Public Service Employee Relations Commission)*, [1999] 3 S.C.R. 3, 176 D.L.R. (4th) 1 (S.C.C).

    A female forest firefighter in British Columbia lost her job because she couldn't run 2.5 kilometres while carrying a 35-kilogram pack, to satisfy a government-imposed standard of fitness required for her job. She showed that this requirement clearly disadvantaged women, who don't have the same aerobic capacity as men. She also argued that there was nothing in her job that required this kind of performance. She made a complaint to the Human Rights Commission of British Columbia. Consider the arguments on both sides. What do you think should be the decision? Would it affect your answer to know that when the test was given about 70 percent of the men taking it passed, but only 35 percent of the women? How could a decision in her favour affect other firefighters and firefighting in general?

4. *R. v. Saplys, Ont. Gen. Div.*, February 18, 1999, as reported in *Lawyers Weekly Consolidated Digest*, Vol. 18.

    The special investigations unit of the RCMP suspected that a corporation was being used for a fraudulent purpose, but had to close the investigation for lack of evidence. They approached Revenue Canada to do an audit. This was done and the information was handed over to the police. This information was used to obtain a search warrant, and charges were subsequently laid. Indicate what complaint the principals of the corporation had and what should be done with the evidence. Should the ends justify the means?

5. *Vancouver (City) v. Jaminer*, B.C.S.C., December 13, 1999, as reported in *Lawyers Weekly Consolidated Digest*, Vol. 19.

    A city by-law was enacted without notice to those affected. The by-law prohibited rooftop signs extending above the roofline of a building to enhance the aesthetics of the urban environment. Jaminer erected such a sign, leased it out for advertising purposes, and was subsequently ordered to remove it by the city. He refused and the city applied to the Supreme Court of British Columbia for an injunction ordering the removal of the sign. Indicate both Charter and procedural arguments that might be available to both sides and the likely outcome. Which result is more efficient in business terms and should this be taken into consideration by the courts?

Chapter 2
Torts and Professional Liability

Learning Objectives

- Define and differentiate a tort from a crime

- Identify several types of intentional torts

- List the elements required to establish negligent conduct

- Trace the development of law related to product liability

- Apply tort principles to professional conduct

- Identify a number of business-related torts

Personal liability involves one person being held accountable when their wrongful conduct causes injury or loss to another. A tort is defined as a private wrong. If the wrongful act causes an injury, the injured person can sue the wrongdoer in a private or civil court action. Some common examples of wrongful conduct, or torts, that may be found in business situations are assault and battery, false imprisonment, trespass, defamation, deceit, nuisance, and negligence, with negligence being by far the most important. A tort is committed when the conduct complained of is inherently wrong. When a contract is breached (contracts are discussed in following chapters) the conduct, or lack thereof, is unacceptable only because the agreement obligates them to do otherwise. But where someone drives carelessly or defames another, the conduct itself is unacceptable, hence wrongful. Criminal conduct also must be distinguished. As discussed in Chapter 1, a crime is offensive conduct considered serious enough for the state to get involved and prosecute the offender. A tort is a civil wrong in the sense that it is the injured party, not the state, that is bringing the action, and the penalties, procedures, and standards of proof are different. Note, however, that specific conduct may be both a crime and a tort, and result in two court procedures, one civil and one criminal (see Figure 2.1).

A tort is a civil wrong

Wrongful conduct may be both a crime and a tort

Figure 2.1 Crime v. Tort

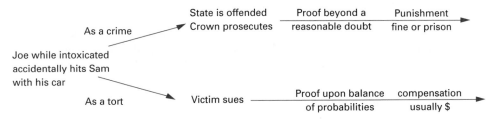

Employer can be vicariously liable.

The reason that a business person has more than a passing interest in tort law is because of **vicarious liability**. An employer is responsible (vicariously liable) for all torts committed by employees in the course of their employment. The employer, usually a company, is responsible for any injuries caused by their employees while doing what they have been employed to do, even where the employees were doing it badly or improperly. The employee is liable as well, but it is usually only the employer who has the resources to pay.

INTENTIONAL TORTS

Intentional torts involve deliberate acts

The listing of torts by categories, as we are about to do, is somewhat misleading. It is only possible to list a few of the recognized categories of torts, and even where conduct does not fit into a well-defined category, the courts will provide a remedy where rights have been violated. These categories are used because it makes the concept easier to understand and because the courts apply different rules and award different remedies depending on the type of tort involved. This first section deals with intentional torts involving deliberate conduct. Note that it is not that the injury was intended, only that the conduct leading to it involves a deliberate act. If the conduct leading to the interference was inadvertent, the appropriate cause of action is negligence, which will be discussed below. (For a summary of the categories of intentional torts, see Table 2.1 on p. 37.)

When one person physically interferes with another, it might be done for the best of motives, and yet it still might qualify as a trespass to person. For example, a medical doctor applying treatment might be doing so to help the patient, but if that treatment is unwanted and consent has been denied, a battery has taken place.

Case Summary 2.1 *Swanson v. Mallow*[1]

Spraying of Pam Is Battery

During a labour dispute at a Safeway store in Regina, three striking workers on two occasions sprayed Pam (cooking oil) on Monica Swanson who was working as a security guard. As a result she suffered laryngitis, headaches, and nausea, and was unable to go back to work for a year. They were charged criminally, but at a preliminary hearing it was decided there was not enough evidence to proceed.

Ms. Swanson also sued in a civil action. At that trial the striking workers were found liable and were assessed damages in the amount of $33 869 for lost income,

trauma, and punitive damages. This illustrates the difference between a criminal and civil action. The criminal action required a higher standard of proof and was dismissed, but the civil action was decided on the balance of probabilities and that standard was met. Labour disputes often involve high emotions on both sides, but when the conduct steps over the line and a tort or crime is committed, the perpetrators are liable for their actions. All concerned should take great care to avoid this kind of physical confrontation.

Assault and Battery

Battery involves physical contact

Assault involves apprehended physical contact

Assault and battery (a form of trespass to person), involves intentional physical interference with another. A **battery** takes place where there is actual physical contact. An **assault** is a threat to harm another. If someone points a gun at a person, an assault has

---

[1] [1991] 5 W.W.R. 454, 94 Sask. R. 217 (Sask. Q.B.).

taken place because of the victim's fear or apprehension of that contact. Even when the person pointing the gun knows there are no bullets, it is still an assault if the victim thinks the gun is loaded. To qualify as an assault, the threat of physical contact must be immediate and physically possible to carry out. If someone threatens to beat you up later, or shakes a fist while you drive off in your car, there is no assault. But if someone steps out in front of you shaking his or her fist, the threat of violence is immediate and possible, and so an actionable assault has taken place. The threatened interference need not be harmful, just unwanted. Medical practitioners are sometimes sued for trespass to person (battery) because they failed to obtain proper consent before a surgical procedure. Even where that procedure is beneficial and the motive is to help, people have the right to decide what happens to their bodies, and a doctor cannot proceed without approval. Such consent can be implied where conditions are life threatening, the patient is unable to give instructions to the doctor, and no guardian is available. But no consent can be implied where there is a clear refusal from the victim.

Threatened contact must be immediate, possible, and unwanted

Defences
Consent is a valid defence to a claim of assault and battery. Kissing would be a trespass to the person, but is considered innocent where the two parties consent. Medical treatment is appropriate and not actionable when the patient consents to the procedure—even where unexpected damage results. In all cases practitioners must take care to ensure that the medical treatment or other conduct goes no farther than the informed consent allows. A hockey player might be protected from being sued by the principle of consent even for a hard check, but if a player were to charge that the other player intentionally speared him with his stick, the consent defence might well be lost. Another important defence for assault and battery is **self-defence**. When attacked, a victim can use reasonable force in response. Such an attack cannot be viewed as an invitation to respond with unrestrained violence. The victim can only use reasonable force or as much force as is necessary to fend off the attack. Further, that reasonable force must be in response to an immediate threat, not one that has passed. Then the response becomes revenge rather than self-defence.

Informed consent effective defence

Self-defence using reasonable force effective defence

Conduct that amounts to assault and battery in tort law can also constitute several different criminal offences under the *Criminal Code* of Canada. These charges range from the actual use of force to the uttering of threats, intimidation, and making harassing phone calls. As in tort law, self-defence and consent will excuse the use of physical force but that force must be reasonable, and consent will not justify assisting a suicide or other specified types of prohibited conduct. Reasonable force can also be used to accomplish a justified arrest or to defend property. A number of other offences such as robbery and homicide also include the prohibited use of physical force or the threat of such force.

There are a number of criminal offences that correspond to assault and battery

Consent or self-defence will not always justify the use of physical force

False Imprisonment
Another type of intentional tort, also amounting to trespass to the person, is **false imprisonment**. Business people dealing with the public will sometimes get into trouble when they suspect someone of shoplifting, or some other inappropriate conduct, and then restrain the person until the police arrive. This amounts to an imprisonment, and when it is done improperly or without authority, it is an actionable false imprisonment. Most people think of an imprisonment as involving a cell, handcuffs, or some other physical restraint. But an imprisonment may take place even where no physical restraint is present. When someone demands that another person accompany her, or even remain in a certain location, and that person complies thinking she has no choice, that person is submitting to the other, and an imprisonment has taken place. Of course,

Complete restraint without authority is an actionable tort

Restraint can be physical or submission

not all such imprisonments are actionable. If the person really has committed a crime for which he can be arrested, even a private citizen has the authority to arrest. But where no crime has taken place, the imprisonment is false and the victim can sue. Note that the police have slightly broader powers of arrest.

Shoplifting, or failing to pay for services, is a serious problem facing people in businesses such as retail stores, hotels, or restaurants. Managers of such businesses are sometimes driven to take decisive action. But they must take great care in doing so, as the potential loss from a false imprisonment allegation can far outweigh the actual losses. The classic example, of a restaurant manager detaining a customer who refuses to pay his bill because he is dissatisfied with the quality of the meal served, is a graphic illustration of employee overreaction and unawareness of the limits of the employee's authority. One such incident cost Marwest Hotel $3500 in damages plus legal expenses over a dispute involving an $8 bottle of wine.[2]

Case Summary 2.2 *Snow v. Brettons Inc.*[3]

Clerk's Error Results in Actionable False Imprisonment

Ms. Snow purchased an item at the defendant's store and upon leaving set off the security alarm. A sales clerk took her by the arm and escorted her back into the store where her bag was searched; it was determined that a tag inadvertently left on an item, which Ms. Snow had properly purchased and had gift wrapped, set off the alarm. Upon leaving, her embarrassment was made worse when she met a co-worker from her own place of employment. She sued the store for false imprisonment. The court held that when she returned with the store clerk to the store, it was reasonable for her to think she had no choice and so an imprisonment had taken place.

It was false because no offence had occurred. Rather, an employee of the store had neglected to remove the tag. Although the incident only lasted five minutes, it caused great embarrassment and the judge awarded damages of $1000 for the false imprisonment. Four walls or physical restraint are not required to constitute an imprisonment. When a person surrenders his or her will to another, thinking he or she has no choice but to go with that person, it is still an imprisonment and actionable if done without authority. This case illustrates how careful a business dealing with the public has to be when dealing with apparent shoplifters.

Trespass

The tort of **trespass to land** involves someone coming on to another's land without permission or authority. A person can be a trespasser without even realizing he is on someone else's property. Someone wandering onto another's property, not realizing she had crossed the boundary line, would be a trespasser. By contrast, a person hit by a car and knocked on to another's property is not. Of course, someone with authority, such as a postal employee delivering mail or an official reading a meter, is not a trespasser. This is true even when that person is acting without permission, provided he doesn't go beyond that authority. The entrance of a meter reader would be authorized, but if the meter reader cut through the back yard to get to the next street, such an unauthorized shortcut would be a trespass. A trespass can also take place indirectly when someone throws something

---

[2] *Bahner v. Marwest Hotel Co.* (1969), 6 D.L.R. (3d) 322 (B.C.S.C.).

[3] Ont. Prov. Ct., (Oct. 16, 1987) as reported in *Lawyers Weekly Consolidated Digest*, Vol. 8.

onto the land or where a permanent incursion takes place, as when a structure is built that encroaches on another's property. Customers can become trespassers when they overstay their welcome, cause destruction, or otherwise break the rules associated with the premises. In this case the proprietor has the right to eject them using reasonable force (no more force than is necessary). This requires that the proprietor first tell the person to leave and give him or her enough time to vacate the premises before having the individual forcefully ejected.

Trespassers may be ejected using reasonable force

There is also a *Criminal Code* offence of trespassing, where a person loitering on another's property at night by a dwelling house is liable to summary conviction. The *Criminal Code* also permits reasonable force to be used to eject a trespasser and to defend real or personal property. Where the trespasser resists, his or her conduct will constitute an assault against the property owner.

Trespass may also be criminal

Trespassers are responsible for any damage they cause on the property. But no damage is actually necessary for the trespass to be actionable by the landowner. When the trespasser is injured on the property, traditionally the occupier of the land was not responsible unless that damage was caused intentionally or recklessly. Most jurisdictions have passed legislation modifying the duty owed by occupiers to those using their land, but even then the duty owed to trespassers is significantly less than the duty owed to others using the property. When a building encroaches on another's land, this is called a continuing trespass and like other forms of trespass the remedy might be damages or an injunction. An injunction would pose a huge problem, requiring the building to be removed at great expense unless a settlement could be negotiated.

Responsibility to trespasser modified by statute

Injunctions used to stop trespassers

Case Summary 2.3 *Epstein v. Cressey Development Corp.*[4]

Necessary Incursion Is Still Trespass

Cressey Development Corporation excavated a lot next to property owned by Mr. Epstein and asked permission to drive supports under Epstein's property to support that excavation. Epstein refused. After unsuccessfully trying other methods to shore up the excavation, Cressey drove the supports under the property anyway. When Epstein found out, he sued for trespass. Cressey claimed the trespass was done out of necessity and that there had been no interference with Epstein's use of his property.

The court held that a trespass had taken place, that damage was caused since future development was now restricted, and that Cressey Development Corporation had been warned by their own engineer that this would amount to trespass. Even so, they went ahead with little concern for Epstein's rights. Punitive damages were justified in this situation. In this case significant damages were awarded, but the award of an injunction to remove the supports would have been much worse since Cressey had completed the construction of the building. Great care should be taken to avoid these situations, and one should never assume that just because such an incursion or other activity is necessary to facilitate your business affairs it justifies interference with another person's property. Your business problems are not the problems of your neighbour.

Nuisance

Private nuisance involves one person using their property in such a way as to interfere with a neighbour's use of their property. This might involve fumes, odours, water, noise, or other substances escaping from one property so as to interfere with a neighbour's

Nuisance involves unusual use of property interfering with neighbour

---

[4] (1992), 89 D.L.R. (4th) 32 (BCCA).

enjoyment of his or her property. Remedies may include damages or an injunction. But the activity complained of must be an inappropriate use of that property. A person moving into an industrial area can't complain about the noise from a factory next door, and someone in a farming area can't complain about normal barnyard smells. But a person in an urban area could complain about smoke from a neighbour's smokehouse drifting onto his property and making it impossible to use the backyard. Also the interference with the use of the neighbour's property must have been reasonably foreseeable; the offender should have anticipated the result. Reasonable foreseeability will be discussed in greater depth under "Negligence" in this chapter.

Defamation

Defamation involves derogatory false statement

Defamation can also be a serious problem for the business person. It involves a false statement about someone to his or her detriment. The statement must not only reflect badly on the victim, but also clearly refer to the person suing. If you said the workers in a particular office were slackers, an individual in that group could not claim defamation since that person could not prove that the statement referred particularly to him or her. It is also possible to defame a product or business. Thus, circulating a false statement that a competitor's brand of beer is contaminated would qualify as defamation. The derogatory statement must also be published to be actionable, which means it must be heard or read by someone other than the two parties involved. This might take the form of a newspaper article, a letter to the editor, or a radio or TV broadcast, but it also could be a letter to the other person's employer, or simply a conversation overheard at a restaurant. Sometimes a statement might appear innocent, but because of some special

Defamation may involve innuendo

knowledge held by the hearer, it becomes derogatory. The statement in a financial paper about a couple at a business convention might appear perfectly innocent, until it's combined with the knowledge of some readers that both are married to other people. This is called an **innuendo** and even where the statement is made in error, it is actionable as **defamation**. **Mistake** is no defence. **Libel** is written defamation whereas spoken defama-

Slander is verbal; libel is written and easier to prove

tion is **slander**. Libel is treated much more seriously, on the theory that it takes a more permanent form and thus can do more damage. Essentially, libel is easier to prove. With slander, except for a few exceptions, actual monetary loss must be shown, whereas with libel it is enough to show that the defamatory statement was made. Legislation has been passed in most jurisdictions declaring broadcasted (over the radio or TV) defamation to

Broadcasted defamation is libel by statute

be libel rather than slander. Communications over the internet are becoming an increasing problem, but there is no question that emails, social networking sites, and internet blogs now pose the greatest danger. It is so easy to thoughtlessly post inappropriate material on a blog or compose emails and send them to many different destinations that this has become an important cause of defamation actions today.

Defences

There are several important defences available to a defamation action, not the least of which is **justification**. So long as the statement is substantially true this represents an effective defence. However, it is important to note that the defendant must prove the statement true rather than the plaintiff having to prove it false. Remember that it is the actual message being communicated (even if it is an innuendo) that must be true, not simply the bare words or the idea that was intended by the communication. Statements made on the floor of the legislature or Parliament, in senior government committees, and as part of trial

Derogatory statements made in Parliament or court are protected

proceedings are considered **absolute privilege**, and cannot form the basis of a defamation action. The free flow of information and the encouragement of debate and free speech are considered to be too important in these circumstances to be hindered by the threat of litigation. Statements made in the context of employment such as the evaluation of another employee's work habits or reports made to the police investigating a case are protected to a lesser extent. This lesser protection is also given to statements made with respect to some matter of mutual interest as with members of professional bodies such as lawyers', accountants', doctors', or dentists' associations. This is called **qualified privilege** and so long as the person made the statement thinking it was true, without malice, and did not communicate it to anyone other than those who needed to know, the victim cannot successfully sue, even if the communication was false and damaging. One of the dangers of using the internet or email is that the message may be communicated too broadly and thus qualified privilege may be lost.

Derogatory comments made pursuant to duty are protected

Case Summary 2.4 *McGarrigle v. Dalhousie University*[5]

Qualified Privilege Protects Employers

Mr. McGarrigle, the coach of the Dalhousie university basketball team, had improperly allowed an academically ineligible player to play in five basketball games in violation of the CIS rules governing the sport. When this happens there is an obligation on the institution to disclose the violation by submitting an appropriate letter to that effect. This was done, but Mr. McGarrigle took the position that some of the contents of that letter were defamatory and sued.

The judge found that Dalhousie had a clear duty to publish the self-disclosure letter to CIS officials and so there is no doubt that this was an occasion of qualified privilege. But a copy of the letter was also sent to the officials of Atlantic University Sport (AUS), which Mr. McGarrigle argued was not required and so any qualified privilege was lost through over publication of the information. This body has no direct role in the disciplinary process and there was no legal duty to send a copy to them. It was clear that the AUS had an interest in what had happened, especially since

they would have to be informed that Dalhousie would be forfeiting those particular games. In all instances the letter had been marked "confidential." This was enough to protect the privilege. Sending the letter to them may have been unwise but it did not disqualify the privilege.

Finally, McGarrigle argued that the defamatory aspects of the letter had been motivated by malice and that this caused any qualified privilege to be lost. But the judge found that the letter related only to the matter of the ineligibility, that it expressed honestly held beliefs, and that there was no dishonesty or ulterior motive in sending a copy to AUS and so there was no malice. The action was dismissed.

The case shows the operation and effect of the defence of qualified privilege in a defamation action but also shows how it can be lost. Over publication and malice will cause any defence of qualified privilege to be lost, but in this case over publication and malice were not established.

Fair comment is another important defence used mostly by the media. People are entitled to have and express opinions on matters of public interest, and so commentaries on plays, exhibitions, sports, or even comments on the actions of politicians and other public figures are protected. As long as the expression of opinion is commentary based on true facts known to the public—even where the opinion is unpopular and most of the public disagrees—and as long as it is a possible conclusion based on the public facts and stated without malice, it is protected. For these reasons harsh or derisive reviews of restaurants, plays, sporting competitions, and the like are not actionable. Politicians are also fair game, but great care must be taken to keep the statement an expression of opinion based on known facts. If the commentary involves statements of fact that are not

Derogatory comments made as fair comment on public matter are protected

---

[5] [2007] N.S.J. No. 108.

true, they are actionable as defamations. You can conclude that a politician's actions were incompetent, but your statement of what happened to lead you to that conclusion had better be accurate. It is interesting that fair comment also protects political cartoons that get their messages across by exaggeration. It should be noted that the Ontario Court of Appeal following the English courts has broken new ground by adding a new defence available to the media.[6] This defence of "responsible journalism" is similar to the concept of due diligence in that if the newspaper can show that the alleged libel involved a matter of public interest and the journalists can show they took reasonable steps to ensure what they were publishing was true, they will be protected even if what they alleged was false. It is generally expected that this defence will be adopted by other provinces and become good law in Canada giving journalists even greater protection than enjoyed in the past.

Legislation in place also limits the exposure of newspapers and other communications media by limiting the amount of damages that can be claimed by the victim if an appropriate apology is published. Still, it must be remembered that defamatory remarks can be extremely dangerous and cause serious damage to the victim. The courts have awarded significant damages. In *Hill v. Church of Scientology of Toronto,*[7] for example, the total damages awarded were $1.6 million, and in a recent Ontario case a jury awarded $3 million to a pilot who was defamed with respect to his work and as a result lost his job and career.[8]

Defamatory libel can also constitute a criminal offence under the *Criminal Code* of Canada, where the published words will injure a person's reputation by "exposing him to hatred, contempt, or ridicule." The usual defences discussed above apply, but the truth of the defamation will only justify its publication if it is also in the public interest. Note also that extortion by defamatory libel, or the threat of it, is also an offence. Publishers can also be liable unless they can show they had no knowledge of the inclusion of the offending words. In *R. v. Lucas*[9] a husband and wife were charged with criminal libel when they picketed a provincial court building. Their signs suggested that a police officer investigating the sexual abuse of children failed in his duty and contributed to or participated in sexually abusive conduct himself. The Supreme Court of Canada found that although the sections of the *Criminal Code* did interfere with freedom of expression, they were justified under section 1 of the *Charter of Rights and Freedoms* to protect the reputation of individuals so defamed. The original sentences imposed at trial were two years less a day for Mr. Lucas and 22 months for his wife, but these were reduced to 18 months and 12 months on appeal. These convictions were upheld by the Supreme Court of Canada.

Libel may also be criminal

NEGLIGENCE

Of all the different ways that liability can be incurred in tort, negligence is by far the most important for the business person. **Negligence** involves inadvertent or careless conduct causing injury or loss to another. At the outset, it must be made clear that

Negligence involves inadvertent conduct causing loss

---

[6] *Cusson v. Quan,* [2007] O.J. No. 4348.

[7] [1995] 2 S.C.R. 1130 (S.C.C.).

[8] *Fennimore v. SkyService Airlines,* as reported in the *Lawyers Weekly* Vol. 27 No. 43, March 21, 2008.

[9] [1998] 1 S.C.R. 439 (S.C.C.).

Table 2.1 Intentional Torts

Intentional Torts	Nature	Defences
Assault and Battery	Assault: threatened battery	Consent: must be informed and complete
	Battery: intentional hitting	Self-defence: must be reasonable force Accident but not a mistake
False Imprisonment	Complete physical or mental restraint without authority	No actual confinement or submission Had authority to imprison
Trespass	Coming on to or putting something on another's land without authority	Had authority to do so Had consent Accident but not a mistake
Nuisance	Use of property so that it interferes with neighbour's	Appropriate use of property for area Interference was not reasonably foreseeable
Defamation	A published false and derogatory statement: spoken (slander) or written (libel)	Truth, absolute privilege, qualified privilege, and fair comment

negligence is not a state of mind. We are not talking about someone being silly or stupid. Negligence involves the failure of one person to live up to a standard of care required in his or her dealings with others. The term "careless," as it is used in this discussion, refers to the failure to live up to that required standard of care. When suing someone for negligence, several things must be established. First, that there was a duty of care. We don't owe a duty to be careful to everyone in the world or even to everybody in our community—only to limited classes or groups of people determined by legal test and social policy, as explained below. Once it is determined that a duty is owed, the next problem is to determine the nature of that duty. Just how careful does a person have to be? To succeed, the plaintiff must show that the conduct fell below a standard of care. Also it must be determined that there was some sort of injury or loss caused by the alleged conduct. (see Table 2.2)

At the outset it is vital to understand the concept of the **reasonable person** in law. While the conduct of average people might be more important in other disciplines, in law we set a standard of required behaviour somewhat higher than what would be expected of an average person. In effect, the court asks what a reasonable, objective bystander would have done in the same circumstances. This reasonable person test requires behaviour that is higher than average but less than perfect. A helpful comparison is the concept of par in a game of golf. Each hole on a golf course has a standard number of strokes associated with it called "par." An average golfer will require more strokes than this number to sink the ball, even though it is possible for a good golfer (or a lucky one) to do it in less. Par, then, is a higher standard or goal, designed to challenge the golfer. It reflects what a good golfer having a good day would likely be able to accomplish. The reasonable person standard in

Reasonable person: better than average but less than perfect

Table 2.2 Requirements of Negligence Action Plaintiff Must Establish	
Duty to Take Care	That injury or loss was reasonably foreseeable (sometimes limited by social policy based on the *Anns* case)
Failure to Take Care	That the conduct complained of fell below the reasonable person standard (or other standard imposed by statute)
Causation and Damage	That the conduct complained of caused loss or injury to the plaintiff

law is similar. It reflects a standard of behaviour we would expect from a prudent person being careful, and while it need not reach perfection, it is clear that average is not good enough.

Duty of Care

One of the most significant civil cases in the 20th century is the famous "snail in the ginger beer bottle" case, *Donoghue v. Stevenson*,[10] which took place in Scotland in the 1930s. The decision made by the House of Lords is followed in most common law jurisdictions. Mrs. Donoghue went to a café with a friend, who bought her a ginger beer float. The ginger beer was served in an opaque bottle, so it was not until the second serving that Mrs. Donoghue discovered it contained a decomposed snail. Mrs. Donoghue became violently ill, but she couldn't successfully sue the café for breach of contract, since her friend bought the ginger beer for her. Contract law is a major area of discussion in the following chapters. Instead, she sued the bottler of the product, Stevenson, in tort for negligence. The case turned upon whether the bottler, Stevenson, owed a duty to be careful to Mrs.

Negligence requires duty of care

Donoghue, the ultimate consumer of the product he produced. The case is famous because it established the test to be used when determining whether a duty of care is owed to another. This is the **reasonable foreseeability test**. Thus, we owe a duty to be careful to anyone we can reasonably foresee (anticipate) might be harmed by our conduct. In this

Existence of duty determined by reasonable foreseeability

case it was clear that Mr. Stevenson should have anticipated that if he was careless in the production of the ginger beer, an ultimate consumer, Mrs. Donoghue, might be injured. Therefore, a duty to be careful was owed to her. This reasonable foreseeability test has become extremely important in the development of the law of negligence and personal liability, although it has been modified in some circumstances. While in normal negligence cases it is clear that foreseability still applies, the Supreme Court of Canada has made it clear that, today, when faced with new or unique problems, the courts are to apply the two-stage *Anns* case test.

The *Anns* case took place in England and involved a number of apartments constructed and let under 999-years leases. The lessors of those apartments brought an action against the city (Merton London Borough Council) for their failure to ensure that the foundation that had failed had been properly constructed. The main question faced by the House of Lords was whether the city owed them a duty of care. Lord Wilberforce found that a duty did exist and in the process formulated and applied the

---

[10] [1932] A.C. 562 (H.L.).

now classic *Anns* two-stage test. This test for determining duty has since been abandoned in England but not in Canada where the Supreme Court has repeatedly reaffirmed its validity.

The first stage of the test is to determine whether there is a degree of proximity or neighbourhood between the parties, such that one person should have realized that his or her conduct placed the victim at risk. This is essentially another way of expressing the reasonable foreseeability test developed in *Donoghue v. Stevenson*. The second question must then be asked: Is there any reason not to impose the duty, to reduce the scope of that duty, to limit the class to whom the duty is owed, or should the damages awarded be reduced? This second part of the *Anns* test allows the courts to modify the nature of the duty where circumstances warrant on the basis of social policy. In Canada then, where an action in negligence takes place and where it does not fall within a category of cases where a duty of care has previously been recognized, the two-staged test characterized as the *Anns* case test will be used to determine if there is a duty of care by determining first if injury or damage was reasonably foreseeable and then asking whether there is any good reason to reduce or eliminate the duty of care. It should be noted that a recent Supreme Court of Canada case has applied this social policy aspect to the first part of the *Anns* test as well.[11] Thus, defining proximity as not only what was reasonably foreseeable but as what was just and fair in the circumstances with the result that there are even fewer findings of duty in new and unique situations where negligence is alleged (see Table 2.2).

Anns case test may limit duty

One recent expansion of the duty of care and a serious problem for commercial hosts in restaurants and pubs was to make them liable to patrons who drink too much and then are injured. It is now well established that these people are owed a duty of care by the commercial establishment even though they are to a great extent the authors of their own misfortune. This duty extends not only to the customers themselves but also to others injured through their intoxicated conduct. For example, in *Laface v. Boknows Hotels Inc. and McWilliams*,[12] the hotel in question had served alcohol to the driver to the extent that they should have know that there was danger of an accident. After leaving the pub, the driver drove his car into a group of people on the roadway causing serious injuries. The appeal court upheld the trial judge's decision to divide liability equally between the driver and the hotel. A similar obligation is imposed on employers who serve alcohol to employees at office parties and on other occasions. This is illustrated by the *Hunt* case that follows. A more difficult question is whether a social host at a party is liable when one of their guests leaves intoxicated and is injured or injures another. In the *Childs v. Desormeaux* case[13] the Supreme Court of Canada dealt with this problem and held that no duty was owed in that situation. Here the hosts did not supply the alcohol that their guest consumed and there was no proof that they even knew that the guest was intoxicated when he left the party. Although it is clear that the Supreme Court was reluctant to extend the duty to such social hosts, the question is still open as to the extent of such social hosts' liability when they do supply the alcohol that leads to the accident.

---

[11] *Cooper v. Hobart*, [2001] 3 S.C.R. 537.

[12] [2006] B.C.J. No. 1111.

[13] [2006] S.C.J. No. 18.

Duty to Protect Worker from Herself

Linda Hunt was a receptionist working part-time for the Sutton Group Inc. when she attended a Christmas party where she had a considerable amount to drink. At 4:00 p.m. she still had responsibilities to clean up after the party, but her employer, seeing she was inebriated, offered to call her husband to come pick her up, to call her a taxi, and even to supply a hotel room. Instead, she remained for two or more hours at the party before she left with several other people and went to a pub. She then set out to drive home in freezing rain and snow. She was seriously injured when her car slid into the path of another vehicle.

The damages were over one million dollars. She sued her employer for putting her into an environment where she was at risk, and she sued the pub for failing to protect her as a patron. Although the court found that her behaviour had contributed to her loss, the employer and the pub were jointly and severally liable for 25 percent of that loss. Joint and several liability means that if one of the defendants can't pay his or her share, the liability assigned to him or her can be collected from the other defendant.

Judicial decisions in Canada have made it clear that employers and commercial establishments serving liquor can be held responsible for injury and loss suffered as a result of serving liquor to the point of intoxication. Care should be taken to ensure that people don't drink to excess and that alternate transportation be arranged when they do. The obvious problem is just what employers must do to protect themselves. In this case the employer went out of his way to try to make other arrangements for Ms. Hunt which she refused. Still he was held partially liable for the damages she suffered. What more could he have done? The result of these cases is a decline in the number of office parties where liquor is served. Stopping the practice is the best solution, but where this is not done it would seem prudent for such hosts (commercial, private, or employers) to make sure people don't drink to excess. It would also be wise to provide taxis or other means for guests to get home when they do drink too much or to provide some other form of accommodation to ensure they don't drink and drive.

Standard of Care

In most negligence cases the existence of a duty of care is self-evident, and the problem is to determine whether there was a failure to live up to the appropriate standard of care. As a general rule our law does not impose a duty to act and so omission (nonfeasance) is not generally actionable unless there is some special relationship imposing a duty. These would include roles such as a lifeguard or guardian, or situations where there is a duty to warn of some danger, as is the case with the occupier of property or the manufacturer of a dangerous product. In most examples of actionable negligence, inappropriate conduct or misfeasance is involved. The question remains, therefore, how careful does a person have to be? The general answer in Canadian law is that a person is required to live up to what would be expected of a reasonable person in the same circumstances. So long as that standard is maintained or surpassed, there has been no negligence even where serious harm has taken place. This is the second major application of the reasonable person test as used in the law of negligence, and is the most significant application of this test in our legal system. Remember that reasonable care is not average but is what is expected of a prudent person being careful. In determining reasonable conduct, the courts will look at several factors. The risk of potential damage will be taken into account. Thus, in a desert where torrential rains are rare, extensive waterproofing of a building would not be expected, especially where the costs of avoiding such an unlikely occurrence would be high. Risk,

The standard of conduct required is determined by reasonable person test

[14] 2002 CanLII 45019 (Ont. C.A.).

cost, and potential loss, therefore, are important factors to be taken into consideration in determining reasonable conduct.

Reasonable care is determined by risk, cost, and potential of loss

In situations where high risk is involved with great potential for damage, the duty to be careful is extremely high. When food handlers and motor vehicle operators cause injury, for example, negligence is easier to prove since the required standard of care is extremely high.

In rare circumstances where someone brings something dangerous on his or her property which escapes, causing injury to a neighbour, liability may be imposed, even where the owner of the property has not caused the escape. This is called strict liability or the rule in *Rylands v. Fletcher*.[15]

Another important factor is the expertise claimed by the person being held to a standard. Doctors, accountants, engineers, and other professionals are expected to have the skills and abilities associated with their profession and to exercise those skills in a reasonable manner. And so the standard expected is that of a reasonable doctor or a reasonable engineer. While it would likely not be negligent for an average person to misdiagnose a person having a stroke or a heart attack, it could well be negligence for an attending physician to make such an error.

Expertise claimed affects reasonableness of conduct

It is often difficult to determine just what caused the loss or injury. Some situations, however, such as a snail in a soft drink, a falling piano, or contaminated food leads one to the conclusion that someone must have been careless. Canadian courts can look at such circumstantial evidence, and, if strong enough, conclude that a presumption of negligence has been established. Then it is up to the defendant to produce evidence that he or she was not negligent. If the defendant cannot, the presumption is confirmed and liability for negligence determined. In the past this was treated under the principle of *res ipsa loquitur*, but the Supreme Court of Canada has decided that these matters are better dealt with by applying the more flexible principle of circumstantial evidence.[16]

Case Summary 2.6 *Kripps v. Touche Ross and Co.*[17]
Accountant Negligent Despite Following Rules

The defendants were a firm of accountants that audited the books of Victoria Mortgage and Housing from 1980 to 1983. These audited statements were used to issue a prospectus and sell debentures to the public. The auditors' refusal to approve the 1984 statements of the company led to its collapse. The debenture holders, who had relied on the previous statements, lost considerably in the collapse and sued the defendant auditors. The debenture holders claimed the auditors had been negligent in providing a favourable audit for the prior years. The problem related to a number of mortgages held by Victoria

Mortgage that were in default. They amounted to one-third of the mortgages held by that company. The bad mortgages had been capitalized as valuable assets along with the unpaid interest, instead of being treated as uncollectible losses.

The auditors defended their actions by stating that this was consistent with the rules that they followed (GAAP, Generally Accepted Accounting Principles and GAAS, Generally Accepted Audit Standards), and so long as they acted within those rules, they could not be acting negligently. The trial judge agreed, but on appeal the court

>

---

[15] (1868), L.R. 3 (H.H.) 330.

[16] *Fontaine v. British Columbia (Official Administrator)*, [1998] 1 S.C.R. 424 (S.C.C.).

[17] (1997), 33 B.C.L.R. (3d) 254, [1997] 6 W.W.R. 421 (B.C.C.A.).

found the auditors negligent. Professionals cannot hide behind the rules they make themselves and claim that they are following the appropriate standard, no matter what the consequences. "GAAP may be their guide to forming this opinion, but auditors are retained to form an opinion on the fairness of the financial statements, not merely on their conformity to GAAP." The auditors knew the mortgages were in default at the time, thus making their audited statements clearly misleading.

This case illustrates the high standard of care required of professionals and the fact that simply adhering to standard practice or rules of conduct set by a professional association may not always be good enough to escape liability.

Historically, special rules were applied to some unique situations. For example, occupiers (the people in possession of property as opposed to the landlord) had a particular responsibility to people using the land and premises, depending on their status. The occupier had to protect an invitee from any unusual danger. Invitees were people on the land for some business purpose. Licensees, who were there out of sufferance or with permission, had to be warned of any hidden danger, but the only duty owed to a trespasser was not to intentionally or recklessly harm him or her. Most jurisdictions have enacted occupier's liability acts, which modify these traditional obligations. Typically, the distinction between invitees and licensees has been abolished, requiring the occupier to take reasonable steps to protect all visitors and their property. The obligations to trespassers remain minimal. If the trespasser is a child, however, the obligations on the occupier are typically greater. The principle is that various features on property can be an attraction to children and extra care must be taken to keep them out and away from danger. In *Tutinka v. Mainland Sand and Gravel*[18] the operator of a gravel pit was aware that it was being used by dirt bike riders, but continued to work the property. In the process they dug away a section just over a hill used by the riders, creating a cliff, which an unsuspecting fifteen-year-old motorcyclist went over. The motorcyclist was seriously injured. Even though the plaintiff had not been given permission to be there, the operator was found to be 75% responsible under the *Occupier's Liability Act* of British Columbia.

There are other examples where legislation has been used to change the standard of care required of certain classes. The unique obligations owed by innkeepers to their guests and common carriers to their customers have been modified by statute in most jurisdictions. But it is important to realize that not every time a statute imposes a duty on someone is a new category of tort created. For example, human rights legislation and privacy legislation both impose duties and rights, but they are not tort obligations unless specifically made so by statute, and the remedies available are limited to those set out in the legislation that creates them. It should also be noted that insurance is a method of avoiding the risks associated with tort liability. In business, of course, insurance becomes a very important aspect of risk avoidance, and the cost of acquiring the various forms of insurance required to operate a business successfully must be factored into the overall cost of doing business. In many jurisdictions certain types of insurance coverage is mandatory, such as automobile insurance

Special statutory standards override common law

Causation and Damage

Finally, to succeed in a negligence action, the plaintiff must demonstrate **causation**, that the conduct complained of was the cause of the injury or damage (see Table 2.2 on p. 38). With intentional torts such as assault and battery, false imprisonment, or trespass,

Breach of duty must have led to loss or damage

---

[18] (1993) 110 D.L.R. (4th) 182 (B.C.C.A.).

Figure 2.2 Negligence

it is not necessary that actual damage be shown. The commission of the tort is enough to warrant payment of damages, although compensation for losses will also be included in any judgment. But with negligence there must be some sort of injury or damage resulting before compensation can be sought from the defendant. Almost getting hurt is not good enough. It follows that the damages must be the direct result of the negligent conduct complained of. The chain of events leading to liability caused by negligence is illustrated in Figure 2.2. If it were established that the driver involved in an accident knew his or her brake lights weren't working, the plaintiff would still have to demonstrate that the lack of brake lights caused the accident. If the accident involved a head-on collision, it would be very unlikely that this failure contributed to the collision. The defendant may have been careless for driving without brake lights, but that failure did not cause the accident. In some situations it can be a very difficult and complex problem for the court to determine just how much of a causal connection is needed for liability for negligence to be imposed. This will be discussed below under the heading "Remoteness."

Defences

Defences that the defendant can raise to eliminate or reduce liability in a negligence action are summarized in Table 2.3.

Contributory Negligence Traditionally, if it could be shown that the person who was suing had also contributed to the loss, he or she would receive no compensation from the defendant. This was first modified to a limited extent in common law and, subsequently, by legislation. Statutes such as Saskatchewan's *Contributory Negligence Act* allow the court to assign proportional liability, making both parties responsible for the loss (see Figure 2.3). For example, in an automobile accident Jones suffered $100 000 damage because of personal injury and Smith only suffered $10 000 damage to his car. If the court determined Smith to be 25 percent at fault and Jones 75 percent, Smith would have to pay Jones $17 500 (Smith pays 25 percent of Jones' loss, $25 000, minus Jones' 75 percent of Smith's loss, $7500) and legal costs. With **contributory negligence**, the court reduces

Where the victim is also negligent, loss is now apportioned

Table 2.3 Defences That the Defendant Can Raise to Eliminate or Reduce Liability in a Negligence Action	
Contributory Negligence	Where the plaintiff is also negligent, the court will apportion the damages.
Voluntary Assumption of Risk	Where the plaintiff has voluntarily put him- or herself in danger—and assumed the legal as well as physical risk—this will be a complete bar to recovery.
Remoteness	Where the causal connection is indirect or consequences out of proportion to expectations, liability may be reduced.

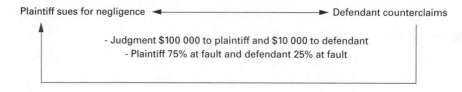

Figure 2.3 Negligence Action

the amount of compensation paid to a victim of negligence when the victim's own carelessness contributed to the loss.

Voluntary Assumption of Risk

Where victim voluntarily assumed the legal risk, there is no remedy

People who deliberately put themselves in harm's way are disqualified from suing for the injury or loss that results. Unlike contributory negligence, this is a complete bar to recovery of loss. This used to be a much more important aspect of negligence law, but to raise this defence today, the defendant must show not only that the injured party voluntarily put himself or herself in danger, but also that he or she did it in such as way as to absolve the defendant of any legal responsibility for the consequences. It must be established that not only did the victim assume the physical risk, but the legal risk as well. This is difficult to prove; consequently, when people act foolishly—taking risks that they shouldn't—the courts usually deal with it as contributory negligence. The courts can then apportion the loss between the parties based on their percentage of fault. This is a much more satisfactory result. Thus, when a drunken individual participated in a tubing race at a winter resort and was seriously injured, contributory negligence was applied rather than **voluntary assumption of risk**, because it could not be established that he had assumed both the legal risk and the physical risk. This was the case even though he had signed a waiver form before commencing the activity.[19] Still, in extreme cases where people knowingly put themselves in harm's way, the court may find voluntary assumption of risk and completely bar recovery.

Rescuers who put themselves into dangerous situations are treated differently. If a person is negligent, putting another at risk, he or she also owes a duty to be careful to someone coming to the rescue of that person. If a bystander pushes a child out of the path of a speeding car, and is injured in the process, she can sue the negligent driver without fear that a claim of voluntary assumption of risk or contributory negligence will bar the action.

Remoteness

Another argument that is sometimes raised in defence of a negligence action is that the injury or loss was too remote. The test used for **remoteness** is the same reasonable foreseeability test used to determine duty of care, but there it applied to the foreseeability of injury generally. Here the question is whether the particular injury in question was reasonably foreseeable. The recent *Mustapha* case[20] decided by the Supreme Court of Canada

---

[19] *Crocker v. Sundance Northwest Resorts Ltd.*, [1988] 1 S.C.R. 1186 (S.C.C.).

[20] *Mustapha v. Culligan of Canada Ltd.*, 2008 SCC 27 (CanLII).

is a good example. Here Mr. Mustapha was changing a water bottle when he saw a fly in the bottle. This caused him great anxiety eventually seriously affecting his health. He developed a phobia with respect to drinking water. He suffered from nightmares, an inability to sleep, was unable to drink water and became seriously depressed. In these product liability cases a duty of care is clearly established on the manufacturer based on the reasonable foreseeability test as established in *Donoghue v. Stevenson*. The trial judge determined that there was a breach of that duty of care because of lax inspection procedures. That failure caused the real, although unusual, injuries and awarded a total of $341 774 in damages.

The Supreme Court of Canada recently overturned this decision. The reasons given are instructive. The Chief Justice found that while there was a duty to be careful and a breach of that duty and that the damages suffered were the result of that failure, the injuries in question were too remote and therefore there was no liability. Physically the injuries were caused by the breach of duty but legally they were too remote. The court found that such injuries have to be reasonably foreseeable to an ordinary person. They must be a real risk and not one that a normal prudent person would consider to be far-fetched. In this case the court found that if the manufacturer had put their mind to it they would not have concluded that what happened was a real risk from their conduct and so no liability is imposed. Basically, the court is saying that Mr. Mustapha's susceptibility to injury was so unusual that it would have been unreasonable to impose a duty on the defendants to avoid the harm. Legal causation will only be established where there is reasonable foreseeability of such an injury to a person of "ordinary fortitude."

> *Where connection is tenuous or the results unexpected, social policy may be applied to reduce or modify duty*

Thus there must be a sufficient causal connection between the conduct complained of and the resulting injury. If that connection is considered to be too remote or too indirect, the requirement of causation will not be met and there will be no liability imposed.

Note that once the causal connection is found, when personal injury is involved, we take our victims the way we find them. Once such injury is foreseeable the plaintiff will be liable even if the degree of injury was unusual. Thus if the person whose hand I negligently injure is a concert pianist, I will be responsible to pay much greater compensation than if the person is a lawyer or accountant. I will not normally be able to claim that because of the unusual occupation of the victim his loss is too remote or that the damages should be limited only to what a normal person would lose. If damage to the hand was foreseeable I must take my victim as I find him and pay the greater compensation. In the *Mustapha* case above, the basic legal causation connection was not found in the first place and so there was no question of taking the victim as found.

> *Responsibility imposed even where unusual occupation or condition causes victim greater loss than normal*

PRODUCT LIABILITY

The *Mustapha* case discussed above indicates some of the difficulties faced by both parties in product liability cases. As discussed in *Donoghue v. Stevenson*, when use of a particular product injures a person, there is normally a choice. The purchaser can sue the seller of the product for breach of contract and/or sue the manufacturer for negligence. Contracts will be discussed in the following chapters, but it is important to note at this stage that an action in contract has the distinct advantage of imposing **strict liability** where the product was defective and caused the injury. There is no need to prove fault on the part of the defendant. However, such a breach of contract action may not be available to the injured party either because he or she was not the person who purchased the product, or because the contract was with the retailer who sold the item, not the manufacturer. The principle that only the parties to a contract have obligations under it is referred to as **privity of contract**. When there is no contractual relation between the parties, the only option is to sue for negligence. The problem is that in a tort action fault must be demonstrated, in addition to showing that the defective product caused the injury. The plaintiff must show that the defendant failed to live up to the standard of a reasonable manufacturer in the circumstances. This can be very difficult to do and is one of the situations where the courts are willing to look at the surrounding events and find that a *prima facie* (clear on the face of it) case of negligence has been established from circumstantial evidence. For example, finding a decomposed snail in a can of soda speaks loudly that someone must have been careless. Either the production process has not been properly designed to avoid this type of thing from happening, or someone made a silly mistake. Once the presumption of negligence has been established through circumstantial evidence, the onus then shifts and the manufacturer must face the daunting task of showing that they did everything reasonable to ensure that this type of injury would not happen. Once it is established that some aspect of the product was defective and caused the injury complained of and that the manufacturer was careless, liability to compensate for that injury will be imposed.

The product liability area is where class action suits are particularly important. Whether defective automobiles or tires, ruptured breast implants, or drugs that cause deformities or heart attacks are involved, when many people are injured as a result of the same complaint against the same manufacturer, a class action approach to the problem is an attractive way to proceed.

In the United States if a person can show that the product was defective and it caused his or her injury, usually that is enough to establish liability. This is called strict liability. Some jurisdictions in Canada have moved away from the traditional approach of requiring the demonstration of negligence in product liability cases. Other provinces have moved in that same direction by imposing contractual warranties on a manufacturer guaranteeing fitness and quality, and extending those rights to anyone who uses the product. This, in effect, wipes out the requirement that the victim be the purchaser of the product as discussed above. Courts in other jurisdictions have found that because of advertising, specifications, and other literature, including manufacturers' warranties, a subsidiary contract exists between the manufacturer and purchaser, making the manufacturer directly liable to the purchaser (see Figure 2.4).

Figure 2.4 Product Liability

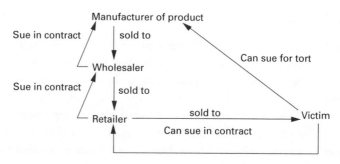

Margin notes:

When a manufacturer is sued, negligence must be established.

But note the use of circumstantial evidence

In some jurisdictions manufacturers may be sued in contract

PROFESSIONAL LIABILITY

A similar situation exists when professionals are involved. They have a direct contractual liability to their clients, and are liable, even without showing fault, when they make errors that cause loss to those clients. However, as they carry out their professional duties, the damage incurred often goes beyond their direct relation to their clients and causes economic or even physical loss or injury to third parties. Those injured claimants then must sue in tort for negligence, and the question for the court to determine is just how far they want to extend such **professional liability** in these circumstances. Historically, the courts refused to provide a remedy where the loss was purely economic, especially where it was caused by words rather than conduct. This changed in Canada in 1965 with the case of *Haig v. Bamford*[21] where investors suffered losses because of a misleading financial statement and successfully sued the negligent accountant who prepared them. In that case the Supreme Court of Canada did not adopt the reasonable foreseeability test, but required that the accountants have actual knowledge that investors would rely on the erroneous statements. For the next 25 years there was some confusion as to when a duty would exist and when it would not. The eventual solution was to supplement the reasonable foreseeability test developed in *Donoghue v. Stevenson* with a Canadian application of the *Anns* case[22] discussed above, which resulted in a much more straightforward and simple approach.

Where an accountant prepares such financial statements they are normally for use by the shareholders to review the performance of the managers in an annual shareholders' meeting. Sometimes, however, they are to be used in a prospectus to attract new investors. The law as developed by the Supreme Court was that a duty was owed when the accountants knew that investors would use them, but no duty existed when they were prepared just for the shareholders to evaluate the management of the corporation.

But a problem arose with the *Hercules* case.[23] Auditors prepared financial reports for a company as part of the normal annual auditing process. These reports were prepared for the shareholders to use in their evaluation of the performance of management. Instead, the shareholders invested further funds in the company on the strength of the audited reports. The invested funds were lost because of errors in the reports, and the investors/ shareholders sued the auditors for negligence. The Supreme Court of Canada applied the two-stage *Anns* case test and held that, while damage to the shareholders was clearly reasonably foreseeable, there was a good policy reason to deny the existence of a duty in this case. The Supreme Court made it clear that they were reluctant to expose accountants and other professionals to open-ended liability where they would be liable for an "indeterminate amount for an indeterminate time to an indeterminate class." Applying this policy, the Supreme Court decided that because the erroneous reports were used for a purpose other than intended, there was no duty and no liability.

Today this approach will be used in any new or unusual situation where duty of care must be determined. This applies even when the careless conduct results in physical injury such as a bridge falling because of a design mistake, and people are injured or suffer loss

Professional liability to clients based on contract

Professional liability to others based on tort and Anns case test

Duty may now be modified or eliminated on policy considerations

Court unwilling to expose professionals to unlimited liability

[21] (1976), 72 D.L.R. (3d) 68 (S.C.C.).

[22] *Anns v. Merton, London Borough Council*, [1977] 2 All E.R. 492 (H.L.).

[23] *Hercules Management Ltd. v. Ernst & Young* (1997), 146 D.L.R. (4th) 577 (S.C.C.).

because of the failure. Just how extensive should the liability be to the people using the bridge? What about those who suffer a loss because they can no longer use the bridge? Once reasonable foreseeability has been determined, the court can then apply the second half of the *Anns* case test and impose limits on the basis of social policy considerations. But even with this limited approach towards duty of care, professionals must always remember that not only are they required to be careful in their dealings with their clients, but they also may be held responsible for damages their conduct causes to others with whom they are not dealing directly.

Higher standard of conduct required of experts

Where professionals are involved, there are also some unique problems in determining the standard of care to which they must adhere. Just how careful must the professional be? The general principle is that the professional, like anyone else, must live up to the standard of a reasonable person in the circumstances. Thus, the standard imposed becomes what is expected of a reasonable lawyer, doctor, accountant, engineer, architect, teacher, or consultant. Wherever a degree of expertise is claimed, that expert or professional is required to have the level of skill and expertise expected of a normal person in that profession. Inexperience is no excuse. Further, the professional is required to exercise that expertise and skill in a reasonable manner. Showing that an expert adhered to the standard practice in a particular profession is usually good enough. The rationale is that professionals will generally act reasonably as they practice their profession. Even this may not always be sufficient. If the court can be convinced that the standard practice in a particular instance is shoddy or inappropriate, liability for negligence will still be imposed.

Standard practice of profession may not be good enough

For example, the Court of Appeal in British Columbia in *Kripps v. Touche Ross*,[24] described above, found that strict adherence to GAAP (Generally Accepted Accounting Principles) and GAAS (Generally Accepted Auditing Standards) was not sufficient to avoid liability for negligence on the part of the defendant accountants when the resulting financial statements misrepresented the condition of the company. If the victim can establish that a duty was owed by the professional, satisfying both parts of the *Anns* case test—that there was a failure to live up to the appropriate standard and that failure caused the injury complained about—liability for negligence will be imposed.

Fiduciary duty requires good faith and clients' interests to be put first

Professionals and other experts also have a fiduciary duty to their clients. This means they have a duty to act in the best interests of their clients, even to the point of putting their clients' interests ahead of their own. Fiduciary duty will be discussed extensively in this text, especially with respect to agency, partnership, and corporations. It is sufficient to say at this point that the nature of a fiduciary duty involves loyalty and good faith. All information that comes to the professional that relates to what is being done for that client is the property of the client. The professional must not disclose it to others or make use of it for any personal gain. Similarly, if the other interests of the professional are in conflict with those of the client (where the professional could serve his own interests at the expense of the client) those conflicting interests must be disclosed, and the professional must step back from any decision-making process where that conflict exists.

Often the professional will have in his or her possession funds from various transactions involving clients. These are trust funds and must be kept scrupulously separate from the professional's other moneys and must never be used for any other purpose than the client's business. A breach of trust action is a very serious matter, and it will usually result

---

[24] (1997), 33 B.C.L.R. (3d) 254, [1997] 6 W.W.R. 421.

in the professional being disqualified from practising his or her profession. This is a particular problem for lawyers, accountants, financial planners, and real estate and insurance agents. Often criminal penalties are also imposed.

Professionals are also answerable to various professional organizations that authorize them to practise their professions. This may be law societies, medical associations, teachers' associations, various accounting organizations, and others, depending on the profession involved. Their powers vary but often these bodies have the authority to determine who can practise the profession and to set the standard of education, ethics, and skills required. Most bodies can also discipline members and disqualify or limit a member's right to practise in the profession if the complaint against the member is serious enough. It must always be remembered that these bodies are subject to law and must adhere to basic human rights legislation; where their decisions violate basic rules of due process, human rights, or other valid regulations, those decisions can be challenged in the courts.

Finally, it should be noted that the risks associated with tort liability can be avoided or significantly reduced for the professional and non-professional as well, simply through the acquisition of appropriate insurance. Insurance has become an essential aspect of doing business. Liability insurance (sometimes called errors and omissions insurance) will protect professionals and others when they make mistakes that cause loss to clients and other people. The insurer not only will compensate the victim for the injury but also will provide appropriate legal representation to cover the insured during the process of the claim. Insurance, however, will not usually protect the insured where the wrongful act was deliberate or fraud was involved. The victim may, in fact, be entitled to compensation in these circumstances, but the insurance company will normally demand repayment from the insured, including any legal expenses incurred. One serious problem with insurance today is the ever-increasing cost of premiums. With the huge awards that are being ordered by the courts for malpractice in all professions, the premiums are generally increasing to the point of becoming unbearable. Consequently, many professionals and business people are simply taking their chances and, where possible, not carrying insurance at all. Some professional bodies, however, require insurance coverage as a condition of practice. They sometimes provide that insurance, often at a high cost, as one of the services provided to their members.

Negligence can also constitute a crime under the *Criminal Code* of Canada, where a person in the performance of a duty does or omits to do something that "shows wanton or reckless disregard for the lives or safety of other persons." This includes failure to ensure that the safety provisions in the workplace and in their sphere of operation are adequate to protect the workers, customers, and the public. If the negligent conduct causes bodily harm the accused is liable to imprisonment up to 14 years, and to life where a death results. These *Criminal Code* provisions extend such liability to corporations and similar organizations as well as those managing them. There are many other provisions of the *Criminal Code* relating to specific conduct that also provide a penalty for negligence. It should be further noted that organizations, including companies, can also be convicted under these provisions, usually with the imposition of significant fines. An example of a typical sentence imposed for criminal negligence is found in *R. v. Jeffery*.[25] The accused was a truck driver who, while intoxicated, caused an accident that resulted in two deaths.

Disciplinary bodies subject to rules of "due process"

Professional risk is reduced by insurance

Negligence may also be criminal

---

[25] Ont. Dist. Ct. 1987, as reported in *Lawyers Weekly Consolidated Digest*, Vol. 7.

The court sentenced the driver to three and a half years, and extended a driving suspension for over 10 years. This case indicates that the primary consideration in such alcohol-related cases should be deterrence.

OTHER BUSINESS TORTS

Other business torts include:

■ Fraud

Negligence is by far the most important tort for the business person or professional. But there are several other related torts of which they should be aware. When a person intentionally misleads another, cheating him or her out of money or obtaining some other advantage, this is a **fraud** or **deceit**. For more detail, see Chapter 4, where fraudulent misrepresentation is discussed as part of the discussion on contract law. Also, defamation has many different forms, and one way it can take place is where false information is intentionally spread to harm the sales of a particular product. This is called injurious falsehood or product defamation.

■ Product defamation

■ Inducing breach of contract

When one person persuades another to breach a contract with a third person, this may constitute inducing breach of contract. Often, one employer "steals" an employee from another employer, persuading that employee to breach his or her employment contract in the process. Whether it is done to obtain the unique skills of that employee, or just to weaken a competitor, the employer usually thinks that the only one that has committed a wrong is the employee. In fact, there is considerable danger for the one inducing the breach. This is because the value of that employee to the business may be much greater than reflected by the salary and consequently the person inducing the breach can be held liable for the loss. This tort can also take place when one person persuades a potential client or customer to breach his contract with a competitor and to deal with his business instead.

Case Summary 2.7 *Drouillard v. Cogeco Cable Inc.*[26]

Even Customers Can Induce Breach of Contract

In 1999 Mr. Drouillard, who was a skilled cable and fibre optic installer, resigned his job with Cogeco Cable Inc. and took employment in the United States. Cogeco was a large cable company servicing Windsor and other areas in southern Ontario. In February 2001, Mr. Drouillard came back to Canada and sought a job with Mastec Canada, where his employment would include working on projects for Cogeco upgrading their fibre optic and internet capacity. He was about to start when the offer of employment was rescinded because Cogeco had informed Mastec that they refused to let him work on any of their projects. In May 2001 he was hired by Mastec, which was then under the impression that the problems with Cogeco had been

resolved. This was not the case and shortly after he started his employment he was terminated again because Cogeco refused to let him work on any of their projects. He tried to get work with other cable installers but because his reputation was now tarnished he failed to obtain employment. He brought this action against Cogeco for 1) interference in economic relations and 2) inducing Mastec to breach its employment contract with him. He eventually found work as a conductor with the CPR but had been laid off that job by the time the matter came to trial.

At trial Cogeco was found liable and ordered to pay damages of $200 000. On appeal the court found that Cogeco had induced Mastec to breach its employment

>

[26] (2007), 282 D.L.R. (4th) 644 (OCA) 25.

contract and so Cogeco was liable for the damages suffered. To establish this tort Mr. Drouillard had to show that there was 1) a valid contract of employment in place, 2) that Cogeco was aware of the contract of employment, 3) that they intended to and did cause it to be breached and 4) as a result Drouillard suffered damage. All of these elements were established and Cogeco's liability affirmed. It should be noted, however, that the award of damages was reduced by 30 percent by taking into consideration what Drouillard had earned from his employment with the CPR. Mitigation is a requirement usually associated with breach of contract and it is interesting to see it applied to tort in this situation.

The case is a good example of the tort of inducing breach of contract and shows what must be established to succeed. Note that it also shows the difference between this tort and its close cousin, unlawfully interfering with economic relations. Mr. Drouillard failed when suing for this tort because the requirement that there be evidence of unlawful conduct had not been met.

In the area of intellectual property there is nothing so valuable as a good name and reputation. Sometimes, by using a similar name, logo, or other identifying characteristic of a brand, one business will try to take advantage of another by misleading people into thinking they are associated with or are part of that reputable business, when in fact they are not. This is an attempt to mislead and is actionable as a **passing-off** action.

■ Passing off

For example, where a retailer sold a handbag line that was a copy of the Hermes line, Hermes Canada sued claiming the tort of passing off. Although there was no name on the handbag it was only on close inspection that the name of a different manufacturer was apparent. This was a clear example of passing off where the customers were deceived into thinking they were purchasing a genuine Hermes handbag when in fact they obtained a copy.[27] This passing-off action is in addition to the remedies provided under the *Trademarks Act* and may even be available where the requirements of a trademark are not met.

Trespass to chattels takes place when someone damages or otherwise interferes with some item of personal property such as a vehicle or other equipment. Slashing a tire would be an example. Taking a car without authority may be a crime, but it is also a tort called **conversion**. Conversion is broader than simple theft and can take place in any situation where one person intentionally deprives another of the possession or use of his personal property. It would even constitute conversion when a person mistakenly took property he thought was his own. Thus conversion can take place by someone taking control over another's property through taking it as their own, but also by hiding it, moving it, destroying it, or locking it up.

■ Trespass to chattels and conversion

The normal remedy where a tort has taken place is damages, which is the awarding of a monetary payment, usually designed to compensate the victim for his or her loss. In rare circumstances, where the conduct was deliberate, punitive damages may also be granted when the object is to punish the wrongdoer rather than simply to compensate. Where a monetary award will not be appropriate, as is usually the case where a passing-off action is involved, the court will sometimes award an injunction ordering the offending conduct to stop. Sometimes an accounting, requiring that a wrongdoer disclose any profits made and pay them over to the victim, will also be ordered.

Note that there are some other non-tort areas where the business person has a duty to maintain a certain standard of conduct in relation to others. These are statutory obligations but do not create tort liability unless clearly so stated in the statute. Thus while

---

[27] *Hermes Canada Inc. v. Henry High Class Kelly Retail Store*, 2004 BCSC 1694 (CanLII).

discrimination in employment may resemble an actionable tort, because it is set out in federal and provincial codes as a violation or human rights it is not a tort. Such a complaint can only be enforced by the board of commission set up for that purpose and is not actionable in the courts. There is also privacy legislation at both the federal and provincial levels, which imposes obligations on businesses with respect to the information they deal with, especially where it relates to individuals. Where businesses fail to adhere to those regulations, they are subject to serious statutory penalties. And in some provinces (British Columbia, Saskatchewan, Manitoba, and Newfoundland and Labrador) the wilful violation of another's privacy has actually been made an actionable tort by statute.

Note increased emphasis on privacy rights

Key Terms

absolute privilege (p. 34)	**negligence** (p. 36)
assault (p. 30)	**passing off** (p. 51)
battery (p. 30)	**private nuisance** (p. 33)
causation (p. 42)	**privity of contract** (p. 46)
contributory negligence (p. 43)	**professional liability** (p. 47)
conversion (p. 51)	**qualified privilege** (p. 35)
deceit (p. 50)	**reasonable foreseeability test** (p. 38)
defamation (p. 34)	**reasonable person** (p. 37)
fair comment (p. 35)	**remoteness** (p. 44)
false imprisonment (p. 31)	**self-defence** (p. 31)
fraud (p. 50)	**slander** (p. 34)
innuendo (p. 34)	**strict liability** (p. 45)
justification (p. 34)	**trespass to land** (p. 32)
libel (p. 34)	**vicarious liability** (p. 30)
mistake (p. 34)	**voluntary assumption of risk** (p. 44)

Questions for Student Review

1. What is a tort? Distinguish between a tort and a crime, and explain when a tort can also constitute a crime.
2. Explain vicarious liability and any limitation on its availability.
3. Distinguish between intentional and inadvertent torts.
4. Explain what is meant by a reasonable person and the reasonable person test.
5. Distinguish between assault and battery, and explain how this distinction might be affected by self-defence.
6. Explain what is required to establish a false imprisonment.
7. Why is trespass to land considered an intentional tort? Under what conditions does a trespass occur? What is a continuing trespass?
8. Explain the obligation of an owner or occupier of land for injuries suffered by a trespasser.
9. Under what circumstances might one neighbour sue another for nuisance?
10. What is meant by defamation? What is an innuendo?
11. Distinguish between libel and slander. Why is the distinction important?

12. Explain the difference between privilege and qualified privileged, and when these defences will be used. What is fair comment?

13. Explain the role of fault with respect to the tort of negligence.

14. What must be established to successfully sue for negligence?

15. Explain the role of the *Donoghue v. Stevenson* and the *Anns* case in determining duty of care.

16. Explain what is meant by strict liability and when it might be imposed on an occupier of property, and how the standard of care imposed on occupiers has been modified by statute.

17. How have the principles of contributory negligence and voluntary assumption of risk been modified in recent times?

18. Explain how the problems with remoteness in a negligence action have been substantially resolved in recent times.

19. If I were to carelessly injure the hand of a musician, on what basis would damages be determined, given the victim's occupation?

20. Why are manufacturers usually sued for negligence rather than for breach of contract? Why is an action in contract preferable for the victim?

21. Explain when a professional's liability will be based on contract and when it will be based on tort. How is the standard imposed with respect to tort determined?

22. Explain what is meant by fiduciary duty and when such a duty arises.

23. Explain the nature of the following torts: deceit, product defamation, inducing breach of contract, passing off, trespass to chattels, and conversion.

Questions for Further Discussion

1. Individuals are sometimes convicted of a crime and then sued in tort for the same conduct. Is it fair or just for one person to face trial twice for the same thing?

2. Is the reasonable person test appropriate for determining what standard of behaviour should be imposed in a negligence action? Would it be more appropriate to determine negligent conduct on the basis of the average person or some other test?

3. In Canada when someone produces a defective product or performs an imperfect service he or she must be shown to have been careless—to have fallen below a community-established standard of behaviour (the reasonable person test)—before he or she can be found liable for negligence. When a person is suing for breach of contract, it is unnecessary to establish fault; the breach is enough. Consider whether the requirement to establish fault where someone's conduct causes another injury ought to be abandoned in a tort action. In other words, should it be enough to show that one person caused the injury for him or her to be liable?

4. Freedom of expression has been guaranteed in our constitution. Yet when people criticize public officials and other public figures, they can be sued for defamation, even if they believe what they say is true. Do you think we should adopt an approach similar to that in the United States and take the position that it is more important to have a frank debate with respect to such public matters, a debate free of the chill imposed by the threat of legal action? Should the protections of privileged communications be applied to all such discussions of matters of public interest, whether the statements are accurate or not? Should the media enjoy special protection in such matters?

Cases for Discussion

1. *Lewvest v. Scotia Towers Ltd.* (1981), 126 D.L.R. (3d) 239 (Nfld. T.D.).

   Scotia Towers Ltd. was constructing a building in St. John's, Newfoundland, and in the process a crane they were operating often swung over the adjoining property owned by Lewvest. Lewvest had not given permission for such an intrusion and sued. Explain the nature of Lewvest's complaint, the arguments on both sides, and the appropriate remedy if the action is successful.

2. *Malette v. Shulman* (1990), 67 D.L.R. (4th) 321 (Ont. C.A.).

   Mrs. Malette was seriously injured in an automobile accident, and at the hospital Dr. Shulman determined she was in need of a blood transfusion to save her life. The nurse, however, discovered a card in the patient's purse indicating she was a Jehovah's Witness. The card gave instruction that under no circumstances should blood or blood products be administered to Mrs. Malette. Dr. Shulman ignored the card and proceeded to administer the transfusion. When the family arrived they repeated the instruction, which Dr. Shulman also overruled. There is no question that the blood transfusion was needed to preserve her life, but upon her recovery Mrs. Malette sued Dr. Shulman for trespass to person (battery). Explain the arguments on both sides and the likely outcome.

3. *Shabsove v. Sentry Department Stores Ltd.*, Ont. Gen. Div., as reported in *Lawyers Weekly Consolidated Digest*, Vol. 15.

   One March day Mrs. Shabsove went to a shopping mall operated by Sentry to go to the bank. She parked close to a bank machine, and when she got out of the car and started to go over to the machine she slipped and fell on the icy surface and suffered a serious injury. She sued the shopping mall for her injury. Explain the likely outcome of the case. How would it affect your answer to know that she was wearing leather-soled loafers, or that the mall had a program in place to salt areas where thawing snow was known to accumulate, but this area had last been salted three weeks previously?

4. *Bruce v. Coliseum Management Ltd.* (1998), 56 B.C.L.R. (3d) 27, 165 D.L.R. (4th) 472 (B.C.C.A.).

   Bruce went to a bar. After a friendly tussle with his friend, the doorman asked him to leave, as he thought the two friends were fighting. The doorman escorted Bruce out, and at the upstairs exit Bruce prevented the doorman from closing the door. Bruce was quite abusive, and eventually the doorman gave him a push that was hard enough to throw him off balance. Bruce fell down the stairs and suffered a serious injury. In this action Bruce is seeking compensation for his injuries from both the doorman and his employer. Explain the nature of his complaint, the arguments on both sides, and his likelihood of success. What factors should be taken into consideration in calculating what damages, if any, should be paid?

5. *Bahner v. Marwest Hotel Co.* (1970), 12 D.L.R. (3d) 646 (B.C.C.A.).

   Mr. Bahner attended the defendant's restaurant with some friends and ordered some wine shortly before midnight. Unknown to Bahner, the laws then in place in British Columbia required all drinks to be removed from the table by midnight. This meant Bahner and his friends only had about 15 minutes to drink the bottle of wine that had been opened by the waiter. When Bahner learned this, he refused to drink or pay for the wine, although he did pay for the rest of his meal. When he proceeded to leave, a security guard told Bahner to remain in the restaurant and to wait until the police arrived. The situation was explained to them and they arrested Mr. Bahner who spent the night in jail. He sued both the restaurant as well as the police for false imprisonment. Explain the likely outcome.

Chapter 3
Formation of Contracts

Learning Objectives

- List the essential elements of a contract

- Describe the process by which consensus is reached

- Explain the principle of consideration

- Recall the requirements of capacity and legality

- Define the element of intention

- Determine whether a written document is required

The process of carrying on business involves transactions, agreements, arrangements, consultations, services, employment, and other forms of interaction—all based on contracts between the parties. An examination of contract law is fundamental to any study of business law, and most of the other topics that will be examined in this text are founded to a large extent on contract law principles.

A contract can be defined as a voluntary exchange of promises or commitments between parties that are legally enforceable in our courts. When people enter into such contracts, they create a world of law unto themselves. They can create new obligations and responsibilities, but they can also modify or remove obligations and responsibilities. When a ticket to an event contains a provision stating that patrons "enter at their own risk" or that the "management is not responsible for injuries or damage," an attempt is being made by contract to remove the risk of liability for negligence that would otherwise be present. Contract law was developed in the courts, and there has been little statutory interference with these common law fundamentals. As we will see in subsequent chapters, however, there are a myriad of examples of statutory modification of contract laws in specific situations, including the sale of goods and consumer protection, both of which will be discussed in the first half of Chapter 5. This chapter will examine the formation of a contract and qualifications that must be met including consensus obtained through offer and acceptance, the exchange of consideration, capacity, legality, and intention. Note that, although it is prudent practice, in most situations there is no requirement that a contract be in writing.

Contract: an exchange of promises enforceable in court

CONSENSUS

Reaching an agreement is at the heart of the formation of a contract (see Figure 3.1). **Consensus** is normally achieved through a process of **offer and acceptance**, which results in a shared commitment where both parties clearly understand the obligations and responsibilities they are assuming. It is a bargaining process that includes enticements,

Offer and acceptance leads to agreement

Figure 3.1 First Element of a Contract

Consensus reached through bargaining

offers, questions, arguments, and counter-offers, until the parties eventually reach an agreement in which a valid offer is accepted. The courts are willing to find that a consensus has been reached by looking at the subsequent behaviour of the parties. If no specific offer or acceptance can be identified and yet the parties have obviously come to common understanding with all the other elements of contract present, it is likely that the court would still find that a contract exists. While we look at the traditional requirements of offer and acceptance here, it is important to remember that a court may find that a consensus exists even where no specific offer or acceptance can be identified. Neither is it necessary that both parties actually have a complete understanding as to what they have agreed. The only requirement of consensus is that the terms are clear and unambiguous. A basic principle of contract law is that the courts will give effect to the reasonable expectations of the parties. If one of them fails to read those terms or misunderstands them, it is not usually an excuse to get out of a contract. But agreement between the parties must be present. The court will not bargain for them. When they leave important terms to be negotiated later, there is no contract. Still, mistakes with respect to the nature, terms, or some other aspect of the contract do take place, and the courts have developed a structured approach to dealing with them. The court usually interprets and enforces those terms, rather than finding there is no agreement. The way courts deal with such mistakes will be dealt with under "Mistake" in the following chapter (see p. 77)

Case Summary 3.1 *Zynik Capital Corporation v. Faris*[1]
Agreement to Enter into an Agreement Not Binding

A shipyard that had operated for many years in North Vancouver ran into financial difficulties and eventually their lands were acquired because of default on a debenture by the Bank of Nova Scotia. Mr. Kassam, through his friendship with executives at the bank, learned of the opportunity to acquire those lands but also learned that in order to do so, because of complicated tax and other factors, he would have to enter into a joint venture with a developer to acquire the lands. As a result Mr. Kassam, on behalf of Zynik, entered into negotiations with Mr. Faris representing Intergulf. Eeventually a "Memorandum of Understanding" was signed between them purporting to set up terms under the two companies to "enter into an 'Agreement' for the purposes of acquiring and developing lands" which were specified as were other important terms. Both men signed the memorandum of understanding. No formal agreement was ever entered into. After further negotiations with the bank, involving complex business arrangements including distressed preferred shares and selling the debt to an offshore entity all to create the most favourable tax advantage, the relationship between Zynik and Intergulf fell apart and the relationship came to an end. Mr. Kassam on behalf of Zynik wrote to Intergulf claiming that they had repudiated the memorandum of understanding, causing the deal with the bank to be frustrated, and that as a result they were responsible for all costs and expenditures that had been incurred. Faris, speaking for Intergulf, took the position that there was no contract and no obligations between them. The issue was whether the Memorandum of Understanding was a binding agreement between the parties. The court found that it was not. While many terms could be left out or implied, there was

>

---

[1] 2007 BCSC 527 (CanLII).

one vital term that was missing. There was no agreed upon amount that would be paid to acquire the debentures and thus the land. There was not even a guideline with respect to the price to be paid and this was fatal to the agreement. This was no more than an agreement to enter into an agreement, which has no legal force.

Offer

The **offer** creates the first legal consequence. It is a tentative promise that contains the terms of the anticipated contract. It is tentative in the sense that the other party need only indicate a willingness to be bound by the stated terms (to accept) to create a binding contract. Before this stage is reached, however, a significant amount of communication can take place between the parties. Pre-contract communications, whether they take the form of advertising or provide product or service information, do not create contractual obligations. They are referred to as invitations to deal or **invitations to treat** and sometimes are confused with offers. It is often difficult to determine at what point we are dealing with an offer rather than an invitation. Most media advertisements, catalogues, brochures, window and floor displays, and even clearly marked and priced goods set out on shelves in self-service situations are invitations to treat rather than offers. There is some controversy over this last point, but it was the subject of a decision of the English Court of Appeal in the *Pharmaceutical Society* case.[2] Legislation required that certain types of drugs had to be sold under the supervision of a pharmacist. When the defendant, Boots, introduced self-service merchandising into the industry, by displaying such controlled drugs on the shelves where they could be selected by the customer and brought up to the front of the store for purchase, it appeared to infringe that legislation. Although the pharmacists were situated at the front of the store by the check-out tills, the Pharmaceutical Society argued that the contract was formed where the customer selected the goods, and thus the sale was unsupervised in violation of the Act. The judge held that the display of the drugs on the shelf was an invitation rather than an offer. The offer was made by the customer picking up the product. The acceptance took place at the front, when the cashier and pharmacist approved the sale, and thus the requirements of supervision were satisfied. Although the reasoning of the judge in this case is suspect, the decision has been followed and is thus good law in Canada, making goods displayed in such self-service situations invitations and not offers. The case is of interest because it is one of the few that makes it clear where an invitation ends and an offer begins.

> Invitations do not create legal obligations

Such an invitation has no legal effect in contract law. The actual offer that leads to an acceptance and eventual contract depends on subsequent communications between the parties. It only takes place when all of the important terms are present, and it is clear that the person making the offer has reached the point where he or she is serious and expects to commit to those terms.

For the communication to be an offer, it must contain all of the important terms of the contract. This usually requires, at a minimum, the identification of the parties to the agreement, the subject matter, and the price to be paid (parties, price, and property). If the parties have added other important terms, they too must be clear. For example, if the goods are to be purchased on credit, the payment schedule and interest payable should also be clear. An agreement to enter into an agreement is not a contract. If Joe agreed to

> An offer is a tentative commitment containing essential terms

---

[2] *Pharmaceutical Society of Great Britain v. Boots Cash Chemists (Southern), Ltd.*, [1953] 1 All E.R. 482 (C.A.); aff'g [1952] 2 All E.R. 456 (Q.B.).

sell his car to Sam for $10 000, "credit terms to be arranged later," there would be no contract, since no final agreement had been reached. All of the important terms of the agreement must be set out or be implied in the agreement. It must be emphasized that putting a contract in writing is always good practice. However, except for a few specific instances that will be discussed below, a written contract is not a legal requirement. Because of this it is possible for parts or even the whole contract to be implied from the circumstances, including the past history of dealings between the parties.

Offer/contract need not be in writing

Note that the object is to reach a consensus, and so the offer must be communicated before it can be accepted. The offeree cannot accept an offer that he does not know about. The problem of communication sometimes arises when the offeror wants to include an **exemption clause** that restricts or limits her liability in the transaction. This must be brought to the attention of the other party at the time the contract is created. For example, a sign at a parking lot may state, "Not responsible for lost, stolen, or damaged vehicles." To be a binding part of the contract, the clause must be communicated to the customer at the time she enters into the contract. Sometimes this is done by including it on the receipt issued at the time the contract is made, or by clearly posting a sign where the ticket is obtained. If it is only communicated after the fact, such as on a bill sent later, or on a sign located in a part of the business where the customer is not likely to see it, that exemption clause will not be a part of the contract. And where that exemption clause appears on the back of the ticket or receipt, there must be something on the front directing the party to the terms on the back.

Exemption clauses must be brought to the other party's attention

Case Summary 3.2 *Brownjohn v. Pillar to Post*[3]

Exemption Clause Must Not Binding

The current practice in the real estate market is to have a home inspected before purchase. When the home turns out to be defective it is also common practice to include the home inspector in the action, claiming that the missed defect on the inspection was at least partially responsible for the loss. Home inspectors are not responsible to tear open or disassemble anything. They simply make a visual inspection. In this case, Pillar to Post provided house inspection services in the Kelowna area of British Columbia and sent a rather inexperienced inspector to provide such a service for Janet Brownjohn. In the inspection Mrs. Brownjohn claimed that the inspector, Mr. Averil, missed a number of important defects and because of this she suffered considerable losses in her purchase. The judge examined the claims and, while dismissing most as trivial or something she should have seen for herself, he did find several significant errors on the part of Mr. Averil

including the age of the furnace and a termite infestation. PTP countered by pointing out the exclusionary clause in their contract limiting their liability for any cause to the inspection fee of $240. The judge found that this was such an all-encompassing limitation clause that it had to be brought to the attention of the client at the time the contract was signed. This was not done and the judge suggested that, if anything, the last thing the inspector wanted to do was to bring her attention to such an expansive limitation clause when trying to attract her business.

The case illustrates the general requirement that any term must be brought to the attention of the parties to be part of the agreement at the time of the contract. Even though this term was included in the contract, it was so important that it had to be underlined or in some other way made to stand out to attract the attention of the client.

---

[3] 2003 BCPC 2 (CanLII).

End of an Offer   Consistent with the bargaining model for the creation of a contract, a number of rules determine when an offer will come to an end (see Table 3.1). Where the offeror states a specific time for expiration, such as "at noon on May 12, 2009," the offer ends when specified. After that time it is too late to accept the offer. If no expiration time has been specified, the offer will end after a reasonable time. What is reasonable depends on the circumstances. If ripe fruit is being offered, a few hours might be appropriate. If property is involved, or heavy-duty equipment, the offer might last a few weeks. The offer will also automatically come to an end with the death or insanity of the offeror. Because the offer is only the first step in the creation of a contract, it imposes no legal obligation on the offeror, who is free to withdraw the offer any time before acceptance, even where he or she has indicated it would remain open. This is called revocation, and so long as the revocation has been communicated to the offeree before acceptance has taken place, it is then too late to accept. There can be no valid acceptance after the offeree learns that the offeror has changed his or her mind. This power to revoke can be given up in a separate option agreement, which is explained below.

The conduct of the offeree can also cause the offer to end. If the offeree communicates a rejection of the offer to the offeror the offer ends. The offeree can't later change her mind, accept, and hold the offeror to the deal. A **counter-offer** by the offeree has the same effect, and if that counter-offer is rejected she can't turn around and force a contract by accepting the original offer. The offeree would have to make another counteroffer, embodying the original terms, and hope that they are still agreeable to the other party. This may seem somewhat complicated, but it has the advantage of eliminating confusion as to just what offer is being accepted and forming the basis of the contract. A common mistake is to assume that selling the subject matter of an offer to someone else automatically ends that offer. This is incorrect. If anything, this is a revocation of the offer by conduct and would have no effect on the offer, unless the other party learned of the sale before accepting. This is a dangerous situation, and the offeror should make sure that the

Offer will end:

- At end of a specified time

- At end of reasonable time

- Upon death or insanity of offeror

- Upon revocation

- Upon rejection

- Upon counter-offer

- Selling item does not end offer

Table 3.1 Bargaining

Invitation	Not an offer; not capable of being accepted to form a contract	
Offer	After expiration of specific time	Original offer ends
Offer	Where not specified, after a reasonable time	Original offer ends
Offer	After communicated revocation	Original offer ends
Offer	After counter-offer or rejection	Original offer ends
Offer	After death or insanity of offeror	Original offer ends
Offer	Where option agreement has been purchased	Original offer continues to end of specified time despite above
Offer	Sale to another	Original offer continues unless revocation
Offer	Qualified acceptance	This is a counter-offer; original offer ends
Offer	Effective acceptance	Results in a binding contract

original offeree knows that he changed his mind before concluding the sale to another. Of course, if the offeree finds out the goods have been sold to someone else, that communicates the revocation indirectly, and it is too late to accept. A person cannot accept an offer when he knows that the offeror has changed his mind.[4]

Option keeps offer open

The right of the offeror to change his mind and revoke the offer anytime he wants is often an impediment to doing business. And so it is possible to create a situation where the offer cannot be revoked and must remain open until expiration at a specified time. This is called an **option agreement**. In effect, a separate contract is entered into where the offeree pays the offeror, usually a small sum, to hold the offer open for the designated time. The offeror is now bound in a separate contract to hold the offer open. Thus the offeror is bound, but the offeree is free to accept or reject the original offer. This gives the offeree some time without the worry that the offer will be revoked or the deal taken up by someone else.

We don't always have the choice to bargain. In some businesses standard form agreements are in place, which create a "take it or leave it" situation. Often one-sided terms are present, including exemption clauses that favour the offeror. It must be emphasized that where such a standard contract is accepted, it is just as binding as any other contract. The only adjustment made for the lack of bargaining is that any ambiguity in a term favouring just one of the parties is interpreted in favour of the other party. Also, some statutory protection has been provided, especially where consumer contracts are involved as will be discussed under "Consumer Protection Legislation" in Chapter 5 (see p. 108).

One-sided contracts may be controlled by statute

Acceptance

Once a valid offer has been made, there is a tentative commitment to be bound on the part of the offeror. The offeree then must make a similar commitment for a contract to be formed. Since the terms of the agreement are embodied in the offer, the offeree's commitment consists merely of an indication of a willingness to be bound by those terms. This may consist of something as simple as a handshake or a signature. Such an acceptance must be total and unconditional. Sometimes an offer will involve several different aspects. The offeree can't pick and choose which part to accept unless that was the intention of the offeror. You have to accept all of the terms of an offer or nothing. Similarly, a conditional acceptance does not qualify. If Joe offers to sell his car to Sam for $5000, and Sam responds, "I accept, providing you fix the rust on the fender," this is a counter-offer rather than an acceptance.

Acceptance is a commitment by the offeree to terms of offer

Acceptance must be complete and unconditional

The general rule is that an acceptance must be communicated for it to be effective. A contract requires a meeting of the minds, and so there is no contract until the offeror is notified of the offeree's acceptance. This can be important since it determines when and where the contract comes into effect. When Joe in Vancouver offers to sell his car to Sam in Montreal by phone, and Sam accepts, also by phone, the acceptance is effective when and where Joe hears the acceptance—in Vancouver. Where the contract is formed can be an important consideration in determining what court has jurisdiction and which province's law should be applied to the transaction.

General rule: acceptance is effective when and where communicated

[4] *Dickinson v. Dodds* (1876), 2 Ch. D. 463 (C.A.).

The offeror may require the offer to be accepted by some specified conduct. When this happens, the conduct required must be something unique, not part of a person's normal routine, and the offeree must respond as directed. If the specified acceptance requires the offeree to "go to work tomorrow as usual," going to work would not constitute acceptance. But if the direction is to put a red ribbon on the front door, doing so would amount to acceptance of the offer. Sometimes the nature of the contract itself requires the actual performance of the contract as the method of acceptance. This is called a **unilateral contract**. The offering of a reward is a good example. When someone places an add offering a $100 reward for the return of a lost dog, the method of acceptance is the actual return of the dog.

Sometimes marketers will send unsolicited goods to a prospective customer stating that if they don't send it back, they've bought it. The general rule is that silence by itself will not be construed as acceptance, and a person in receipt of such goods is not required to go to the trouble to return them. Note that care should be taken not to use such goods, as this would affirm the contract. Simply store the goods for a reasonable time, and if they're not reclaimed by the marketer, dispose of them. Only where there is a pre-existing business relationship will silence be an appropriate acceptance. If you have been receiving a regular supply of a product from a business, it is quite appropriate for that business to send a note: "If we don't hear otherwise, we will renew your order as of May 20, 2009." Because of the already established relationship, there is a duty to communicate a cancellation in these circumstances. A few years ago a company providing cable services notified their customers that they would be supplying them with extra channels at an added cost unless the customer notified the company that they didn't want the additional service. Because of the pre-existing service relationship, silence in these circumstances would have affirmed the new arrangement. The public was outraged, however, and the company was forced to back off. This is the danger of joining a CD- or book-of-the-month club. Once the relationship is established, it is hard to terminate it.

There is one important exception to the rule that an acceptance must be communicated to be effective. This is the **post-box rule**. As contract law developed, the postal service was the accepted method of doing business at a distance. The inherent delay in communications created uncertainty as to what point a contract actually came into existence. The solution was the rule that if it was appropriate to respond by mail, the acceptance was effective when and where it was posted. In the example above of selling a car, if the mails, instead of the phone, were used—with Joe in Vancouver sending a letter to Sam in Montreal offering to sell his car for $5000 and Sam responding with a letter of acceptance—that acceptance would be effective when it was mailed in Montreal. If Joe had required acceptance before Saturday, and the letter was mailed Friday, there would be a valid contract, even though Joe would not know of it until the letter was actually received by Joe—likely sometime in the following week. Also, since the contract was formed in Quebec, this could be an important factor in determining what court would have jurisdiction and what provincial law would apply to the contract. Note that the post-box rule only applies where it is reasonable to respond by mail. There is usually no problem posting an acceptance where the offer is sent by mail. But where the offer is presented in some other way, such as in person, past dealings between the parties, as well as the nature of the subject matter of the contract, will be important factors in determining if response by mail was reasonable. If ripe fruit were being offered, a response by mail would likely be unacceptable. To avoid the problem, the appropriate means of acceptance should be specified in the offer.

Acceptance by conduct

Acceptance by performance

No acceptance by silence

Exception: Where use of mail is reasonable, acceptance is effective when and where posted

Case Summary 3.3 *Eastern Power Ltd. v. Azienda Communale Energia and Ambiente*[5]

Post-Box Rule Not Applied to Fax

Azienda, an Italian company, negotiated a cooperation agreement with Eastern Power Ltd., which was based in Ontario. When Azienda terminated the agreement and refused to pay the bill for costs submitted by Eastern Power, the Ontario company brought this action against Azienda in an Ontario court. In determining if they had jurisdiction, the Ontario court had to decide, among other things, where the contract was made. Negotiations took place by facsimile. The final acceptance of the offer was also sent by fax by the Ontario company to Azienda in Italy. Claiming the post-box rule exception applied, Eastern Power argued that acceptance was effective when and where the fax was sent in Ontario. The court rejected this argument, stating that the use of facsimile transmissions involved instantaneous communication, much like a telephone, and so there was no justification for applying the post-box exception. Since the fax was received in Italy, the contract arose in Italy. Consequently, Ontario was an inappropriate place to sue.

In recent times there has been a profound change in the nature of business communications. The mails are still used to a significant extent, but fax and email have become commonplace. An important question faced by the courts was whether the post-box rule should be extended to other forms of communications. It has been extended to the use of telegrams, but should it be extended further? The question was answered in the *Entores* case[6] where the English Court of Appeal held that when telex (similar to a modern fax) and other forms of instantaneous communication were used, there was no need for the post-box rule. Thus, where fax is used, the acceptance is only effective when and where it is received by the offeror. Although there may be some small delay when email is involved, it is not likely that any court would expand the rule in that direction. Today the post-box rule is restricted to the use of the postal service, telegrams, and possibly couriers. It must be emphasized that the post-box rule is an exception to the requirement that an acceptance be communicated before it is effective. There is no indication that the rule will be applied to other forms of communications between the parties as they bargain. In fact, in the English case of *Henthorne v. Fraser*,[7] which was important in establishing the rule in the first place, the court made it clear that the rule did not apply to a mailed revocation, which was not effective until received. See Table 3.2 for a summary of the rules of acceptance. Several provinces have passed legislation specifically directed at transactions using electronic means of communication such as the internet. British Columbia,

The post-box rule will not apply where a fax is used

Exception only applies to an acceptance

Table 3.2 Acceptance

Offer	Acceptance, general rule	Acceptance is effective when and where offeror hears of acceptance
Offer	Acceptance by performance	Unilateral contract accepted upon performance of contract term
Offer	Acceptance, post-box rule	Acceptance effective when and where posted, if use of post was appropriate

---

[5] (1999), 178 D.L.R. (4th) 409 (Ont. C.A.).

[6] *Entores Ltd. v. Miles Far East Corp.*, [1955] 2 All E.R. 493 (C.A.).

[7] [1892] 2 Ch. 27 (Ch.D.).

for example, has legislated that documents communicated in this way are deemed to be sent when entered into the system and outside of their control, and deemed to be received when they are in the system and could have been accessed by the addressee.[8]

CONSIDERATION

The second qualification that must be met for the formation of a contract is the exchange of **consideration** (see Figure 3.2). In keeping with the bargaining model, both parties must get some benefit from the deal. This may take the form of money, service, goods, or some other type of benefit. Note that it is not necessary for the consideration to actually change hands at the time of the acceptance; rather, both parties must make a commitment to give the other some form of consideration pursuant to the agreement. This is often referred to as the exchange of promises.

Exchange of promises/benefits required

People sometimes promise to give a gift or do something for someone else and expect nothing in return. Such one-sided promises (called **gratuitous promises**) are not legally enforceable. Of course, once a gift has been given, the giver cannot force its return; rather, it is the promise to give such a gift that cannot be enforced. If I give you a fur coat, it's yours. But if I promise to give you a fur coat and change my mind, there is nothing legally you can do about it.

In business it is sometimes difficult to tell whether there has been an exchange of consideration or not. While the court won't worry about whether the consideration is reasonable (that would be interfering in the bargaining process), the benefit must be specific. A promise to pay "something" or a "reasonable price" is generally not good enough, as there is no specific commitment and the matter will require further negotiation in the future. The exception is where services are requested. Then, on the basis of the equitable principle of *quantum meruit*, the requester is obligated to pay a reasonable amount for the services delivered. If you ask a plumber to fix a leak in your basement and after the leak is fixed the plumber hands you a bill, you will have to pay it if it is reasonable, even though you didn't agree to a price beforehand.

What is promised must also be possible, legal, and of some value. A commitment to bring a pet dog back from the dead for $1000 would not be legally enforceable because, at least in the eyes of the law, it is not possible to bring a dog back to life. A promise to pay someone $500 to perform an illegal act such as buying drugs or assaulting someone also fails to qualify, because a promise to commit an illegal act is not valid consideration. Nor would a promise to return friendship or love and affection normally constitute valid consideration as no value can be put on such affection. As mentioned above, it is not necessary that the consideration be fair, only that there be some consideration on both sides. However, if the transaction is grossly one-sided, it may support an allegation of fraud or the claim of incapacity.

Consideration need not be reasonable but must be legal, possible, and have some value

Figure 3.2 Consideration Involves an Exchange of Commitments

Binding contract

Offeree ◄──────────────► **Offeror**

agrees to pay $100 for
offeree's bike

agrees to give bike
for offeror's promise of $100

---

[8] *Electronic Transactions Act*, S.B.C. (2001) c.10 s.18.

To determine if there is consideration it is often much easier to look at the price to be paid rather than the benefit to be received. If I promise to pay $50 to John to mow my aunt's lawn, it is hard to identify what specific benefit I will get out of the deal. But if we look at it from the point of view of what is to be paid (in the sense of what is being given up, not just money) it is clear that both of us are paying a price. We both have by agreement changed our legal position in relation to each other. John is now obligated to mow the lawn, which he was not obligated to do before the agreement, and I am obligated to pay the $50. There has been an exchange of commitments, which constitutes consideration.

Both parties must pay a price

For example, in business one person is often required to sign a **guarantee** before a financial institution will loan money to a debtor. What does the guarantor get out of it? It is better to look at the commitments. The guarantor is now responsible for paying the loan if the debtor defaults. His or her legal position has changed in accordance with the agreement. The bank now commits to advance the funds to the debtor, something they otherwise would not have done. They also have changed their legal position pursuant to the deal, and so there is consideration on both sides. Both have paid a price in the sense that they have assumed obligations that they didn't have before. But if the money is advanced before the guarantee is extracted, as sometimes happens, it may well be a gratuitous promise and not binding. The guarantor has made a commitment, but the bank does not change its legal position, since it has already advanced the money. This is an example of past consideration. Where the benefit has been given before the deal is struck, it cannot be part of an exchange and hence the expression "past consideration is no consideration."

Past consideration is no consideration

Case Summary 3.4 *Mackenzie v. Mackenzie*[9]

Past Consideration Is No Consideration

Linda MacKenzie and her husband built a house on land given to her husband by her mother. Her father-in-law assisted in the construction and paid for some of the materials. He also claimed to have loaned his son considerable funds before the house was constructed. Shortly before the house was completed Linda and David MacKenzie signed a mortgage in favour of her father-in-law for $25 000 at 10% interest. She claims she didn't understand what she was signing. No money changed hands and the father-in-law stated at that time that he had "already advanced the $25 000 to his son." This mortgage was not registered until 3 months after the son died 14 years after it was made. (Note that before the house had been completed Linda and her husband had been separated for 6 months) The father-in-law is claiming on the mortgage which has accumulated to $112 000. The judge in finding that there was no consideration to support the mortgage found that any monies given the son had been given before the mortgage was signed and therefore past consideration. Past consideration is no consideration and will not support the contract. He found that any money that had been given to the son prior to the building of the house was a gift given out of love and affection. In his judgment the judge suggested that because of the separation of his son and the son's wife before the completion of the house, the mortgage was to ensure that in the event of the marriage failing that she would not get the home. This is supported by the fact that the mortgage was not registered until shortly after the son's death.

The case illustrates the bargaining nature of the contract, which requires consideration on both sides. Here there was no such bargain as any consideration had been given before the agreement was entered into.

---

[9] 1996 CanLII 3698 (PE S.C.T.D.).

Gratuitous Promises   Sometimes there is an existing legal relationship or obligation that the parties want to change. In general, any obligation created by contract can be changed by agreement. But there has to be consideration on both sides to support the change. If a builder had a contract to finish renovating your house by June 10 and fell behind, you might well agree to pay an extra $2000 so that more help could be hired to get the job done on time. At first glance it looks like there is consideration on both sides, but in fact there is not. You have made a commitment to pay more, but the builder is in exactly the same legal position that he was in before you made that promise—to finish the job by June 10. He has made no new commitment and so this is a one-sided or gratuitous promise not binding on the promisor. It is true that the builder has agreed to hire extra help and this will cost him more, but he would have had to do that anyway to fulfill the original agreement. The commitment has not changed. You would not be obligated to pay the $2000 promised, unless the builder agreed to do something extra for it.

Paying less to satisfy a debt is a similar problem. If I owe you $1000 and I offer to pay you $800 if you will take it in full satisfaction of the debt, the reduction of the debt is one-sided. You get nothing out of it. Yes, you will be paid, but I was obligated to do that before you agreed to take the lesser payment. So unless I agree to do something extra such as pay early, after getting the $800 you should still be able to sue me for the other $200. But this is another one of those situations where the necessities of business overshadow the logic of the law. It is often better to settle debts this way—with certainty. As a result, legislation has been passed in most jurisdictions to the effect that if a creditor agrees to take less in full satisfaction of a debt and in fact takes the money, he or she can't turn around and sue for the remainder. The debt is settled.[10]

Taking less in satisfaction of a debt made binding by statute

Exceptions   There are two exceptions to the unenforceability of gratuitous or one-sided promises (see Table 3.3). **Promissory estoppel** is a difficult concept best understood by example. In the example above where you agree to pay a builder an extra $2000 to get the renovation of your house done by June 10 as originally agreed, that promise is clearly gratuitous as the builder's legal position has not changed. Even if he hires extra help he is only doing what he was already committed to do—finish the job by June 10. He cannot sue to enforce that promise. But what if you had actually paid the extra $2000 and then read this text and realized that the promise was gratuitous. Could you

Table 3.3 Consideration and Alternatives

A makes promise to B	Under seal w/o consideration	B can sue A to enforce promise
A makes promise to B	With mutual consideration	Result is a binding contract, so B can sue A to enforce promise
A makes promise to B	Bare promise w/o consideration	Promissory estoppel; B can defend if A sues and thus ignores promise, but B cannot sue A

[10] Examples are British Columbia's *Law and Equity Act*, R.S.B.C. 1996, c. 253, s. 43, and Ontario's *Mercantile Law Amendment Act*, R.S.O. 1990, c. M-10, s. 16.

sue to get the $2000 back from the builder? To do so you would have to deny the validity of your own promise and you are estopped or prevented from doing so. The builder can show that he has relied on your promise by hiring extra help and can raise the defence of promissory estoppel.

This defence is rarely available since it is the person who made the promise who has to sue, and that only happens when there is some pre-existing contract that is being modified by the gratuitous promise. Promissory estoppel, then, will only be used where there is a gratuitous promise, and then only where it can be used as a defence. The expression is that promissory estoppel can only be used "as a shield and not as a sword."

The second exception is the use of the **seal**. The use of the seal predates the requirement of consideration and was used to indicate a person's commitment to the deed or transaction in question. That historical recognition of seals continues, and today when a wafer or design is pressed into a document, it has a similar effect. Contract law and the need for consideration never replaced the sanctity of the seal, and today where a seal has been affixed to a document there is no need to establish consideration. Financial institutions will usually affix seals to credit transactions involving a guarantor to avoid any possible question of lack of consideration. Note that the presence of a seal does not replace the need for consensus or any other requirement of contract law, only consideration. In some jurisdictions specialized corporate documents must be under seal to be effective, and some specialized documents prepared by lawyers and notaries are also placed under seal. But as a general rule, the seal is not a requirement in modern contract law.

Reliance upon one-sided promise may be used as a defence

Where there is a seal, no consideration is required

Case Summary 3.5 *Gilbert Steel Ltd. v. University Construction Ltd.*[11]

Promise to Pay Higher Price Not Supported by Consideration

Gilbert Steel agreed to supply steel at a specific price to University Construction for the construction of a number of buildings. The cost for steel went up, and upon request, University Construction agreed to pay Gilbert a higher price than previously agreed for the steel they supplied. University made regular payments as the job progressed, but not enough to cover the increase in price. When the job was completed Gilbert Steel sued University Construction for the shortfall. University Construction claimed they were not obligated to pay the agreed-upon increase based on the lack of consideration supporting the change. The court agreed.

University Construction had agreed to pay a higher price, but Gilbert Steel had not agreed to do anything in return for the change. Note that promissory estoppel was raised by Gilbert Steel. This was rejected by the court, since promissory estoppel can only be "used as a shield, not as a sword," and Gilbert Steel was suing to enforce the gratuitous promise. Had University Construction made the higher payments and then sued to recover the excess paid, it could well be that Gilbert Steel could have used University Construction's promise to pay the higher amount as a defence on the basis of promissory estoppel.

CAPACITY

As a rule the courts don't interfere with the parties' freedom to contract. There are, however, some people who are considered incapable of negotiating a contract.

---

[11] (1976), 67 D.L.R. (3d) 606 (Ont. C.A.).

Infants

The age of majority at common law used to be 21. In Canada this has been reduced to 18 or 19, depending on the province. Anyone under that age is considered to be an infant and is protected to the extent that the contracts they make with adults are binding on the adults, but voidable (not binding) on the infant. The terms *void* and *voidable* will come up throughout the discussion of contract law (see Figure 3.3). Void means there never was a contract and both parties are free from any obligation under the agreement. A voidable contract is valid, but one of the parties, because of some problem, has the right to escape if he or she chooses to do so. This is the case with infants. The adult is bound by the contract, but the infant can escape if he or she so chooses. Of course, the infant can't have it both ways and must return any goods obtained under the agreement. If the infant purchases a car on credit from a merchant and then stops making payments, she has no further obligation with respect to the payments but must return the car. There are significant exceptions to the infant's right to escape from contracts. Infants are bound to pay a reasonable price when they contract for necessities. Such necessities include food, clothing, lodging, and transportation. Infants are also bound by their beneficial contracts of service. These are contracts that are determined to be in the infant's best interest such as an apprenticeship arrangement.

> Infants not bound by contracts but adults are

> Infants are bound by beneficial contracts of service and for necessities

---

Case Summary 3.6 *Mosher v. Benson*[12]

Car Is Not a Necessity, Contract Voidable

Kyle Mosher was only 17 years old when he purchased a car from Peter Benson. In this action he is asking to have the transaction reversed on the basis that he was a minor at the time of the contract. He also claimed that the car was not roadworthy and that he had been charged an excessive price considering the condition. The judge found that there were no expressed or implied warranties with respect to the physical condition of the vehicle given the fact that it was a private sale.

The age of majority in Nova Scotia is 19 and so the contract of sale was with an infant and is therefore voidable unless it is for a necessity. The judge then considered whether the sale of a car qualified as a necessity. The judge referred to the *Law of Contract in Canada*,[13] which stated when discussing necessities "Curiously enough, a

car has been held not a necessary, even in these days, even as in Pysett v. Lampman where the car was used by the minor in the business of selling fish by which he earned a living."

In this case there was no claim that the car was needed for any special use and so there is no question that it could be considered a necessity. The contract was with an infant for a non-necessity and was therefore voidable and the judge ordered that the parties be restored to their original positions. The seller was required to return the purchase price paid as well the filing fee for bringing this action and Mr. Mosher was ordered to return the car.

This case illustrates the way contracts with infants are treated, as well as indicating the appropriate remedy when a contract is determined to be voidable.

The British Columbia *Infants Act*[14] is unique in that it declares that *all* contracts with infants are **unenforceable** against the infant except those specifically made enforceable by statute such as student loans. In British Columbia even contracts for necessities and beneficial contracts of service are unenforceable against the infant. An unenforceable contract

---

[12] 2008 NSSM 72 (CanLII).

[13] Gerald Fridman, *The Law of Contract in Canada*, 5th ed., (Toronto: Thompson Carswell, 2006).

[14] R.S.B.C. 1996, c. 225.

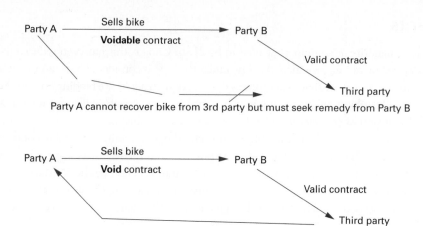

Figure 3.3 Void and Voidable Contracts

only prevents the adult from suing the infant to enforce the contract; it does not empower the infant to get out of the deal once she has performed as required in the contract. The infant has only done what he or she agreed to do, and the courts will stay out of it. Of course, this can lead to an unfair result, and the court has the power to give relief to both the adult and the infant where appropriate.

In every jurisdiction, if the infant ratifies the contract after becoming an adult, he is bound by it. This may be done directly in writing or by implication, such as receiving some further benefit or making additional payments.

Note that this protection of infants in contract law does not extend to tort liability. Infants are as liable for torts committed by them as anyone else, subject of course to what reasonable standard of behaviour could be expected of that infant. The adult can't get around the protection provided to an infant in contract law by suing in tort instead. For example, if an infant damages a rented car, the rental company could not sue in contract, but may try to sue in tort claiming negligence on the part of the infant. This would not be allowed. Parents, as a general rule, are not responsible for the contracts entered into by their children unless they have authorized that contract or they have agreed to be a guarantor or co-debtor. Nor are parents responsible for the torts committed by their children. Only where the adults themselves are negligent, as would be the case if they allowed a child access to a loaded gun, will they be held personally liable. In fact, this has been changed by statute in several jurisdictions where parents have not only been made responsible for torts but in some cases responsible even for the criminal conduct of their children.

Infant can ratify when adult

Infants are liable for their own torts.

Parents may be made liable by statute

Insanity and Intoxication

A contract supposedly involves a meeting of the minds, but where one of those minds is insane or intoxicated, they may be able to escape the contract. The person or his representative trying to escape a contract for a non-necessity—something other than food or lodging—on the basis of insanity must be able to establish three things. First, it must be shown that the contracting party was so insane that he didn't understand the nature of the transaction that he entered into. Anything short of this, and the contract is binding.

Second, it must be shown that the other party knew, or should have known, of the insanity. A central principle in contract law is that the courts will enforce the reasonable expectations of the parties. So if a person has no idea that she is dealing with someone whose mind is gone, and there is nothing in the situation that should have alerted her to that fact, that contract will be enforceable. In the case of *Hardman v. Falk*,[15] after terms for the sale of a property were negotiated with two daughters, the women introduced the purchasers to their elderly and sickly mother, the owner of the property. The terms were then explained to the woman and she signed the documents with an X. The daughters explained that their mother was too feeble to sign her name. Later the daughters tried to get out of the deal on the basis of their mother's insanity at the time of the contract. The court found that her mind was gone at the time of the contract. But even though she was visibly old and sickly, there was nothing to alert the purchasers to her insanity, and so the contract for the sale of the property was valid. Third, if a person regains his sanity, that person must take steps to quickly repudiate the agreement. If the person has bought shares, for example, he can't wait to see if those shares have gone up or down in price before repudiating.

> Where one party is insane or intoxicated, there is no contract if the other person should have known

This latter requirement is more important where the mental impairment is caused by intoxication, since sobriety usually follows. Whether the intoxication is caused by drugs or alcohol, the requirements for escaping liability under the contract are the same: that the person was so impaired he or she didn't understand the transaction; that the other person knew or ought to have known of the intoxication; and that the agreement is repudiated quickly upon becoming sober. Insanity will be a defence to a criminal charge where the accused didn't understand what he or she was doing or that it was wrong. Intoxication, however, in most cases will not constitute a defence to a crime. Note that where a person has been committed to a mental institution, a trustee is appointed to look after his or her affairs. The person may be given an allowance, and any contracts he or she enters into beyond that are simply not binding—not even contracts for necessities.

There are several other situations where the **capacity** to contract might be a problem. Where corporations and societies are involved, the extent of their capacity to contract depends on the legislation that creates them. This is not a problem where ordinary corporations are involved, but when dealing with Crown corporations, government agencies, or even universities, municipalities, and trade unions, their powers are often limited. Any doubt should be resolved by checking the appropriate statute. A different problem exists when dealing with foreign governments and their representatives. Because governments are sovereign, they may be immune from criminal prosecution or civil action in our courts. A few years ago a woman was struck and killed in Ottawa by an intoxicated foreign government official. The Canadian courts could do nothing because of diplomatic immunity. The official was recalled, however, and tried in his own country. Finally, it should be noted that the capacity of status Indians is also limited to some extent under the provisions of the *Indian Act*.[16] This was intended to protect them from exploitation and is a right that remains despite the provision of the *Charter of Rights and Freedoms*. When dealing with First Nations people (whether as individuals as groups or the bands themselves) who are registered as status Indians it would be prudent to review the relevant provisions of the *Indian Act* that relate to the transaction.

> Statutory bodies may have limited capacity

> Diplomats protected

> Aboriginal people are protected

[15] [1953] 3 D.L.R. 129 (B.C.C.A).

[16] R.S.C. 1985, c. 1–5.

LEGALITY

Contracts to commit a crime or other illegal acts are void

Contracts that have an unlawful objective or where the consideration is illegal are void. Examples are contracts to commit a crime or tort; contracts involving an immoral act including prostitution; contracts to sell government secrets or to bribe officials; and contracts that obstruct justice, such as paying someone to go to jail and thus defeating the deterrent nature of a jail sentence. Note that where a statute prohibits a certain act, the terms of the statute itself must be examined to determine the consequences. The prohibited agreement may or may not be void, depending on the provisions of the statute. Gambling was illegal according to common law but now is permitted, providing the terms of appropriate statutes are complied with. Without such permits there are significant penalties under the *Criminal Code* for gambling in various forms, for placing bets for others, and for operating the premises involved in such activities.

Insurance arrangements also face the danger of being illegal contracts—a form of wagering—unless they are intended to cover a loss. To collect you must demonstrate that you have an **insurable interest** in what was insured, meaning that the insurance payout must compensate for a loss and not constitute a windfall. Contracts where merchants agree to sell their merchandise at a common price (price fixing) also raise questions of **legality**. Under the federal *Competition Act* it is only where competition is unduly restrained by such contracts that the agreements are prohibited. The *Competition Act* imposes significant criminal penalties for various forms of agreements between businesses that have the effect of unduly injuring or limiting competition, including conspiracy and bid-rigging.

Perhaps the most important business situation where the question of the legality of an agreement may arise occurs when a business is sold and a provision is included prohibiting the seller from carrying on a similar business. Such a provision is permissible only where it is reasonable, meaning that it goes no further than is necessary to protect the goodwill of the business being sold. If Joe sells Sam a barbershop, and a term is included that prohibits Joe from carrying on the trade of a barber, this would be void. It goes too far. The idea is that if Joe were to immediately start up a new business near the old one, this would defeat the goodwill of the one sold because he would attract all of his old customers. But if Joe opens up a barbershop in another province or five years later, this poses no danger. Such a contract should include a time limitation and an area limitation that goes no further than is necessary to protect the business being sold from such unfair competition. In this example the limitations of not opening up another barber shop within two years and within 40 kilometres of the original business might be more appropriate. It must also not harm the public interest. If only one barber were left, who then could charge exorbitant prices, this might be sufficient reason to void the contract. A similar problem arises when employers impose such terms on their employees that require them not to work in a similar industry after termination. This condition may be necessary to protect trade secrets or special customer relations, but the term should also be reasonable and not go further than necessary to prevent the anticipated evil. It should be noted, however, that the courts are less inclined to enforce such restrictive covenants against employees, especially where they are prevented from carrying on their trade or profession.

Restrictive covenants must be necessary and reasonable

Case Summary 3.7 *KRG Insurance Brokers (Western) Inc. v. Shafron*[17]

Reasonable Restrictive Covenant Enforced

Morley Shafron worked through his incorporated company Morley Shafron Agencies Ltd. and then sold his shares in that company to KRG Insurance Brokers (Western) Inc. He continued to work for them and as a term of his employment contract agreed upon leaving not to work in the same industry for a period of 3 years "within the metropolitan city of Vancouver." In 2000 Mr. Shafron left KRG and went to work for an insurance company in Richmond, British Columbia, a city immediately to the south and adjacent to the city of Vancouver. KRG sued claiming a breach of the restrictive covenant. The Court of Appeal found that the restrictive covenant, while at the upper limit, was reasonable with respect to time but that there was no such thing as the "Metropolitan city of Vancouver" Following a Supreme Court of Canada judgment in *Burgess v. Industrial Frictions & Supply Co. Ltd.,*[18] the judge found that while a restrictive covenant with respect to employment was *prima facie* offensive unless there were special circumstances present to justify it, the opposite was true with respect to a restrictive covenant with respect to the sale of a business where the goodwill

associated with the business was being protected. Such contracts should be enforced where reasonable.

Applying this principle to this case, the court of appeal found that the relationship was not a typical employment one since the parties were of equal bargaining power and the customer base of KRG was largely loyal to Mr. Shafron, requiring such a covenant to protect the goodwill of the business. The court then adopted the "Remedial Flexibility" approach used in the Burgess case and decided that the intention of the parties was to extend the restrictive covenant to the adjacent municipalities close to where KRG had their business. This would include the city of Richmond and so Mr. Shafron was found to be in breach of the noncompetition clause and had to pay considerable compensation based on the 3-year period he was in breach.

This case illustrates the more flexible approach to interpreting these clauses that the Supreme Court of Canada has recently adopted. It also shows the court's reluctance to allow too great a restriction to be imposed when simple employment contracts are involved.

INTENTION

The parties must intend to be legally bound by their agreement, but a person can't get out of an agreement just by saying he or she was only kidding. As mentioned above, the court will give effect to the reasonable expectations of the parties. Therefore, the question isn't so much whether you intended to be bound, but whether the other party reasonably thought he or she was entering into a legally binding agreement. In some situations, such as family arrangements, it would not be normal for the arrangements to be legally binding. Thus, where such domestic relations are involved, there is a presumption that there was no **intention** to be legally bound. This means that unless the other party can produce evidence to rebut or overcome this presumption, there is no legally enforceable agreement. An agreement by a parent to pay a child an allowance would be such a situation. Business agreements are the opposite. There is a presumption that business and commercial contracts are legally binding, and to get out of one you would have to produce evidence that indicated an opposite intention. Sometimes people in business enter into understandings that they don't want to be legally enforceable. But to overcome

Parties must intend legal consequences to result from contract

In domestic or social relationships there is presumption of no intention

In commercial transactions there is a presumption of intention

---

[17] 2007 BCCA 79 (CanLII).

[18] (1987), 12 B.C.L.R. (2d) 85 (C.A.) at 95.

that presumption, they must clearly state that the arrangement is not intended to be a binding contract or have any legally enforceable effect on the parties. Business and family affairs may intersect, or the agreement may involve exaggerated terms. For instance, during a golf game a person might say, "I'll give you a million dollars if you make that putt." Each situation must be looked at separately and the reasonable person test applied. The question is: Was it reasonable for the other contracting party to have expected legal consequences to flow from the agreement? Only if the answer is yes and the other elements necessary to form a contract are present will a legally enforceable contract exist.

Presumptions may be rebutted

FORMAL REQUIREMENTS

Historically, the form of the document was important in determining whether it was binding. The use of the seal as discussed above is an example, but today these formal requirements have largely been removed.

Seal may be required by statute

Writing

It must be emphasized that it is always good practice to put an agreement into written form. It is surprising how even the best-intentioned people will remember the same agreement differently. Still, people are usually surprised when they find out that a verbal contract is every bit as binding as a written one. The writing is important because it is evidence of the contract. There are a few situations, however, where a contract will not be enforceable unless it is in writing. Several statutes are in place requiring writing for specific types of transactions. The most important is the *Statute of Frauds*, originally passed in England in the 17th century. This statute requires evidence in writing for contracts dealing with interests in land, such as the purchase and sale of land, including easements, leases, etc., as well as agreements where one person assumes responsibility for the debt of another. Other less common provisions include contracts not to be completed within one year, a personal commitment of an executor to pay the debt of the estate, and agreements where someone promises another something if they get married. In some jurisdictions the sale of goods acts require that items sold over a given amount be accompanied by writing (a receipt). Some jurisdictions have repealed their statutes of frauds, and others have severely limited its application. In most jurisdictions it is expected that agreements dealing with land—except for a short-term lease of less than three years—and agreements to be responsible for the debt of another, such as a guarantee, will require written evidence. Note that most jurisdictions have passed electronic documents acts that give electronic documents and signatures the same status as written ones.

Writing may be required by statute

Statute of Frauds requires evidence in writing in specific situations

Sale of goods act requires writing in some jurisdictions

When written evidence is not present, such agreements are unenforceable. As discussed above this means that without such writing one party cannot sue in court to force the other to perform. But if a party has already performed her obligations under the contract she has only done what she should have and can't use the courts to get out of the deal. Also, if there has been partial payment or partial performance (providing that it is only consistent with the existence of the agreement), as a rule that will take the place of the writing requirement, and the contract will be enforceable.

Where writing is required but absent, the contract is unenforceable

Partial performance satisfies writing requirement

Case Summary 3.8 *Atlantis Transportation Services Inc. v. Air Canada*[19]

Various Documents Taken Together Satisfy *Statute of Frauds*

Atlantis Transportation Services Inc. provided delivery services over a number of years for Air Canada. Because the business of Air Canada grew considerably during that time, Atlantis had to expand their fleet and incur other expenses. At one point a five-year contract had been agreed to, but Air Canada terminated it after only two years. Atlantis sued. Air Canada took the position that they had never agreed to the five-year term. Secondly, they argued that even if they had agreed to the term, the *Statute of Frauds* required that any agreement to be performed beyond a one-year period had to be in writing. Since it was not, it could not be enforced. The court found first that Air Canada had agreed to a five-year term and also that the requirements of the *Statute of Frauds* had been met. Even though the actual agreement was not in writing, there were sufficient other documents, including letters, invoices, and company minutes, that clearly indicated the existence of the contract; therefore, the requirement of written evidence was satisfied. This provision has since been repealed in Ontario along with other modifications made in Ontario and other provinces to their *Statute of Frauds* legislation, but it does indicate the operation of the *Statute* as well as what constitutes compliance with the writing requirement.

In summary, where there has been consensus in the form of offer and acceptance, consideration has been exchanged, both parties have capacity to contract, the agreement is legal, and there was intention to be bound, a legally enforceable contract has been created.

Key Terms

capacity (p. 69)

consensus (p. 55)

consideration (p. 63)

counter-offer (p. 59)

exemption clause (p. 58)

gratuitous promises (p. 63)

guarantee (p. 64)

insurable interest (p. 70)

intention (p. 71)

invitation to treat (p. 57)

legality (p. 70)

offer (p. 57)

offer and acceptance (p. 55)

option agreement (p. 60)

post-box rule (p. 61)

promissory estoppel (p. 65)

quantum meruit (p. 63)

seal (p. 66)

unenforceable (p. 67)

unilateral contract (p. 61)

Questions for Student Review

1. Explain consensus, its importance in contract law, and how such consensus is reached.
2. Distinguish an offer from an invitation to treat.
3. What must be contained in an offer for it to form a binding contract?
4. What role does the requirement of writing play in the formation of a contract?
5. What is an exemption clause and how is it treated by the courts?
6. Under what circumstances can an offer end before acceptance?
7. Explain the requirements for an option agreement to be binding?
8. What is required for acceptance of an offer and how can such acceptance be accomplished?

---

[19] Ont. Gen. Div., as reported in *Lawyers Weekly Consolidated Digest*, Vol. 15.

9. When and where is an acceptance effective?

10. What is the effect of the post-box rule and when does it apply? To what forms of communications does it apply?

11. When a unilateral contract is involved, how is acceptance accomplished?

12. When will an acceptance sent by email or fax be effective?

13. Explain what is meant by consideration and the contract rule associated with it.

14. Explain what is meant by past consideration and why the designation is important.

15. What is the effect in most jurisdictions of a creditor taking less in full satisfaction of a debt? Why?

16. Explain what is meant by promissory estoppel and why it is important.

17. What is the relationship between a sealed contract and the requirement of consideration?

18. Explain the effect of a contract entered into between an infant and an adult on the parties to it. When will infants be bound by their contracts?

19. What must be proved to escape liability of contracts on the basis of insanity or intoxication? List other situations where capacity may be a problem.

20. What is required for a restrictive covenant to be enforceable?

21. Explain what constitutes intention on the part of parties to a contract.

22. Explain the provisions of the *Statute of Frauds* and when a contract must be in writing.

23. What is the effect if the requirements of the *Statute of Frauds* are not met? Will anything else other than actual writing satisfy the requirements of the *Statute of Frauds*?

Questions for Further Discussion

1. Consider the creation and use of the post-box rule in terms of its original purpose, whether it met that objective, and whether its continued use can be justified today. In your answer consider whether the rule ought to be applied to communications between the parties other than acceptance and to different forms of communications such as email and the internet generally.

2. It is arguable that the requirement of consideration in a contract serves no other purpose than to indicate that the parties intend their agreement to be binding. Do you think that the continued requirement of consideration in contract law serves any valid purpose today? What about the separate requirement of intention?

3. Consider the fact that in most jurisdictions only some forms of contracts have to be evidenced in writing to be enforceable. Many jurisdictions have made important changes to these requirements. What do you think? Should only written contracts be enforceable in court? Should writing ever be required? In your answer consider the costs and use of legal resources as well as whether the purposes of justice in a broad sense are served by your recommendations.

4. People who are insane are given special treatment with respect to the contracts they enter into. If they are so insane they don't know what they are doing and the other party knew or ought to have known of that insanity, there is no contract. Should the only question be whether there was insanity? Would that be fair to merchants? Why don't we treat contracts with infants the same way and allow the infant to escape the contract only if the adult with whom they were dealing knew they were contracting with an infant?

Cases for Discussion

1. *Canadian Imperial Bank of Commerce v. Milhomens*, 2004 SKQB 168 (CanLII)

   Milhomens claimed that he was insane and didn't understand the nature of what he was doing when he was granted a Visa credit card by the CIBC. While he was using it they increased his limit until eventually his indebtedness was $18 104.29 as of 1 October 2003 plus 18.5 percent interest to the date of the trial. This action was brought by the bank claiming that amount. There was medical evidence produced showing that Milhomens had a long psychiatric history. What other information would he have to show to escape liability on his Visa card? Explain what arguments could be raised by the bank to overcome the insanity argument raised by Milhomens. Explain the likely outcome

2. *Lilly v. Phillips*, 2006 CanLII 29280 (ON S.C.)

   Sandra Phillips won $675 000 in the Cash for Life lottery and her friend Eunice Lilly in this case is claiming half of it. They played together in a bowling league. For years on their weekly bowling night they had jointly shared in the purchase of 50/50 $2.00 lottery tickets and on the few occasions when they had won a small amount they had shared the proceeds, but it was clear that the practice to share was only on nights when they were both present for the league play. At the bowling league's Christmas party in 2003 the league executives decided to use the excess end of year funds (left over from regular registration fees that all members paid) to purchase Scratch to Win Cash for Life lottery tickets and give them out to attendees to encourage attendance. At the Christmas party there was also bowling but it was not league play and was just for fun. When they both attended they both received tickets and at the 2002 party they both won $4.00. Ms. Lilly testified that it was her understanding that if they were to win any large amounts it would be shared. But she couldn't give any indication of what would happen if one was absent from the party. At the 2003 Christmas party only Ms. Phillips attended while Ms. Lilly went to another party. Phillips accepted a ticket for herself and one for the plaintiff even though she was not there. Ms. Phillips ticket won $676 000. Although there was no specific agreement with respect to the sharing of the lottery win, indicate what arguments could be advanced by both parties and the likely outcome.

3. *Rogers & Rogers Inc. v. Pinehurst Woodworking Company Inc.*, 2005 CanLII 45977 (ON S.C.)

   Allen and Sue Rogers carried on business in New York State through their incorporated company Rogers and Rogers Inc. supplying and installing store fixtures into higher-end retail stores. Their clients included companies such as Estee Lauder, Cartier, Chanel, Movado, Giorgio Armani, Yurman, and Burberry.

   Pinehurst Woodworking Company Inc. is a larger Ontario company manufacturing such store fixtures and one of the clients that they supplied their products to was Rogers and Rogers. The standard form contract Rogers and Rogers had with Pinehurst and other suppliers contained a non-competition clause stating that any dealings or product inquires from clients were to be directed through Roger and Rogers.

   The plaintiffs alleged that they had informed Pinehurst of an impending opportunity to supply store fixtures to Burberry and that after a falling out between the companies Pinehurst, in violation of their contractual obligation and fiduciary duty to Rogers and Rogers, bid directly on the job and were successful, defeating Roger and Rogers in the process. Indicate the arguments that could be raised on both sides and the likely outcome.

4. *Gendis Inc. v. Richardson Oil & Gas Ltd.* (2000), 148 Man. R. (2d) 19, 224 W.A.C. 19, [2000] 9 W.W.R. 1, 6 B.L.R. (3d) 193 (Man. C.A.)

The chief executive officer of Gendis and the managing director of Richardson Oil and Gas met and negotiated a deal, whereby Gendis would purchase Richardson's share of a privately owned oil company for $39 million, plus certain designated incentive payments (Gendis and Richardson each owned 50 percent of that company at the beginning of the negotiations). At the end of the negotiations both men agreed that they had a deal, and they also agreed that Gendis would supply written documents to confirm the deal and add the necessary details. When the written documents were supplied, Richardson refused to sign them and refused to complete the transaction. When Gendis sued, Richardson claimed that what had been agreed at the negotiation session had not been finalized, and there was no intention to create a binding contract at this stage. What do you think? What is the likely outcome?

5. *Toombs v. Mueller* (1974), 47 D.L.R. (3d) 709 (Alta. S.C.)

Mueller sold land to Toombs pursuant to an oral contract. The only tangible evidence of the contract was that Toombs paid regular mortgage payments and took possession of the land. Toombs is bringing this action and asking for specific performance to enforce the oral contract. Mueller is saying that since the contract is not in writing, he is not bound by it. What do you think? Give arguments on both sides. Consider the jurisdiction within which you reside. What if Mueller were bringing an application to have Toombs evicted from the property? Would this make any difference to your answer? See *Re Whissell Enterprises Ltd. and Eastcal Development Ltd.* (1980), 116 D.L.R. (3d) 174 (Alta. C.A.).

Chapter 4
Enforcing Contractual Obligations

Learning Objectives

■ List the events that can bring a contract to an end

■ Identify the various mistakes that can end or otherwise affect a contract

■ Describe four forms of misrepresentation

■ Explain the effects of duress and undue influence on a contract

■ Consider the implications of privity and assignment for a contract

■ Describe how a contract can be breached or otherwise ended

■ Outline the remedies that are available for breach of contract

At the heart of most business dealings is the understanding that courts will enforce contractual agreements if there is a dispute between the parties. When both parties are happy with the outcome it is not necessary that the contract be legally enforceable. It's only when the parties think the agreement is not being honoured that the legal validity of such arrangements and their enforceability in court becomes an important issue. Those disputes can revolve around the existence of the contract, complaints about the conduct of the parties at the time of agreement, or the performance of the obligations arising from it. The prior chapter dealt with what was needed for a legally enforceable contract to exist. This chapter looks at disputes that arise with respect to the start of the contractual relationship, including mistakes as to the nature, terms, or other aspects of the agreement; misrepresentation; duress; and undue influence. The concept of privity and the assignment of contractual obligations are examined. The chapter concludes by examining problems related to the proper performance of the terms of the agreement.

MISTAKE

When contracts are challenged, the argument often revolves around the interpretation of particular terms. Often the parties have a different understanding of the wording or effect of the terms of an agreement. Such mistakes can take place in three ways (see Figure 4.1).

When both parties have made the same serious error, the resulting **shared mistake** may destroy consensus and result in no contract between them. The contract is said to be **void** in such circumstances, for example, where both parties think they are dealing with one parcel of land and in fact they are dealing with another, or where both parties share a belief that an event will take place and it doesn't. If this kind of shared misapprehension

Parties making the same mistake may destroy consensus

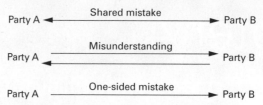

Figure 4.1 Mistakes in Interpreting Terms

is not the fault of the parties and is serious enough to actually destroy the basis of the agreement, it can cause the contract to be void for lack of consensus. Such shared mistakes are rare. Sometimes, where a mistake is made in recording the agreement, the courts will respond to a request to **rectify** the agreement so that it corresponds to the original understanding. But for rectification to take place the actual terms of the agreement must be clearly understood by both parties at the time of contract and the error is simply in the recording of that agreement. Thus, if the parties agreed to sell and purchase a boat for $50 000, and it was mistakenly written down as $5000, the court may be willing to supply the missing zero.

Court may correct mistake through rectification

The second type of mistake occurs when both parties have a different understanding of the terms of a contract. Such **misunderstandings** are the most common disputes in contract litigation and are usually resolved by the court imposing the most reasonable interpretation of those terms on the parties. For example, if I thought the terms of the contract required that you include the sheepskin seat covers with the sale of your car, and you refused to supply them, the court would look at the terms of the contract to determine whether they were included. The court would determine the most reasonable interpretation of the terms. If the car was shown with the seat covers on, it is likely they would be included. It is only where the court finds both interpretations equally reasonable that the mistake will destroy the contract. Thus, two British merchants who agreed on the sale and purchase of the cargo of the ship *Peerless*, on route from Bombay, India to Liverpool, England, ran into difficulty when it was discovered that there were two ships of that name making that passage. The purchaser intended one ship's cargo and the seller the other. Both positions were equally reasonable; consequently, the court found that there was no contract.[1]

When parties disagree, court will apply reasonable interpretation

The third type of mistake is where only one of the parties is in error. Such **one-sided mistakes** will normally not affect the existence of the contract. This is where the principle of *caveat emptor* (let the buyer beware) is applied. When one party has been induced to make the mistake by misleading statements made by the other, this is an actionable misrepresentation and discussed below. But when that person misleads himself or herself, normally he or she has no recourse. On rare occasions a person might sign a document by mistake, thinking it is about something different than it actually is. If that mistake goes to the nature of the agreement in its entirety, not just some aspect of it such as the price, the document may be void. The principle is **non est factum** (it is not my act), and while it used to be very important, the Supreme Court of Canada has now determined that negligence may block such a claim.[2] The problem is that it is difficult to make an error about the essential nature of a document, for example, mistaking a mortgage for a guarantee, unless you haven't read it—and not reading it qualifies as negligence that may block the claim.

One-sided mistakes usually have no effect on contract

But non est factum can cause void contract

---

[1] *Raffles v. Wichelhaus* (1894), 2 H. & C. 906, 159 E.R. 375 (E.D.).

[2] *Marvco Colour Research Ltd. V. Harris*, [1982] 2 S.C.R. 774.

Case Summary 4.1 *Green Lane Environmental Group Ltd. v. Leach*[3]

Contract Enforced Despite One-Sided Mistake

Green Lane agreed in a simple one-page contract with Leach to remove approximately 2000 cubic metres of soil from a specified location. Leach calculated it would involve 122 truck loads with costs estimated to be approximately $80 000. Instead when the job was completed Leach received a bill for $236 582.89. The reason for the difference was how the volume removed was calculated. Green Lane based their measurement on how much soil would be removed if each of the 122 trucks had been loaded to the capacity of the truck, which totalled 5471 cubic metres. In fact the trucks had not been loaded to capacity. Whereas Leach based their calculation on the weight and volume of the soil actually removed which amounted to 2486 cubic metres. Green Lane stated that it was industry practice to calculate the volume to be charged on the basis of the capacity of the trucks. The trial judge found that a mutual (misunderstanding) mistake had been made between the parties and found that the appropriate solution would be to apply the industry standard approach and awarded Green the higher amount.

On appeal the court disagreed. They found the contract to be clear that $40 per cubic metre would be paid for approximately 2000 cubic metres. The contract was clear that the amount to be paid was to be based on the amount of soil actually removed, which totalled 2486 metres, and the price to be paid by Leach was only $99 440.00 ($40 × 2486) plus GST. This was an example of a unilateral mistake on the part of Green Lane. If they had wanted to use the other basis for calculation they should have made this clear to Leach. They were bound by the clear terms of the contract even though they had made a one-sided error.

This case nicely illustrates the difference between a mutual (misunderstanding) mistake and a unilateral (one-sided) mistake and the effect on the parties.

Exemption Clauses

As mentioned in Chapter 3, an area where disputed contract terms often arise is over exemption clauses, sometimes referred to as exculpatory, exclusion, or limitation clauses. These are provisions that favour one side, usually exempting that side from liability for failure to perform some aspect of the contract. While the courts do apply such clauses they do so very narrowly. Any ambiguity will be interpreted at the expense of the party favoured by the clause. If a hotel has a sign saying that they are "not responsible for lost or stolen goods," if those goods were destroyed by fire the hotel would not be protected.

Exemption clauses limit liability

Exemption clauses strictly interpreted

Exemption clauses must be brought to the attention of the other contracting party. Today, it is generally accepted that any unusual clause like this should be highlighted in some way and not buried in the general language of the contract. The language used should be concise and easily understood, and where possible it is wise to have the other contracting party initial the clause. If the notification is by sign, as would likely be the case in a parking lot or restaurant, that sign must be at a location where it is clearly visible to the customer.

Exemption clauses are usually incorporated into what are called **standard-form contracts**. Contract law is based on a bargaining model, but, in fact, parties are often in unequal bargaining positions. Try bargaining with an airline over the terms included in a ticket or a car dealer over the terms included in the warranty. In those circumstances the courts are particularly vigilant in interpreting such exemption clauses as narrowly as possible.

---

[3] 2005 CanLII 7877 (ON C.A.).

> ## Case Summary 4.2 *Boutcev v. DHL International Express Ltd.*[4]
> ## Exclusion Clause Not Properly Brought to the Attention of Customer
>
> When two boxes that were supposed to contain computers arrived empty at their destination, the plaintiff, Boutcev, sued the shipper, DHL International Express Ltd., for compensation. The shipper refused to pay and denied all liability, referring to an exemption clause contained in very small print on the back of the waybill. The judge found that the clause was illegible, saying it was "pain-fully small and defied reading with the naked eye." He refused to enforce it, holding in favour of the plaintiff. Parties to an agreement are only bound by the terms that are reasonably brought to their attention, and to ensure that such exclusion clauses are enforceable, the party drawing up the contract should put them in bold type or otherwise highlight them in some way.

MISREPRESENTATION

Misrepresentation involves false and misleading statements

Misrepresentation involves false and misleading statements that induce a person to enter into a contract. Note that the term false includes half-truths, where what is *not* mentioned makes the statement misleading. Telling a prospective investor that a finance company has several million dollars in assets in the form of outstanding loans is misleading if the investor is not also told that half of those loans are unsecured and unrecoverable. The matter is simplified if the false statement becomes a term of the contract and, consequently, the injured party can sue for breach of contract. Breach of contract will be discussed as a separate topic below. Often, however, these misleading statements never become part of the contract, even though they are persuasive and the very reason the person enters into the agreement in the first place. If you purchase property because the vendor told you a new resort will open nearby, the purchase agreement would normally make no reference to the new resort. Still, if you relied on that false information to persuade you to purchase the property, you will likely have recourse under the law of misrepresentation.

If a false statement is a term of contract, the remedy is to sue for breach

False statements that induce a contract are also actionable

To be actionable, a false statement must be a statement of fact, not an opinion

For a statement to be an actionable misrepresentation, normally it must be a statement of fact, not a statement of opinion. You are entitled to have the opinion that you are selling a "great little car in good shape." It is only when an expert makes the statement that the opinion can be an actionable misrepresentation. When a mechanic says the car he is selling is a "great little car in good shape," the statement had better be true. But in most cases the false statement must be a statement of fact to be an actionable misrepresentation. Even the non-expert will be liable if he falsely claims as a fact that the engine of the car he is selling has recently been rebuilt or replaced. When marketing products or services, legislated advertising standards must be followed. Even when those standards are adhered to, if the message is false or misleading, individual customers may be able to sue for misrepresentation. Consumer protection legislation, which is in place in all jurisdictions, broadens the responsibility of employers for misleading statements made by their salespeople. Consumer protection legislation will also be discussed under "Consumer Protection Legislation" in Chapter 5 (see p. 108).

---

[4] Alta. Q.B., 2001, as reported in *Lawyers Weekly Consolidated Digest*, Vol. 20.

Silence will not normally be misrepresentation. Only when there is a legislated duty or some special relationships between the parties requiring disclosure will failure to make such a disclosure constitute misrepresentation. A recent development in contract law is the recognition in a growing number of relationships that there is a **duty of good faith** between the parties. Where such a duty is present there is an obligation to disclose pertinent information. The failure to do so may well be considered misrepresentation and can be challenged in court. Even in a business transaction where someone withholds information that would lead the other party to change his or her mind, the person withholding information could be violating the duty to act in good faith. Of course, if the misleading statement did not induce the other party to contract, there is no remedy. Suppose the vendor of a property told you of a new resort opening nearby and you purchased the property to build a home or for some other purpose not affected by that claim. You will have no complaint if the statement later turns out to be false, since it did not induce you to enter into the contract in the first place. When the false statement does induce a person to enter a contract, the misrepresentation may be considered innocent, fraudulent, or negligent (see Table 4.1 for a summary of the types of misrepresentation and their remedies).

> Silence is not misrepresentation except where duty of good faith or relationship

Innocent Misrepresentation

A distinction has to be drawn between someone who intentionally misleads and a situation where there is no such intention and no knowledge of the error being made, or **innocent misrepresentation**. When a person misleads another without knowing, and he or she is otherwise without fault, the misrepresentation is said to be innocent. The recourse is limited to the equitable remedy of **rescission**. Rescission involves the court attempting to restore the parties to their original positions. Thus, if a seller had innocently misrepresented the year of production of a car sold to you, and this was important enough to induce you to enter into that transaction, you could seek to have the contract rescinded. You would return the car, and the seller would be required to return the purchase price as well as any incidental costs you may have incurred, such as repair and maintenance expenses. A problem arises where the goods have been destroyed, resold, or are otherwise not available to return to the other party. Rescission is then not possible. Where the misrepresentation has been innocent, no other remedy is available. The remedy of rescission will also be refused where the victim of the misrepresentation has in turn done something inappropriate, such as causing unreasonable delay or having cheated or misled the other party. To obtain an equitable remedy such as rescission, the person seeking it must "come with clean hands." Rescission will also be refused where the contract has been affirmed. This means that the victim has done something to acknowledge the validity of the contract after learning of the misrepresentation, such as trying to resell the goods to someone else.

> Where misrepresentation is innocent, the only remedy is rescission

Table 4.1 Remedies

Innocent misrepresentation	Rescission only
Fraudulent misrepresentation	Rescission and/or damages (tort)
Negligent misstatement	Rescission and/or damages (tort)
Misstatement—becomes a term of the contract	Rescission, damages, and other breach of contract remedies

Case Summary 4.3 *Samson v. Lockwood*[5]

Rescission Not Available Where Contract Affirmed

The defendants produced a brochure advertising property that stated that a building of 150 000 square feet could be built on it. Unknown to the defendants, because of a change in local bylaws, a building of only 30 000 square feet could be built. The plaintiff, after having read the brochure, agreed to purchase the property and put a substantial deposit down on the transaction. Before the actual transfer of that property, land values in the area dropped significantly. The plaintiff tried to sell the property, and when this proved impossible, he refused to go through with the transaction, claiming misrepresentation and demanding the return of the deposit. The court held that the plaintiff was not permitted to rescind the contract in this case. He knew of the error six months before the agreed-upon date for the completion of the transaction, and yet he still indicated a willingness to complete. The plaintiff also attempted to sell the property to others long after learning of the error and before land values dropped. This amounted to affirmation of the contract after he already knew of the innocent misrepresentation. The result was that the purchase agreement was binding on him, despite the innocent misrepresentation in the brochure. The plaintiff was required to forfeit all of the deposit that he had paid.

Damages are not available where misrepresentation is innocent

It must be emphasized that where the misrepresentation has been innocent, the only remedy is rescission. Damages or the payment of monetary compensation to the victim is not available for innocent misrepresentation.

Fraudulent Misrepresentation

Fraudulent misrepresentation occurs when a person knowingly misleads

Fraudulent misrepresentation takes place when one person intentionally and knowingly misleads another and induces him or her to enter into a contract. If it can be shown that you didn't believe that what you were saying was true, you have committed a fraud and the remedies available to the defendant are expanded. Where the misrepresentation is fraudulent, the victim can seek rescission of the contract, or he or she can seek a remedy of damages for the tort of deceit, or both.

Remedy for fraud can be damages and/or rescission

As mentioned earlier, damages involve the wrongdoer paying money to the victim to compensate for his or her losses. Because this is a tort remedy the objective is to put the victim into the position he or she would have been in had the misrepresentation never taken place. In rare circumstances where the fraud is serious enough, the court will award **punitive damages**, which is an attempt to punish the wrongdoer rather than to compensate the victim. In such cases the victim will be awarded more money than he or she has actually lost. Victims will often sue for innocent misrepresentation, even though the presence of fraud is apparent. This can be confusing until you appreciate the strategy involved. Establishing fraud and intention is much more difficult. Where the remedy sought is only rescission, the victim will usually take the easier route of suing for innocent

Innocent misrepresentation is easier to prove than fraud

misrepresentation. Note also that an innocent misrepresentation can become fraud if the person who made the statement later learns it is false and fails to correct the false impression left with the victim.

---

[5] (1998), 40 O.R. (3d) 161, 39 B.L.R. (2d) 82 (Ont. C.A.).

Negligent Misrepresentation

Historically there was no difference between innocent and **negligent misrepresentation**. Since the victim was not knowingly misled, the only remedy available was rescission. In recent years, however, the courts have also awarded damages where it can be established that the wrongdoer should have been more careful. In such cases negligence is established. The legal rules associated with the tort of negligence were discussed in Chapter 2. To summarize, the remedy of rescission is available whether the misrepresentation is innocent, fraudulent, or negligent. But the remedy of damages is restricted to circumstances where it can be established that the misrepresentation was fraudulent, negligent, or where the misleading term became part of the agreement.

Damages also available where misrepresentation was negligent

Case Summary 4.4 *BG Checo International v. B.C. Hydro*[6]

Where Misrepresentation Is Negligent, the Victim Can Sue in Contract or in Tort

B.C. Hydro was erecting a transmission line and put out a request for tenders to erect the towers and string the required lines. BG Checo was the successful bidder, but they based their bid on erroneous information they had been given with respect to the condition of the right of way. They were informed by B.C. Hydro that it would be cleared by another party, when, in fact, they had to clear it themselves. As a result, they incurred considerable extra expense.

In this action Checo is seeking to recover those extra costs from B.C. Hydro, claiming misrepresentation and breach of contract. The main issue was whether the action should be brought in tort for negligence or for breach of contract. The matter went all the way to the Supreme Court of Canada with the defendant advocating the more traditional approach—where a contract is involved, any remedies should be restricted to breach of contract. The court rejected this position holding that Checo had the right to sue in tort for negligent misrepresentation or for breach of contract. The importance of this decision is that the court declared that when the conduct complained of could be characterized as either a breach of contract or negligence, the victim had a right to sue in either tort or contract. "The parties may by their contract limit the duty one owes to the other or waive the right to sue in tort, but subject to this, the right to sue concurrently in tort and contract remains." The difference gives the plaintiff more options and the court more flexibility in awarding damages. The case is also interesting in that it differentiates between fraudulent and negligent misrepresentation, thus providing a tort remedy for the parties even when their relationship is primarily based on contract.

Criminal Fraud

Inducing someone to enter a transaction through intentionally misleading statements can also constitute a crime with potentially significant penalties. There are many specific provisions where various forms of fraudulent activity are prohibited, but for this discussion the most significant are sections 361–365 of the *Criminal Code*, which prohibit knowingly making false representations that are intended to induce someone to act on that representation. This includes obtaining credit, the extension of credit, or some other benefit for themselves or someone else under false pretenses, including misleading statements about the financial condition of the applicant or others. Knowingly paying with a cheque without sufficient funds to back it (N.S.F.) or executing some other valuable security by making

Fraudulent misrepresentation may constitute a crime

---

[6] (1993), 99 D.L.R. (4th) 577 (S.C.C.).

false representations are also specifically prohibited. Obtaining food, beverages, or accommodation by false pretenses is also included. Section 380 contains provisions generally prohibiting fraudulent activities that cheat the public "of any property, money, or valuable consideration or service." This is followed by a number of specific offences, including using the mails to defraud and fraudulent manipulation of stock exchange transactions. A significant aspect of these provisions relates to offences involving falsifying, destruction, or manipulation of books, employee records, prospectus, and other documents with intent to defraud. Impersonating others and passing-off is also prohibited. As mentioned in Chapter 3, passing-off involves leading someone to believe that he or she is dealing with one business, when they are not. For example, selling knock-off copies of Rolex watches or products of other well-known manufacturers is a criminal offense. The penalties for such frauds vary with the nature of the offense, the value of what has been lost, or the importance of the documents involved. For example, where the subject of the fraud is a testamentary document such as a will, or where the amounts involved are over $5000, or where the fraud affects the market price of shares, stocks, or merchandise offered for sale to the public, it will be treated as an indictable offence with a potential prison term of up to 14 years. If less than $5000, it will be treated as a summary conviction offence with potential imprisonment of two years.

DURESS AND UNDUE INFLUENCE

Duress and undue influence also involve disputes related to the formation of contract. **Duress** occurs when the free will to bargain is lost because coercion, involving threat of violence, imprisonment, scandal, damage to property, or even inappropriate financial pressure is exercised by one of the parties. If someone threatens to harm your family or vandalize your business to force you to enter into a contract, the agreement would be voidable because of duress. Another example of duress would be an employer who finds an employee stealing stock or money and agrees not to report him or her to the police if the employee will agree to repay the money by working overtime at regular wage or for some other advantage. The

Threats, a form of duress, make the contract voidable

term **voidable** means that the victim can get out of the contract unless a third party has become involved. If you sold your car to A under threat, you could sue to have it returned because you sold it under duress. But if A had already resold the car to B, you can't force B to give it up. Your only recourse is against A, the person who threatened you. Historically, duress was only available where the threats were threats of violence or imprisonment to the contracting party or his family. In Canada this has been expanded and duress can also be claimed where the threats are against property or take the form of economic duress. A classic example of such **economic duress** took place when a landlord put inordinate pressure on a tenant to sign a lease with unfavourable provisions. The tenant had taken over a prior lease from a tenant who had left several months' rent unpaid. She did so with the understanding that she was not obligated to pay that back rent. But the rent remained unpaid, and the landlord insisted that she was responsible for it. But she was completely committed to carrying on her business at that location and so, under tremendous pressure, she signed a new lease where she assumed the back rent obligation. The court held that the landlord knew she had to sign to avoid "catastrophic financial losses." This economic duress made the transaction unconscionable, and released her of her obligations.[7]

---

[7] *Canada Life Assurance Co. v. Stewart* (1994), 118 D.L.R. (4th) 67 (N.S.C.A.).

Uttering threats of physical violence to a person, to his or her property, or even to his or her animals can amount to the criminal offence of assault. Obtaining some advantage from people by threats or intimidation can constitute the criminal offense of extortion with serious penalties. Duress, as discussed above, may constitute criminal harassment or intimidation, which are also offences under the *Criminal Code*. These offences are also punishable by indictment up to 10 years in prison or by summary conviction up to two years in prison. The *Criminal Code* also makes it a summary conviction offence for an employer to threaten or intimidate an employee with respect to his or her trade union activities.

Note that when a person is compelled to commit an offence by threats of death or immediate bodily harm, that can constitute a valid defence except where the crime involves very serious crimes such as high treason, murder, abduction, sexual assault, or robbery.

Undue influence is more common. It also involves the loss of free will to bargain causing the resulting contract to be voidable. But instead of force, the unique influence of the other contracting party takes away the free will of the victim. In certain types of relationships undue influence is presumed. Examples include professionals such as lawyers, doctors, and trustees taking advantage of their clients as well as guardians contracting with wards, religious advisors with parishioners, and adults with infant children or aging parents. The presumption of undue influence means that in the absence of other evidence to the contrary, simply showing that the relationship exists is enough for the court to allow the victim to escape the contract on the basis of undue influence. Professionals doing business with their clients often find themselves in such relationships, and they are well advised to ensure that the client obtains independent legal advice before committing to the transaction. That will normally provide sufficient evidence to overcome the presumption of undue influence. There are other situations, however, where undue influence can arise based on the unique circumstances involved. For example, when Oscar learned he was dying of cancer, he transferred some of his estate to his nephew. When his brother, Arthur, found out, he got angry and demanded that Oscar transfer the rest of his estate to him and his wife. Arthur's yelling at his brother and pressuring him to go to the lawyer and change his will the next day was clear evidence of undue influence, and the transactions and will were set aside.[8] Where there is no legal presumption based on the relationship between the parties, the person trying to escape the contract must produce evidence of actual undue influence. This is much harder to do.

The principle of **unconscionability** is related to undue influence. This is also a recently developed area of contract law that allows the court to set aside or modify the contract on the basis of vulnerability, such as poverty or mental impairment (short of incapacity), that has allowed one party to unfairly take advantage of the other. In effect, it must be shown that because of these factors the bargaining position of the parties was unequal, resulting in an unjust contract that was grossly unfair to the victim. Note that simple economic advantage will not create an unconscionable transaction. If you are charged a high rate of interest on a loan because you are a high risk, this is not an unfair or unconscionable contract. Most provinces have statutes regulating unconscionable transactions involving loans or mortgages, but unconscionability has now been expanded into contract law generally.

> Undue influence involves abuse of a trusting relationship making a contract voidable

> Undue influence presumed in some situations

> Unconscionable contract when vulnerable people taken advantage of

---

[8] *Francoeur v. Francoeur Estates*, 2001 MBQB 298 (CanLII).

PRIVITY AND ASSIGNMENT

Privity means only the parties to contract are bound by it

The problems of privity and assignment are concerned with determining who has rights and claims under the contract and who can sue to enforce those claims. **Privity of contract** is a basic principle of contract law under which only the parties to a contract have rights. Strangers to the contract are not bound by it, nor can they enforce its provisions. In the example used in Chapter 2, *Donoghue v. Stevenson*,[9] Mrs. Donoghue, after finding a decomposed snail in her ginger beer, could not sue the seller because she was not privy to the contract. Her friend bought the drink for her. Her only alternative was to sue the bottler/manufacturer for negligence. The same principle of privity prevents shareholders or investors in corporations from suing accountants or others who negligently do business for that corporation, such as providing incorrect audited financial statements. The corporation is considered a separate person, and the contract is between that company and the accountant—not the shareholder or investor. The only option for the shareholder is to sue in tort for negligence.

Privity exceptions:

■ Interests in land

■ Trusts

■ Life insurance

There have always been some specific exceptions to the privity rule. Three important exceptions are: 1) interests in land that go with the land—thus a lease will bind not only the original owner and tenant but also any person to whom that land was sold during the term of the lease; 2) trust arrangements—where a person puts property in trust with a trustee for the benefit of some third party, that third party can enforce the trust though a stranger to the contract; 3) life insurance—where the beneficiary is able to enforce the policy taken out by the deceased. Note as well that in some jurisdictions the restrictions of privity have been removed by statute, allowing, for example, the consumer of a product to sue the manufacturer for breach of contract even though the original contract was with the dealer.

Agency and novation do not violate the privity principle

Note that when agents act for principals in dealings with third parties, the principle of privity does not enter into the situation, since the resulting contract is between the principal and the third party, and the agent is merely a go-between. Similarly, where one person takes over the obligations of another in a contractual relationship with a third party (called a **novation**), there is no privity problem since that new relationship requires a complete new contract between the newcomer and the original contracting parties. All three must agree to the change substituting a new contract for the old one. Note that such a new contract can be implied from the conduct of the parties. For example, where Jones has a business delivering baked goods to various supermarkets there is a contract between Jones and those individual supermarkets. If Jones sells the business to Smith (assuming Smith and Jones are sole proprietors and no corporation is involved) and Smith started making the deliveries, the supermarkets would not have to accept since their contract was directly with Jones, not Smith. The change between Jones and Smith could not be imposed on them. They must agree. But if they did permit Smith to make the deliveries, by implication they have consented to the change and a novation has taken place. Their contract is now with Smith not Jones.

Privity rules are changing

In addition to the statutory exceptions mentioned above, the courts have also shown a willingness to move away from the privity rule. For example, in the case of *London Drugs Ltd. v. Kuehne & Nagel International Ltd.*,[10] Kuehne & Nagel was storing valuable goods for London Drugs, and there was an exemption clause in that storage contract that limited

---

[9] [1932] A.C. 562 (H.L.).

[10] [1993] 1 W.W.R. 1 (S.C.C.).

any liability for loss to $40. Employees of Kuehne & Nagel caused considerable damage by careless handling of goods, and London Drugs sued them directly for the loss. Even though the employees were not party to the contract limiting liability to $40, the Supreme Court of Canada extended that protection to those employees, thus ignoring the rule of privity that normally would have applied.

Assignment

Perhaps the most significant area where the rules of privity have been modified involves the **assignment** of contractual rights (see Figure 4.2). Assignment involves the assignor transferring a benefit to which they are entitled under a contract to a third party, called the assignee. In effect, they are selling an entitlement or claim to someone else. For example, if a debtor owes money to a creditor, that creditor can assign the claim to a third party. Merchants selling goods on credit, such as car dealerships, often do this. Their business is selling cars, not extending credit. So they assign the credit transaction they have entered into with their customer to a finance company for a fee, and the payments are then made to the finance company.

> Contract benefits can be transferred or assigned to a non-party

The problems arise when the person owing the obligation that has been assigned fails to perform. Because of the rule of privity, the assignee cannot sue directly; the assignor and assignee must join together to sue the debtor. This is a cumbersome process and most jurisdictions have enacted statutes that allow the assignee to sue directly if certain criteria are met. This is called a **statutory assignment**, and to qualify the assignment must be absolute. This means it must be complete and unconditional; it must be in writing; and proper notice of the assignment must be given to the person owing the obligation that has been assigned. In the example above, the car dealership would make the assignment of the original debt owed by the purchaser to the finance company in writing. The finance company would then send a copy of that assignment to the debtor, asking that all future payments be made to them. In the event of default, the requirements for a statutory assignment have been met and the finance company can sue the debtor directly.

> Statutory assignments can be enforced directly

Finally, it should also be noted that only benefits can be assigned, not obligations. In this example, if a car were defective, the dealership would still be responsible for their breach of contract, no matter what their agreement with the finance company said. The dealership cannot assign such obligations. For that reason, in any assignment, the assignee is said to take "subject to the equities." Thus, if the car dealership doesn't honour the warranty when something goes wrong, the purchaser would have an excuse not to continue paying the finance company. The assignee can be in no better position with respect to the contract than was the assignor.

> Only benefits can be assigned, not obligations

Figure 4.2 Assignment

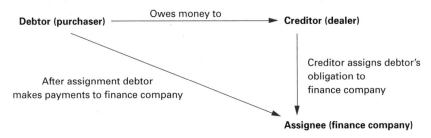

Case Summary 4.5 *Trans Canada Credit Corp. v. Zaluski et al.*[11]

Promissory Note Enforceable Despite Salesman's Fraud

Green was a salesman representing Niagara Compact Vacuum Cleaner Company when he persuaded and pressured the Zaluski family into signing a conditional sales agreement and promissory note for the purchase of a vacuum cleaner. Niagara, in turn, assigned their interest in the transaction to Trans Canada Credit. When Zaluski made no payments, Trans Canada Credit sued Zaluski on the strength of the assigned conditional sales agreement and on the promissory note.

The court found that Green was guilty of fraud, which tainted the sale, thus giving Zaluski a good defence against Green and his principal Niagara. This defence also extended to Trans Canada Credit, which, as the assignee of the conditional sales agreement, could

be in no better position than Niagara. But Trans Canada had sued on the promissory note, and this led to a different result. Once the negotiable instrument, such as a promissory note, gets into the hands of an innocent third party (called a *holder in due course*) they can enforce it independently of any failure on the part of the original party. Trans Canada Credit, as such a holder in due course, was in a position to enforce the promissory note, and therefore Zaluski had to pay. Negotiable instruments are extremely dangerous, and people should be careful when they enter into them. A more detailed discussion of negotiable instruments follows. Zaluski, in turn, successfully sued Niagara for the return of the money he had to pay Trans Canada Credit.

Case Summary 4.5 *Trans Canada Credit Corp. v. Zaluski et al.*

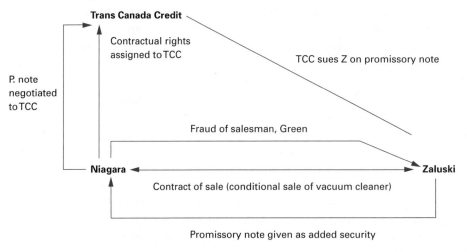

Negotiable Instruments

The position of a third party can be quite different when a negotiable instrument is involved. **Negotiable instruments** have an ancient origin but are now controlled by the federal *Bills of Exchange Act*.[12] These instruments are passed between people and represent claims for funds owing. The key to understanding negotiable instruments is to appreciate their free transferability from party to party. To facilitate this they have to be enforceable at face value. This is accomplished by first allowing the holder to collect on it even though no notice of the various transfers that may have taken place has been given to the original

---

[11] (1969), 5 D.L.R. (3d) 702 (Ont. Co. Ct.).

[12] R.S.C. 1985, c. B-4.

Figure 4.3 Promissory Note

debtor. Secondly, and more importantly, they are made enforceable at face value by giving an innocent party (called a **holder in due course**) who acquires possession the right to collect on it whether the original contractual obligations have been met or not—short of outright fraud or forgery with respect to the instrument itself. This must be contrasted with assignment where the assignee takes subject to any claims between those initial parties to the transaction. That's why Trans Canada Credit couldn't sue on the strength of the original debt they had been assigned in the *Zaluski* case above. The transaction was tainted by the fraud of the salesman, Green. But Zaluski also signed a promissory note, which is a negotiable instrument, and because Trans Canada qualified as a holder in due course with respect to that promissory note they could enforce it directly against Zaluski. The defenses with respect to assignment do not apply when a negotiable instrument and a holder in due course are involved. For this reason most credit transactions include a promissory note so that the position of any third party acquiring rights under it can be protected.

> Holder in due course must be innocent

> Holder in due course gets better rights than parties

Thus, where a purchaser gives a cheque in payment for a car and there has been misrepresentation, he or she can stop payment on the cheque as long as it is in the hands of the person to whom it is made out. But if that cheque is transferred to an innocent third party, including the payee's bank, the purchaser/drawer will have to pay, even though there has been misrepresentation.

Negotiable instruments include cheques, bills of exchange (sometimes called drafts), and promissory notes, which can be used to advance credit and to transfer funds.

> Negotiable instruments take the form of:

A **promissory note** is an instrument whereby one person promises another to pay a certain sum of money at some future date or on demand (see Figure 4.3).

> ■ Promissory notes

A **cheque** involves three parties. The drawer orders a bank where he or she has an account to pay a certain sum of money to a third party, who is called the payee. The drawer delivers the cheque to the payee, who normally then takes it to the bank and presents it for payment (see Figure 4.4).

> ■ Cheques

A **bill of exchange** or a *draft*, which also involves three parties (drawer, drawee, and payee), is similar but broader. A cheque must be drawn on a bank, but the bill of exchange can be drawn on any person or business. Also, the bill of exchange can be made payable at some future time, whereas the cheque must be payable on demand (see Figure 4.5).

> ■ Bills of exchange or drafts

It must also be emphasized that when one of the persons in possession of the cheque or other negotiable instrument endorses the back before transferring it, he or she can also be held liable for the amount of the cheque if the original drawer fails to pay. There are several different types of endorsement, but where the holder merely signs his or her name

Figure 4.4 Cheque

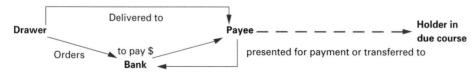

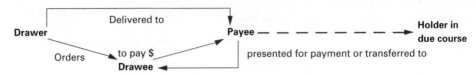

Figure 4.5 Bill of Exchange

(a blank endorsement), it becomes a bearer instrument negotiated simply by passing it from one person to another. Where the holder adds the words "pay to the order of" it is an order instrument and the next person must also endorse it before transferring. In both cases the endorser has added his or her credit to the instrument and must be prepared to pay if the drawer fails to do so.

Normally, the endorser adds credit to a negotiable instrument

DISCHARGING CONTRACTUAL OBLIGATIONS
Performance

Most disputes with respect to contracts arise because of incomplete or improper performance of contractual obligations (see Table 4.2). This is called **breach of contract**, and there is a significant problem in determining just how imperfect performance has to be before it becomes a serious enough breach to discharge the other party's obligations. A contract is **discharged by performance** once both parties have performed as required under the agreement and there are no further outstanding obligations. The terms of an agreement can be characterized as major terms, called **conditions**, and minor terms, called **warranties**. Be careful not to confuse the term warranty, as it is used here, with the assurance given by a manufacturer with respect to the quality of a product produced by them and sold to consumers (a manufacturer's warranty). That is a specialized use of the term. The more correct use of warranty refers to any term of lesser importance (a minor term) in all contractual relationships. You can tell if a term is a condition or a warranty by applying the reasonable person test. Ask yourself if the contracting party had known ahead of time that the term was going to be breached, whether he would still have entered into the contract. If he would have walked away, the term is a condition, but if it is likely that the contracting party still would have entered into the contract, the term is of lesser importance or a warranty.

Contractual obligations can be ended by performance

If a condition is breached after the contract is in place, the victim can elect to treat the contract as discharged. He or she doesn't have to perform the obligation under the

Table 4.2 How to End Contractual Obligations	
Performance	Discharge by performance takes place where there is complete performance or where failure to perform is minor.
Breach	Breach of a condition discharges the victim of his or her obligations under the contract.
Frustration	Discharge by frustration takes place where performance is made "impossible" by some outside event
Agreement	Obligations can be modified or ended by a new agreement.

agreement since the contract has been discharged by breach. But if a warranty is breached, the failure is not considered serious enough to discharge the contract or end the obligations of the non-breaching party. Thus, the contract is still in effect, and the non-breaching party must still perform his or her side of the agreement. There has been a breach, however, and the non-breaching party does have the right to seek compensation in the form of damages from the breaching party.

A similar result takes place when a condition is breached in some minor way. Even though a major term has been breached, the failure is so minor that the contract is considered substantially performed and the non-breaching party is still required to perform his or her obligations under the agreement. This is referred to as **substantial performance**. Of course, here there is also a right to seek compensation for the loss from the breaching party. If you were to order a new car from a dealership and it was delivered with regular wheels rather than the racing rims you specified, this would be a breach of warranty. You could not refuse to take delivery of the car and would have to pay the agreed-upon price, reduced by what it would cost to replace the wheels. If the car was delivered without an engine or a different model altogether was sent, this would be a breach of condition, and you could refuse delivery and would not have to pay for the car. If you operated a fleet of cars and ordered 1000 cars from the dealership and only 999 were delivered, this would be substantial performance of a condition of the contract (the delivery of 1000 cars). You would still have to pay, but only for the 999 delivered cars.

When money is involved, there are some special rules. A cheque, even a certified cheque, is not the same as cash. If the contract calls for the payment of a specified amount of money, that means Canadian legal tender unless otherwise specified. Cheques can be used if that has been agreed to or has been the accepted method of doing business in the past. But when in doubt, make sure that actual Bank of Canada bank notes are delivered. Even Canadian coins do not qualify as legal tender over a specified amount. For example, under the *Currency Act*[13] anything over 25 pennies is not considered legal tender. All coins have restrictions in this way; the amount that can be used varies with the denomination of the coin. However, there is no similar limitation on bills.

It should also be noted that one party can't prevent the other from performing and then claim to be relieved of her obligations because the other party has failed to properly perform her contractual obligations. As long as the performing party is ready, willing, and able to perform and has attempted to do so, that **tender of performance** is considered equivalent to proper performance of the contract. Suppose I agree to paint your house and arrive at the time specified with the appropriate paint and brushes, and you refuse to let me in. I have lived up to my contractual obligation. If you fail to pay me, you are the one in breach, not me. Again, money is treated differently. If I owe you money and come ready to pay it at an appropriate time and place, and you refuse to take it, I still owe you the money. But there is one significant change in my obligation. Normally, it is the debtor's obligation to seek out the creditor to make payment. But I have done that, and now the obligation will be upon you to seek to collect the money from me. You must bear any expenses (including court costs) arising in that process.

Breach of warranty still considered performance

Substantial performance still considered performance

Note limited definition of legal tender

Except with money, proper tender is considered performance

---

[13] R.S.C. 1985, c. C-52.

Breach

As noted, a serious breach of contract can discharge the other party of his or her obligations under the contract. This breach of contract could take place by incomplete or improper performance of the contractual obligations. The breach can also occur through **repudiation**. This involves one of the parties informing the other that he is refusing to perform his contractual obligations, or doing something that makes proper performance impossible (implied repudiation). Where the repudiation takes place before performance is due, it is called **anticipatory breach**, and the victim of that breach has two options. He can either ignore the repudiation and continue to demand performance, or treat the contract as discharged and make other arrangements. Treating the contract as ended allows the victim to make other arrangements and to sue right away rather than waiting for the actual failure before suing. If the victim must hire someone else to do the job, for example, any higher costs can be recovered in that action. On the other hand, if the victim continues to demand performance, the damages eventually recovered may be higher, but there is also the danger that some unexpected event such as a fire, natural disaster, or even sickness may make the contract impossible to perform. Such an event would discharge both parties of their obligations by frustration (discussed below). Worse, the victim of the repudiation may find that he is no longer in a position to perform, making him the one in breach.

If the refusal to perform comes after performance is due, this is just another form of breach through failure to properly perform contractual obligations. The remedies available for such a breach will be discussed below.

Repudiation involves refusal to perform

Anticipatory breach: can treat contract as ended by breach or demand performance

■ **But is bound by choice**

Case Summary 4.6 *Trio Roofing Systems Inc. v. Atlas Corp.*[14]

Failure to Pay Repudiates Contract

Atlas Corporation was a general contractor that had built several schools in the past, using Trio Roofing as a subcontractor on two of them. On the first of those two jobs Trio had been "shortchanged." They had largely completed the first job and, as per the contract, they submitted requests for payment every month. They requested payment for 80 percent for one month and were paid, the next month they requested payment for 95 percent, were authorized payment of 85 percent by the architect but were only paid 80 percent. This shortfall may have been an oversight, but the effect was that Trio did not get what they expected or what they were entitled to. This was in effect a breach of the first contract. Because of this failure Trio lost confidence and did not start the second project when requested. Atlas treated this as Trio abandoning the second contract and hired another roofer to do the job at an extra cost of $17 000. In this action Atlas is demanding that Trio compensate it for that $17 000 on the basis of breach of contract. Trio takes the position that in fact it was Atlas that had repudiated their contract (by failing to pay as agreed) and that as a result it was Atlas that had breached and because of the breach of the first contract Trio was entitled to walk away from the second contract. They, therefore, had no responsibility for the extra $17 000 Atlas had to pay to roof the second school. The court agreed with Trio and found that they were not liable for the $17 000 claimed and that Atlas owed them $35 000 still owing on the first contract. Even if the shortfall in pay had not constituted a repudiation, the hiring of the other roofer so quickly, before the matter could be sorted out, would certainly be repudiation of the second contract by conduct since the hiring of the other roofer made it impossible for Trio to perform the contract.

>

---

[14] 2004 CanLII 19581 (ON S.C.).

> This is a good example of repudiation in the form of anticipatory breach. The actions of Atlas failing to pay as required on the first contract was sufficient to lead Trio to expect that they would be shortchanged or payment would be delayed on the second job. This constituted an anticipatory breach and Trio was entitled to walk away.

As noted above, exemption clauses are often included in contracts to lessen the liability of one party at the expense of another. This is an attempt to make something that would normally constitute a breach of contract, imposing liability on the breaching party, only a minor breach of warranty—if indeed a breach at all. The courts have responded by interpreting such clauses very narrowly; only in the clearest of cases have the courts given effect to them and in some situations the courts will ignore the exemption clause altogether. For example, where an automobile is purchased, the contract will usually include an exemption clause that will limit the liability of the seller and manufacturer from responsibility for certain types of defects in the car. But when the defect is so fundamental as to make the car essentially worthless, even where the exemption clause appears to cover it, the courts will often ignore the provision and hold the seller responsible anyway. This is called **fundamental breach**. The idea is that the purchaser never would have intended such a complete exclusion of responsibility when they originally entered into the contract. An alternative approach is that the courts will find a fundamental breach and not apply the exemption clause where to do so would lead to an "unconscionable, unfair or unreasonable" result.

Exemption clause ignored where fundamental breach

Finally, it should be noted that under rare circumstances a breach of contract can amount to a criminal offence with serious penalties. For such a breach to constitute a crime under section 422 of the *Criminal Code*, the breaching party must know, or have reasonable cause to believe, that the breach will result in danger to human life, serious bodily injury, or serious property damage, or that the breach will delay a train, or even deprive a city (or a significant part of it) of light, power, gas, or water. See Table 4.3 for a summary of the types of performance and breach.

Table 4.3 Performance and Breach

Performance and Breach		Options of the Other Party
Repudiation		
Before performance is due	Election	Can treat obligations as ended and sue or wait for performance
After performance is due	Breach	Can treat obligations as ended and sue
Failure to perform	Breach	Can treat obligations as ended and sue
Partial performance		
Serious failure	Breach	Can treat obligations as ended and sue
Minor failure	Performance	Must perform obligations, but can sue for compensation
Complete performance	Performance	Must fulfill contractual obligations
Performance tendered but refused		
Goods and services	Performance	Must fulfill contractual obligations
Money		Money still owed, but no obligation to seek out creditor

Frustration

Frustration ends contractual obligations

A contract discharged through **frustration** is a recognition that the parties should not be penalized when events happen that are out of their control. Frustration usually takes place when performance becomes impossible, such as when the subject matter of the contract is destroyed through no fault of the parties before performance. A contract can also be frustrated when performance is still technically possible, but would lead to a completely different result because of the changing circumstances. For example, if you were to rent an apartment in Vancouver during the winter Olympics and the Olympics were cancelled for some reason, that would likely frustrate your contract. It would be possible to still occupy the apartment, but the whole basis for the contract has gone and now to require you to go through with it would be something essentially (or fundamentally) different from what you intended, especially when you consider the extraordinarily high rental rate you would be paying.

Frustration involves impossibility of performance or fundamental change

The kinds of situations that can lead to a contract being frustrated are personal illness or destruction of the subject matter, an event the contract was based on being cancelled or changed, and interference by government (such as changing the law, refusing permits and licences, or expropriating property). For a contract to be frustrated the changing events leading to frustration must be unforeseen and outside the control of either party and prevent the proper performance of the contract. Such events destroy the foundation of the contract and make performance impossible or something completely different from what was contemplated. Suppose that Jones contracted to build a house for Smith, but was denied a permit due to a change in government regulation. That would likely be frustration. But if he was denied that permit because of his failure to supply necessary plans or other documentation, that would be breach of contract, since the matter was within his control. This is referred to as *self-induced frustration*, which is simply a breach of contract.

Self-induced frustration is breach of contract

Sometimes a provision will be put into the contract stating what will happen and who will bear the loss in the event of such frustrating events. If that is the case, the provisions of the contract will prevail.

Case Summary 4.7 *Cassidy v. Canada Publishing Corp.*[15]

Change of Curriculum Frustrates Contract

Ms. Cassidy had a contract to work as part of an authoring team to produce a social studies text to be used in the public schools. Her contribution, among other things, was to provide a chapter on criminal law. But the Ministry of Education changed the curriculum requirements so that a criminal law chapter was no longer required. In response, the defendant dropped the plaintiff from the writing team and provided no compensation for the considerable amount of work that she had already done. The court found that there was a contract here, but that it had been frustrated by the change in curriculum. Although it was still technically possible for the arrangement to continue, "the substantial revision of the curriculum amounted to a frustrating event," excusing the parties of further performance. It is interesting to note that although the court found frustration, they ordered a considerable amount of compensation for the work the plaintiff had already done, and which benefited the publisher, to be paid to the plaintiff as required under the *Frustrated Contracts Act* (discussed immediately below).

[15] B.C.S.C., as reported February 3, 1989, in *Lawyers Weekly Consolidated Digest*, Vol. 8.

Historically, the effect of a frustrated contract was simply "let the loss lie where it falls." Both parties were discharged of any further obligations, keeping any benefits and bearing any losses that had been incurred to that point. But that was seen to be unfair, and today all jurisdictions have enacted frustrated contracts acts that overcome much of this unfairness. Essentially, if either party has benefited by a partially performed contract, he or she will have to pay for that benefit as was the case in *Cassidy v. Canada Publishing* above. If a deposit has been paid and no benefit has been received, the deposit must be returned. Note that a portion of that deposit can be retained to compensate for costs incurred in preparing to perform the contract. The British Columbia *Frustrated Contracts Act* goes further by requiring the parties to share equally any costs incurred, even where no deposit has been paid.

Frustrated contracts acts require payment for benefits received and the return or apportionment of any deposit

Agreement

Changing legal relationships through agreement is the basis of contract law. Just as contractual obligations are created by agreement, they can be modified or ended by agreement as well. But for a **discharge by agreement** to take place, all of the elements necessary to form a contract must be present. The problems usually arise with respect to the requirements of consensus and consideration. One party cannot impose such changes on the other without his or her consent. If one party decides to pay less, or not go through with the contract without the agreement of the other party, that is simply a breach of contract.

Contract can be modified by new contract

But all ingredients including consideration must be present

The lack of consideration is a more difficult problem. Where both parties are relieved of some obligation—or get something more by the change—there is no problem. But sometimes the parties agree to changes to end or modify a contract that benefit only one side. In these circumstances the party benefited must agree to do something extra for the changes to be binding; otherwise, the person benefiting from the gratuitous promise cannot enforce it. Still, where the person making the gratuitous change to the agreement changes his or her mind and then brings an action to enforce that original provision, the other party, who has relied on the change, may be able to raise promissory estoppel as a defence. It should be noted that in almost all instances where promissory estoppel has been applied by the court, the gratuitous modification of a prior contractual obligation was involved. Consideration and promissory estoppel are discussed in detail in Chapter 3.

Finally, it should be noted that the original contract might include conditions that will end or modify the obligations. In some circumstances the contract may include an option for one of the parties to terminate under certain specified conditions, but more commonly there will be a condition precedent or a condition subsequent included. When someone buys a house subject to selling his or her old one or subject to arranging financing at a particular rate, that is a **condition precedent**. Until it is met, there is no obligation under that contract. Contracts involving continuing obligations will often include terms specifying when that obligation will end, such as a contract to supply food services until a particular construction project is finished. This is a **condition subsequent**.

Note condition precedents and conditions subsequent in contract

Remedies for Breach

When a dispute arises over the formation of a contract, judicial remedies are designed to put the parties in the position they were in before the contract was entered into. Thus, where there has been misrepresentation or the contract is void or voidable, the court will usually grant rescission and attempt to put the parties back to their pre-agreement positions. But when the dispute relates to improper or incomplete performance, the remedies attempt to put the injured party in the position they would have been in had the contract been properly performed. In the first case the courts look back, and in the second they look forward. Note that rescission is also used as a remedy for breach of contract in combination with damages. This nullifies the original contract and excuses the victim from any further contractual obligation. And then the victim of the breach would be entitled to a reasonable price for work done under the principle of *quantum meruit* discussed below.

Case Summary 4.8 *968703 Ontario Ltd. v. Vernon*[16]

Early Failure Justifies Termination of Contract

Vernon agreed to have the assets of his business sold at auction. The terms of the contract required all proceeds to be deposited in a bank account and then Vernon was to get the first $450 000, the auctioneer was to get the next $150 000, and the rest was to be split between them on a 70/40 basis. But after the first two days of the auction, the auctioneer kept the entire $100 000 brought in, and Vernon refused to allow the auctioneer back on his property. The auction company continued to hold onto the money and sued for lost profits resulting from the breach of contract.

Vernon countersued, also for breach of contract. The court held that the auctioneer's continued failure to deposit the money as agreed was a substantial breach of contract. The auctioneer had also breached a fiduciary duty that he or she had to Vernon by selling some of Vernon's assets at a lower price than was appropriate to a company with which the auctioneer was associated. These failures entitled Vernon to rescind the contract and treat it as if there never was a contract, thus undoing any obligations Vernon had in association with it.

Remedy of damages involves money payment

Damages   The primary remedy for a breach of contract is the awarding of damages. This is an order for the breaching party to pay monetary compensation to the victim of the breach in an attempt to put her in the position she would have been in had the contract been properly performed. Where someone agrees in contract to sell his yacht to one person for $100 000 and then sells it to another, he might well be sued for breach of contract. If the victim of the breach had to pay $110 000 to obtain a similar yacht, the damages awarded would be the difference ($10 000) plus any costs incurred. These amounts are usually given to compensate for monetary loss, but in some cases, where appropriate, the courts today are also willing to provide monetary compensation for emotional stress or pain. For example, in medical malpractice actions and in wrongful dismissal cases, the courts will often take into consideration any pain and mental upset in the damage award. A classic example where damages for mental distress were awarded involved a hospital that in breach of contract improperly disclosed confidential information that implied the plaintiff may have been infected with AIDS.[17] Normally, punitive damages designed to punish the breaching party rather than compensate the victim for the loss are not available for breach of contract. They are sometimes awarded where a tort such as fraud is also involved, or in other special circumstances.

The parties can agree in the contract to limit the amount of damages to be paid in the event of a breach. For example, an electrician may have a term in his contract that

---

[16] 2002 CanLII 35158 (Ont. C.A.).

[17] *Peters–Brown v. Regina District Health Board*, [1996] 1 W.W.R. 337 (Sask. Q.B.).

he loses $50 per day for every day he is late on a contract. These are called **liquidated damages**. A prepaid **deposit** is a form of liquidated damages. When someone purchases a new car, he or she will usually be required to pay a certain amount as a deposit before delivery. If the purchaser fails to go through with the deal, that amount will be forfeited as a pre-estimation by the parties as to what damages will be paid in the event of breach. Another form of prepayment that must be distinguished is a **down payment**. This is simply the first payment of the purchase price and is not forfeited in the event of breach. The terms used are not conclusive, but where the contract does not provide that the prepaid amount is to be forfeited upon breach, it is a down payment and is not directly available as damages. For such liquidated damages clauses to be enforceable they must be an honest attempt by the parties to pre-estimate what damages would be suffered in the event of a breach and not to unreasonably penalize the breaching party.

Liquidated damages are pre-agreed payments for breach in contract

There are significant limitations on the availability of damages in contract law. First, the victim must mitigate her loss. That means the victim must take all reasonable steps to minimize that loss. Failure to do so will reduce the damages awarded to what should have been lost had there been proper **mitigation**. For example, when someone is wrongfully dismissed from his employment, he has an obligation to mitigate by trying to find another job. Any damage award for wrongful dismissal will be reduced by what the person earns (or should have earned) from that alternate employment. Second, the victim of the breach can only receive compensation in an amount that was reasonably foreseeable by the breaching party at the time they entered into the agreement. This means that unreasonable or unexpected losses are too **remote** and cannot be claimed. In one case a victim of fraudulent misrepresentation was induced to enter a franchise agreement to purchase and service soft drink and food dispensers. The court awarded compensatory damages, including the recovery of the initial investment, and also awarded punitive damages for the fraud. But the plaintiff had also put a deposit down on a van to be used to service the dispensers, which had to be forfeited when the franchise arrangement failed. He also sought compensation for the loss of his deposit on the van, but the court held that the purchase of the van was not part of the franchise agreement and was therefore too remote and could not be recovered.[18]

Mitigation requires victim to keep damages low

Damages only payable where reasonably foreseeable

Sometimes monetary compensation will not sufficiently compensate the victim of a breach. The Courts of Chancery developed several remedies that are still available when a contract is breached. Note, however, these equitable remedies are not available when money damages would provide adequate compensation, where there has been wrongdoing on the part of the person seeking the remedy (including unreasonable delay), and when some innocent third party would be adversely affected.

Equitable remedies require good behaviour of victim

Specific Performance   This is an equitable remedy that requires the breaching party to perform his or her part of the contract. Where the goods involved are unique, such as a painting by a famous artist, no amount of money will compensate if the seller changes his or her mind. A specific performance remedy involves the court ordering the breaching party to actually transfer the painting to the buyer. Land transactions are often remedied by an order for specific performance because each plot of land is unique.

Specific performance requires carrying out original contractual obligation

Injunction   An injunction is used in contract and in tort to stop a person from doing something that is wrong. If the party breaching a contract is involved in some activity inconsistent with the proper performance of the contract, the court may order him or her

Injunction requires the end of conduct that is breaching a contract

---

[18] *Lapensee v. First Choice Industries Ltd.* (1992), 46 C.P.R. (3d) 115 (Ont. Gen. Div.).

Table 4.4 Remedies

Remedies	Type	Nature
Damages	Common law	Money compensation limited by mitigation and remoteness
Liquidated Damages	Contract	Deposit forfeited or contract terms limit damages to be paid
Specific Performance	Equitable	Order to perform contract terms
Injunction	Equitable	Order not to act inconsistent with contract terms
Accounting	Equitable	Order to disclose and pay over profits to victim
Quantum Meruit	Equitable	Order to pay reasonable amount for services supplied

to stop doing it. If I rented a hall from you to put on a concert and you changed your mind, I could seek an injunction to prevent you from renting that hall to anyone else. I could also seek an order of specific performance forcing you to let me use it as per the original contract.

Accounting   There are other types of specialized equitable remedies. An accounting is available when profits have been diverted and it is difficult to determine just what injury has taken place. The court can order the breaching party to disclose financial records and dealings, and to pay any profits obtained through their wrongdoing to the aggrieved party.

Accounting requires disclosure of profits and their surrender to victim

Quantum Meruit   This remedy is applied where the contract is breached before all work has been done or when no specific consideration has been agreed upon for services rendered. Here, the court orders a reasonable amount to be paid for what has been done. If you seek help from a plumber or mechanic, often you don't agree on a price ahead of time. You are then required to pay a reasonable price on the basis of *quantum meruit*, which is what you are billed, unless you immediately protest and dispute the amount claimed. See Table 4.4 for a summary of the remedies for a contract breach.

Quantum meruit requires reasonable payment for services given

---

Case Summary 4.9 *Alumitech Architectural Glass & Metal Ltd. v. J.W. Lindsay Enterprises Ltd.*[19]

Payment Owed for Work Done with or Without a Contract

Both Alumitech (defendant) and J.W. Lindsay Enterprises (plaintiff) bid on a job at Dalhousie University and J.W. Lindsay Enterprises got the job. Alumitech made a separate deal with J.W. Lindsay Enterprises to do some of the work but eventually a dispute arose as to how Alumitech was to be paid. One thought there was to be a flat rate price and the other thought the payment was to be based on a unit price per square foot completed. The court found that there was no consensus between the parties, the price being a very important term of the agreement. With no consensus there was no contract but there had been a considerable amount of work done and the court awarded a remedy to Alumitech based on the principle of *quantum meruit*. Applying this remedy the court then determined a fair and reasonable price for the work that had been done and the award was based on that. This amounted to a calculation based on the costs incurred plus a small allowance for profit. *Quantum meruit* is an equitable remedy where someone receiving a benefit is required to pay a reasonable price for that benefit received even in the absence of a binding contract.

---

[19] 2006 NSSC 14 (CanLII).

Key Terms

anticipatory breach (p. 92)

assignment (p. 87)

bill of exchange (p. 89)

breach of contract (p. 90)

cheque (p. 89)

condition precedent (p. 95)

condition subsequent (p. 95)

conditions (p. 90)

deposit (p. 97)

discharge by agreement (p. 95)

discharge by performance (p. 90)

down payment (p. 97)

duress (p. 84)

duty of good faith (p. 81)

economic duress (p. 84)

fraudulent misrepresentation (p. 82)

frustration (p. 94)

fundamental breach (p. 93)

holder in due course (p. 89)

innocent misrepresentation (p. 81)

liquidated damages (p. 97)

misunderstanding (p. 78)

mitigation (p. 97)

negligent misrepresentation (p. 83)

negotiable instruments (p. 88)

non est factum (p. 78)

novation (p. 86)

one-sided mistake (p. 78)

privity of contract (p. 86)

promissory note (p. 89)

punitive damages (p. 82)

rectify (p. 78)

remote (p. 97)

repudiation (p. 92)

rescission (p. 81)

shared mistake (p. 77)

standard-form contracts (p. 79)

statutory assignment (p. 87)

substantial performance (p. 90)

tender of performance (p. 91)

unconscionability (p. 85)

undue influence (p. 85)

void (p. 77)

voidable (p. 84)

warranties (p. 90)

Questions for Student Review

1. Distinguish between a shared mistake, a misunderstanding, and a one-sided mistake and explain how a court would deal with each of these problems.

2. Distinguish between innocent, fraudulent, and negligent misrepresentation, and indicate the remedies available for each.

3. Explain why it is easier to succeed with an action for innocent misrepresentation than for fraudulent or negligent misrepresentation.

4. Distinguish between a void and voidable contract. Why is this important to the discussion of duress and undue influence?

5. Explain what is meant by a presumption with respect to undue influence, the effect of such a presumption, and under what circumstances those presumptions will occur.

6. When will the courts find a contract to be unconscionable? What effect will that have on the position of the parties?

7. What is meant by privity of contract? Indicate any exceptions.

8. Explain what is meant by assignment in contract law, and indicate any limitations on what can be assigned.

9. What is necessary for an assignment to qualify as a statutory assignment? What is the importance of such a designation?

10. What does it mean to say the assignee is "subject to the equities"?

11. Define a negotiable instrument and distinguish between a cheque, a bill of exchange, and a promissory note.

12. Explain the position of an endorser of a negotiable instrument.

13. What is necessary for a person to qualify as a holder in due course? Why is that designation significant?

14. Distinguish between conditions and warranties, and explain how this can affect the discharge of contractual obligations.

15. Explain what is meant by substantial performance and how that can affect the discharge of contractual obligations.

16. Explain what is meant by repudiation and, in particular, the effect of anticipatory breach on the position of the parties to a contract.

17. What will cause a contract to be discharged though frustration and what are the consequences?

18. How has the effect of a frustrated contract been modified by statute?

19. What is necessary for a contract to be discharged or modified by agreement?

20. Explain the role promissory estoppel sometimes plays in the discharge or modification of a contract by agreement.

21. Distinguish between a condition precedent and a condition subsequent.

22. Explain what is meant by fundamental breach and how it relates to the enforcement of exemption clauses in a contract.

23. Explain the remedy of damages as it applies to breach of contract.

24. Explain how damages for breach of contract are calculated and any limitations on their availability.

25. How are equitable remedies treated differently from an award of damages for breach of contract?

26. Distinguish between specific performance, an injunction, an accounting, and *quantum meruit.*

Questions for Further Discussion

1. The law of contract is to a large extent based on the barter model. The guiding principle of this model is that the parties are in an equal bargaining position negotiating balanced terms with which the courts shouldn't interfere. However, in recent years the courts are showing an increasing willingness to overturn terms such as exculpatory clauses, or they are stepping in to protect individuals on the basis of good faith or unconscionability. Consider whether in the process of attempting to ensure fairness in contract law the courts and legislatures have unduly interfered with the underlying principle of the parties' freedom to contract as they wish. Should the guiding principle or the assumption that the parties are in an equal bargaining position be abandoned and the courts take on more of a protective role?

2. Discuss the principle of privity of contract and whether it has any place in modern law. In your answer consider the problems it presents when the person injured by products or services supplied under contract is not the party who originally contracted for that product

or service. Also look at the growing number of exceptions, including assignment of contractual rights and negotiable instruments, and consider whether the retention of privity causes more harm than it overcomes.

3. Consider the discharge of a contract through frustration. There are several restrictions on the application of frustration such as the fact that the interfering event must be unexpected and out of the control of either party. Also, legislation has been passed modifying the common law position of "let the loss lie where it falls." Consider whether anyone should be allowed to escape his or her contractual obligations on the basis of frustration. Should the application of the principle be broader so that there are not so many limitations involved? Does the statutory interference reduce the problem or make it worse? Is there any place for the doctrine of frustration in modern contract law?

4. It makes little difference to the nature of the injuries suffered by the victim of false statements if they were misled intentionally or inadvertently. However, it makes a significant difference to the remedies available to the victims if they were misled intentionally or innocently. The victims of intentional misrepresentations can sue for damages, whereas the victim of an innocent misrepresentation can only ask for rescission. Should a distinction be drawn between fraudulent and innocent misrepresentation in determining the availability of damages as a remedy?

Cases for Discussion

1. *Kettunen v. Sicamous Firemen's Club*, B.C.S.C., as reported in *Lawyers Weekly Consolidated Digest*, Vol. 19.

   Kettunen attended a campground where a "mud bog race" was being held. Even though she was some distance from the race course, one of the drivers lost control and the vehicle struck Mrs. Kettunen, causing her injury. She sued Sicamous Firemen's club, the operators of the campground, and the race. When Kettunen signed in as a camper, one of the documents contained a waiver of liability and indemnity. This is a particular kind of limitation clause exempting one party from liability for failure to perform what would otherwise be an obligation under the contract. Should the victim be precluded from seeking compensation on the basis of this waiver of liability? How would your answer be affected by knowing that the clause was long, in small print, was difficult to read, and was not drawn to her attention?

2. *Whitby Hydro Electric Commission v. Kurz,* [2005] O.J. No. 56.

   Karl and Katherine Kurz opened a factory in 1967 and opened an account with Whitby Hydro Electric Commission for power service. They eventually incorporated the business in 1975 and from then on the bills were paid by the company. The company eventually failed, having run up considerable arrears in the payments to Whitby, and Whitby demanded that Mr. and Mrs. Kurz pay those areas personally. Explain why Whitby felt that Mr. and Mrs. Kurz were personally liable and indicate any defenses that they could raise to this claim.

3. *Liu v. Coal Harbour Properties Partnership,* 2006 BCCA 385

   A purchaser paid a $391 000 deposit towards the purchase of land valued at almost $2 million. Before the sale was completed a dispute arose with respect to the number of parking stalls to be included on the property and this apparently soured the deal. The purchaser refused to go through with the contract and demanded the return of their deposit. The court found that the vendor did nothing to prevent the deal from going through and that it was the purchaser that made a considered decision after receiving professional advice not to go though with the deal. Explain whether the purchaser should get the deposit back. Give the arguments for both sides.

4. *McDermid et al. v. Food-Vale Stores (1972) Ltd. et al.* (1980), 117 D.L.R. (3d) 483 (Alta. Q.B.).

When Food-Vale Stores (1972) Ltd. bought a food store from McDermid, a provision of the purchase agreement required Food-Vale to supply heat to a neighbouring store for 10 years. Unfortunately, five months later a fire destroyed the Food-Vale store, along with the equipment needed to generate and supply the heat to the neighbouring store. As a result, Food-Vale ceased to supply the promised heat and was sued by McDermid. Explain what Food-Vale might raise in its defence. Explain the arguments on both sides and discuss the likely outcome.

5. *Canlin Ltd. v. Thiokol Fibres Canada, Ltd.* (1983), 142 D.L.R. (3d) 450 (Ont. C.A.).

Canlin manufactured swimming pool covers and purchased their material from Thiokol Fibres. Unfortunately, one batch of material was defective, but this was not discovered until dissatisfied customers complained and demanded compensation. Canlin not only had to meet these expenses, but also lost a considerable amount of future business because of the harm to their reputation. In this action they are asking for compensation from Thiokol for these losses. Explain the arguments that Thiokol might raise in its defence. Explain the likely outcome.

6. *Byle v. Byle* (1990), 65 D.L.R. (4th) 641 (B.C.C.A.).

Various members of the Byle family were involved in a real estate business that went sour when one son physically threatened one of his siblings. Fearing for their other children, the parents conveyed certain land to the verbally abusive son and gave him other advantages. This action is being brought by the parents and other family members to overturn those transactions. What arguments can be raised by the various parties to this action? Explain the likely outcome.

Chapter 5

Legislation in the Marketplace

Learning Objectives

- Describe the function and form of *Sale of Goods Act*
- Outline the duties of sellers and buyers
- Describe the nature and purpose of consumer protection legislation
- Discuss the role of federal legislation in controlling competition in the marketplace
- Consider the forms and purpose of securing transactions
- Describe the process and objectives of bankruptcy

Our economic system is, to a large extent, based on a free market system, which in turn depends on the capacity of contracting parties to bargain freely. The courts, as a rule, will not interfere with people's freedom to make whatever bargain they want. Still, there are a number of situations where statutes have been passed to modify or interfere with that process. This chapter will examine some of the special situations where legislation controls or imposes special rules on sales transactions. The *Sale of Goods Act* applies to all contracts where goods are sold, whether they involve consumers or business transactions. **Consumer protection legislation** in its various forms is aimed at policing the marketplace, adjusting the balance between consumer and merchant, and establishing recourse for the worst abuses. A significant portion of business and consumer transactions involve some form of security to ensure payment, and a significant portion of this chapter sets out the general principles involved in such **secured transactions**. Unfortunately, businesses fail and individuals often find themselves overwhelmed by debt. A brief discussion of the *Bankruptcy and Insolvency Act*, which provides relief for the debtor and protection for the creditor, is the final topic of this chapter.

Statutes modify business law

THE *SALE OF GOODS ACT*

The primary purpose of the sale of goods acts in place in all common law provinces is to supply missing terms that the parties didn't think to include in there contract of sale. Because of this it is one of the few examples of statutes where the parties can override its provisions by clearly providing for a different result in their agreement. Remember, the *Sale of Goods Act* applies to all transactions where goods are sold, not just retail sales; therefore, it has important implications for all levels of business.

Sale of Goods Act supplies missing terms

Goods or Services

For the *Act* to apply, goods must be transferred/sold

It must be emphasized that for the *Sale of Goods Act* to apply, there must be an actual sale where the goods are transferred from a seller to a purchaser. Simply using goods as security for a loan is not a sale, even though a bill of sale may be involved unless, as with a conditional sale agreement, possession and the title to the goods are eventually transferred to the purchaser.

The Act only applies where goods are sold. This requires that money be paid and that goods, as opposed to land or services, are involved. Goods or chattels are tangible, movable property such as pens, cars, boats, and even locomotives. Where mixed goods and services are involved, if the transaction is primarily for a service such as an artist painting a portrait, the Act will not apply. However where the service is incidental to obtaining the goods, as when a meal is supplied at a restaurant, the *Sale of Goods Act* will apply to the transaction. Where the service and goods can be separated as with a mechanic repairing a car, the Act applies to the parts supplied but not to the labour.

Case Summary 5.1 *Gee v. White Spot Ltd.; Pan et al. v. White Spot Ltd.*[1]

Contaminated Food Covered by *Sale of Goods Act*

Two customers suffered botulism poisoning from consuming food they obtained at the White Spot restaurant in Vancouver; they sued. They relied on section 18 of the B.C. *Sale of Goods Act* that requires goods to be of merchantable quality and fit for normal use. The restaurant claimed they provided a service—not a good—and that the Act did not apply. The judge, however, agreed with the plaintiff:

> I agree with counsel's submission that an item on the menu offered for a fixed price is an offering of a finished

product and is primarily an offering of the sale of a good or goods and not primarily an offering of a sale or services.

The contaminated food was not fit for the purpose for which it was sold and was not of merchantable quality. The contract of sale, therefore, had been breached and the White Spot was liable for the injuries. This case shows how important the implied terms of the *Sale of Goods Act* can be, especially since the damages awarded were substantial.

Title and Risk

Under the *Act* risk follows title, except . . .

■ in the case of CIF, FOB, COD, and bill of lading

It is important to determine which party will bear the risk of damage to those goods while the transaction is proceeding. Under the *Sale of Goods Act* "risk follows title," meaning that whoever has the title to the goods when they are damaged must bear the loss. This is one area that is often overridden by the parties in the agreement by including such phrases as CIF, FOB, or COD. With **CIF** (cost, insurance, and freight) contracts, one party is responsible for arranging the insurance and the transportation of the goods, thus assuming the risk. In **FOB** (free on board) contracts, the parties specify that title and risk will transfer at a specific place, for example, FOB the seller's loading dock. **COD** contracts (cash on delivery) require the purchase price to be paid and title and risk transfer when the goods are delivered to the purchaser. **Bills of lading** can also be used to control risk and title. When

---

[1] (1986), 32 D.L.R. (4th) 238 (B.C.C.A.).

the goods are given to a common carrier, the seller can designate himself to receive those goods at their destination thus retaining control over them during transport.

In situations where such provisions are not made, risk will follow title and the transfer of title (the property in the goods) will be determined by the operation of five rules set out in the *Sale of Goods Act* (see Table 5.1).

Rule #1 Where the goods sold are specific, identified, and nothing further has to be done to them, title transfers immediately upon the contract of sale being made. The purchaser bears the risk even though payment or delivery may take place at some later date and the goods continue in the hands of the seller.

Rule #2 If something has to be done to those goods to put them in a deliverable state, such as fixing a scratch or adjusting a part, title transfers when the repair is made and the customer is given notice that the goods are ready.

Rule #3 If the goods have to be weighed or measured to determine price, title will transfer once that has been done and notice given.

Rule #4 When goods are taken on approval or sale with the right to return them if not satisfied, title and risk transfers when the purchaser notifies the seller of his or her acceptance, or when the purchaser acts towards those goods in a way consistent with having accepted them. For example, if cloth is involved and you make a dress out of it, the cloth is yours. You can no longer return it.

Rule #5 When goods have not yet been made, or where they have been selected from a sample or a floor model, etc., title only transfers after the particular goods to be purchased have been made (or selected and committed to the transaction) with the assent of the other party (usually the purchaser). In rules #2 and #3, actual notice is required, but the wording in #5 is broader; therefore, assent or approval can be implied. Suppose I were to leave my car at a tire store specifying four new tires were to be installed while I was shopping in the mall. Title would not transfer immediately. But when the seller chose the four tires and installed them on my wheel rims they would be committed unconditionally to the transaction. My assent would be implied, since I left the merchant to make the choice and to install the tires on my car.

Five rules determine when title transfers

Table 5.1 Title and Risk

Situation	Rule	Result
The sale of specific goods in a deliverable state	#1	Title transfers immediately upon creation of the contract of sale.
The sale of specific goods needing repairs, etc.	#2	Title transfers when work is done and the purchaser is notified.
The sale of specific goods needing to be weighed or measured	#3	Title transfers when this is done and the purchaser is notified.
The sale of goods on approval	#4	Title transfers to the purchaser with - Notification to seller of approval - Passage of a reasonable time - Treatment of goods as the purchaser's own
The sale of goods that are not yet selected (from many) or not yet made at the time of contract	#5	Title transfers when goods are unconditionally committed to contract with assent (expressed or implied)

Obligations of the Seller

Some of the most important provisions in the *Sale of Goods Act* relate to the seller's responsibility for the goods sold. Although the Act varies to some extent from province to province, there are usually four sections imposing conditions and warranties on the seller with respect to the nature of the goods supplied. As was the case with contracts generally, warranties are less important terms, and conditions are major terms the breach of which will free the purchaser from his obligation to go through with the contract. This may make the difference between the right to return the goods to the seller for a refund or only to have the goods repaired or replaced. Note that the parties are free to designate a provision as a condition, thus making it important, when otherwise it would only be a warranty. All provinces have similar terms.

Breach of condition ends contractual obligations

Breach of warranty does not end contractual obligations

Title   There are several implied terms with respect to title. There is an implied condition that the seller must deliver **good title** to the goods to the purchaser. If it turns out later that the goods were stolen, whether the seller knew it or not, the purchaser can get his or her money back. There is an implied warranty requiring the purchaser to provide **quiet possession** with respect to the goods supplied. This means that the goods have to be usable as intended without interference. For example, if you purchased a cell phone but it couldn't work on any of the available networks, that would be a breach of quiet possession. Finally, there is an implied warranty that the goods will be free of any **charge or encumbrance**. This refers to a lien that gives a creditor the right to seize the goods upon default where the goods have been used as security for a loan.

Obligations of seller under the Act:
- *To deliver good title*

- *To deliver quiet possession*

- *To deliver goods free of liens*

Case Summary 5.2 *Gencab of Canada Ltd. v. Murray–Jensen Manufacturing Ltd.*[2]

Breach of Quiet Possession Provides Remedy

Dominion Electric sold dies and equipment and the right to produce a particular product to Gencab, which in turn sold those dies and equipment to Murray–Jensen Manufacturing. When Dominion Electric relied on their patent rights and prevented Murray–Jensen from using the dies and equipment to produce the product in question, Murray–Jensen sued Gencab for breach of contract, claiming that their right of quiet possession of the goods sold had been breached under section 13 of Ontario's *Sale of Goods Act*. The court held that Dominion's patent rights, which prevent the use of the goods sold, did interfere with their quiet possession and found Gencab liable for the breach. This case illustrates the nature of the right of quiet possession.

Case Summary 5.2 *Gencab of Canada Ltd. v. Murray–Jensen Manufacturing Ltd.*

Description or Sample   If the goods are bought by **description** or by **sample** and what is delivered does not match the description or sample, the *Sale of Goods Act* implies conditions into the contract that permit the purchaser to refuse delivery. A purchaser buying a truckload of apples based on a sample Spartan would be able to refuse delivery if

Goods must match description or sample

---

[2] (1980), 114 D.L.R. (3d) 92 (Ont. H.C.J.).

Macintosh apples were delivered. Sale by description not only covers situations where goods are bought through a catalogue or ordered from an advertisement, but also includes any purchase of goods that have been mass-produced. Since you don't choose one particular item over another, as they are all the same, you are relying on specifications (description) to make the purchase, and the goods must match that specification, picture, box, pamphlet, etc.

Quality Perhaps the most important implied obligation of the seller relates to the **fitness and quality** of the goods sold. The *Sale of Goods Act* requires that when goods are sold by description (which now is taken to mean all mass-produced goods), those goods must be of merchantable quality. This means essentially that the goods must be free of any defects that would render them unusable or interfere with their effectiveness. If they are defective in some way or fail earlier than expected, a condition of the contract has been breached, and a refund can be demanded. British Columbia has taken this even further, requiring the goods to be "durable for a reasonable period of time."

Goods must be of merchantable quality

The Act also provides that when the purchaser relies on a seller's recommendation for goods that will do a specific job, the goods must be fit for that purpose. If you go to a paint store asking for a product to cover a concrete floor and the product supplied then peels off the floor, a condition has been breached and you can recover not only the purchase price but also any costs you incur in stripping and repainting the floor.

Goods must be fit for the purpose purchased

Sellers often attempt to override these implied conditions of fitness and quality (see Table 5.2). A new product warranty is an attempt by the seller and manufacturer to limit the liability that would otherwise be implied by the provisions of the *Sale of Goods Act*. These warranties usually limit the time of the obligation to 90 days for electronic products, for example, or to a few years for automobiles. They also typically restrict the remedy available to repair or replace the product, and specifically exclude all other warranties express or implied.

Limited warranties try to override these obligations

In commercial transactions such limitation or **exemption clauses** will generally be enforced unless they completely change the nature of the obligation or can be said to be "unfair unreasonable or unconscionable." However, in consumer transactions most jurisdictions in Canada and many in the United States have included in their consumer

Exemption clauses may limit liability

Table 5.2 Implied Conditions and Warranties

Seller's obligations with respect to title	Seller must deliver property/good title	Condition
	Seller must deliver quiet possession	Warranty
	Goods must be free of charge or encumbrance	Warranty
When goods bought by description	Goods must correspond to description	Condition
Purchaser relies on advice of seller	Goods must be reasonably fit for purpose required	Condition
When goods bought by description	Goods must be of merchantable quality	Condition
When goods bought by sample	Goods must correspond to sample and be free of hidden defects	Condition

protection legislation provisions that prohibit such all-encompassing limitation provisions. For example, if you check a manufacturer's warranty for a new automobile or electronic product it will likely include a statement to the effect that, "Some states or provinces do not allow limitation on how long an implied warranty lasts or the exclusion of incidental or consequential damage so the above limitation or exclusion may not apply to you."

In commercial transactions the importance of such clauses as well as the extensive application of the *Sale of Goods Act* is illustrated by *Hunter Engineering Co. v. Syncrude Canada Ltd.*[3] In this case massive gears were sold as vital components of the huge conveyor belts used to convey the oil sands as they were extracted in the tar sands project of northern Alberta. The gears were defective, and the court held that the fitness and quality provision of the *Sale of Goods Act* applied, making Hunter Engineering liable to Syncrude for the defective parts. They had failed to contract out of that provision by including a carefully worded, limited warranty. It is interesting to note that another supplier of identical defective gears, Allis Chalmers, was not responsible because they had effectively limited their liability.

The Act implies many other important terms into sale of goods transactions. We can only mention a few here. Where no purchase price is stated, a reasonable price is implied. Where no date is specified, payment is due at a reasonable time, which is normally taken as the time of delivery. If the purchaser defaults and fails to take delivery of the goods or fails to pay for them, the seller is entitled to the normal contractual remedies discussed in Chapter 4. In addition, the seller has the right to **stoppage in *transitu***. This means that if the goods are in the hands of a transporter and being delivered to the purchaser, the seller can intercept those goods and recover them from the transporter. Even if they do get into the hands of the purchaser, the seller has a limited right to recover them in the event of the purchaser's bankruptcy under the federal *Bankruptcy and Insolvency Act*. Where title has transferred and the full price is due and payable, the seller can sue for the whole price in the event of a default—not just for lost profits and costs—a much more attractive remedy. Finally, it should be mentioned that each province has passed an international *Sale of Goods Act* covering international sales transactions. International business transactions are a specific topic discussed in Chapter 10

If the purchaser defaults, the seller can stop goods in transit

If bankruptcy, seller has limited right to recover goods

CONSUMER PROTECTION LEGISLATION

As we use the term here, **consumer** refers to someone purchasing a product for his or her own use, not for resale and normally not for use in a business activity. Historically, the common law approach to consumer transactions has been *caveat emptor*, sometimes translated as, "let the buyer beware." However, this is one area where the many abuses have prompted governments at both the federal and provincial levels to enact legislation designed to protect the consumer.

Both federal and provincial consumer protection legislation

Provincial Legislation

While the legislation varies substantially from province to province, in the next few pages we will highlight some of the basic principles that the different provinces' legislation has in common.

---

[3] [1989] 1 S.C.R. 426 (S.C.C.).

Quality and Fitness   The first type of protection provided relates to the quality of products and services supplied. As mentioned above, the *Sale of Goods Act* implies certain conditions and warranties related to title, fitness, quality, and nature (description) of goods supplied. Normally, the parties can override these provisions, but where consumer transactions are involved, most provinces have prohibited any attempt to do so. B.C.'s *Sale of Goods Act* includes these prohibitions, but in other provinces they are included in special consumer protection legislation. Thus, products must be fit for their purpose and of an acceptable quality, and sellers are liable for any failure, no matter what other provisions may be included in a limited warranty or other limitation clause in the contract. In some provinces, for example in Saskatchewan and New Brunswick, these provisions not only apply to retailers but to manufacturers as well. People suffering injury or loss because of defective products always had the right to sue the supplier or manufacturer of the goods in tort for negligence. The advantage of this legislation is that it provides a contract remedy where it is not necessary to show fault, only that the contract was breached. As mentioned in Chapter 4, where the product is dangerous and the seller breaches while knowing there is a risk to health or injury to property, criminal prosecution may result.

Consumer goods must be of minimum quality

Case Summary 5.3 *Prebushewski v. Dodge City Auto (1984) Ltd.*[4]

Breach of Warranty

Shawna Prebushewski purchased a new top-of-the-line Dodge Ram 4 X 4 truck. She also purchased an extended warranty. She borrowed $43 198.80 from the bank to finance the purchase. About 16 months later she parked her truck near her employment where it caught fire and was destroyed. It was determined that the cause of the fire was a defective daytime running light module and Ms. Prebushewski made a claim against the seller of the vehicle and the manufacturer (Dodge City Auto (1984) Ltd. and Chrysler Canada Ltd.) under the warranty agreement, claiming the fire was the result of a manufacturing defect. The dealer and the manufacturer refused the claim and simply told Ms. Prebushewski to make a claim to her insurer. She did this but after the claim was paid out the proceeds were not enough to cover what was still owed the bank, which was $11 383.65. She then sued the manufacturer and the dealer.

At trial the manufacturer's representative admitted that they had been aware of these faulty daytime running light modules for several years and had not informed customers nor had they issued a recall. The trial judge determined that the statutory warranty provisions of the Saskatchewan *Consumer Protection Act* had been breached and awarded general damages to Ms. Prebushewski to replace her truck and other expenses in the amount of $41 969.83 and also ordered exemplary damages (punitive damages) of an additional $25 000 on the basis that the violation of the *Consumer Protection Act* had been wilful. The award of exemplary damages was overturned on appeal, but was reinstated at the Supreme Court of Canada level. The case illustrates how powerful and effective such consumer protection provisions can be.

Business Practices   Statutes, variously called a *Trade Practices Act* or *Business Practices Act*, are designed to protect consumers from unacceptable practices. They prohibit misleading and deceptive practices generally, and then list a number of unacceptable practices specifically. All involve different ways that merchants may deceive the consumer, whether intentionally or by mistake. These statutes also control unconscionable transactions

Abusive and deceptive trade practices are controlled

---

[4] S.C.C., [2005] 1 S.C.R. 649, (2005) 253 D.L.R. (4th) 209, (2005) 333.

Unconscionable transactions are
controlled

Salespersons' statements form part
of the contract

Abusive merchants subject to fine,
injunction, and loss of licence

Cooling-off period for door-to-door
sales

True cost of borrowing must be
disclosed

where the consumer is taken advantage of because of factors such as undue pressure, a particular vulnerability results in the victim paying an unfair price, or some other harsh or adverse terms that are imposed in the contract. Such unconscionable transactions are unenforceable against the consumer. Some jurisdictions limit this unconscionability protection to mortgage contracts where the courts have been given the power to modify, limit the obligations, or otherwise change the terms of the agreement to make them more equitable. In most provinces, legislation also makes any false or misleading statement made in the course of the sale, whether in advertising or by the salesperson, a term of the contract, thus making it actionable as a breach with all of the normal remedies available. Other remedies against the merchant engaging in unacceptable business practices include injunctions and damages, fines, and other penalties. These provincial statutes aimed at consumer protection are typical examples of statutes creating provincial offences.

Specific Businesses Controlled   Consumer protection acts in place in most provinces are designed to control specific types of businesses that are prone to abuse. Where door-to-door sales (direct sales) are involved, cooling-off periods, as well as other protections, are provided. Where **executory contracts** are involved (contracts to be performed in the future), a written contract is required and the consumer's obligations, before performance, are limited. Referral selling and the delivery of unsolicited goods are also controlled. Referral selling involves giving a discount when the purchaser provides a list of names for the seller to contact. Responsibility for unsolicited credit cards, and for lost and stolen credit cards, is also severely restricted. Legislation that requires the true cost of borrowing be disclosed in all loan transactions is also in place. Sometimes the practice of including bonuses or using different methods of calculating the effect of compounding interest will lead people to pay much more for their loans than they expected. Now the actual rate and costs associated with the transaction, including the total amount to be paid, must be made clear at the outset. The practice of buying income tax returns and making short-term loans before payday are also controlled. These practices often involve huge interest rates exceeding the criminal interest rate of 60 percent per year (section 347(1) of the *Criminal Code*). Most jurisdictions also control organizations that supply their customers' credit information to others, as well as debt-collecting practices. These are just some of the provisions that are typically included in such consumer protection statutes. These Acts also control businesses such pre-paid funeral services and burial plots, food plan sales, future service contracts such a gym memberships, etc.

Case Summary 5.4 *Pro Gas and Heating v. Hayes*[5]

Extra Protections Where Direct Sellers Involved

Mrs. Hayes had an arrangement with Pro Gas & Heating for routine maintenance of her furnace and natural gas fireplaces, and while in her home a representative persuaded her that she needed a new boiler. She entered a contract to that effect, agreeing to pay a total of $3000 for the boiler and its installation. She gave a post-dated cheque for half of this amount as a deposit. A short while later she had second thoughts and stopped payment on the cheque.

In this action Pro Gas is suing claiming $1500 in damages (the amount of the stopped cheque which constituted a deposit). Mrs. Hayes claimed that this was a direct sale (in her home and away from their normal place of business) in which under the *Consumer Protection Act*, she

[5] (1978), 90 D.L.R. (3d) 695 (B.C.S.C.).

>

had ten days to rescind the agreement. In fact she had notified Pro Gas that she had changed her mind and did not wish to go through with the agreement within that ten-day period. It turned out that she did replace the boiler through another unrelated company.

The judge found that this was a direct sale, that she did have 10 days to rescind her agreement, and that she had done that within the stated period. He also found that the contract she signed did not have a cancelation provision in it notifying her of this right as required under the *Consumer Protection Act*. She did not have to pay Pro Gas the amount of the cheque on which she had stopped payment.

This case illustrates that where direct sales are involved most provinces have given consumers even greater protection providing for a cooling-off period and the requirement of notice of these rights.

Consumer Bureaus   Provincial statutes aimed at consumer protection are typical examples of statutes that create provincial offences. Government agencies are set up to investigate abusive practices and to resolve disputes. Typically, such organizations have the power to investigate, to search and seize records, to assist the consumer to obtain remedies, and to impose fines and other penalties in their own right. Large fines can be effective, but these bodies also often have the right to take away a licence and put the offender out of business. In many cases these consumer protection statutes provide for dual enforcement. The consumer, or even the designated government official, is given the option of proceeding in a civil action seeking damages and/or seeking an injunction to stop the offending conduct. But that government official will usually also have the power of treating the offending conduct as an offence punishable by fine and imprisonment. Although these offences are not criminal in a technical sense, (only the federal government can pass criminal law) they can have the same impact and are referred to as **quasi-criminal offences**. The procedure involved for prosecution is set out in provincial legislation such as Ontario's *Provincial Offences Act*.[6] Because there is the potential of a significant fine and imprisonment, the *Charter of Rights* protections relating to legal process (sections 7–14) and other criminal prosecution requirements, including the "presumption of innocence" and "proof beyond a reasonable doubt" discussed in Chapter 1, generally apply.

Powerful government agencies enforce rules

Case Summary 5.5 *Director of Trade Practices v. Ideal Credit Referral Services Ltd. et al.*[7]
The Power to Enforce Is Considerable

Ideal Credit resided in British Columbia and advertised to U.S. customers that they would provide guaranteed credit, even for bad risks. They used phrases such as "bankruptcies O.K.," and "guaranteed results." This was a scam. The customers were required to pay $300 as a processing fee. Ideal would then do a $15 credit check and invariably turn down the credit application and pocket the difference. The director of trade practices applied to the court under the *Trade Practices Act* for an injunction to stop this "deceptive or unconscionable act." But Ideal countered that since the customers were in the United States, the B.C. Act did not apply. The trial court agreed with Ideal, but on appeal the court held that the *Trade Practices Act* prohibited any deceptive or misleading practices that took place in the province, even where the victims were elsewhere.

This case shows the extensive reach of the *Trade Practices Act* but raises the question of just how far this should go. What about providing gambling services for other locations, or offering pornographic or other materials considered immoral in one province to those in other provinces or countries?

[6] R.S.O. 1990, c. P. 33.

[7] (1997), 145 D.L.R. (4th) 20 (B.C.C.A.).

The Future   In 2002 Ontario enacted a comprehensive consumer protection statute, the *Consumer Protection Act*,[8] which likely points the way that consumer statutes will go in other jurisdictions as well. It not only ensures that warranties for fitness and quality set out in the *Sale of Goods Act* cannot be overridden in a consumer purchase agreement by a limited warranty, but also extends that protection to leases and services as well. The Act includes the provisions previously found in the former *Consumer Protection Act* and *Business Practices Act* of that province. Thus, there is a list of specified unfair practices that are prohibited, including unconscionable representations as well as the remedies and procedures to follow when these provisions and others are violated. Extensive powers are given under the Act to search, seize, make orders, create offences, etc. The current *Consumer Protection Act* also sets out regulations and prohibitions with respect to specific businesses and business activities, including agreements requiring future performance (such as the payment of price) time-share agreements; personal development agreements such as provided by fitness clubs; agreements made over the internet; the repair of motor vehicles and other goods; and credit transactions in general. The current *Consumer Protection Act* and regulations also have extensive provisions to govern internet consumer transactions. The recently enacted *Business Practices and Consumer Protection Act*[9] of British Columbia is a similar comprehensive consumer protection statute.

Non-government agencies also help consumers

   There are other non-government, consumer-oriented organizations, both profit and non-profit, that can be helpful to the disadvantaged consumer. The Better Business Bureau is a unique organization consisting of and supported by member businesses. The idea is that reputable businesses are served by weeding out unscrupulous businesses that damage other members of the business community. The bureau issues reports, but also provides a service directly to the public where they can inquire about specific businesses to learn of any complaints that have been made.

Federal Legislation

The federal government also has significant consumer protection legislation enforced by government departments. These control hazardous products, govern the bankruptcy process, and control anti-competition business practices. They also investigate and resolve consumer complaints. They have considerable power and funds to support research, investigation, hearings, and education.

The Federal *Competition Act*

A free market system is considered vital to our economy. It benefits business by making businesses more efficient as they become more competitive and benefits consumers with lower prices and better selection in the marketplace. But there is a tendency for businesses to try and manipulate that market to their advantage. The federal *Competition Act* is designed to prevent that manipulation. The stated purpose of the Act "is to maintain and

---

[8] 2002, S.O. 2002, c.30, Sch. A.

[9] 2004, S.B.C. c. 2.

encourage competition in Canada."[10] The *Competition Tribunal Act*[11] is supportive legislation creating an enforcement body to implement the provisions of the *Competition Act* and other similar federal legislation.

The anti-competitive practices controlled by the *Competition Act* range from mergers and acquisitions designed to create monopolies and reduce competition to direct interference in the marketplace in the form of price fixing or false advertising. The tools used to prevent such conduct also range from persuasion and pressure to the imposition of civil or criminal penalties. Note that the kinds of offensive conduct set out below is not intended to be a comprehensive review of the Act but only to set out significant examples of the kinds of activities and practices controlled. Throughout the discussion it should always be remembered that economic principles usually determine the outcomes, not technical legal rules.

Competition Act controls mergers and abusive practices

Interference with Competition

Conspiracies that unduly lessen competition are prohibited. Note that not all such agreements are prohibited, only those that have the effect of "unduly lessening" competition. A **conspiracy** involves businesses getting together and, through agreement, trying to control the market and prices. The basic principle here is that any agreement or arrangement between businesses that has the effect of unduly restricting competition constitutes an offence. Where merchants agree together not to sell a product below a certain price, or agree not to open a store or compete in a given area, their conduct is prohibited if it unduly restricts competition. Where these agreements attempt to increase prices by restricting production, transport, storage, supply, or increasing the price of insurance, the businesses have committed an indictable offence. Any attempt at **bid rigging** is also an indictable offence. This involves competitors conspiring together to control the bids on a particular project so that they can control the winning bid and charge a higher price. With respect to banks and other financial institutions, any agreement to fix rates of interest and prices charged for services also constitutes an indictable offence punishable with fines up to $10 million and up to five years' imprisonment.

Prohibited practice must unduly lessen competition

Perhaps the most common form of conspiracy in restraint of trade is simple **price fixing**. This involves two or more parties agreeing together not to sell products below a specified price. Remember that to be an offence this has to be an undue restraint of trade. The largest settlement for price fixing took place in 2005, settling several separate class actions started in 1999 and involving a complex conspiracy of price fixing and market sharing of the sale of vitamins in Canada. The settlement involved a consent order for $140 million.[12]

Offences include manipulating the market through the control of the resale price or credit

Pyramid Selling

Where people pay a fee to participate in a multilevel organization, which is not based on the sale of a product, this is an offence with substantial fines and jail terms. Under the *Competition Act* (section 55.1) the fine is at the discretion of the court and may include a penalty of up to five years' imprisonment. Under the *Criminal Code* (section 206(1)e) such schemes constitute a summary conviction offence. See Table 5.3 for a summary of offences against competition.

Pyramid selling is prohibited

---

[10] *Competition Act*, R.S.C. 1985, c. C-34.

[11] R.S.C. 1985 c. 19 (2nd Supp.).

[12] *Ford v. F. Hoffman-La Roche Ltd.* (2005), 74 O.R. (3d) 758.

Table 5.3 Offences Against Competition

- Conspiracies
- Restricting supply, production, storage, and transportation
- Bid rigging
- Banks controlling interest rates and service charges
- Giving one customer, but not others, a better rate, discount, or advantage
- Suppliers controlling the resale price to consumers (retail)
- False and misleading representations
- Double ticketing
- Telemarketers not disclosing required information or misleading the consumer
- Multilevel schemes not disclosing required information
- Pyramid selling schemes

Case Summary 5.6 *R. v. CLP Canmarket Lifestyle Products Corp.*[13]

Pyramid Marketing Schemes Are Also Prohibited Under the *Competition Act*

The defendant established a multilevel marketing scheme where new distributors, who had to pay a $30 registration fee to participate, were recruited by other distributors. The defendant company was charged under the *Combines Investigation Act* with creating an illegal pyramid scheme. (Note that the current federal *Competition Act* has replaced the *Combines Investigation Act* and has a similar provision in section 55.1.) The accused argued that this covered the expense of a "career kit" needed to sell its products, but the court agreed with the prosecution that this amounted to a fee charged to participate, and it didn't matter what the fee was used for. Even though the amount could be legitimately justified, it still constituted a fee charged for participating and thus created an illegal pyramid. The problem with pyramid schemes is this: Where the sale of a product is not involved, the higher levels in such a scheme can simply skim funds from the lower levels, cheating them out of their money. Multilevel marketing schemes must be careful not to cross the line and become an illegal pyramid. The question does arise in this case whether we have gone too far and are simply interfering with an effective method of doing business.

Deceptive Marketing Practices   Table 5.4 provides a list of deceptive marketing practices. These prohibitions against deceptive and misleading practices are designed to protect the consumer. Any false or misleading representation made to the public with respect to the promotion of a product is reviewable. Any claim with respect to life expectancy or performance that is not based on proper testing, and any misleading warranty promises that are not likely to be carried out, constitute reviewable conduct. Testimonials or tests used to promote a product must only be used where such a test or testimonial has been published and permission has been given to use it. When goods are being sold at a "bargain" price and a regular price is referred to as the one normally offered by that particular retailer or others, they must be able to show that a reasonable volume of the product was sold at that higher price. The *Sears* case is a good example. Sears advertised a particular brand of tires as being on sale. The ad said, "Save 45%," when in fact

---

[13] Man. Q.B., 1989, as reported in *Lawyers Weekly Consolidated Digest*, Vol. 8.

Table 5.4 Deceptive Marketing Practices

- False and misleading representations
- Warranty or performance claims not supported by tests
- Unsupported tests and testimonials
- Bargain prices not supported by goods sold at regular prices
- Selling at a higher price than advertised
- Bait-and-switch selling
- Failure to disclose chances and value of prizes in a contest
- Failure to base contestants on skill or at random

Deceptive marketing practices include:
- False and misleading representations
- Warranty or performance claims not supported by tests
- Unsupported tests and testimonials
- Bargain prices not supported by goods sold at regular prices
- Bait and switch tactics

they regularly sold only about 2 percent of those tires at the posted cost. The ad inflated the regular cost of the tires, making the sales price appear more attractive. This constituted misleading advertising, which could bring "harm to consumers, business competitors, and competition in general." The penalty included a payment of $500 000 and a commitment not to do it again.[14]

The practice of **bait and switch** is also prohibited. This is where a product is advertised at one price, but not enough are supplied so that the customer can be persuaded to buy a higher-priced alternative. **Double ticketing,** where two prices are placed on an item and the merchant sells at the higher price, is also prohibited.

Where there are attempts to manipulate the market using "deceit, falsehood, or other fraudulent means," such actions are indictable offences under the *Criminal Code* with a potential penalty of up to 10 years' imprisonment.

Full Disclosure   The Act requires that merchants make full disclosure of all relevant information in many situations. For example, where games or contests are involved, the number of prizes and chances of winning must be disclosed and the winners must be chosen at random or on the basis of a skill. Telemarketing operations must disclose such information as the identity of the seller and the nature and true price of the product being sold. Where multi-level marketing schemes are involved, representations as to earnings and sales (both actual and expected) must be fair and accurate. Of course, in all situations any false or misleading representation is an offence.

Telemarketers must disclose all pertinent information

Multilevel schemes must also make full disclosure

Other Matters Reviewable by the Tribunal   Often a supplier will manipulate the sale of a product at the retail level by restricting the supply of their product only to merchants that will sell at the suggested retail price, or tie the sale of one product to another. Where a supplier sells a product below cost to drive out a competitor that is **predatory pricing** and also reviewable.

Schemes that tie the sale of products to others or restrict who can buy are reviewable by tribunal

Predatory pricing also reviewable by tribunal

Mergers and Acquisitions   There is a growing trend today toward mergers and acquisitions. This can lead to less competition on the one hand but can also, through economies of scale, create a more efficient business. A main objective of the *Competition Act* and its supporting legislation is to balance these considerations. Where businesses of any size have merged through the acquisition of assets or the purchase of shares so that

The goal is to balance the loss of competition against increased efficiency

---

[14] *Commissioner of Competition v. Sears Canada Inc.* Comp. Trib. No. CT-2002-004.

Tribunal can review mergers and acquisitions

competition is lessened, the Competition Tribunal has the power to review the acquisition and order, among other things, the dissolution of the resulting corporation where competition has been lessened unduly. Where the merger is with a supplier, a competitor, or a customer the merger will be in more danger of being disallowed as unduly lessening competition than if the merger is with an unrelated business. Table 5.5 provides a summary of matters reviewable by the Competition Tribunal.

Not all mergers that reduce competition are prohibited

Case Summary 5.7 *Canada (Commissioner of Competition) v. Superior Propane Inc.*[15]

Increased Efficiency Overrides Lessening of Competition

Two propane companies decided to merge, and the matter was brought before the Competition Tribunal by the Competition Commissioner. It was determined that the merger would significantly lessen competition in the field, but also that the merger would greatly increase efficiency; consequently, the merger was permitted to go ahead.

The greater efficiencies derived from the merger outweighed the significant reduction in competition. At first, the tribunal only considered production of propane and costs, but on the application of the commissioner, the Federal Court ordered the Competition Tribunal to look at social considerations as well. They reconsidered the matter, looked at all factors, and reached the same decision. Again, the case was appealed, but this time the Federal Court upheld the decision of the tribunal allowing the merger. The case illustrates how increased efficiency can be more important than reduced competition in allowing mergers. The case also dramatizes the role of the Competition Commissioner in relation to the Competition Tribunal. The commissioner acts like a prosecutor bringing matters before the tribunal for their determination, and then, if not satisfied, he or she can further appeal to the Federal Court.

Other federal statutes include the *Food and Drugs Act*, which regulates dangerous food and pharmaceuticals. (Note that mandatory nutritional labeling was recently established for prepackaged food products and beverages under food and drug regulations.) There is also a *Hazardous Products Act*, which regulates dangerous products, prohibits some products, and requires appropriate warnings on others. These federal statutes also create specific criminal offences for certain kinds of prohibited conduct.

Table 5.5 Matters Reviewable by the Competition Tribunal

- Suppliers only selling goods to some retailers
- Selling of one product tied to the sale of another
- Abuses of power
- Selling products below cost to defeat a competitor
- Mergers and acquisitions that affect competition

---

[15] (2003), 223 D.L.R. (4th) 55 (F.C.C.A.).

SECURED TRANSACTIONS

As a general rule, the simple promise embodied in a contract to repay debt is not good enough for a creditor to loan money. Whether in the consumer world or in arranging business financing, some extra assurance is required to ensure that the creditor will be repaid. This is usually accomplished by the debtor providing security, and giving the creditor first claim on some asset at least equal to the value of the debt. In the event of default the creditor has first claim on that asset (see Figure 5.1). Any form of property can be used to create such security. Real property (land and permanent structures built on that land) is normally the preferred form of security, but other forms of property can also be used. The use of real property as security will be discussed in a subsequent chapter.

Security arrangements assure creditor of repayment

Real property and personal property used as security

Personal property, both tangible in the form of goods or chattels, and intangible in the form of a right or claim one party has against another, can also be used as security. Share certificates, bonds, and negotiable instruments such as cheques and promissory notes are examples of intangible personable property. The documents involved merely represent the actual claim or right. The personal property security acts (*P.P.S.A.*) in place in all English-speaking provinces control secured transactions involving personal property. Historically, there were separate statutes in place for the different ways that personal property could be used as security. **Conditional sales**, **chattel mortgages**, and **assignment of book accounts** each had their own statute. Today these separate statutes have all been replaced by the *Personal Property Security Act*, but it should be noted that there still has to be a contract creating the secured transaction and these often take the form of those traditional agreements (conditional sales, chattel mortgages, and assignment of book accounts). A significant advantage of the *Personal Property Security Act* is to bring all transactions involving personal property as security under one statutory umbrella, with one consistent approach—no matter what form the security takes. A second advantage is that the Act allows any form of personal property—tangible or intangible—to be used. This flexibility creates a much more comprehensive system. An important change under the Act is that no matter what the contract says, title now stays with the borrower, but the rights given to the creditor remain the same as with traditional conditional sales and chattel mortgages where title was transferred to the creditor to support the security.

P.P.S.A. accommodates all forms of personal property as security

Conditional sales, chattel mortgages, and assignment of book accounts now under *P.P.S.A.*, but these standard forms of contract still often used in credit transactions.

Now title remains with the borrower

A security is created by giving the creditor first claim against the assets used as security. This is accomplished in a unique way under the Act. The transaction should be

Figure 5.1 Secured Transactions

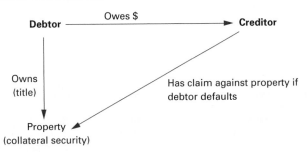

viewed in three stages—first the agreement; second, attachment; and third, perfection (see Figure 5.2). In fact, these steps often take place simultaneously, but conceptually distinguishing among the stages makes it easier to understand. The contract sets out the rights and obligations between the parties and designates the asset (such as a vehicle) to be used as security. The creditor still has no claim against the car, having provided no actual benefit to the debtor at this stage. **Attachment** takes place when value is given under the contract to the debtor. At that point the creditor obtains a claim against the asset. If money is involved, attachment takes place when the money is provided to the debtor. But what happens where the debtor resells those assets to some third party or uses them as security in another transaction? The whole idea of security is to give the creditor a first claim in these circumstances. It would be unjust to allow the creditor to retake those goods from the third party, who has no way of knowing of the creditor's claim in the asset. To solve this problem a registry has been created so third parties dealing with the assets can check to see if someone else has a claim against them. There is, therefore, an obligation on the creditor with the secured interest in the asset to register that claim in the appropriate registry.

This final stage is called **perfection**, which is primarily accomplished through **registration**. Anyone dealing with such goods is well advised to search the registry before purchase. Perfection gives the creditor a prior claim to the property that is good against any subsequent holder or claimant. If Jones, through a chattel mortgage agreement that uses his car as security, borrows money from Ace Credit Union, the credit union has no claim against the car until they advance the funds. At that point their security attaches. This gives them a claim against the car while in Jones' possession, but not if it is resold. The credit union then perfects their secured interest by registering the claim. This is accomplished by filing a simple, standard form at the appropriate registry. Now anyone interested in buying or taking the vehicle as security in another transaction can search the registry to determine if there are any prior claims (called liens or charges). Finding such a claim should dissuade the buyer from the transaction because the credit union's registered claim now has priority.

Perfection can also take place by the creditor taking possession of the property used as security. This is usually done where intangible claims, such as stock certificates, bonds, or negotiable instruments, are used to secure the loan. However, the original document, not a photocopy, is required to accomplish perfection by possession. The creditor's security is established by the fact that the possession of the original document prevents it from being used to support another transaction. The key to understanding the *Personal Property Security Act* is to understand the process of attachment and perfection: attachment gives the creditor a claim to the property or goods against the debtor, and perfection gives the creditor a claim to the property or goods against all others.

Attachment gives the creditor rights against the debtor

Perfection by registration

Perfection gives the creditor rights to security good against all subsequent claimants

Perfection by possession

Figure 5.2 The Process

Creation of contract	Attachment	Perfection
Contents of agreement determine rights of parties	Value given for security taken	1. By registration or 2. By taking possession of property (security) (not repossession)

Case Summary 5.8 *Doran, Re, 2006 NSSC 123*[16]

Leases with Option to Purchase Must Also Be Perfected

Mr. Doran and his wife rented furniture from Easyhome in November 2003. The terms of the rental agreement provided for payment by the week and an option to purchase the furniture. The contract also made it clear that this was not a conditional sale or a credit transaction. Almost two years later, after making regular payments, Mr. and Mrs. Doran made an assignment in bankruptcy transferring their assets over to a trustee in bankruptcy. Easyhome claimed that they were the true owners of the furniture and demanded its return. The trustee in bankruptcy refused, claiming that this was a credit transaction where personal property in the form of the furniture was used as security and the *Personal Property Security Act* of the province required that Easyhome's interest in the furniture be perfected by registration, which it wasn't. Easyhome took the position that this was not a lease for credit situation but a true lease arrangement where Easyhome retained ownership and had never given it up. As such the *Personal Property Security* Act did not apply and it did not have to be registered.

The issue then was whether this was a true lease where the lessor retained the ownership of what was leased and would be returned eventually, or whether it was the type of lease contemplated in the *P.P.S.A.*, where it was another method of securing repayment of the debt.

The judge found that, although it was arranged on a weekly basis, this was a long-term lease, and because there was an option to purchase the subject matter, it was the kind of lease contemplated under the *Personal Property Security* Act. Since it had not been perfected through registration, the trustee in bankruptcy had priority and Easyhome lost their claim to the furniture. It is interesting to note that some forms of assets including furniture can be retained by the bankrupt, but that did not apply in this case because at the time of the assignment in bankruptcy they didn't actually own the furniture; they just had an option to purchase it.

Not only does this case illustrate the requirement that leases with options to purchase are also covered by the *Personal Property Security* acts, it also illustrates that the danger of failing to perfect even applies when the property is assigned to a trustee in bankruptcy. The case also introduces the topic of bankruptcy, which will be dealt with subsequently in this chapter.

In actual practice the operation of the *Personal Property Security Act* can be quite complicated, especially where a variety of claims are involved. But once attachment and perfection described above are understood, the basic principle is relatively straightforward. In the event of default, the essential right of the creditor is to obtain and resell the property used as security. Where the tangible personal property involves goods that are not in the possession of the creditor, this process entails repossessing those goods from the debtor. It must be emphasized that where the contract gives the creditor this right upon default, there is no need to get a court order or otherwise involve official government services. Repossession is usually accomplished through employees or the services of a private agent called a bailiff. It is important to note that no force or violence can be used. Where a car is locked in a garage or furniture is in a house, a court order must be obtained to get them.

Once possession has been acquired, the goods can be sold to recover the debt. But anyone who has an interest, including the original debtor, must be notified of the sale and given a chance to redeem the goods by making appropriate payment. The seller must make an effort to obtain a fair price upon sale. This is usually done at public auction, although it can be done by private sale, providing the process is "commercially reasonable."

Creditor has the right to repossess and resell upon default

Court order not needed to repossess

But force cannot be used

Creditor must give the debtor notice and the opportunity to redeem the goods before resale

---

[16] (CanLII) (2006), 243 N.S.R. (2d) 139.

Any excess obtained from the sale over the amount owing, less the costs of the process, must be paid to the debtor. If there is a deficit or shortfall, that amount is still owed by the debtor. If the sale was done properly, further steps can be taken to collect the debt. Note that in some provinces, where consumer sales are involved, such a shortfall will not be recoverable.

If resale is properly handled, creditor has the right to sue for deficit

---

Case Summary 5.9 *General Motors Acceptance Corp. of Canada Ltd. v. Snowden et al.*[17]

A Creditor's Right to Deficit Can Be Easily Lost

Snowden purchased a car and arranged financing though General Motors Acceptance. When he defaulted on the payments, they repossessed and resold the vehicle under the *Conditional Sales Act* of New Brunswick. They sold the vehicle at an auction restricted to licensed automobile dealers; the amount recovered fell short of what was owed by about $6000. Snowden refused to pay the difference, claiming that the sale had not taken place in good faith. The court found that the creditor failed to satisfy the court that they had obtained the best price for the car. This auction involved wholesale prices, with the dealers purchasing at a lower price so they could resell at a profit. A retail sale would have brought a better price for the car. The creditor's action to sue for the remainder of the outstanding debt was refused. Although this is an older case and the result may not apply in other jurisdictions, it illustrates just how careful creditors have to be to comply with the requirements of notice and process of sale when reselling goods used as security after a default and repossession.

Other Forms of Security

A problem has always existed in the construction industry where suppliers of labour and materials deal with contractors. Because the contractor normally doesn't own the property, the suppliers of goods or subcontractors have nothing to claim against if they are not paid. This has been remedied in all provinces with builders' lien/construction lien/mechanics' lien acts, which give suppliers and subcontractors a claim against the property if they are not paid (see Figure 5.3). A subcontractor can now register a lien against the property, which can eventually force a sale of the property if the subcontractor is not paid. The property owner is protected from this possibility by retaining a **holdback** (7–20 percent of the amount owing to the contractor, depending on the province) and making this available to satisfy the claims of the subcontractors or suppliers. Upon payment of the funds held back, an application can be made to the court to have the liens removed, and thus the property owner will have no further obligation even where the amounts claimed exceed the amount of the holdback.

Builders' liens protect contractors, sub trades, workers, and suppliers

The **guarantee** is another way to create security. It involves three parties—the creditor, the debtor, and the guarantor. (see Figure 5.4). Instead of some property being put up as security, the guarantee involves someone else (the guarantor) agreeing to be responsible for the debt if the debtor defaults. Note that the guarantor has no obligation under this agreement until the debtor actually defaults and so, unlike cosigning for a debt, the guarantor doesn't actually owe the money until there is a default. Note that the guarantee is one of the forms of contract discussed in Chapter 3 that must be evidenced in writing

Guarantee: One person agrees to pay if debtor does not

---

[17] (1990), 76 D.L.R. (4th) 519 (N.B.C.A.).

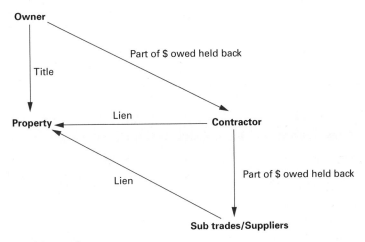

Figure 5.3 Builders' Liens

to be enforceable. Often these agreements are put under seal to avoid any problem with consideration.

It should be noted that any defence that the debtor has against the creditor is also available to the guarantor, with the exception of bankruptcy and infancy. Thus, if the debtor purchases a car on time and there is a default, the creditor can turn to the guarantor for payment. But if the car is defective or there has been fraud involved, the creditor/ seller cannot demand payment from the guarantor instead of the debtor. Both can claim the defective product or fraud as a defence.

If the guarantor is called upon to pay the creditor, he or she steps into the shoes of the creditor and assumes the rights of the creditor. If, for example, there is some additional form of security involved such as a charge against the debtor's car, the guarantor assumes the creditor's right to repossess that car from the debtor. It is also important to note that if the creditor and debtor get together and change the terms of the agreement to advance more credit, change the interest rates, or otherwise modify the agreement without the permission of the guarantor, the guarantor will not be bound by the new terms and will also be released from the original obligations. Thus a creditor must always remember to

> Guarantor has the same defences as debtor

> Guarantor steps into the shoes of the creditor upon payment

Figure 5.4 Guarantee

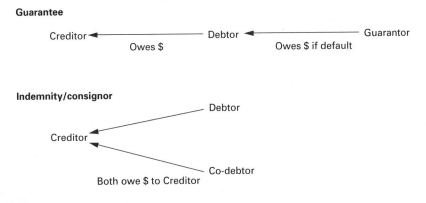

involve the guarantor in any arrangements they make with the debtor that may affect the agreement.

Case Summary 5.10 *Guinness Tower Holdings Ltd. et al. v. Extranic Technologies Inc. et al.*[18]

Changes to Contract Release Guarantor from Obligation

The plaintiff landlord entered into a lease agreement with Extranic Technologies Inc. for the purpose of teaching English as a second language (ESL) to students on the premises. Mr. Eric Hsiao guaranteed the lease. The contract provided for a 5-year lease with an option to renew and to extend the leased premises to a larger area. In June 2002 Extranic started their ESL classes but soon found they needed more space. They exercised their option to amend the lease and expand the premises. This involved signing a lease amending agreement with the landlord, but because of complaints this new agreement prohibited them from teaching ESL classes, which was a major part of their business. It also introduced a clause giving the landlord the right to cancel the expansion portion of their lease with only 30-days notice. This amendment agreement was signed by representatives of the landlord and Extranic, but was not signed by the guarantor Mr. Hsiao, who was not notified of the change.

The business failed and Extranic abandoned the premises. The landlord is claiming damages from Mr. Hsiao as guarantor on the lease. But Mr. Hsiao takes the position that the lease terms were changed without his consent and according to common law and equity because his position was weakened by the change he is released from the guarantee. The right to cancel the expansion portion of the lease on 30-days notice and the prohibition of ESL classes on the premises were serious changes that weakened the position of the guarantor. The judge agreed. It was pointed out that parties were free to override this right for a guarantor to be released by changes by so stating in the original contract, but they had to do this clearly and this had not been done in this instance. Mr. Hsiao was released as guarantor and had no further obligation under the lease.

This case points out how careful a creditor must be to ensure that the position of the guarantor is not weakened by any further dealings between the creditor and debtor without including the guarantor in the process.

BANKRUPTCY AND INSOLVENCY

No discussion of creditor/debtor relationships would be complete without an examination of the law of bankruptcy. People often confuse the terms bankruptcy and insolvency. When a person is **insolvent**, it simply means that he or she is unable to pay his or her bills as they become due. **Bankruptcy**, on the other hand, involves a process whereby the debtor's assets are actually transferred to an official, who then distributes them to the unpaid creditors. Bankruptcy is becoming much more common today. For the 12-month period ending 31 October 2008 there were 93 085 bankruptcies filed (86 911 consumer bankruptcies and 6 174 business bankruptcies).[19] These figures will likely increase dramatically over the next 12 months as the recession worsens. The federal *Bankruptcy and Insolvency Act*[20] provides a uniform process of bankruptcy across Canada. The object of the legislation is to preserve as much of the assets of the bankrupt debtor as possible for the benefit of the creditors. At the same time, the intention is to promote rehabilitation

---

[18] 2004 BCSC 367 (CanLII).

[19] Office of the Superintendent of Bankruptcy Canada, "Insolvency Statistics in Canada," October 2008, http://www.ic.gc.ca/eic/site/bsf-osb.nsf/eng/br02074.html.

[20] R.S.C. 1985, c. B-3.

of the debtor so that he or she will have an insurmountable burden of debt removed and will again become a productive member of society.

There are two ways that bankruptcy can be accomplished. When a debtor voluntarily transfers his or her assets to a **trustee in bankruptcy** (a private professional authorized to act in the area), it is called an **assignment in bankruptcy**. When the debtor is forced into bankruptcy by his or her creditors, they must obtain a **receiving order** from the court to forcibly transfer those assets to the trustee. To obtain a receiving order the debtor must owe at least $1000 and have committed an act of bankruptcy such as a fraudulent preference (paying one creditor in preference to another), a fraudulent conveyance (transferring property to a spouse or friend to keep it out of the hands of a creditor), or fleeing the jurisdiction to avoid debts. These also constitute bankruptcy offences and are discussed below. However, the most common act of bankruptcy is insolvency, where the debtor has simply been unable to pay debts as they come due.

The function of the trustee, in addition to counselling individual debtors, is to look after the assets and preserve them, doing whatever is necessary to protect their value. This may involve making repairs, doing maintenance, or, where an operating business is involved, actually managing that business. But usually a trustee will determine the priorities among the creditors, sell assets where necessary, and distribute the proceeds to those creditors on the basis of their entitlement.

Secured creditors, as discussed above, retain their privileged position with respect to the assets taken as security. The trustee must surrender the asset to them or pay out the amount owed. Where there is a shortfall and the amount obtained in selling the security does not cover the debt, the secured creditors will become unsecured creditors for the remaining amount owed. In such cases, they usually only obtain a percentage of that amount along with the other unsecured creditors. **Preferred creditors** are paid next. Some examples include funeral expenses, costs of the bankruptcy process itself, some taxes, and other fees such as employment insurance and workers' compensation. Also included are a limited amount of unpaid wages of employees and up to three months' back rent owed to a landlord. Note that unremitted federal withholding payments for GST, CPP, EI, and income tax take priority over secured creditors. Finally, any amount left over is distributed to the **unsecured creditors**. Each receives a percentage of what was originally owed. Often the amount the unsecured creditors receive is a very small portion of the actual debt; this underlines the wisdom of taking security when a debt is created, as discussed above. Note that the trustee will often allow the bankrupt to keep certain assets that are difficult to sell and some assets such as tools and furniture, as well as pensions and RRSP investments, which are exempt from seizure. Note that other assets may be exempt depending on the province.

If the bankrupt commits a **bankruptcy offence**, such as failing to disclose information, lying, or transferring property to a spouse or friend, this is a punishable offence and may ultimately interfere with him or her being discharged from the bankruptcy. The listed offences under the *Bankruptcy and Insolvency Act* are criminal offences with fines up to $10 000 or three years in jail, if treated as indictable offences. False claims made by creditors face similar penalties. The fraudulent transfer of property with the intent to defraud creditors is also an indictable offence under section 393(1) of the *Criminal Code* with a maximum term of imprisonment of two years.

Where the bankrupt is an individual, after nine months an application is automatically made to the court for the **discharge** of the bankrupt. If it is the first bankruptcy, the

Assignment is voluntary, but bankruptcy may also be forced by a receiving order.

Assets are distributed:
- First to secured creditors

- Then to preferred creditors

- Finally to unsecured creditors

Some possessions are exempt

Bankruptcy offences prohibited and penalized

individual will automatically be discharged, unless the discharge is opposed by one of the creditors or there has been a bankruptcy offence committed. If less than 50 cents on the dollar is paid, the court will sometimes impose a **conditional discharge**, requiring the bankrupt to make some further payments. But usually once a person has been discharged, he or she is then free of any former indebtedness. This means that even if that person were to win a lottery worth millions, those former creditors would have no claim, since the debts would have been discharged through bankruptcy. Note that some debts survive the bankruptcy process and will not be eliminated by a discharge. These include student loans less than seven years old, family maintenance obligations, child support, and court-imposed fines.

Discharge ends obligations

Note exceptions

Corporations do not survive bankruptcy

A corporation can also go through the bankruptcy process but will not be ultimately discharged. After the bankruptcy process all assets are distributed and the corporation is left as an empty shell or dissolved, although this is normally not worth the expense. Creditors, shareholders, and others may have other recourse against the directors, principals, and officers of the corporation. This will be discussed in Chapter 7.

Case Summary 5.11 *Re Southwick, Trask and Trask*[21]

Bankrupt Must Make Payments after a Conditional Discharge

This case illustrates bankruptcy and the principles taken into consideration in discharging the bankrupt. The bankrupt operated a call centre that employed a number of people. There were considerable debts, both secured and unsecured, that totaled about $2 million. When a significant client failed to pay a large account, the business became insolvent. As a result, personal bankruptcy was forced upon Mr. Trask and his wife, who had signed personal guarantees. Because the assets were less than 50 cents on the dollar, the court agreed that there would be a conditional discharge; this meant the bankrupt should be required to make further payment after discharge.

The trustee and other creditors recommended that Mr. Trask and his wife should pay a further $54 000. This amount was claimed on the basis that the couple had $354 000 in RRSPs that were exempt, and they had managed to borrow $160 000 from their family to pay off claims on their home and cottage, which had been used as security for the business loans. The judge, however, rejected this recommendation.

He made it clear, first, that the bankruptcies resulted from business misfortune, not from any wrongdoing. He found that the legislature had specifically exempted RRSPs from the bankruptcy process, and so they should not be taken into consideration nor forced into liquidation when deciding what should be paid in a conditional discharge. He looked at the superintendent of bankruptcy guidelines, which stated the bankrupt should be left with 25 to 30 percent of his or her income per month to live on. The Trasks' income was calculated to be about $1000 per month, and so the payment would be only $750 for a period of 24 months or a lump sum payment of $18 000 (the present value of that amount). The judge acknowledged that one of the purposes of a conditional discharge was to accomplish a fair distribution to creditors, but this had to be balanced against the goal of rehabilitating the bankrupt. Clearly, in this case the judge looked at the lack of blameworthiness of the bankrupt and what the Trasks could afford to pay, more than at the losses of the creditors.

There are alternatives to the bankruptcy process, the most obvious consisting of simply negotiating alternative arrangements with creditors, including consolidating one's obligations. Where that fails, the *Bankruptcy and Insolvency Act* provides a formal alternative

---

[21] 2003 N.S.S.C. 160, 44 C.B.R. (4th) 134, 216 N.S.R. (2d) 190 (N.S.S.C.).

to the bankruptcy process. If individual debtors owe less than $75 000, they can make a proposal to their creditors to pay less than the full amount owed, and/or over a longer time. If the offer is accepted and properly fulfilled, a certificate is issued and the debtor is then released from those obligations without having gone through bankruptcy. Failure to live up to such an accepted proposal will automatically result in bankruptcy. Debt counseling is involved and the arrangements are usually made through the trustee/ administrator. This is a **Division Two proposal**.

Division Two proposal is an alternative for individuals

The arrangements for companies and larger debtors owing over $75 000 is more formal and complex; they involve more oversight and fall under a **Division One proposal**.

Division One proposal is an alternative to bankruptcy for a company

A singular advantage for both Division One and Division Two proposals is that any action being taken to seize property is stopped until the time allotted for the proposal process has been completed. Even then, an application can be brought to the court to extend this time. This has led to some abuses. Large corporations with very large debt obligations often proceed using a different federal statute, the *Companies' Creditors Arrangement Act* (C.C.A.A.),[22] which has a similar effect and allows some additional flexibility.

*C.C.A. A.*also provides alternative to bankruptcy for company

Usually secured creditors of large corporations will include terms in the original contract that give them the right to take over the management of that corporation in the event of default. This is called **receivership** and is often confused with bankruptcy. Receivership eliminates the need to go through the bankruptcy process, but the effect can be just as devastating on the business. A professional receiver is appointed by the creditor and literally takes over the business, displacing the directors and other managers in the process. Table 5.6 provides a summary of the consequences of bankruptcy.

Receivership is not bankruptcy

Table 5.6 Consequences of Bankruptcy

Debtor	Options	Result
Debtor owing under $75 000	- Voluntary assignment	Loss of assets and ultimate discharge
	- Receiving order (forced)	Loss of assets and ultimate discharge
	- Division Two proposal	Pay as agreed; no bankruptcy
Debtor owing over $75 000	- Voluntary assignment	Loss of assets and ultimate discharge
	- Receiving order (forced)	Loss of assets and ultimate discharge
	- Division One proposal	Pay as agreed; no bankruptcy
Corporations	- Receiving order (forced)	Loss of assets but no discharge; corporation dies
	- Division One proposal	Pay as agreed; no bankruptcy; corporation survives
	- Receivership (forced)	No bankruptcy but creditors take over company

---

[22] R.S.C. 1985, c. C-36.

Key Terms

assignment in bankruptcy (p. 123)

assignment of book accounts (p. 117)

attachment (p. 118)

bait and switch (p. 115)

bankruptcy offence (p. 123)

bankruptcy (p. 122)

bid rigging (p. 113)

bill of lading (p. 104)

charge or encumbrance (p. 106)

chattel mortgages (p. 117)

clauses (p. 107)

CIF (p. 104)

COD (p. 104)

conditional discharge (p. 124)

conditional sales (p. 117)

conspiracy (p. 113)

consumer protection legislation (p. 103)

consumer (p. 108)

description (p. 106)

discharge (p. 123)

Division One proposal (p. 125)

Division Two proposal (p. 125)

double ticketing (p. 115)

executory contracts (p. 110)

exemption clause (p. 107)

fitness and quality (p. 107)

FOB (p. 104)

good title (p. 106)

guarantee (p. 120)

holdback (p. 120)

insolvent (p. 122)

perfection (p. 118)

predatory pricing (p. 115)

preferred creditor (p. 123)

price fixing (p. 113)

quasi-criminal offences (p. 111)

quiet possession (p. 106)

receivership (p. 125)

receiving order (p. 123)

registration (p. 118)

sample (p. 106)

secured creditor (p. 123)

secured transaction (p. 103)

stoppage in *transitu* (p. 108)

trustee in bankruptcy (p. 123)

unsecured creditor (p. 123)

Questions for Student Review

1. Explain the role played by the *Sale of Goods Act* and the qualifications that must be met for the Act to apply to a particular transaction.

2. How is the person who bears the risk determined under the *Sale of Goods Act?* Explain how this can be modified by the parties.

3. Explain the five rules that determine when title will pass under the *Sale of Goods Act.*

4. Explain the obligations imposed on a seller with respect to title, sale by sample and description, fitness and quality, and merchantable quality.

5. Discuss the nature of limitation or exemption clauses and their effect on the provisions of the *Sale of Goods Act.*

6. When a default takes place, what are the rights of the seller with respect to goods that are in transit and with respect to goods that are in the hands of a bankrupt?

7. Describe the abusive business practices that are controlled by trade practices or business practices statutes. Describe how the statutes' provisions are enforced.

8. Explain what is meant by a cooling-off period and explain how pyramid and referral selling schemes are controlled under consumer protection legislation.

9. Explain the purpose of the federal *Competition Act.* and list five competition offences.

10. Explain what is meant by bid rigging, double ticketing, and predatory pricing.

11. List and explain five deceptive marketing practices, and explain how they are treated differently from offences against competition.

12. What kind of matters are reviewable by the Competition Tribunal? What is the purpose of such a review?

13. Indicate other federal statutes that have a consumer protection aspect to them.

14. Explain what is meant by a secured transaction, indicating the special position of the creditor.

15. Distinguish between a conditional sale and a chattel mortgage, and indicate the effect of the *Personal Property Security Act* on such transactions.

16. Distinguish between attachment and perfection, and describe how perfection can be accomplished.

17. Describe the rights of the creditor when there is a default under the *Personal Property Security Act.* What must the creditor do to protect his or her right to sue for a deficit?

18. Explain the significance of a holdback under the builders' liens or construction lien statutes.

19. Distinguish between an indemnity and a guarantee.

20. Explain the position of a guarantor with respect to the debtor's obligations and how those obligations are affected by subsequent dealings between the parties.

21. Distinguish between insolvency and bankruptcy, and between an assignment and a receiving order, and explain the role of a trustee in bankruptcy.

22. Distinguish between an act of bankruptcy and a bankruptcy offence.

23. Explain the positions of secured, preferred, and unsecured creditors in the event of a bankruptcy.

24. Explain the effect of a discharge on the bankrupt.

25. Explain the difference between the provisions of the Division One and Division Two proposals.

Questions for Further Discussion

1. The purpose of the *Sale of Goods Act* is to imply terms into any contract of sale where the parties haven't specifically agreed otherwise. In some provinces a few of these terms are imposed and any attempt to override them is void. Some other provinces accomplish the same thing through separate consumer protection legislation. Consider whether the parties should be able to contract out of any of the terms of the *Sale of Goods Act.* Should such restrictions apply to both consumer and business transactions? Should there be any provision of the *Sale of Goods Act* that the parties can't override in their own agreement? Consider also consumer legislation generally. Should such legislation ever interfere with the parties' rights to have whatever terms they deem appropriate in a contract, whether it relates to a consumer transaction or not? Do such restrictions unduly interfere with the commercial process?

2. Does the process of taking collateral security unfairly assist secured creditors over unsecured creditors? Does the requirement of registration sufficiently answer any criticism? In your answer consider the process of bankruptcy and how secured creditors are given preferred treatment, often leaving an unsecured creditor with nothing.

3. Competition lies at the heart of the capitalist enterprise. Is government regulation necessary and does it achieve intended aims? What are some of the negative impacts of regulating competition? What other methods of controlling competition might be more effective?

4. Consider the bankruptcy process. It seems to be inconsistent with every principle of fundamental contract law and commercial relations. Is it fair to the creditors and debtor? What about discharge? Should debtors be allowed to escape their obligations in this way? Can you come up with a better alternative? Why prohibit student loans from being discharged through bankruptcy? Should there be other exceptions?

Cases for Discussion

1. *Mustapha v. Culligan of Canada Ltd.*, 2008 SCC 27 (CanLII), (2008), 238 O.A.C. 130

    Mr. Mustapha suffered considerable trauma when, in the process of replacing a used jug of water with a new one, he discovered dead flies in his sealed jug of water. He had a particular sensitivity to this and suffered an unusual reaction. When he complained to the water producer they offered him a few free water bottles and the cleaning of his dispenser as settlement. He was offended and sued. Explain the basis of his complaint and the likely outcome. What do you think should be the remedy Mr. Mustapha should receive, if anything? How would it affect your answer to discover that Mr. Mustapha suffered an unusual reaction, becoming argumentative and edgy, losing his sense of humour, and becoming unable to drink bottled water?

2. *Lasby v. Royal City Chrysler Plymouth* (1987), 37 D.L.R. (4th) 243 (Ont. H.C.J.).

    Mrs. Lasby bought a used car from a dealer when the salesman, Mr. McDonald, told her that it had been driven by one of the dealership's executives and had a powerful six-cylinder engine. She had refused other cars because she wanted a six-cylinder car. The next day when she noticed the car was only a four-cylinder engine, she called the salesman. He told her that Chrysler no longer made a six-cylinder and that a four-cylinder was the biggest engine they made. In fact, that was false, as Mrs. Lasby found out later from her mechanic. It turned out that the car had not been executive-driven; it had been leased and had only a 2.2-litre, four-cylinder engine (instead of the larger 2.6-litre engine). She demanded her money back, but the sales manager refused, saying she "had bought the car and that was that." The salesman denied ever having made false statements to her, and the company refused any remedy. Mrs. Lasby brought this action and continued to drive the car. By the time it got to court 22 months after the purchase, the car had 40 000 kilometres on it. Explain the likely outcome of the action and the appropriate remedy if Mrs. Lasby wins.

3. *Goodfellow Inc. v. Heather Building Supplies Ltd.* (1996), 141 D.L.R. (4th) 282 (N.S.C.A.).

    Heather Building Supplies Ltd. sold and delivered lumber to Goodfellow Inc., but made it clear that the lumber was not theirs until it was paid for. Goodfellow failed to pay. Heather seized the lumber, but before they could move it back to their premises, a notice was served on them that Goodfellow was making a proposal under the *Bankruptcy and Insolvency Act*. Explain the position of the parties under the Act. What is the likely outcome of the case? Would it affect your answer to know that no attempt was made by Heather to register their interest in the lumber?

4. *Re M. C. United Masonry Ltd.* (1993), 142 D.L.R. (3d) 470 (Ont. C.A.).

    Goldfarb, Shulman, Winter and Co. were a firm of chartered accountants providing various accounting and consulting services to M.C. United Masonry Ltd. and other related companies. The amount owed to the accountants was over $100 000. M.C.

United guaranteed this amount and conveyed certain share certificates they held in another company (Palm Hill Investments Ltd.) to the accounting firm to be held by them as security for the guarantee. The security arrangement was not registered under the *Personal Property Security Act*. M.C. United Masonry Ltd. was forced into bankruptcy and the trustee demanded the return of the share certificates, effectively denying Goldfarb their position as a secured creditor as claimed on the basis of the share certificates. Discuss the arguments available to both parties. Have the requirements for priority under the *Personal Property Security Act* been satisfied in this case?

5. *R. v. Clarke Transport Canada Inc.* (1995), 130 D.L.R. (4th) 500 (Ont. Gen. Div.).

A group of five companies provided freight forwarding services through container shipments in the Toronto area. They would take orders from customers, charge on the basis of weight, fill a container with those orders, and transport the goods by rail. All five agreed to control prices. They exchanged information and promised not to undercut each other's prices. Explain how their conduct would be viewed under the *Competition Act*. What arguments might they raise in their defence?

6. *R. v. Lorne Wilson Transportation Ltd. and Travelways School Transit Ltd.* (1982), 138 D.L.R. (3d) 690 (Ont. C.A.).

In this case several companies bidding on providing school bus services got together to control the price. When charged they argued that no offence is committed when the other party knows of the cooperation between the bidders. (They claimed the school board knew because of the identical bids that were presented.) They also argued that there was no *mens rea* (the requirement of intention needed for a criminal conviction). Explain what offence they were being charged with and the likelihood of conviction.

Chapter 6
Agency and Employment

Learning Objectives

- Explain the roles and limitations placed on agents
- Discuss the liability of principals and agents
- Describe the fiduciary duty of agents and principals
- List appropriate process for disciplining and terminating employees
- Discuss the role of unions in employment
- Outline the obligations of employers in providing a safe work environment
- Consider the impact of criminal activity on businesses

An essential aspect of any business activity is the various relationships through which business transactions are accomplished. These relationships may involve owners, managers, employees, agents, and independent contractors. They may also include consultants, lawyers, and accountants, as well as those who carry out the various functions associated with corporations such as directors, officers, and shareholders. Each of these relationships involves unique responsibilities, rights, obligations, and benefits, all of which should be taken into consideration when a person makes decisions with respect to his or her business, including whether that business should be carried on through a proprietorship, a partnership, a corporation, or a combination of these methods. The functions and relationships associated with the different methods of carrying on business (proprietorships, partnerships, and corporations) will be the subject of the following chapter. In this chapter we will look at agency and employment.

An independent contractor works for him- or herself

It is important to distinguish between independent contractors, employees, and agents. An **independent contractor** performs a specific service described in a contract. Normally, this is not an ongoing obligation. The contractor does the job and moves on. Essentially, a contractor works for himself or herself, as when a builder agrees to build a house for someone or a lawyer incorporates a company for a client. Consultants and auditors are other examples of independent contractors who provide a contracted service to a business. The nature of these relationships is governed by the general rules of contract law discussed in prior chapters.

An employee works for the employer in an ongoing relationship

An **employee**, on the other hand, is more committed to an employer in an on-going relationship and is subject to more control from the principal and to specialized rules governing employment, which will be discussed below, but the first topic to be examined in this chapter is the law of agency.

AGENCY

The study of agency law is important because most business activity is carried on through agents and agency forms a significant component of the law of partnership and corporations to be discussed in Chapter 7. An agent is someone who represents another person (the principal) in dealings with a third party (see Figure 6.1). Both employees and independent contractors can find themselves acting as agents depending on the nature of their duties. For example, a plumber may be acting as an agent when he orders fixtures in the name of the property owner, but not when installing those fixtures into the building. Travel and insurance agents are examples of independent contractors acting as agents, whereas a store clerk or a restaurant server are examples of employees acting as agents. Of course, not all employees are agents nor are all independent contractors agents. It depends on the duties they have been given. The **agency relationship** is usually created by contract, but in rare cases it can be created gratuitously where the agent acts as a volunteer. The important thing is to find that there has been a granting of authority to act on behalf of the principal. These duties usually consist of the agent entering into contracts on behalf of their principal, but this is not always the case. Lawyers will often file documents and accountants file tax returns for clients. They are representing their clients but are not entering into contracts on their behalf.

> An agent represents a principal in dealings with a third party
>
> An agent may be an employee or an independent contractor
>
> Agency is usually created by contract
>
> Agency depends on granting of authority
>
> Agents usually enter into contracts on behalf of their principals

Principal/Third-Party Relationship

The unique aspect of agency law relates to the relationship between a principal and a third party, created when an agent functions as an intermediary. The primary consideration is to determine under what circumstances the third party will be able to hold the principal responsible for the conduct of the agent in contract law and/or in tort law.

Authority   In contract law the answer is deceptively straightforward. The principal and third party will be bound in contract when the agent had authority to bind the principal. The problem lies with respect to how that authority is obtained. When the principal has directly granted the authority to act, it is called **expressed authority** and will support the contract. But authority to act can also be implied from the surrounding circumstances.

Figure 6.1 Agent's Authority

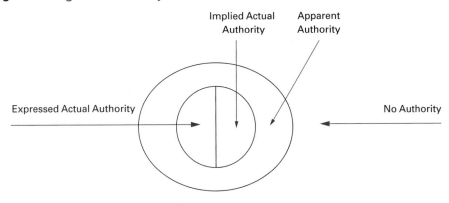

(An agent may have actual authority [expressed or implied] or apparent authority)

For example, a gas station attendant would have the **implied authority** to sell gas whether the employer has specifically stated he has such authority or not. Of course there is no implied authority to sell the gas station itself. Such expressed or implied authority is referred to as an agent's **actual authority**.

Principal also bound where agent acts within apparent authority

The extent of an agent's **apparent authority** is a little more difficult to understand. Sometimes the principal may make it clear to an agent that his authority is limited, but not make that limitation clear to a third party. If the principal has done something to lead a third party to believe the agent has authority, even when he does not, the third party can rely on that representation and so the agent is said to act within his apparent authority. For example, where a clerk in an auto supply store has been told she cannot make any sale over $100 without the manager's express approval, she has a limitation on her authority. If, despite such instructions, the clerk sells an engine manifold for $300 without getting approval, the contract is still binding on the store. There is no expressed authority and you can't imply authority where there have been express instructions to the contrary.

Agent has apparent authority when principal leads another to that belief

Rather this is an example of apparent authority or agency by **estoppel**. Where the principal has led the third party to believe the agent has authority, the principal cannot later deny that authority. The principal put the clerk in a position where it would appear to a customer that she had the authority to make such a sale. The principal is thus estopped from denying the agent had authority. Be careful not to confuse this with promissory estoppel discussed in Chapter 3. That involved a promise whereas this involves the assertion of some fact indicating the agent has authority to act.

Case Summary 6.1 *Doiron v. Devon Capital Corp.*[1]

The Consequences of Allowing Others to Believe Someone Is Your Agent

The plaintiffs wanted some short-term investments and turned to Mr. Demmers, who had looked after their pension fund and insurance matters as a representative of Manulife. He persuaded them to invest in Devon, calling the corporation "a no-risk investment." This proved to be bad advice and the plaintiffs lost all of their funds. They unsuccessfully sought compensation from Demmers, who had become bankrupt. In this action the plaintiffs sought compensation from Manulife. It was clear that the plaintiffs thought Demmers was an employee of Manulife and that the Devon investment was one of their products. In fact, Manulife had taken pains to set out in their contract that Demmers was not an employee, but was an independent contractor.

Even though the Devon investment was not one of Manulife's products and their contract with Demmers made it clear that he was an independent contractor, the court held Manulife liable for Demmers' negligence in recommending this investment. Demmers had offices in the Manulife building and was encouraged to refer to himself as their representative. When someone phoned him, the call went through the Manulife operator. Demmers was required to work for Manulife exclusively. These factors encouraged those dealing with him to believe he was working for Manulife. This gave Demmers apparent authority to act for Manulife and created the impression that Manulife was responsible for his actions. This case illustrates the difference between an independent contractor and an employee, but it also shows the importance of finding apparent authority, which can make the principal responsible for the agent's actions even when there is no actual authority.

[1] [2002] 10 W.W.R. 439, 2002 ABQB 664 (Alta. Q.B.).

Ratification   There is an obvious overlap between apparent authority and implied authority. The distinction is only important where there have been express instructions to the agent not to act and he does so anyway. Of course, where the agent exceeds both his actual and apparent authority the principal is not bound. Still, if the principal likes the deal he can ratify the agreement making it a binding contract. This can be done intentionally by the principal expressly ratifying the transaction, or it can be done inadvertently by the principal taking some benefit under the agreement. In effect the principal is giving the agent authority to act after the fact, and that grant of authority works retroactively as if the agent always had authority. This is confusing but it is really the only way such **ratification** could create a binding contract.

    In fact there are some restrictions on when a contract can be ratified. First, it must have been possible to enter into the contract at the time of ratification. For example, you can't ratify a contract of insurance after the house has burned down. Second, it must have been possible for the principal to enter into the contract at the time the agent purported to act. You can't ratify a contract if you were insane at the time the contract was entered into by the agent. And finally the ratification must take place within a reasonable time of the agent's unauthorized conduct.

Vicarious Liability   What is the responsibility of the principal for torts committed by the agent? Where the agent is also an employee, the liability of the principal for the agent's conduct is based on the principles of vicarious liability as discussed in Chapter 2. Essentially, when the conduct of the employee is closely related to the job he is employed to do the employer /principal will be liable as well as the employee. (see Figure 6.2). If a company's purchasing agent negligently struck a pedestrian on her way to a meeting with suppliers, she would be liable, but so would her employer. She was acting within the scope of her employment when she committed the tort in question. However, if she were driving home or had diverted to do some personal chore, she would be on a "frolic of her own" and the company would not be responsible for her conduct. The question is not always clear and the Supreme Court of Canada has determined that it is more an application of policy considerations. Chief Justice McLachlin stated "The fundamental question is whether the wrongful act is sufficiently related to conduct authorized by the employer to justify the imposition of vicarious liability."[2] This leaves room for those acting outside their actual job responsibilities to still impose vicarious liability on their employers. The more difficult question relates to when a principal will be liable for torts committed by an agent who is not his or her employee. Liability for the acts of independent contractors such as lawyers, accountants, insurance agents, and real estate agents is much more restricted. The principal will only be liable if the tort causing injury took place during the actual exercise of the authority that the principal has given the agent. The agent has to be in the process of actually transacting the business he or she was authorized to do. Usually this is restricted to the tort of fraud and negligent misstatement associated with the negotiation or enactment of the contract itself. Where my real estate agent negligently runs over someone on the way to show my house, I would not be held vicariously liable for her tort, but if she fraudulently or negligently misrepresented some aspect of the house to a customer, I could be held vicariously liable for that tort. Of course, if the principal gave the false information to the agent, who then innocently passed it on, the agent would be completely innocent and it would be the principal alone who would be directly liable for the fraud or negligent statement.

---

[2] *Bazley v. Curry*, [1999] 2 S.C.R. 534, (1999), 174 D.L.R. (4th) 45 (SCC).

Agent can be given authority by ratification either intentionally or by implication

Ratification works retroactively

Restrictions on ratification

Vicarious liability will be imposed where an agent is also an employee and . . .

Where employee/agent commits tort in course of employment

Liability of principal for agent's torts are limited where the agent is an independent contractor

Principals will be responsible for their own torts committed through the agent

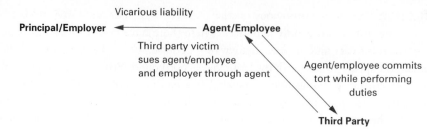

Figure 6.2 Vicarious Liability

Note that in the statutes of many jurisdictions the owner of a motor vehicle is vicariously liable when they loan out their vehicle.[3] Essentially, if you loan your car to someone and he gets into an accident that is his fault, you are responsible along with the driver.

The Agent/Third-Party Relationship

As a general rule, the third party has no claim against the agent since the agent simply acts as an intermediary. The resulting contract is between the principal and a third party, and if not satisfied, the third party must look to the principal for a remedy. For the same reason, the agent has no claim against the third party and must look to the principal for any payment for services rendered. It is only when the agent has exceeded all authority to act that the third party can sue the agent for claiming authority not possessed. This is a tort action for "breach of warranty of authority," and gives the third party the right to obtain compensation from the agent for what was lost because of the unauthorized transaction.

Normally, the agent can neither sue nor be sued under the contract

Exception: Agent may be sued for breach of warranty of authority

---

Case Summary 6.2 *Maple Engineering & Construction Canada Ltd. v. 1373988 Ontario Inc.*[4]
Make It Clear When You Are Acting for a Company

The plaintiff Maple Engineering was a general building contractor and had successfully bid on the construction of a building in the Municipality of Muskoka. The defendant, Peter Bisson, was the owner, director, and sole shareholder of 1373988 Ontario Inc. (doing business as ACI) and, using the letterhead of ACI, had submitted a bid as a subcontractor to supply woodwork products on that project. Bisson received a formal construction contract from Maple, but after a negative credit check of Maple, Bisson refused to sign. Maple had to turn to another supplier and pay a higher price.

In this action Maple seeks damages from Bisson for breach of contract and damages claimed for the extra amount they had to pay the other subcontractor.

The court found that a contract had been breached and damages in the amount of $50 000 were awarded. The problem was just who should pay. 1373988 Ontario Inc.

was a properly incorporated Ontario company but Maple thought they were dealing with ACI through its agent Bisson. The court determined that Bisson had misled Maple, albeit innocently, into believing they were dealing with ACI. ACI in fact did not exist and so Bisson did not have the authority he claimed to represent it. Mr. Bisson was liable personally for the damages because he did not have the authority to act for ACI, which he led Maple to believe he had. This is an example of breach of warranty of authority. Note that Bisson thought he was acting through the legitimate 1373988 Ontario Inc. throughout. He thought that ACI was simply the trade name of the company. This is a common error and had Bisson informed Maple of that fact he would have avoided personal liability. The point is that if you represent yourself as acting for a specific principal you had better have the authority to do so.

---

[3] *Motor Vehicle Act*, R.S.B.C. 1996 c. 318, s. 86 (1).

[4] 2004 CanLII 46655 (ON S.C.).

When an agent doesn't disclose to the third party that he is acting as an agent, or refuses to disclose who he is acting for, it is referred to as an **undisclosed agency** situation. For example, a developer is often reluctant to disclose they are behind a particular project for fear that the information would push up the price of the land being acquired. The developer or principal would then employ an agent to make the purchase without disclosing whom they are acting for or the full nature of the project.

If things go wrong, the third party has to sue the agent. In that process the identity of the principal is normally disclosed and then a choice must be made to continue the action against the agent or to sue the principal instead. Once the choice is made, the third party is bound by it and cannot change its mind, even if it turns out that the party being sued has no funds. It should also be noted that there are some situations where a contract entered into by an agent for an undisclosed principal will not be binding—in contracts where identity is important, for instance. Thus, a famous tenor cannot agree to perform a concert and then send an understudy claiming he was acting as an agent for an undisclosed principal.

Exception: Agent may be sued where acting for undisclosed principal

Third party can sue agent or undisclosed principal, but bound by choice

Third party not bound where identity of undisclosed principal is important

The Agent/Principal Relationship

The relationship between the third party and the principal is governed by the contract creating the relationship. The rights of the agent to payment for services and expenses and just what the agent is authorized to do should be set out in that agreement.

Fiduciary Duty Although the principal has some obligations to the agent, such as the payment of expenses, salaries, and any fees already agreed to in the contract itself, the more interesting obligations in this relationship rest on the agent who has a fiduciary duty to the principal (see Table 6.1). A **fiduciary duty** is basically an obligation to act in the best interests of the principal. This is referred to as an "utmost good faith relationship" and arises where trust has been placed in another by someone particularly vulnerable if that trust is broken. As a fiduciary, the agent cannot take advantage of a business opportunity that comes to her because of her position. That business opportunity belongs to the principal. Where there is a conflict between the agent's personal interests and that of the principal, the agent must disclose it and put her own interest aside. If the agent has an interest in the property being offered to the principal, she must fully disclose that fact and not make a profit on the deal without the consent of the principal. Similarly, any information the agent acquires with respect to transactions she is involved in belongs to the principal and must be communicated to the principal. An agent must act for only one

Agent has fiduciary duty to principal

Agent must exercise utmost good faith to principal

Agent must make full disclosure to principal

Table 6.1 Agent's Fiduciary Duty

- Must not take advantage of principal's business opportunities
- Must submerge his or her own interests in favour of principal's
- Must disclose conflict of interest
- Must not take benefit from both parties
- Must disclose information to principal
- Must not compete with principal
- Must not make profit at expense of principal

principal and cannot take a benefit from both sides. These are called kickbacks and for an agent to take even a small gratuity such as liquor, a trip, or some other benefit from a supplier would be a violation of this fiduciary duty.

Agent must put principal's interest ahead of his or her own

The agent cannot make a personal profit from the deal, other than the commission or other payment coming from the principal. For example, if a real estate agent finds an unsophisticated principal willing to sell a house at a low price, he cannot purchase the property himself, even if done through a partner or a company. The agent's duty is to get the principal the best price possible and that duty would conflict with his own interests in this situation. Also, the agent cannot compete with the principal. If the agent is selling one particular product for the principal, he cannot promote his own product or someone else's product instead. To continue with the real estate example, if the real estate agent is selling a house for a principal and finds an interested buyer, the agent will be in violation of his fiduciary duty if he tries to sell the prospective purchaser his own property instead.

It is a criminal offence for an agent to accept secret benefits

Where such a fiduciary duty is breached the principal can demand an accounting. He can require the agent to disclose any profits personally made from the transaction and then to pay those profits to the principal. The agent would also be deprived of any commission in these circumstances. Section 426 of the *Criminal Code* makes it a criminal offence for agents or employees to accept a secret commission or other benefit (or indeed for anyone to pay or offer such a secret commission) to act against the interests of their principal or employer, or to show favour or disfavour to a particular party in the business dealings of their principal. This is an indictable offence, and the penalty imposed can be up to five years in prison, with both the agent/employee and the person making the offer subject to be charged. In addition, there are specific offences related to agents involved in unique activities such as fraudulently dealing with minerals; title documents to land; or participating in, acquiring, or operating premises used for gambling or other prohibited activities. Thus, these agents not only face civil action, including the loss of their commissions for such breaches of fiduciary duty, but also may face criminal prosecution in certain circumstances.

Agent must also exercise reasonable competence and appropriate skill

In addition to a fiduciary duty, the agent also has an obligation to act competently in carrying out those duties. An employee or agent who carelessly performs his or her responsibilities, causing the employer or principal losses, may be required to pay compensation in a negligence or breach of contract action brought by the principal or employer.

Case Summary 6.3 *Krasniuk v. Gabbs*[5]

An Agent Must Disclose Information to the Principal

Maria and Barry Krasniuk contracted with Donna Gabbs, a real estate agent, to sell their home. They made it clear to Ms. Gabbs that they needed $137 000 from the sale to pay off their debts. The house was listed for $149 900. But it didn't sell. The price was reduced to $144 450 and then to $139 500, and eventually sold for $130 000. The problem was that Mr. and Mrs. Balgobin, the ultimate purchasers, were seriously interested in the house. They had verbally offered $135 00 and then $137 000 for the house and Gabbs had failed to inform the Krasniuks of these offers. When they discovered that the Balgobins had been willing to pay the higher price and that Ms. Gabbs had

>

---

[5] 2002 MBQB 14 (CanLII), [2002] 3 W.W.R. 364 (2002), 161 Man. R. (2d) 274.

failed to inform them about these offers they sued for the loss (the difference between the $137 000 offered and the $130 000 of the eventual sale) and for the return of any real estate commission paid. Gabbs responded by referring to a section of the *Real Estate Brokers Act* stating that only offers in writing had to be communicated to the sellers. The judge considered this but noted that the section referred to was created for a different purpose relating to the payment of commissions and so the common law fiduciary duty to make full disclosure of all information relating to the agency had not changed. Gabbs had a fiduciary duty to the Krasniuks to act in their best interests and to disclose any relevant information related to the sale. She failed in this duty and was liable for the loss as well as required to surrender any commission paid to her.

Note that when dealing with land most professionals understand that offers have to be in writing to be enforceable. Here it is likely that Gabbs simply had that in mind when she failed to communicate the information, but it is important to understand that this was information that should have been disclosed even if it didn't constitute a legal offer.

It should also be noted that it is the agent's job to carry out the responsibilities assigned to him or her. As a general rule the agent cannot delegate those responsibilities to others. There are many exceptions to this rule, usually based on industry practice. Thus, it is common for real estate agents to use sub-agents to fulfill their responsibility. Accountants and lawyers will also normally involve others in fulfilling their responsibilities to their clients.

In general, an agent cannot delegate

Ending the Agency Relationship

An agent's actual authority to act for the principal will normally be terminated when the job is finished, when the agent receives different instructions from the principal, or when the employment or agency relationship is changed or terminated. The authority to act will also end where the project involved becomes illegal or the principal dies, goes bankrupt, or becomes insane. Although an agent's actual authority may be terminated in this way there is still the problem of apparent authority. This is one reason the principal should avoid the creation of such apparent authority in the first place. Where that is not possible, the employer must take steps to notify all customers and suppliers who would normally deal with the agent that the relationship has been terminated.

Agency ends with termination of authority

Death, bankruptcy, or insanity terminates authority . . .

But apparent authority may continue

Most jurisdictions now permit a power of attorney to be created that will continue after the principal becomes mentally incapacitated, thus allowing a trusted friend or relative to manage the incapacitated principal's affairs. This usually must be done under the supervision of a public trustee or some other government official.

EMPLOYMENT

Employment is based on a special relationship that is historically recognized under the common law as one of master and servant. That term catches the essence of this special relationship, which involves unique obligations of commitment, duty, and loyalty. Today, the employment relationship is based on contract, and normal contract law applies—especially to the employment's creation, the duties to be performed, the consideration, and the terms of termination.

Contract law applies to employment

There are three main areas with which we are concerned regarding employment. The common law of master/servant applies in those areas that are not covered by collective bargaining and where no unions are involved. It deals primarily with the law of termination and wrongful dismissal. Secondly, we will look at those special relationships where collective bargaining determines the workplace environment, and where unions and management must comply with the law set out in specialized statutes. There has also been a considerable amount of legislation passed that deals with employee rights and benefits, and this will be the final topic of discussion in this section.

The first question to be determined is whether or not an employment relationship exists. Today there are many statutes in place that provide a definition of employment, such as the *Employment Standards Act*, the *Workers' Compensation Act,* and the *Employment Insurance Act*. These are important, but the definition given is restricted to the operation of the particular statute within which it is found. No general statutory definition of employment is provided. The reason it is important to determine whether an employment relationship exists outside of these statutes is usually to determine the extent of the employer's liability for wrongful acts committed by their employees. As discussed above, such vicarious liability is usually restricted to the employment relationship, with the employer being responsible for wrongful acts of employees where the act committed is closely connected to the employment. The injured victim can seek redress from both the employee who caused the injury and the employer who profited from the work being performed. Since the employer is usually in a much better position to pay such compensation, it is vital, from the point of view of the victim, that an employment relationship is established. Employment also must be established for an employee to have access to those rights associated with master/servant law, including reasonable notice or pay in lieu of notice when terminated.

Historically, the test used to determine employment was based on the degree of control exercised. Independent contractors work for themselves, doing the job agreed to in the contract. They control their own hours and how they do the work. Employees, on the other hand, work for and under the direction of the employer and can be told not only what to do, but how to do it. If a painter was hired as an employee to paint an apartment building, he would be expected to come to work at a specified time, take limited breaks during the day, and leave for the night when instructed. He could also be told which rooms to do first and even the length of brush stokes to use in the process, whereas a painter hired as an independent contractor would have agreed to do the job and to meet certain specifications such as colour, number of coats, and quality of paint. But since the painter would be working for himself, he would determine the hours of work and process used. So long as the painter finishes by the time specified and does an adequate job, the owner of the property would have no complaint. Thus, the employee is subject to rules and control whereas the contractor is independent of those controls (see Figure 6.3).

Sometimes this **control test** is not adequate for determining employment, and so a supplemental test has been developed based on an employee's relationship to the business.

Specialized statutes have own definitions of employment

Vicarious liability based primarily on employment

Employment exists when employee can be told what to do and how to do it

Figure 6.3 Employee v. Contractor

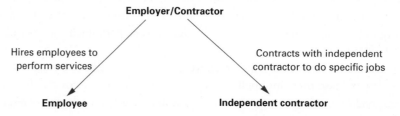

This is called the **organization test**. If the individual is found to be an integral and essential part of the business organization, he or she is an employee for purposes of vicarious liability, even though the actual control exercised over him or her is limited. A salesperson may look like an independent contractor selling by commission only, supplying her own car, and determining her own hours. But if she can only sell for that one business, must report to it for sales meetings, has an office or desk located at the business, and is part of the main sales force, then she can be said to be an integral part of that organization and an employee of the business. The employer will be held vicariously liable for wrongful acts committed in the process of this employment. But remember that the employer will only be responsible for conduct that takes place that is closely related to the employment, and not when the employee is "on a frolic of her own." The employer will also have significantly greater obligations to an employee, as opposed to an independent contractor, if that salesperson's employment is terminated.

Employment exists when employee is an essential element of employer's organization

Employer liable for torts of employee within scope of employment

Employment Duties   In general, an employer has an obligation to provide a safe workplace, appropriate direction, tools where necessary, wages, and reimbursement for expenses, as well as any other specific obligations set out in the employment contract. The employee must be reasonably competent, have the skills claimed, and must also be honest, punctual, loyal, and perform the work agreed to. Where the employee is a manager or key to the business, there may be a fiduciary duty owed to the employer, but generally there is no fiduciary duty owed by an ordinary employee.

Only managers or key employees have fiduciary duty

Case Summary 6.4 *Western Tank & Lining Ltd. v. Skrobutan*[6]

Vulnerability of Company Creates Fiduciary Duty in Employees

Western Tank and Lining employed two salesmen in Manitoba, two in British Columbia, and one in Alberta. The two salesmen in Manitoba resigned, went into partnership, bought out another company, and entered into competition with Western. They took two other employees of the company with them. They submitted one quote in competition with Western even before leaving. Western sued, claiming they had violated their fiduciary duty to the company, and asked for an injunction. They were successful. In this case the judge found that the employees had a fiduciary duty that continued after their employment ended. He reasoned that even though there was no restrictive covenant preventing them from competing, the nature of the relationship was such that there was a duty not to compete in any case.

The judge determined that, "There is no comprehensive list of standard relationships giving rise to fiduciary duties. Rather, the focus is on the nature of the relationship

between the employer and the employee in question." Here the relationship was such that the company was completely vulnerable to the actions of the two salesmen since they were the whole face of the company in Manitoba. They were in fact more than salesmen and were responsible for all of the business of the company in that province. The salesmen had been entrusted with the "whole show." Note that the one-year injunction imposed was binding on the entire newly formed partnership. When one partner is bound by fiduciary duty all partners are bound. There are a number of other cases where employees are not bound by fiduciary duties when they leave and it seems that it is not only the position held that is determinative but also the nature of the relationship and the nature of the duties performed. In this case the relationship of trust was such that the company was completely vulnerable to the conduct of the employees giving rise to the fiduciary duty, which continued even after employment ended.

---

[6] 2006 MBQB 205 (CanLII) [2006] 12 W.W.R. 376; (2006), 207 Man. R. (2d) 176.

TERMINATION

For our purposes the most important aspect of the law of master/servant relates to the termination of that employment and the notice that must be given, usually by the employer (see Figure 6.4). The employment contract itself sometimes contains terms with respect to the ending of the employment relationship. Under the common law an employer must give the employee **reasonable notice** of the termination, unless there is just cause, which is discussed below. Most of the litigation with respect to wrongful dismissal involves disputes over the adequacy of the notice to terminate given to the employee. It should be noted at the outset that it is notice, or pay in lieu of notice, that must be given.

In Canada the required notice will be based on such factors as length of service, the importance of the job, the age of the employee, and the likelihood of finding other employment. The longer the service and the more important the job, the longer the notice period must be. Where long-term employment is involved, the required notice can approach two years. A very rough rule of thumb is one month for every year of employment, but remember that other factors may affect the amount of notice required. The *Employment Standards Acts* in place in most Canadian jurisdictions set out a minimum amount of notice that must be given by an employer when terminating an employee. This ranges usually from one week up to a maximum of eight weeks in British Columbia and Ontario, for example, depending on the length of employment. However, those statutes make it clear that if there are higher standards, either in other statutes or at common law, those higher standards will prevail. Note as well that the amount that must be paid in lieu of notice is more than just the actual wages that would have been earned; it also includes benefits such as dental, medical, and disability insurance premiums; pension contributions; and even bonuses when they are normally paid to all employees and are not based on merit.

It would be a mistake for an employer to assume that these amounts must be offered to all terminated employees. Often the employee will be willing to settle for less, since he or she will get the money right away, avoid the costs of litigation and lawyers' fees, and will avoid having his or her payout reduced by income from other employment (the obligation to mitigate). Still, if the matter does go to court, it is important to consider that judgments involving these considerable amounts are a potential outcome. It is also important to make the parting of an employee as painless as possible, not just to avoid confrontation and potential lawsuits, but because it is the right thing to do. Great care should be taken not to add to the trauma of the terminated employee, but to provide assistance in counselling, upgrading, and in finding alternate employment. Human resources departments today should have specialists in place to assist in this process. This is the essence of the decision

Employment contract may be for specific period

Reasonable notice or pay in lieu of notice required

Length of notice determined by kind and length of service

But statutory requirements must be met

Good practice to negotiate termination

Figure 6.4 Notice of Termination of Employment

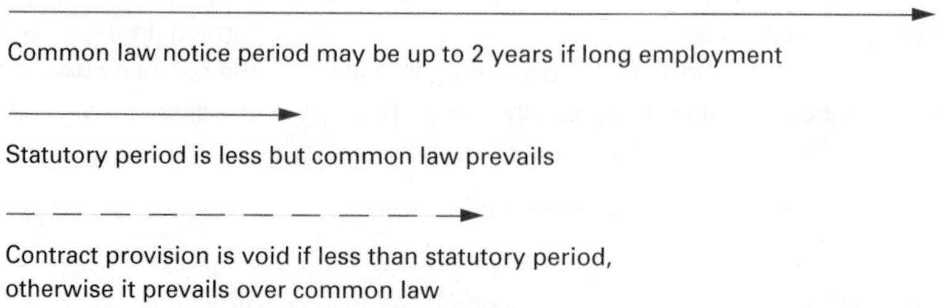

Common law notice period may be up to 2 years if long employment

Statutory period is less but common law prevails

Contract provision is void if less than statutory period, otherwise it prevails over common law

of the Supreme Court of Canada in the *Machtinger* case where it was determined that the contractual notice period of two weeks was void, as it was in conflict with the statute which required four weeks. But since the common law notice (reasonable notice) was higher than the statutory minimum, the Supreme Court applied the higher standard, restoring the trial court's award of 7 months notice for Machtinger and 7½ months for Lefebvre.[7]

Notice requirement may be set out in contract, but must be more than statutory minimum

Just Cause   An employer is not required to give any notice of termination where there has been **just cause** on the part of the employee. If the employee has stolen from or otherwise been dishonest with the employer, has acted immorally, or has been convicted of some crime that will interfere with his or her ability to perform the job or otherwise harm the employer, has disobeyed a lawful instruction, or has committed some actionable wrong while on the job, such actions can amount to just cause supporting immediate dismissal without notice or other compensation. Where an employee lies on a resumé and the employer finds out, that destroys trust and also amounts to just cause. Remember that accusations are not enough and before termination the employer should investigate such claims of wrongful conduct, making sure that the employee is given an opportunity to explain his or her side of the matter. Terminating an employee on unsubstantiated allegations can result in expensive litigation and substantial damage payments for wrongful dismissal.

No notice required where just cause

The employer also has to be careful to make sure the conduct complained of actually does amount to just cause. Not every falsehood, argument, or immoral act will constitute just cause. For example, in *Carroll v. Emco Corporation*[8] the owner of a restaurant found out that his manager had been making enquiries about starting his own restaurant and his employment was terminated. The manager sued for wrongful dismissal. The restaurant owner claimed that the manager had breached his fiduciary duty to the business, but the court disagreed. It determined that the manager was free to contemplate and even to scout out such opportunities without breaching any duty to his employer. The damages paid out were substantial.

Employee incompetence can also constitute just cause, but employers often lose the right to dismiss an employee on this ground because of their own past conduct. Where they have given annual raises or bonuses to the employee, they have led that employee to believe that the level of performance was adequate. In the process employers lose the ability to claim incompetence. When faced with such a problem, the employer should clearly inform the employee of his or her shortcomings with respect to the job and give the employee a chance to improve before proceeding to termination. Hopefully, there will be in place some form of regular employee evaluation, which will identify problems before they become too serious. The employee will then be invited to participate in making a plan to overcome that problem or shortcoming, including making concrete attainable goals such as taking courses, sensitivity training, and the like. Where the employee follows through and overcomes the problem, the business has regained a valuable employee. But where that employee fails to meet the goals after being given the opportunity and help to improve, the employer is on much more solid ground when the employment is terminated.

Incompetence often difficult to establish

The same principle applies where a person has committed some less serious form of unacceptable conduct such as minor theft, lying to supervisors, erratic behaviour, and the like.

---

[7] *Lefebvre v. HOJ Industries Ltd.*; *Machtinger v. HOJ Industries Ltd (1992)*, 91 D.L.R. (4th) 491 (S.C.C.).

[8] [2007] B.C.J. No. 737.

Often the conduct, while serious, may not be enough to constitute just cause and a cautious employer, after carefully determining the exact nature of the inappropriate conduct, will provide for some program of **progressive discipline**. Providing a reprimand or other form of discipline and counseling after a first offence, and in the process making sure the employee understands what is and is not acceptable, should be part of such a program. Giving the employee a second chance will often produce a better employee. With each repeated offence the discipline can become progressively harsher, eventually leading to termination. The repeated offences establish a pattern of wrongful conduct that will support a much stronger case of just cause for termination. Of course, very serious misconduct may support immediate termination.

Historically, illness that prevented an employee from working also constituted just cause for dismissal. Although this is not the fault of the employee, if he or she can no longer do the job, the employment contract has been frustrated. Today, human rights legislation requires that the employer make all reasonable efforts to accommodate a disabled employee. If that employee can do some work, the employer should find the individual a job that he or she can do—even if it is part time—providing it doesn't place an unreasonable burden on the business. If the disability causing the interruption in the employee's ability to work is only temporary, this will not support termination of employment. Only where the disability results in a permanent incapacity to return to work will the employment contract be terminated by frustration. Today, long-term disability plans and pensions go a long way to overcome the dilemma posed by sick employees who can no longer work.

Reasonable accommodation required for disabled workers

Case Summary 6.5 *Wilmot v. Ulnooweg Development Group Inc.*[9]

Frustrated Contracts Require Permanent Disability

Terry Ann Wilmot had been employed by Ulnooweg Development group for 12 years when that employment was terminated because of numerous absences caused by illness. Before that time she had a history as an excellent employee, conscientious and diligent, who had never been disciplined for misconduct of any kind. Her sickness took the form of depression and panic attacks. There is no question about Ms. Wilmot's condition, but the problem is to determine just how sick a person has to be for the employment contract to be considered frustrated and terminated. The human rights codes of all provinces impose a duty to accommodate disabled workers. Just where does this duty to accommodate end and the employer have the right to terminate the employment relationship? There is evidence that her absences made a negative impact on the company and on the other people working with her. Finally, the company told

her that she could only come back if she was prepared to work on a full-time basis. She could not do this and her employment was terminated. She sued for wrongful dismissal.

The court held that the contract could only be considered frustrated where the disability made return to work impossible. And this had to be a permanent condition. In this case it was determined that her return would not likely take place within a year period. The judge found that this was not permanent and found she had been wrongfully dismissed. While an employee's inability to work may constitute frustration of the employment contract, that is only where the disability is permanent and of a nature so that the employee cannot do other work. Otherwise the employer has a duty to accommodate to the point of undue hardship on the business.

[9] 2007 NSCA 49 (CanLII) (2007), 283 D.L.R. (4th) 237.

Lack of work because of a downturn in the economy does not amount to just cause for dismissal. That is not to say that an employer cannot terminate employees when the need arises, but the employer must provide reasonable notice and satisfy other statutory requirements. Often such conditions prompt a layoff where the employment is suspended until there is more work to do. Note that the employee may be entitled to treat such long-term lay-offs as termination, which triggers the above-mentioned employer obligations of notice and severance pay if permitted in the applicable employment standards legislation.

Lack of work is not just cause

Wrongful Dismissal

A wrongful dismissal action in Canada almost always involves a dispute over whether an adequate amount of notice or pay in lieu has been given by the employer to the employee. Either the employer is claiming just cause and has given no notice at all, or the employee is claiming that although she received some notice or severance, it was not enough. When just cause is present, even if discovered after the termination has taken place, the employee will fail in her wrongful dismissal action.

When an employee does sue for wrongful dismissal, the compensation claimed is usually based on what should have been earned, given the difference between the amounts of notice the employee was given and what she should have been given. Thus, if the employee received two months' notice and should have been given ten, the employee will claim an amount of damages equivalent to what she would have earned in that extra eight months. The compensation may also be increased on the basis of how that termination took place. Employers sometimes try to justify the termination on the basis of just cause, such as theft or lying, when there is none. The employer may also degrade the employee or otherwise harm her reputation, publicly causing further mental anguish. Today, the courts will take these aggravating factors into consideration and award a longer period of compensation. The Supreme Court of Canada in *Wallace v. United Grain Growers Ltd.*[10] decided that the employer owed the employee a duty of good faith in the process of termination and that it was appropriate for the court to take into consideration the way that the employee was terminated—including any mental distress caused—and extend the notice period required accordingly. In that case Justice Frank Iaccobucci stated, "The obligation of good faith and fair dealing is incapable of precise definition. However, at a minimum, I believe that in the course of dismissal employers ought to be candid, reasonable, honest, and forthright with their employees and should refrain from engaging in conduct that is unfair or is in bad faith by being, for example, untruthful, misleading, or unduly insensitive." As a result today there are many examples of cases where several months of required notice have been added to a wrongful dismissal award because of the highhanded or brutal manner in which the employment has been terminated. But there must be clear indication of unfair conduct or bad faith on the part of the employer. It is currently the practice in most wrongful dismissal actions to claim "Wallace Damages" even where the employer's conduct has been substantially appropriate. The judges have indicated that they will not tolerate substantial trial time being wasted on such claims where they are frivolous or where only minor complaints with respect to the employers conduct are present. As a general rule the courts are unwilling to add punitive damages to this mix and then only where there has been a separate tort committed such as defamation.

Wrongful dismissal damages based on what notice should have been given

Bad faith of employer may justify extended notice period

---

[10] (1997) 3 S.C.R. 701. 152 D.L.R. (4th) 1 (S.C.C.).

Note that in some jurisdictions where the appropriate legislation allows a separate action and punitive damages, this separate class of wrongdoing can include human rights complaints such as racial discrimination or sexual harassment. The *Human Rights Code of Ontario*[11] has recently been amended to allow such separate claims.

Case Summary 6.6 *Honda Canada Inc. v. Keyes*[12]

Award of Punitive Damages Overturned

After working for Honda for 14 years, Mr. Keyes became ill with chronic fatigue syndrome. Honda required Keyes to provide doctor's notes to support each of many absences and to be assessed by their doctor before he was eventually terminated. Keyes alleged that there was a conspiracy to force him out and successfully sued for wrongful dismissal. At trial the judge concluded that there was considerable wrongdoing on the part of Honda in the dismissal process and extended the notice period from 15 to 24 months because of "egregious bad faith" on the part of Honda (Wallace damages). The trial judge also awarded punitive damages for discrimination and harassment of $500 000. On appeal the punitive damages were reduced to $100 000 and on further appeal to the Supreme Court of Canada the award of punitive damages was eliminated entirely. The Supreme Court

found that there was no evidence of harassment or discrimination. While there was some wrongdoing on the part of Honda it fell far short of what was necessary to award punitive damages, which should only be awarded where conduct amounts "to advertent wrongful acts that are so malicious and outrageous that they are deserving of punishment on their own." The Supreme Court also reversed the trial judge's decision to extend the notice period from 15 to 24 months (Wallace damages) because the trial judge had been mistaken in finding such bad faith present.

Because of the Supreme Court reversal this case isn't as significant as once thought, but it is instructive of how the courts should be extremely reluctant to award punitive damages and that "Wallace damages" should only be awarded in serious cases of bad faith.

Terminated employee must mitigate loss

A terminated employee must make a reasonable effort to mitigate his losses. The main purpose of the notice period is to give the employee an opportunity to find another job and if that is successful damages will be reduced by whatever he earns from other employment during the notice period. The employee who should have received ten months' notice and only received two would have a right to claim for the difference. But if the employee found other employment after three months at the same rate of pay or higher, he would be entitled to only one month's additional compensation, making the wrongful dismissal action a waste of time and resources. Reinstatement is not generally an option in a wrongful dismissal action. It is a possibility, however, where a statutory requirement has been breached, such as dismissing an employee because of pregnancy or some other human rights violation. Also, where collective bargaining is involved, the grievance procedure often gives the arbitrator the power to reinstate. Even in these situations, there is usually a reluctance to order reinstatement because of animosity between the parties.

Wrongful dismissal may take form of constructive dismissal

Constructive Dismissal   Sometimes by demoting, transferring, or otherwise changing the employment conditions, an employer will try to make an employee so uncomfortable that she will quit, thus avoiding the requirements of notice and termination. Whether it was done intentionally or simply as part of the restructuring of the business, it is the

---

[11] *Human Rights Code Amendment Act*, S.O. 2006, c.30.

[12] 2008 SCC 39 (CanLII) (2008), 66 C.C.E.L. (3d) 159.

employer who has created a situation that makes it difficult or impossible for the employee to continue. Consequently, it is the employer who has breached the employment contract, not the employee, when they refuse the change or quit. The employee can successfully sue for wrongful dismissal in such circumstances. The employee's obligation to mitigate may require her to take an alternate position unless the atmosphere has been so poisoned or the potential harm to her reputation makes such an option impractical. Examples of constructive dismissal include: dismissal of an employee for refusing to relocate when that was not included as a term of the contract when hired; forcing an employee to retire by changing her duties; termination upon refusal of a foreman in a paper mill to be on call every sixth weekend without pay; and the refusal of an employee to take a lower-paying position because of company downsizing. Even the practice of laying off a non-union employee for a period of time because of lack of work can constitute constructive dismissal, although this may depend on the employment standards legislation in place in that jurisdiction. Note that the employer consulting with the employee before the changes are made can often avoid the problems associated with constructive dismissal. An understanding of the employee's personal situation and needs will often give the employer cause to rethink and direct communication will often overcome the employee's reluctance to make the change. Where possible there might be an opportunity for the employee to try out the new arrangement before a permanent commitment is made, thus reducing the fear of change. The following case is a good example of constructive dismissal.

Case Summary 6.7 *Fisher v. Lakeland Mills Ltd.*[13]

Forced Retirement Amounts to Constructive Dismissal

Mrs. Fisher had worked for Lakeland for 15 years when she turned 65 in 2002. She asked and received assurance that she could work for the company for as long as she wanted. In 2003 she was required to do extra training and acquire computer skills. She had difficulty with the new demands and felt great pressure to retire and finally did so. She stated that she felt her immediate supervisor "wanted to get rid of her because she couldn't do the job." When she talked to the president of the company he did nothing to change this impression. After retiring she considered what had happened and sued for wrongful dismissal.

At trial the court determined that where an employer unilaterally "makes a fundamental or substantial change to an employee's contract of employment—a change that violates the contract's terms—the employer is committing a fundamental breach of the contract that results in its termination and entitles the employee to consider himself or herself constructively dismissed. The employee can then claim damages from the employer in lieu of reasonable notice."

The judge concluded that the demands placed on Mrs. Fisher amounted to such fundamental changes and that she felt compelled to retire as a result. This case was upheld on appeal and illustrates not only what constitutes constructive dismissal, but emphasizes a growing problem of how to handle a body of aging employees especially with the removal of mandatory retirement laws in all jurisdictions.

Termination by the Employee

Finally, we should look at termination of employment by the employee. The employee has a right to quit for cause when he or she is given dangerous or illegal instructions, is not properly paid, is put into dangerous situations, can no longer perform his or her duties

Employee can quit where just cause or pursuant to contract provision

---

[13] *Fisher v. Lakeland Mills Ltd.*, 2005 BCSC 64 (CanLII).

because of disability or illness, or where important terms of the employment contract are otherwise breached. Where the employment contract or other subsequent agreement provides for notice or has other terms relating to termination, those provisions will prevail.

Otherwise employee must also provide reasonable notice

Usually, however, there is no such provision and the employee is required to give reasonable notice of termination. What constitutes reasonable notice on the part of the employee, however, is considerably less, unless that employee plays some special role so that his or her leaving on short notice would be particularly damaging to the employer. This might be the case where the employee is a manager or salesperson having exclusive dealings with the company's customers or where the employee had some particular skill or expertise that would be difficult to replace. Even then, it is unlikely that lengthy periods of notice would be required.

Employees liable for misuse of confidential information or other wrong

Employees may be liable to their employers for wrongful or inappropriate conduct when leaving. When they leave to work for a competitor they sometimes take with them confidential customer lists, secret formulas or practices, or other information, the disclosure of which causes harm to the former employer's competitive position. Sometimes employees, while still employed, will approach the customers and try to persuade them to go with them to their new business. Such activities may amount to a breach of trust, a breach of fiduciary duty, or a violation of the duty of confidentiality and could be the cause of legal action by the employer.

Often an employment contract will contain a restrictive covenant preventing an employee, upon termination, from working in a similar industry for a period of time. Such provisions are designed to prevent unfair competition by those employees or the disclosure or misuse of confidential information to competitors. Sometimes employers require long-term employees to enter into restrictive covenants long after the initial hiring. When this happens there may be a problem with consideration. Clearly the employer should provide some added inducement for the employee to sign, but simply the promise of continued employment could constitute sufficient consideration provided there is a clear intention on the part of the employer to terminate the employment if he doesn't sign. Of course, if the employment is terminated all of the requirements discussed above with respect to reasonable notice will apply. As discussed in Chapter 3, such restrictive covenants must be reasonable in that they must be necessary to protect a valid interest of the employer and go no further than necessary to accomplish that goal. In determining the reasonableness of the provision in the employment contract, the court will also look at the effect it has on the employee. If it prevents the employee from working in his or her profession, it is less likely to be enforced. The case set out below illustrates the reluctance of the court to enforce such provisions on employees.

Case Summary 6.8 *947535 Ontario Ltd. v. Jex*[14]

Unreasonable Restrictive Covenants Void

The defendants were employed as tax consultants in an H & R Block franchise owned by the plaintiff in Owen Sound, Ontario. They were long-time employees but were terminated every year at the end of tax season and later rehired for the next. In 1993, the franchise was sold and

when the employees were hired back they were required to sign a non-competition agreement as part of their renewed employment. This provision required them not to prepare any tax returns or solicit any of the company's clients for two years after termination within the city or for a distance

>

---

[14] (2003), 37 B.L.R. (3d) 152 (Ont. S.C.J.).

of 40 kilometres from the city limits. In January 2000, instead of going back to work for the owners of the franchise, they opened up a new business in direct competition next door to where they used to work. That year they served 562 former clients of their previous employer. This action was brought by the current owner of the franchise, seeking an injunction. Among other things the court had to deal with the reasonableness of the restrictive covenant.

The court held that not only was the distance limitation unreasonable, but also the two-year restriction. The actual franchise from H & R Block only gave the plaintiff a right to operate within the city limits of Owen Sound. And although the distance included a department store where the plaintiffs operated another similar business,

the defendants never worked at that location and so could not unreasonably compete. The court determined that the 40 kilometre distance from the city limits was too broad and unreasonable. The court also found that since the defendants were only temporary employees hired and terminated each year, the two-year restriction was also too broad and unreasonable. There were additional reasons for the decision, but the case clearly illustrates how such non-competition provisions must go no further than necessary to protect the goodwill of the business. Where such provisions are found to be unreasonable they are void, leaving no restrictions at all. Note that the fact that these were only temporary employees was taken into consideration in determining the reasonableness of the provisions.

COLLECTIVE BARGAINING

Low wages and poor working conditions prompted workers to band together in the 19th century in an effort to improve their lot. The resulting trade unions were initially resisted, sometimes violently, but throughout the 20th century they managed to achieve respectability and acceptance. The passage of the U.S. *National Labor Relations Act* (the *Wagner Act*) of 1935 (after which Canadian labour legislation was patterned) was designed to put an end to labour strife. The Act recognized the employees' right to organize collectively, but required the union to show they had the support of a majority of the workers. Once majority support was established, the union was certified as the exclusive bargaining agent for the employees, and the employer could then deal only with the union and not make special arrangements with individual employees. In all jurisdictions in Canada labour relations boards have been established to handle disputes arising with respect to collective bargaining and related labour matters. See Table 6.2 for a summary of the types of disputes and their consequences.

Workers band together to combat poor working conditions

Violence associated with trade union movement

Canada follows American approach

Certification process reduces confrontation

Table 6.2 Types of Disputes and the Consequences

Recognition dispute	To get the employer to bargain with the union instead of individual employees	Certification process
Jurisdictional dispute	Rival unions contend over who should do what job or who should represent workers	Certification process or application to board
Rights dispute	Disagreement over the meaning of terms in the collective agreement	Grievance procedure and ultimately arbitration
Interest dispute	Disagreement over what should be included in the next collective agreement	Mediation and ultimately strike, lockout, and picketing

Organization

Employees have right to bargain collectively

All Canadian jurisdictions recognize that there is a general right for employees to be members of a trade union and to bargain collectively through a bargaining agent. The Supreme Court of Canada has recently confirmed this as a right under the *Charter of Rights and Freedoms*.[15] Management, however, is normally excluded from the bargaining unit and some categories of employees such as police, firefighters, and health workers, who provide essential services will usually have only limited rights to take job action.

A trade union seeking recognition as the bargaining agent for a group of employees must make application to the labour relations board for **certification**. They must show that they have a certain portion of the designated workforce signed up as members of the union, for example, 45 percent in British Columbia and 40 percent in Ontario, and similar percentages in other provinces. The process usually begins with disgruntled employees approaching a union such as the Teamsters, or union organizers will approach the employees to sign them up as members. In most cases, this won't take place on the employer's premises or during working hours, although an employer will sometimes allow it to keep on good terms with the union and to be aware of what is happening.

Recognition disputes reduced through certification process

Historically, most of the violence took place at this stage in the process called a **recognition dispute**, but today this is all dealt with through the certification process. Often a company will have several different categories of employees, and different unions will represent them. Disputes can arise between the different trade unions as to which body should represent a particular group of workers or which union's members ought to be doing a particular job. For example, should the member of the carpenters' union install the new metal studs in a building or should a steelworker? This is called a **jurisdictional dispute** and is also resolved by application to the labour relations board. Once the particular bargaining unit has been identified and the requisite number of employees signed up, an application is made to the board for certification of the union as the bargaining agent for that group of employees. In some jurisdictions, if the union can show they have signed up a large number of employees (over 50 percent federally[16]), the union can be certified without a vote. But in most jurisdictions the next step requires that a government-supervised certification vote take place. There are some jurisdictional differences, but normally if a majority of those voting support union representation, the union is then certified as the official bargaining agent for those employees. The result is that the employer from that point on must deal with the union exclusively, and can no longer make separate deals with individual workers.

Jurisdictional disputes also resolved through certification or by application to board

Certification requires signing up members and making an application

Followed by government supervised vote

Certification granted with majority vote

Even though it is a right for employees to be represented by a union and to bargain collectively, some employers will attempt to interfere with the process. Trying to intimidate or threaten employees, creating employer-dominated bargaining units, or even changing pay or conditions of work to undermine the certification drive are usually considered **unfair labour practices** and prohibited. Firing employees for their union

---

[15] *Health Services and Support-Facilities Subsector Bargaining Assn. v. British Columbia*, [2007] 2 S.C.R. 391; (2007), 283 D.L.R. (4th) 40.

[16] *Canada Labour Code*, R.S.C. 1985, c. L-2, ss. 28–29.

activities is not only a violation of labour legislation, but under section 425 of the *Criminal Code* it is a criminal offence for an employer to fire or refuse to hire someone because of his or her trade union activity or to threaten or otherwise intimidate employees from joining a trade union. It is also a criminal offence for employers to conspire together to do those things. This refers to the past practice of creating a blacklist of employees in a particular industry. These acts are punishable as summary conviction offences with the potential of up to a two-year prison term. In the face of such unfair labour practices, in some jurisdictions the board can certify the union without a vote if it is convinced that it is no longer possible to determine the true feelings of the workforce through a representative vote. Still, freedom of speech is guaranteed in the *Charter of Rights and Freedoms* and the employer retains the right to make comments and express opinions with respect to the organization process and its effect on the business, providing those comments don't amount to threats or intimidation. Still, there are limits. An employer who played messages repeatedly throughout the workday requiring employees to listen went too far and it amounted to intimidation and interference with an employee's free choice about union representation.[17]

Intimidation and coercion prohibited

But employer free to express honest opinions

In some jurisdictions it is possible for a group of employers to band together and be certified as an association for bargaining purposes. An example in British Columbia is the Forest Industrial Relations or FIR, an association of forest companies that bargain with the forestry unions through a common bargaining agent.

Bargaining

Once certified, the process of collective bargaining begins. Either party can serve notice on the other to commence bargaining. Then representatives from both parties meet and negotiate with the object of reaching a collective agreement. When they do reach an agreement, it must be presented to the members of the union—the employees—for **ratification**. If there is an employer association involved, they too must ratify the contract, and once ratified there is a binding collective agreement in place. Often, however, there is a deadlock. One of the important developments in Canadian law has been the imposition of **mediation**, sometimes referred to as **conciliation**, into the process. Either party or the government can request the intervention of a mediator who will assist the parties in their efforts to reach an agreement. The mediator acts as a go-between, trying to find common ground between the parties. During this mediation process neither party can take any further job action. If mediation is successful, a collective agreement will result, but if the mediator feels that his or her efforts are no longer helpful, the mediator will "book out" of the dispute. The parties are then free to take further job action.

Parties must bargain in good faith

Mediation available to assist bargaining

If they do reach an agreement, there are some mandatory provisions that must be included. For example, any dispute that arises after the agreement is in place (called a **rights dispute**) must be handled through a grievance process set out in the contract itself and culminate in arbitration of the dispute. Strikes and lockouts are not permitted to resolve disputes with respect to current collective agreements. When such a strike does take place it is referred to as an illegal strike or a wildcat strike, and the court will have little hesitation in issuing an injunction to bring it to an end. A collective

Contract must provide for arbitration of rights dispute

---

[17] *RMH Teleservices International Inc. (Re)* ([2003] B.C. L.R.B.D. No. 345).

agreement must be for a period of at least one year. Normally, a prior agreement will expire before serious bargaining takes place. As a result, when a new agreement is finally reached, it will be applied retroactively to the expiration of the prior agreement. Thus, even with the minimum one-year requirement, the parties can find themselves back into bargaining almost immediately, making contracts of longer duration much more attractive.

Once an agreement is in place and the parties have become used to bargaining with each other, subsequent collective bargaining will often be accomplished in a more orderly fashion. But often reaching the first agreement poses difficult if not insurmountable obstacles; because of this, in most jurisdictions the labour relations board retains the right to impose a first contract. Often just the threat of this will encourage the parties to be reasonable and conclude an agreement without the need for such intervention.

Unions will often insist that a **union shop** clause, which requires any future employees to join the union, be included in their agreements. Note that an exception is made for individuals that have religious objections. Sometimes the contract will require that only members of a union be hired. This is called a **closed shop** agreement. Dockworkers, who are sent out to a job from a union hiring hall, are an example of this arrangement. A compromise where employees don't have to join the union is referred to as a **Rand Formula** agreement. In this form of collective agreement employees need not be members of the union, but they must pay dues and are subject to the terms of the collective agreement negotiated. Most collective agreements will also have a clause requiring the employer to deduct union dues directly off the employees' pay (a **check-off provision**). This has the advantage of saving the union from the trouble of collecting dues directly from their members, some of whom may not be enthusiastic about contributing.

Job Action

If the parties cannot reach an agreement, normally a strike or lockout will follow. Such actions are only permitted where there is an **interest dispute**, which is a dispute over the terms to be included into the new collective agreement. After the parties have bargained in good faith, and all mediators involved have booked out without an agreement reached, each party is free to serve **notice** (72 hours in British Columbia) on the other of a strike or lockout. A **strike** involves the employees withdrawing their services by stopping work, although this may not involve closing down the whole operation. Often only some workers will be pulled off the job in different locations for study sessions, rotating, or escalating strike action, to put further pressure on the employer. A **lockout** involves the employer closing down the operation and denying work to the employees. This is often done to control the timing of the work stoppage, so that it will have the least possible impact on the business, for instance, when stockpiles of products have been accumulated. Note that once such notice has been given, the job action need not necessarily commence at the expiration of the notice period. Often the continuing threat of immediate job action will be used as a pressure tactic at the bargaining table during negotiations. Employee benefits such as health, dental, and insurance coverage will normally continue while the strike or lockout continues, but the employees will have to pay the entire premium.

Case Summary 6.9 *United Food and Commercial Workers, Local 1518 v. KMart Canada Ltd. et al.*[18]

Right of Expression Protected by Charter

Employees lawfully on strike at one KMart department store decided to pass out leaflets at another KMart location. This was determined to be secondary picketing, and an injunction was imposed to stop the practice. The matter went to the Supreme Court of Canada. The court first determined that handing out leaflets in this way did constitute picketing as defined in the B.C. *Labour Relations Code* and that picketing at a location other than the one struck constituted secondary picketing, which was prohibited under the statute. The court then looked at the definition of picketing in the statute and determined that it was too broad and interfered with the *Charter of Rights* guarantee of freedom of expression. There was no intimidation or physical confrontation here, which was often present with normal picketing, but just the communication of accurate information persuading people not to deal with the store. It was argued that this was a reasonable limit under section 1 of the Charter, but the Supreme Court found that while restricting secondary picketing might well be upheld as a reasonable limit under section 1, the prohibition against distributing leaflets extended this restriction further than was necessary. The B.C. government was given six months to change the definition of picketing in the statute so as to not include this type of activity.

Employers will usually try to keep the business running with management personnel doing all of the essential jobs, or in those jurisdictions where it is permitted, with replacement workers. Aside from the strike, one of the strongest weapons in the union arsenal is **picketing**. This involves the employees and often other sympathetic union members posting themselves at strategic entrances to a job site (or marching around the job site) carrying signs displaying their grievances and trying to persuade customers, suppliers, and other workers not to deal with the employer. The idea is to shut the business down completely during the duration of the strike or lockout.

Union members can picket during lawful strike

Note that people have the right to cross a picket line if they want to. But this will sometimes lead to frustration on the part of the striking workers, and violence or intimidation may take place. Courts and labour boards usually will not tolerate this, and upon application by the employer, they will order the number of picketers limited to a reasonable amount. But there is a strong ethic among union members never to cross a picket line; truck drivers, rail workers, and other union members who would be picking up or delivering will normally not cross a picket line, effectively cutting the business off with the possibility of preventing its continued operation. That is the strength of the strike and picketing process. It is usually very difficult in most jurisdictions for a company to continue its operations once a picket line has been established. In some jurisdictions only the location where the particular group of employees on strike works can be picketed. In others the union can picket anywhere the employer carries on business.

Strong tradition of honouring picket line

Note that trade unions must be democratic and free of discrimination and other human rights violations. They are also required to properly represent their employees in dealings with the employers. If they fail to do so, the legislation permits the dissatisfied employee/union member to bring an action against the union itself for compensation.

Trade unions must be democratic, not discriminate, and properly represent members

---

[18] (1999), 176 D.L.R. (4th) 607 (S.C.C.).

OTHER LEGISLATION

Only a fraction of workers are represented by trade unions, and so a considerable body of employee welfare legislation has been passed in all jurisdictions to protect employee rights and curb abuses by employers. There are many examples of statutes that have been passed to better the plight of workers, both socially and on the job. The original factory conditions that employees found themselves working in during the industrial revolution were often dangerous and unhealthy in the extreme. Employees who became sick or were injured because of conditions on the job were simply terminated and left without recourse or compensation. Workers' compensation statutes were designed to overcome those problems. Employers are required to contribute to a fund that works like insurance, providing compensation to workers who become ill or are injured on the job. Sick or injured employees make a claim against the fund for compensation. Workers injured on the job cannot normally sue the employer or a fellow employee who causes them injury. Rather, their recourse is to seek compensation under the **workers' compensation** legislation.

A second aspect of workers' compensation legislation, often contained in a separate statute, authorizes a government-appointed body to set and enforce health and safety standards in the workplace. This includes rules with respect to matters such as ventilation, workplace safety, and the use of safety equipment. This can include the use of hard hats, safety shoes, railings, harnesses, and the like. Inspectors who have authority to levy penalties and even close the job down where necessary enforce these standards. The trend today is to impose more significant fines and penalties for violation of these safety rules. In reaction to the Westray mining disaster in Nova Scotia where 26 men were killed, the criminal negligence provisions of the *Criminal Code* have been broadened, making organizations more criminally responsible for the negligent action of their representatives that cause injury to others. It should also be noted that with the increased practice of outsourcing workers, a responsibility for their health and safety has also been extended. Thus where cleaning, security, catering, and other similar services are provided by other employers, the business to which those services are provided are as responsible for their health and safety as they are for its own employees.

Employment insurance legislation is designed to provide a soft landing for those who are laid off. Both the employer and employees contribute to a fund. When laid off, the employee makes a claim and receives a set payment for a designated number of weeks to help bridge the gap until he or she finds other work. Also the **human rights legislation** discussed in Chapter 1 has its greatest application in the field of employment. Discrimination on the basis of race, religion, ethnic origin, gender, disability, and sexual orientation with regard to hiring, promotion, or any other aspect of employment is prohibited, as is sexual harassment. In the past all complaints had to go to human rights boards, which have broad powers of investigation and enforcement. But the courts have shown an increased willingness to take such violations into consideration in awarding compensation in other actions such as wrongful dismissal. Some provinces have changed their human rights legislation to support this new direction (such as the *Ontario Human Rights Code*[19]).

Workers' compensation statutes compensate injured workers

Occupational health and safety statutes ensure worker safety

Employment insurance statutes help workers between jobs

Human rights statutes protect workers discriminated against in employment

---

[19] R.S.O. 1990, c. H.19.

A particular problem for employers is how to deal with employees with a substance abuse problem, especially where there are safety concerns. Should mandatory drug testing be allowed? Is this discrimination? Remember that a drug or alcohol addiction is considered a disability and the employer has a duty to accommodate. There are some conflicting decisions but it is likely that where safety is a serious concern mandatory drug testing is permissible. Even then where there is addiction the employer has a duty to accommodate and to the point of suffering undue hardship find other work for the employee and provide other help. It is interesting to note that an employee who violates a company's no-drug policy as a recreational user can be disciplined but the addict has a disability and must be accommodated.

Most jurisdictions have incorporated a number of different statutes setting out various standards for the workplace into one comprehensive statute (called the *Employment Standards Act* in British Columbia and Ontario). The Acts set up standards that apply to all employees and cannot be waived by contract. The only exception is where a higher standard exists in common law or has been agreed to in a collective agreement. These statutes cover such areas as the amount of notice or pay that must be given in the event of termination; the number of hours to be worked in a day, a week, or a month; what amount of overtime to be paid if these figures are exceeded; pay for statutory holidays and annual vacation; and specified leaves for pregnancy, bereavement, parenting, and the like. These statutes also set up government boards that have the power to hear complaints, investigate, enter the workplace, gather evidence, inspect records, impose penalties, and otherwise enforce the legislation. This discussion is intended to give just a summary of the kinds of provisions that have been enacted. For specifics you should look up the particular statutes that apply in your jurisdiction. Note that contravention by employers of the provisions and standards established under these statutes can constitute a provincial offence and expose the offending party to significant fines, and, in some cases, imprisonment. For example, in the Ontario *Workplace Safety and Insurance Act* fines of up to $25 000 can be imposed on an individual and $100 000 on a corporation. In that province's *Employment Standards Act* the maximum penalty for repeated serious offences can be as high as $500 000 and up to a year in prison. Even where provision for such penalties has been in place, the trend today is towards increasing enforcement and to more vigorously pursue violators.

Employment standards statutes provide for holiday pay, leaves, overtime, termination, etc.

SUPERVISING EMPLOYEES

At the outset it is important to emphasize that nothing will substitute for creating a good relationship with employees so that loyalty and respect are fostered. And like any business activity it is important to develop clear and comprehensive employment policies that are known by managers and employees alike and carefully followed by all. Those policies should include not only rules that are consistent with fair employment practices but a system of education for the employees and managers as well as a fair disciplinary process that is clearly understood and consistently applied.

In this section we will examine some of the common workforce problems with legal implications that such policies should be designed to prevent. We have already dealt with wrongful conduct that constitutes just cause for termination. Often such conduct is obvious, but at other times it may be known that wrongful conduct such as theft has taken place but the culprit may remain unknown. Unfounded accusations based on rumour or suspicion leading to precipitous action such as termination may cause the employer more grief than the inappropriate conduct. Or the theft or other wrongful conduct may be minor and not enough to constitute cause for termination. Large corporations usually have security sections that can investigate suspected wrongdoers within the workforce and human resources departments that deal with hiring and firing employees as well as other disciplinary processes. They should be carefully trained to understand employee rights so that they will not violate those rights in the investigation and disciplinary processes.

It is usually the owner or managers in smaller businesses that are left to do such investigations, but the same principles apply. They must take great care to respect the rights of the employee in the process. Often the manager, upon hearing an allegation of wrongful conduct, will terminate the employee immediately. But it is now clearly established that the employee has the same right to due process as we find in dealing with any disciplinary body. Basically, that means that the employee must be told the nature of the allegations and evidence against him and be given an opportunity to explain or refute them.

Termination should not automatically be the outcome in all cases of wrongful conduct or violation of company policies. For a minor infraction it may be appropriate to reprimand the employee, write the employee up, or even in more serious instances suspend the employee without pay for a period. Be careful here, as this might constitute constructive dismissal, especially where senior staff or long-term employees are involved. The process of reprimanding, writing up, and suspending creates a process of progressive discipline. Good employees who make mistakes are retained and made better employees. Incompetent, disruptive, or dishonest employees are identified and weeded out. This process of progressive discipline will identify problem employees and create a paper trail of evidence establishing a pattern of behaviours that may, when taken together, constitute just cause for termination. The same process is involved with incompetent employees. An evaluation review should be regularly performed with problems clearly identified to the employee. Together goals are set and promises made such as taking courses to become current or overcome weaknesses, or in the case of addicted employees, commitments to complete treatment programs. These commitments are subsequently reviewed and new promises made. If the employee fulfills the promises and reaches the goals, a more productive employee is saved for the business. Where the employee fails to meet these goals or live up to the promises, it establishes a pattern of unsatisfactory performance, which may justify termination or demotion. Always the disciplinary processes must be well documented with the view of these records being available for subsequent litigation.

One of the greatest challenges to many businesses is to deal with shoplifting and employee theft. Theft is set out in section 322 of the *Criminal Code*. There are also a number of similar listed offences, all providing for significant penalty. Fraud is similar but involves cheating people out of their valuables through deceit and falsehood. Employees also sometimes sabotage the business by causing some form of physical damage to tools and equipment; interfering with software, data, or computer equipment; or contaminating information or goods. This constitutes mischief (section 430) or one of the various property-related offences discussed in Chapter 8. Most of these theft-like offences expose the perpetrator to a maximum term of imprisonment of 10 years where the amounts involved exceed $5000 and the Crown proceeds by way of indictment. Fraud is set out in section 380 with a penalty of up to 14 years where amounts over $5000 are involved. Shoplifting by customers is also theft, but it usually involves lesser amounts and is punishable by indictment or summary conviction with a term of imprisonment of up to two years.

Examples of theft and theft-like activity

The challenges for businesses relate to detection and prevention. All businesses have to balance the costs of security, surveillance, and enforcement against the losses incurred. Of course, too tight security can also have the negative effect of destroying employee morale and loyalty and damaging customer goodwill. No one likes going into a store and having his or her bags searched, and the presence of security cameras and other forms of surveillance are sometimes taken by employees as an invitation to try to beat them. It is likely that the best counter to employee theft is the promotion of employee loyalty, but this will depend on the nature of the business. Where small valuable items are involved such as precious jewels, watches, or valuable tools, most employees and customers would expect and tolerate a reasonable amount of surveillance and security, providing it is not too intrusive.

Extensive surveillance often resented

In all cases where surveillance is involved, it is important that employees are made aware of it from the outset; otherwise, there is not only the danger of losing employee loyalty but also of being accused of violating that employee's right to privacy. When countering shoplifting, well-trained security people and other employees are vital. A business will often lose much more as a result of a judgment for assault, defamation, or false imprisonment brought on by an overzealous or misguided employee than from the shoplifting itself.

Employee training vital to avoid litigation

Employee theft and fraud has to be treated somewhat differently. Often the existence of the theft is discovered before anyone in particular is suspected. At this stage the police can be brought in to investigate, but sometimes it is better for internal security people to investigate first. Again, the rights of employees have to be respected. There is no general right to search employees, their lockers, or computers unless there are reasonable grounds to suppose that a particular employee committed the theft. Police can obtain a search warrant, but that option is not available to managers or even their security services without involving the police. If it is made clear when employees are first employed that there is surveillance in place and that telephones and computers will be monitored, there is little likelihood of infringing on an employee's rights, providing the business owns the phones and computers. But it is doubtful that such notice will entitle an employer to search an employee or his or her locker without police involvement.

Police have more power

Of course, where shoplifting or employee theft is involved, prosecution is often not effective due to the high standard of proof that must be established by the prosecution. Another serious disadvantage is the disruption to the business caused by the investigation, evidence gathering, and prosecution process; the long delays; and the damage that the publicity can bring to the business. Often it is better where employees are involved to simply terminate the employee, assuming enough evidence has been gathered to establish just cause. Unless the amounts for a particular individual are significant, it is generally not worth the trouble, time, and expense to pursue theft or frauds by customers in a civil action. For this reason businesses often simply include such shoplifting, customer fraud, and employee theft as a cost of doing business, and add it to the cost of the merchandise or service provided. This, of course, is entirely unsatisfactory but does drive home the importance of putting the emphasis on prevention rather than enforcement.

Termination often only effective remedy for employee theft

If a decision is made not to involve the police, there is the danger of the business itself, the managers, or the owner who made that decision being charged with the criminal offence of obstructing justice. This comes with the potential of 10 years' imprisonment when treated as an indictable offence. For example, suppose an employee has been stealing for some time. When he is found out, the employer promises not to tell the police if that employee agrees to repay the money by working longer hours. Or suppose a youthful shoplifter is caught and the parents promise to repay the amount and a fee for overhead if the police are not brought in.[20] This is likely an obstruction of justice, as it amounts to withholding evidence of a crime from the police. Similarly, where an ad is placed in a newspaper offering a reward for the return of stolen goods "no questions asked," both the person who placed the ad and the business that published it have committed a summary conviction offence under section 143 of the *Criminal Code*.

Legal pitfalls when legal advice or police involvement is lacking

While prevention is important, detection of fraud is vital. Often such crimes, committed by trusted employees, go on for years because there is no structure in place for detection. Proper processes of supervision and control, including appropriate security and surveillance, serve the double purpose of discouraging crime and detecting it when it takes place. Here again, care must be taken not to infringe on the privacy rights of employees. The rights to privacy and employers right to interfere with those rights will be discussed as separate topic in Chapter 9. Whether there is simple abuse by an employee who makes personal use of a company's tools, equipment, or other facilities, or whether these resources are being used to commit a criminal act or to defraud the company, the practice will likely be reduced with proper surveillance. A business is more likely to have the right to monitor an employee's use of company equipment such as computers, phones, and other telecommunications equipment if they inform the employees that they are subject to such monitoring at the outset. They also have the right to use closed-circuit TV to monitor various plant and office locations, again with appropriate pre-notification. In fact, such notification should be made a term of the contract of employment. This might be more difficult where a union is involved, and their agreement and cooperation are required. It is likely that anything beyond normal supervision of unionized employees will be considered a breach of an employee's privacy rights, unless there are reasonable grounds for launching an investigation. Note that such privacy legislation varies from province to province. While such close monitoring of an employee's activities and use of equipment may be taken as distrust and reduce loyalty, if the expectation is made part of the corporate culture from the outset, it will likely be more readily tolerated by all levels of employees.

Careful supervision, security, and surveillance can avoid problems

Employers must take care not to infringe the rights of employees

Even when no crime has been detected, there are often telltale clues that should alert management to a potential problem. When an employee shows a marked change in personality or there is evidence of a serious drinking problem or drug abuse, this should at least trigger concern for the employee's welfare, but it may also indicate a serious problem with reference to his or her job performance or some criminal activity. High debt load or other financial difficulties, gambling problems, and even an employee avoiding taking a vacation may also be symptoms of a serious job-related problem, especially if the opportunity is present for the misappropriation of funds.

Expert help should be obtained when a crime is suspected

When an individual employee is suspected of criminal activity or other wrongdoing, great care must be taken in the investigation and punishment process. The first stage is usually a forensic audit to determine the extent of the fraud and find evidence of the wrongdoing. Lawyers should be brought in at this stage to ensure that evidence is

---

[20] *(B.D.C.) v. Arkin* (1996), 138 D.L.R. (4th) 309, [1996] 8 W.W.R. 100 (Man. Q.B.).

preserved and the investigation does not interfere with the rights of the employee. Overenthusiastic investigators have been known to breach privacy rights, defame individuals, and trespass, putting at risk any further action and subjecting the corporation to a wrongful dismissal action. Sometimes a gentler, less threatening approach will be more productive.

A decision has to be made at this stage whether the goal is simply the dismissal of the employee, the recovery of what has been lost, or an actual criminal prosecution. If the goal is simply to get rid of the employee, there is the danger of a wrongful dismissal action or even an action for defamation if the grounds for the dismissal are theft or fraud and that is made public. Such an unfounded accusation can significantly increase the damages awarded. The employee should be given an opportunity to respond to any charges against him or her, and any other employees involved must be made to understand that everything associated with the investigation is completely confidential. The dismissal process itself should be done privately, preserving the dignity of the terminated employee so as to avoid defamation by innuendo.

Improper process can have serious repercussion to business

If the goal is to recover the money, great care must be exercised not to intimidate or coerce the employee by threats of prosecution. Any agreement not to inform the police in return for the employee's cooperation and the return of the money is an indictable offence under sections 141 and 142 of the *Criminal Code* and is punishable with imprisonment up to five years. Also, if there is any chance of recovering the funds, action must be taken immediately to preserve those funds and any evidence of the wrongdoing. This may include police involvement, obtaining *ex parte* injunctions and court orders to freeze assets.

Employer should move quickly when fraud discovered

Where internal fraud or theft is involved, the corporation often will not be interested in pursuing a criminal prosecution because of damaging publicity, the disruption of the business, time-commitment of key personnel, the disclosure of confidential corporate information, the lengthy legal process, and the difficulties of getting a conviction. Still, it may well be that for the preservation of the company's reputation or as a deterrent to others, criminal prosecution will be appropriate. In this case it is advisable to involve the police at the earliest stage. Police have greater powers of investigation and greater investigatory expertise. They can obtain search warrants and are more likely to ensure that the process followed is correct and does not interfere with the rights of the suspected wrongdoer. While the primary focus of criminal prosecution is conviction and punishment, the prosecution process also has the potential of a restitution order in the event of a conviction. If the matter can be settled with the cooperation of the prosecutor before that stage, the restoration of the funds taken can be a condition of the settlement. The threat of jail might be a stronger inducement to return the funds, since doing so can significantly reduce any sentence imposed by the court.

Police involvement and prosecution can have beneficial results

One considerable problem with involving the police is that the corporate crime specialists are often overextended and overworked and may not have the resources to properly investigate the complaint in a timely manner. Private professional legal and forensic experts can be hired by the corporation to investigate. They then provide information to the police, thus overcoming this problem to some extent. But in some cases the police simply do not have the resources and will refuse to get involved, especially where there is a civil remedy available. Still, insurance policies usually require that at least a police report be filed.

Key Terms

actual authority (p. 132)	**jurisdictional dispute** (p. 148)
agency relationship (p. 131)	**just cause** (p. 141)
apparent authority (p. 132)	**lockout** (p. 150)
certification (p. 148)	**mediation** (p. 149)
check-off provision (p. 150)	**notice** (p. 150)
closed shop (p. 150)	**organization test** (p. 139)
conciliation (p. 149)	**picketing** (p. 151)
control test (p. 138)	**progressive discipline** (p. 142)
employee (p. 130)	**Rand Formula** (p. 150)
employment insurance (p. 152)	**ratification** (pp. 133, 149)
Employment Standards Act (p. 153)	**reasonable notice** (p. 140)
estoppel (p. 132)	**recognition dispute** (p. 148)
expressed authority (p. 131)	**rights dispute** (p. 149)
fiduciary duty (p. 135)	**strike** (p. 150)
human rights legislation (p. 152)	**undisclosed agency** (p. 135)
implied authority (p. 132)	**unfair labour practices** (p. 148)
independent contractor (p. 130)	**union shop** (p. 150)
interest dispute (p. 150)	**workers' compensation** (p. 152)

Questions for Student Review

1. Explain why the topics of agency and employment are important with respect to the study of business law.

2. Distinguish between independent contractors, employees, and agents. Explain why that distinction is important.

3. Distinguish between actual, apparent, and implied authority.

4. Explain what is meant by ratification, how ratification may arise, and its effect on the contracting parties.

5. Explain under what circumstances a principal will be responsible for the wrongful acts committed by an agent who is an employee and by an agent who is an independent contractor.

6. Explain what is meant by an undisclosed agency. What options are available to a third party when an agent acts for such an undisclosed principal?

7. Explain the nature of an agent's obligations to the principal, and what is meant by fiduciary duty.

8. Define employment and distinguish between the control test and the organization test.

9. Explain under what circumstances an employer will be vicariously liable for the torts committed by an employee and for contracts entered into by an employee.

10. Explain how the employment relationship may be terminated. In the absence of contractual provisions, how much notice is required? Include a discussion of constructive dismissal and what effect that will have on the requirement of notice.

11. Define just cause. Give examples, and explain what effect it has on the requirement of notice.

12. What are an employer's obligations with respect to disabled workers?

13. How are damages assessed in a wrongful dismissal action, and how is that award affected by bad faith on the part of the employer or an employee's failure to mitigate?

14. Explain the employee's obligations with respect to notice to quit, fiduciary duty, and confidential information.

15. Describe the certification process in your jurisdiction.

16. Distinguish between recognition, jurisdiction, interest, and rights disputes. Indicate how each of these types of deputes must be resolved.

17. Explain what is meant by unfair labour practices and how they are dealt with in Canadian law.

18. Explain what is meant by the obligation for the parties to bargain in good faith and the role mediation plays in the collective bargaining process.

19. Distinguish between a strike and a lockout, and indicate how much notice must be given and any other restrictions or requirements on strike or lockout in your jurisdiction.

20. What is meant by picketing? Why is it so effective and what limitations on the right to picket are there in your jurisdiction?

21. Explain what is meant by a union shop, a closed shop, and the right of "check-off."

22. Explain the purpose and effect of workers' compensation legislation, occupational health and safety statutes, employment insurance statutes, and human rights statutes with respect to employment.

23. List the standards imposed by employment standards statutes in your jurisdiction.

24. Describe effective strategies to avoid or deal with unlawful and inappropriate behaviours by employees.

25. What dangers does a business face with respect to the investigation and enforcement aspects of employee crime?

Questions for Further Discussion

1. A principal who enters into a contract that specifically limits the agent's authority to act still faces the possibility of being bound by acts the agent performs outside that actual authority. This is because of the agent's apparent authority. Why should the principal bear responsibility to the third party when it was the agent who violated the authority limitation? Would it not be more appropriate for the third party to turn to the agent for compensation for any losses suffered when the agent violates his or her authority? In your discussion consider the matter from the point of view of the principal, the agent, and the third party.

2. Employers are held vicariously liable for torts committed by their employees in the course of their employment. Some have questioned the fairness of this process since it is the employee who is committing the wrongful act, not the employer. This is an example of holding the employer strictly liable for the employee's wrongdoing even though they are completely innocent. We don't even impose that kind of liability on parents for the wrongful acts committed by their children. Discuss the appropriateness of holding one person such as an employer responsible for the acts of another. Look at the question from the point of view of all parties involved and also consider the public interest. Consider as well that the Supreme Court of Canada has broadened when an employer will be vicariously

liable for the acts of employees. The test now is not whether he was doing his job but whether the act was closely enough connected to his employment to impose liability.

3.   In Canada we have developed the practice of requiring employers to give employees extensive notice or pay in lieu of notice when terminating without cause. Most provinces have enacted employment standards acts where the required statutory notice is much less than the common law requirement. But these statutes also provide that the longer term (in either the statute or the common law) should prevail. Is it appropriate or fair to employers to impose such lengthy notice periods? Should the declared statutory period simply override any prior common law approach, as would normally be the case with statutes? On the other hand, do you think that when a term is included in the employment contract that reduces this notice period it should be allowed to stand? Think about the relative bargaining positions of the employer and employee at the time of hiring when these special terms are normally agreed to.

4.   Do you feel that unions have too much power today? Look at the legislation in place in your jurisdiction and discuss whether it accomplishes a balanced approach between the needs of employees and their right to bargain collectively, and the freedom of action required by an employer to carry on its business.

Cases for Discussion

1.   *Calgary Hardwood & Veneer Ltd. et al. v. Canadian National Railway Co.* (1979), 100 D.L.R. (3d) 302 (Alta. S.C.).

Thomas Young worked as an Industrial Development Officer for the Canadian National Railway Company. For two years he had been dealing with Calgary Hardwood & Veneer Ltd. to sell them certain lands owned by the C.N.R in Calgary. Finally, he made an offer to the purchaser to the effect that if they could get municipal approval for the use they were intending to make of the land, then the C.N.R. would "agree to sell" it under the terms negotiated. Calgary Hardwood did obtain the necessary approval and accepted the C.N.R. offer presented to them by Mr. Young. But the C.N.R. then took the position that Mr. Young didn't have the necessary authority to make such an offer, and they refused to go through with the sale. For the entire two years, the C.N.R. officials were aware of the negotiations Mr. Young was carrying on with the purchaser, but they said nothing. Indicate the arguments on both sides as to the validity of the contract of sale of the land. Would it affect your answer to know that on some of the negotiation sessions with the purchaser Mr. Young was accompanied by other C.N.R. officials?

2.   *Ocean City Realty Ltd. v. A & M Holdings Ltd. et al.* (1987), 36 D.L.R. (4th) 94 (B.C.C.A.).

Mrs. Forbes was a salesperson working for Ocean City Realty when she arranged for Halbower to purchase commercial property in Victoria from A & M Holdings. But in order for the deal to proceed, the purchaser, Halbower, insisted that Mrs. Forbes surrender half of her commission to them. She agreed to do this but did not inform the seller. Even though A & M Holdings didn't lose any money in the process, when they found out about the agreement to pay over half the commission to the purchaser they refused to pay any commission to the agent. Explain the basis for their complaint and the likelihood of success.

3.   *Adga Group Consultants Inc. v. Lane,* 2008 CanLII 39605 (ON S.C.D.C.).

Mr. Lane suffered from a bipolar condition, which caused mood swings from manic to depressive states. When stable he was a very capable worker, but could be very disruptive when in a manic phase. He was trained as an electrical engineer and had been employed successfully in sensitive industries in the past requiring a high security clearance. He worked for a time for Siemens but when they discovered his disorder they terminated his employment. Mr. Lane brought a complaint to the Ontario Human Rights Tribunal, which was eventually settled between the parties. He then worked for Linmor who were aware of his problem and were able to work around the disruptions. He was highly rated as a valued, hardworking, and productive employee. In September 2001 Lane applied for a job at Adga, but did not disclose that he suffered from the bipolar disorder. He was hired but 10 days later he had a manic episode and was terminated immediately. Note that the level of work involved working on NATO military contracts and was quite stressful. It was also time sensitive requiring prompt performance of software development contracts. Lane brought a complaint to the Ontario Human Rights Tribunal. How should the Tribunal respond to this complaint?

4. *McKinley v. BC Tel et al.* (2001), 200 D.L.R. (4th) 385 (S.C.C.).

   Martin McKinley was a chartered accountant who worked as a controller for several BC Tel companies. He developed high blood pressure, a condition which at first was controlled by medication. Eventually, under his doctor's advice he had to take a leave of absence from his employment. He discussed with his superior his desire to return to work in a less responsible position, but no such position was offered even though such positions opened up in the organization. The company made him a severance offer that was rejected. His employment was terminated and this action for wrongful dismissal was brought against BC Tel. At the time of his termination McKinley had been employed by BC Tel for 17 years. When his employment was terminated, he lost his short-term and long-term disability benefits. He complained to the Human Rights Commission and brought this wrongful dismissal action. He also claimed that the company had dismissed him in a "high-handed and flagrant manner," amounting to "intentional infliction of mental suffering." This was denied by the company. They claimed that the employment relationship had been frustrated and that they had offered a reasonable severance package. What would McKinley's complaint to the Human Rights Commission consist of? Did the company have just cause for termination? If not, what would be an appropriate remedy in these circumstances? If the company had been guilty of bad faith in the termination process, how would this affect the remedies to be awarded? How would it affect your answer to know that well into the trial the company was allowed to change their defence to just cause for dismissal? The new defence was based on a letter they discovered, which indicated that the doctor had recommended a type of medication that would allow him to return to work and that McKinley's withholding of this letter amounted to dishonesty justifying the termination.

5. *Lane v. Carson Group Inc.* 208 N.S.R. (2d) 60, 2002 NSSC 218, [2002] N.S.J. No. 428 (N.S.S.C.).

   Patrick Lane had worked as a salesman for the defendant for 25 years; he had a territory covering all of the Atlantic Provinces. Some adjustments had been made over the years, but all with consultation and his consent. In 2000, a new sales manager first refused to pay for Mr. Lane's travel expenses that had been paid in the past and then reduced his assigned territory substantially by assigning Newfoundland and Cape Breton to another salesperson. That represented 25 to 30 percent of his income. In response to these actions by the new sales manager, Mr. Lane resigned. He then brought this action for wrongful dismissal. Explain the basis for his action and the likelihood of success and if successful what remedy he should obtain. How would it affect your answer to know that the original employment contract provided that he would be entitled to only 2 weeks notice upon termination?

6. *Pepsi-Cola Canada Beverages (West) Ltd. v. R.W.D.S.U.*, Local 558 (2002), 208 D.L.R. (4th) 385 (S.C.C.).

   The union in question obtained certification as the bargaining agent for the employees working at the Pepsi-Cola bottling plant in Saskatchewan. The employer and union bargained collectively but were unable to reach an agreement, and a legal strike took place, followed by a lockout. A bitter confrontation ensued, including employees taking over the company's warehouse facilities. An injunction was issued and the company resumed business with replacement workers. The union members then extended their picketing to secondary locations, including retail outlets where Pepsi products were sold, as well as a hotel where several replacement workers were staying, and in front of the homes of several Pepsi managers. They carried placards, chanted slogans, screamed insults, and uttered threats of harm at these locations. This action was brought by the employer; they applied for an injunction to stop picketing at these secondary locations. Explain the grounds for their complaint and the likelihood of their success. Indicate any arguments that might be raised by the union in their defence. Would it affect your answer to know that there was no statute prohibiting secondary picketing in place in Saskatchewan as there is in some provinces?

7. *Kelly v. Linamar Corporation*, 2005 CanLII 42487 (ON S.C.).

   Kelly had worked for Linamar Corp. for 14 years. The company was the largest employer in the town and had a reputation as a good corporate citizen. He was working as a materials manager supervising 12 other employees when he was arrested after the discovery of child pornography on his personal computer (at home). He had a good employment record; nevertheless, upon learning of the arrest; the company immediately terminated his employment. He sued for wrongful dismissal.

   Do you think that the actions of the corporation were justified in these circumstances? How could they have handled the termination differently? Would it make a difference to your answer if it turned out that eventually he was acquitted of the charge? How would it affect your answer to learn that the corporation had a good reputation in the community especially because of charity work done to support children?

Chapter 7
Methods of Carrying on Business

Learning Objectives

- Distinguish the three basic methods of carrying on business
- Compare the advantages and disadvantages of sole proprietorship and partnership
- Understand the methods and objectives of incorporating
- Consider the duties and obligations of directors and shareholders
- Review ethical business practices
- Understand the various methods of funding corporate activities

Choosing a method for doing business is one of the most important topics in this text. The methods have been developed to facilitate the commercial needs of society by spreading the control and risk of doing business among those involved. People should exercise great care when starting a business to ensure that the structure chosen is the best one for their particular needs.

Take care in choosing method to carry on business

Although there are other business models, we will look primarily at sole proprietorship, partnership, and incorporation. The sole proprietor involves one person operating a business alone without going through the process of incorporation. A partnership involves two or more people carrying on business together without going through the process of incorporation. And the corporation involves any number of people going through the process of incorporation where documents are filed with a government agency and a certificate is issued, thus creating a new entity—the corporation—which is the vehicle for carrying on the business. It shouldn't be assumed that a corporation is the best way to carry on a business. Each structure has its advantages and disadvantages, but it is important to point out that often what is a disadvantage to one person is an advantage to another. As a result, we discuss business structures, except in a few instances, more in terms of their characteristics rather than advantages or disadvantages. In this chapter we will first examine the general characteristics that apply to all business approaches. Then unique methods will be identified along with the rights and obligations of those involved in the business and those who do business with them.

COMMON ELEMENTS

Each one of these structures is designed for the purpose of carrying on business and making profits for those involved. Government regulations present a series of hurdles that all businesses must face. For example, both federal and provincial income taxes must be paid

Government regulations impact all businesses

and business people must keep sufficient records of their dealings to account for those tax obligations. There may also be property taxes owed to a city or municipality. Where services or products are offered federal GST must be collected from customers, and, depending on the jurisdiction, there may be an obligation to collect provincial sales tax. Those funds must then be remitted to the appropriate level of government. A certain portion of employees' pay must be retained for income tax purposes, and employers must pay employment insurance, workers' compensation, and Canada Pension Plan premiums. In some cases, depending on the nature of the business, it may be necessary to obtain a provincial or municipal licence and adhere to the regulations associated with that licence. For example, most businesses dealing with the public will need a municipal business licence, and some businesses such as real estate, insurance, and travel agencies will need a provincial licence to operate. Professionals such as lawyers, doctors, dentists, accountants, and real estate agents must also meet stringent qualifications and maintain membership in good standing in their respective professional organizations.

In addition, there are privacy and confidentiality obligations, human rights regulations, pollution controls, and health and safety standards that must be complied with. Carrying on business today is a highly regulated activity and an understanding of the regulations that affect your business is crucial to its success.

THE SOLE PROPRIETOR

Sole proprietor works for himself or herself

A **sole proprietor** works for himself or herself (see Figure 7.1). There are no special processes or formalities that must take place to create a sole proprietorship other than the registration of a business name. Even that is only required when the business name is different than the sole proprietor's. A person is a sole proprietor as soon as she embarks on some business activity alone. When a child opens a lemonade stand she is a sole proprietor. Sole proprietor then is the term used to describe someone who starts up a business on her own without going through any formal process such as incorporation.

No formal process required

As a general rule the sole proprietor has complete control of the business. There is no one else to tell her what to do and she is answerable only to herself. The record and reporting burden is lighter and there are fewer government regulations. Any profits made from the business belong to the sole proprietor, and any obligations of the business are those of the sole proprietor. Thus, the sole proprietor and the business are one. It is interesting to note that in the case of *R. v. AFC Soccer*[1] criminal charges were brought against AFC Soccer for certain copyright violations and AFC Soccer was convicted. But AFC Soccer was simply the business name that Arree Arunkiet had properly registered for his sole proprietorship and the Appeal Court overturned the conviction, finding that AFC Soccer did not exist. It was not an incorporated body and since all charges had been dropped against Mr. Arunkiet the conviction against the non-existent company could not stand.

Sole proprietor has unlimited liability

The main problem with a sole proprietor is that there is **unlimited liability**. This means that any debts associated with the business are those of the sole proprietor, and her

Figure 7.1 Sole Proprietor Relationship

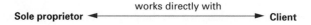

works directly with

Sole proprietor ◄───────────────────► Client

---

[1] (2004) 240 D.L.R. (4th) 178 Man C.A.

personal assets will be vulnerable to creditors. There is no separation made between the sole proprietor and her business activities. The sole proprietor will be vicariously liable for an employee's wrongful conduct that takes place within the scope of the employment. It is usually this unlimited liability that discourages people from carrying on business as a sole proprietor. However, many of these disadvantages can be offset by obtaining adequate insurance coverage.

Personal assets are at risk for business debt

Perhaps the primary disadvantage of operating a business alone is also its greatest advantage. While others can invest in the business, they become creditors of the sole proprietor, not participants in the business. The sole proprietor remains in control. To become participants, a partnership or corporation must be created. In many jurisdictions professionals cannot incorporate. A dentist may incorporate a company to hire the staff, assistants, and supply the office space and equipment, but not the performance of the dental service itself. If such a professional is by himself, he must act as a sole proprietor. If the professional decides to band together with other professionals who then carry on business together, they must do so as a partnership. Some jurisdictions now allow such professionals to form professional corporations, but in most cases they retain personal responsibility for their professional activities.

Some professionals can't incorporate

One of the greatest disadvantages to a sole proprietor involves income tax. Since the income of the business and that of the person owning it are one, it is considered personal income and taxed at that rate. Most business people will pay a much higher rate of personal taxes than they would if they operated through a corporation. Through the corporation the business person has the advantage of paying at a lower rate and then reinvesting the funds, thus delaying personal taxes so that there is more money available for investment. This is especially true where a small business is entitled to the small business deduction. Funds to be distributed can be taken out at a more convenient time when personal income is low. If the business is eventually sold there is a one-time capital tax allowance that can be claimed. Also, there are mechanisms available so that the corporation can be used to redirect income to a spouse or other family member. Such income splitting allows the parties to take advantage of the lowest personal tax rates. These tax advantages are continually changing, but it is clear that there are significant tax advantages that can be obtained by carrying on a business through a corporation. The converse is also true, that while a sole proprietor will have income come straight into his hands, business losses also will come directly to him so that those losses may be balanced against personal income directly.

Because of these factors most sole proprietorships fall into the class of small businesses. They are often found in the construction and forestry sectors where one-man or small operations subcontracting with larger general contractors are common. And most professionals who practice by themselves do so as sole proprietors although professional corporations, where permitted, are becoming much more popular.

Case Summary 7.1 *Atlantic Glass and Storefronts Ltd. v. Price*[2]
Unlimited Liability Continued After Incorporation

Mr. Price originally operated "Fins, Furs and Feathers" as a sole proprietor but neglected to register the change under the *Partnerships and Business Names Registration Act* when he incorporated the business as P.R. Enterprises Ltd. When the company failed to pay their supplier—Atlantic Glass and Storefronts Ltd.—the supplier sued Mr. Price

>

[2] (1974), 48 D.L.R. (3d) 471 (N.S. Co. Ct.).

directly instead of the company. Price clamed he was protected as a shareholder of the company and that the company was liable for the debt, not him. But the court found against him since he was still registered as a sole proprietor and he had done nothing to inform Atlantic Glass of the change. As far as Atlantic Glass and the court were concerned that was still the case, and Price was personally liable for the debt. This case shows how important it is to follow the correct procedures when incorporating a business and following up by naming the company as the contracting party and indicating that you (the shareholder/director) are merely acting in a representative capacity. All correspondence should be under the company name and contracts should be in the name of the company with the individual signing doing so as its representative. It also illustrates the different responsibilities of a shareholder and a sole proprietor. This is an older case but the obligation to inform those you are dealing with that they are dealing with a corporation and not you as an individual remains an essential requirement in all jurisdictions.

PARTNERSHIP

Partners work together to earn a profit

A **partnership** is defined as "the relation between persons carrying on a business in common with a view to profit."[3] Essentially, they are a group of sole proprietors who have agreed to carry on their business together without going through the incorporation process (see Figure 7.2). No formal process is needed other than, in some cases, registration with the appropriate government agency. Historically, this was the common method of carrying on business and a considerable body of judge-made law was developed to deal with partnerships. In 1890, as part of the movement towards codifying commercial law in England, this body of law was summarized in partnership acts. Each common law province in Canada has adopted a version of the *Partnership Act*. Today, in many jurisdictions doctors, lawyers, dentists, and accountants can only carry on business as sole proprietors or in partnerships. It should be noted that there are some common law obligations that, while not included in the *Partnership Act*, still apply. The fiduciary duty owed by one partner to another is an example.

No formal process needed to form partnership

Common law case law is codified by partnership acts

Creation

Partnership should be created by contract

Partnerships should be created by express contract where the parties clearly indicate in writing the nature of the rights and obligations between them. Many of the provisions of partnership acts that deal with the relationship between the partners can be modified by agreement. Considerable deliberation and negotiation should be devoted to determining just what changes should be made. For example, under the *Partnership Act* all partners have an equal share of the decision-making power, and are entitled to an equal share of

Some provisions of partnership can be modified by contract

Figure 7.2 Partnership Relationship

---

[3] *Partnership Act*, R.S.O. 1990, c. P.5, s.2

the profits. This can be modified to create different classes of partners, with the senior partners having more control and receiving a greater share of the profits. The provisions of the Acts will apply, unless the partners have agreed otherwise.

Partnership acts govern relations between partners where there is no contract

Case Summary 7.2 *Backman v. Canada*[4]

The Name Alone Will Not Create a Partnership

Although this is a taxation case, basic partnership law determines its outcome. Mr. Backman got together with several other Canadians and through a series of transactions became the assignees of the interests of certain American partners who had been carrying on a money-losing venture with respect to the construction of an apartment complex in Texas. They also acquired a small interest in a failed oil and gas property. The idea was to have those losses flow through to the Canadian partners who could then use the partnership losses against their personal income for Canadian income tax purposes.

But the Supreme Court of Canada determined that they were not a partnership and so were not entitled to claim the losses in Canada. To claim these losses through a partnership they had to qualify as a partnership under provincial or territorial law in Canada. To do that the individuals must show that they are 1) carrying on a business, 2) in common, and 3) with a view towards profit. It is not necessary that a new business be involved nor that it be a long-term undertaking. It could be limited to only one short-term project, but here the apartment building was sold and there was no "continuity

of business." The major problem was with the requirement that it be undertaken with a view towards profit. This project was clearly not undertaken to obtain a profit but just the opposite. By examining the intention of the parties it was clear that the activity was undertaken to claim the losses for Canadian income tax purposes and that does not satisfy the provincial requirement for the creation of a partnership in Canada. It is not necessary that profits have actually been made, only that that was an object of the project. Even if making a profit was only a secondary consideration that would be enough, but here claiming the American losses was the sole purpose of the endeavour. Merely calling yourselves a partnership isn't enough to satisfy the legal definition of a partnership, although it may impose liability on the parties who so claim. In this case because there was no objective of making a profit there was no partnership created and the tax losses could not be claimed. Although this is a tax case it nicely underlines the three elements necessary for a partnership to arise: that a business be involved, that it be carried on in common, and with a view toward profit.

A contract, whether it is expressed or implied, is not necessary for the creation of a partnership. The definition in the Act simply requires that the parties work together in some business where they are trying to make a profit. Such a relationship can be created inadvertently. What has to be determined is what constitutes carrying on business and when is that done in common. Normally, one event, such as a group of students getting together to put on a dance or party, will not constitute carrying on a business. But if that group of students promotes a series of dances and they do it for profit, then they are engaged in the business of promoting dances, and a partnership has been created. This has important consequences in terms of liability for those students. Note that when large companies band together to participate jointly in a particular project, such as developing a mine or an oil well, that will be enough to constitute carrying on a partnership, even though it is only for the one project.

Partnership can be created inadvertently

Carrying on business together can create a partnership

A court will usually find that individuals are carrying on the business in common where it can be shown that the parties have contributed to the capital necessary to carry

---

[4] [2001] 1 S.C.R. 367; (2001), 196 D.L.R. (4th) 193 (SCC).

on the business, and where they each participate and have a say in the management of the business, or where they will share in the profits from the enterprise. **Profit**, as used here, means the net proceeds of the business after expenses have been deducted. The sharing of fees (gross receipts) is not enough. For example, if a lawyer were to kick back a given percentage of what she was paid for transferring property to the real estate agent who referred a client to her, this might be unethical, but it would not by itself establish a partnership. But if the lawyer paid over a given percentage of her profits (after expenses have been deducted), that would be evidence of a partnership. The *Partnership Act* specifically lists a number of activities that by themselves will not establish a partnership. For example, sharing rental profit from a jointly owned property, or an employee commission or bonus based on the performance of a business, will not cause the person being paid to be considered a partner in the business.

It should also be noted that the liability of a partnership will be imposed on a person who represents himself or allows himself to be held out as a partner. If an accountant introduces his friend to a client, referring to him as his partner in circumstances where it is reasonable for the client to believe that there is a business relationship between them, and the friend does not correct the statement, that friend will not be able to deny it later if the client sues him as a partner. This is an example of the principle of estoppel, which was explained in the previous chapter in the discussion relating to the apparent authority of an agent (see p. 132). Note that this doesn't create a partnership; it simply prevents individuals called partners from denying it for liability purposes.

Sharing profits indicates partnership

But note exceptions listed in Partnership Act

Representation of partnership can create liability

Case Summary 7.3 *Brown Economic Assessments Inc. v. Stevenson*[5]

Allowing Yourself to Be Called a Partner Imposes Liability

Cara Brown, the president of Brown Economic Assessments Inc., was in the business of providing economic consulting services. This included estimates of lost income with respect to accident victims and the like. She met with R. L. Stevenson in Edmonton and he represented himself as a senior partner and litigator in the firm of "Stevenson Gillis Hjelte Tangjerd, Barristers and Solicitors" of Saskatoon and he showed her a letterhead and business card to that effect. There was also subsequent correspondence between them under that letterhead. Ms. Brown agreed to and did provide her consulting service to him but was not paid and brought this action against all of the partners for an amount outstanding of $23 242 plus costs and interest. Stevenson by the time of the trial was bankrupt and so the question dealt with the liability of the other partners for the services Stevenson had obtained. But those alleged partners all claimed that there was no partnership. The trial judge found that in fact there was no partnership, but that these individuals had allowed themselves "unwittingly" to be held out as partners by Stevenson because of the letterhead. In fact they were a group of lawyers sharing office space, but they maintained separate trust accounts, didn't carry on their business in common, and did not share any profits net or gross. On appeal the court found that both at common law and under the relevant section of the Saskatchewan *Partnership Act* where these individuals had allowed themselves to be held out as partners as was the case here based on the letterhead and other communications between the parties, then they were estopped or prevented from denying that they were partners and were liable to pay the debt incurred by Stevenson. Even if there is no partnership between individuals this case shows the danger of allowing yourself to be called a partner. As was the case with agency where you knowingly permit someone to think that a person is your partner, you cannot later deny that he was your partner.

---

[5] [2003] 11 W.W.R. 101; (2003), 233 Sask. R. 149 (SKQB).

Liability of Partners

Each partner is responsible for the debts and obligations of the partnership. This includes obligations based on tort, breach of trust, or contract. Each partner is vicariously liable for the torts of employees and other partners that are committed in association with the partnership business. If one partner carelessly injures a pedestrian while delivering documents, the other partners will also be responsible for those injuries. When one partner commits a breach of trust, such as diverting money she is holding in trust for a client for her own use, the other partners are equally responsible. And with respect to contracts, each partner is considered an agent of the other partners, so that any contract entered into by one partner with respect to the partnership business is binding on them all. If one partner in a flower store business purchases flowers from a distributor, the other partners are parties to that contract as well and liable under it, even though they may not have authorized the purchase and have no knowledge of the transaction. This liability is unlimited. Just as with the sole proprietor, the debts of the partnership are the debts of the individual partners.

All partners are liable for all debts and obligations of partnership

Liability of partners unlimited

Case Summary 7.4 *McDonic et al. v. Hetherington et al.*[6]

Other Partners Are Liable for Their Partner's Negligence

Watt was a partner in a law firm and lost money on several imprudent investments he made for two elderly sisters. When they died, their estate sued all of the partners for the money lost. Watt had used the firm's trust accounts to transfer the money; the partners were aware of the investments; the other partners sometimes signed the cheques; and some of the money was loaned to employees and their relatives. As a result, the court found that the investments were made as part of the partnership business, and all partners were liable for the loss.

If the resources of the partnership business are not enough to meet its obligations, each partner will be required to pay them out of his or her personal assets. If the business fails, the partners will not only lose their business but may lose their homes, cars, and other personal assets to satisfy the claims of the creditors. In the example where a partner injures a pedestrian while carrying out company business, if the injuries are significant and there is inadequate insurance, it is quite likely that all the partners would have to pay from their personal assets. If there are several partners and only one of them has assets, that partner will be required to pay the entire claim and will be left with the hollow hope of collecting from the others as their circumstances improve. Thus, it is vitally important that business people exercise great care in choosing partners who are trustworthy and financially sound. The great danger about unlimited liability in partnership is that one partner will not only be liable for his or her own mistakes but also completely responsible for the mistakes of the other partners and employees as well.

Personal assets are at risk for partnership debts and liabilities

While many of the provisions of the *Partnership Act* can be modified by the partners, terms that relate to their liability to outsiders cannot be changed. Thus, the partners could set out a term in their partnership agreement that a particular partner would only be

Unlimited liability unaffected by partnership agreement

---

[6] (1997), 142 D.L.R. (4th) 648 (Ont. C.A.).

responsible for 15 percent of any losses. But if a customer, creditor, or outsider had a claim of, for example, $50 000 against the partnership, and the other partners had no funds, that partner could be required to pay the entire $50 000, despite the provision of the agreement to the contrary.

A new partner coming into the partnership will not be responsible for prior debts and obligations unless he agrees to take on that responsibility. But a retiring partner is not in as favourable a position. As a general rule he will not be responsible for debts that are incurred after he ceases to be a partner. However, as long as people dealing with the partnership still think that person is a partner, he will be liable to them on the basis of apparent authority. Every partner is an agent of every other partner. For this reason it is vitally important that the retiring partner provide notification to others that he has left. This usually requires specific notification to current customers, suppliers, and clients as well as a public notice of the retirement published in a newspaper or trade publication. Even then if there are ongoing obligations that continue after he leaves, that retiring partner is still obligated. A lease with a term extending beyond his retirement is a good example. It is a good idea to get the remaining partners to agree to indemnify the retiring partner for any obligations that arise after he leaves.

It is usually this threat of unlimited liability that persuades business people to avoid the partnership model of doing business and to incorporate. But much of the liability risk associated with partnership can be overcome by acquiring sufficient insurance coverage. As will be seen below, often the advantage of limited liability found in corporations is more of a myth than reality. Also, there is a growing trend to use limited partnerships and the newly developed **limited liability partnerships** to overcome this liability problem. These modified partnerships will be discussed below.

The Partner Relationship   Even though some terms of the *Partnership Act* can be modified in a partnership agreement, it is the relationship between the partners and their rights and obligations to each other as set out in the *Partnership Act* that makes partnership unique. With respect to the day-to-day operation of the business, a majority vote prevails, but one of the most significant features of a partnership is that no major decisions can be made without unanimous agreement of the partners. Where a decision must be made to admit a new partner, to borrow or invest money, to dissolve the partnership, or to embark on some new business venture—even if only one partner out of 10 opposes the decision—that one veto will prevail. All partners are equal. They share the profits equally; they have equal access to the partnership books and records; and they all share in the management of the partnership with an equal say in its operation. Because partners carry on business together, they cannot earn a salary from the business. Each partner is entitled to an equal share of the profits, and arrangements are usually made so that they will take a monthly draw against those profits. An end-of-the-year adjustment is then made so that the draws equal each partner's profit entitlement. Any expenses incurred should also be repaid before the profits are determined.

One of the most important features with respect to partners' obligations is the special duty owed by each partner to the others. Partners are agents of each other and as such owe a fiduciary duty to their principal (the other partners) as was discussed in Chapter 6. They must act in the best interest of the partnership, even to the extent of putting the interests of the partnership business ahead of their own. Thus they can't take advantage of business opportunities that come to them because of their position, but must make them available to the partnership. If a partner in a real estate agency learns of a particularly good deal on commercial property, she must bring it to the partnership rather than make the investment alone. If she fails to do this and makes a profit on the deal, she may be required to pay over that profit to the partnership. If she loses money, the losses are hers alone. Similarly, the partner must disclose any **conflict of interest**; avoid competition with the partnership; not use any partnership property for her own purposes; and properly account for all expenses, income, and benefits received. Of course, where one partner sets out to cheat others, she will be subject to damages and other civil remedies. In serious cases of intentional fraud, she may also be subject to criminal prosecution and the imposition of significant fines or imprisonment. This applies whether she is committing that fraud against a fellow partner or a client.

Case Summary 7.5 *Schmidt v. Peat Marwick Thorne*[7]

Consequences of Breaching Fiduciary Duty to Partnership

Mr. Schmidt worked as a partner in the Abbotsford accounting firm of Peat Marwick Thorne, when he informed the partnership that he wanted to retire and help his sons on their farms. The partnership agreement notice period was reduced considerably and the firm agreed to pay out Mr. Schmidt over $125 000 for goodwill from a previous merger, $65 000 work in progress, a $55 800 "disposition fee" payable over five years, and a two-year consulting contract to cover the transition. The agreement also included a term that if he did enter into practice again the "disposition fee would not be payable," but that there would be no other ramifications.

In fact, he never did intend to retire but had arranged to join another accounting firm, Ernst and Young, and take his clients with him. He eventually took 65 clients with him and had actually been soliciting several other accountants of the firm to go with him during the time he had been negotiating the early retirement agreement. The firm learned of his plans just after he left and stopped payment on the cheques they had issued. Schmidt brought this action to enforce the early retirement contract. The court held that Schmidt had misled the firm when he had

negotiated the early retirement contract and therefore it was voidable. He was entitled to negotiate an early retirement contract, but not to mislead his partners in the process. Peat Marwick Thorne was within its rights to rescind the agreement on the basis of the misrepresentation and so that contract no longer applied. Under the Peat Marwick Thorne partnership agreement that now applied, a withdrawing partner was not entitled to any payment for goodwill but could take clients with them upon payment of a 75% fee of the last year's fees for those clients.

Schmidt was entitled to leave and take his clients with him upon paying this standard 75% fee but he was not entitled to the terms that had been obtained through misrepresentation. He not only lost the money he had negotiated upon leaving but also had to pay 75% of the fees earned from the clients he took with him (75% of $175 000). In total he lost over $300 000. In this case Schmidt had breached both his common law fiduciary duty and that imposed by the *Partnership Act* to act toward his partners with utmost fairness and good faith.

This is the default position as set out in the *Partnership Act*, but it is often modified by agreement. The importance of a carefully negotiated partnership agreement cannot be overemphasized. **Partnership agreements** are often used to create different classes of

Relations between partners can be modified by agreement

---

[7] B.C. S.C., Aug. 18/92, as reported in J. Spencer, "Didn't retire but joined rival, accountant liable to B.C. firm," *Lawyers Weekly* 12 no. 18 (September 11 1992).

partners so that they are no longer equal. Senior partners will have a greater say in the operation of the business. Also, a partner's right to an equal share of profits may be modified by agreement. In a partnership of 8, for example, the two senior partners may be entitled to 20 percent of the profits each, while the six junior partners would only be entitled to 10 percent. Partnership agreements often contain terms restricting a partner's authority to act on behalf of the partnership and limiting their responsibility for losses. It is important to remember that these provisions only give rights to compensation from each other after claims by outsiders have been satisfied. The partnership agreement will not affect the rights of the people with whom the partners are dealing. Other provisions often included in partnership agreements establish the contribution expected from each partner in terms of capital and service, the maintenance and access to books and accounts, how disputes between the partners are to be resolved, provisions relating to the retirement of partners, and the dissolution of the partnership.

It should also be noted that the same tax considerations apply to the partnership as with the sole proprietor. Because the income of the partnership business is also the income of the partners, they must pay taxes on it at their personal rate. For this reason many professionals create separate corporations to provide services to the practice. While they may not be able to incorporate the actual practice of their profession, they create a corporation to handle the rental or ownership of property; to employ secretaries, managers, and other staff; and to rent or purchase the equipment needed. The partnership pays a fee to the corporation for these services. The shareholders of the service corporation can be the partners' spouse or other family members, thus effectively splitting income for tax purposes.

Dissolution

Partnership dissolves upon death or bankruptcy

Under the partnership acts a partnership is dissolved automatically upon the death or bankruptcy/insolvency of a partner. Where there are more than two partners this can have disastrous consequences for the business. This is one of the areas where the provisions of the partnership acts vary from province to province. For example, in British Columbia when there are more than two partners and one of them dies or becomes bankrupt, the partnership only dissolves with respect to that one partner, but the firm continues.[8] In Ontario, where there are more than two partners and one dies the whole partnership dissolves in the event of the "death or insolvency of a partner."[9] In fact, just what will cause a partnership to be dissolved is one of the most important provisions of the *Partnership Act* that is normally modified in a partnership agreement. Usually, the partners will agree that the partnership will not dissolve except with respect to that one partner, and they will arrange sufficient insurance to pay out the claims of that partner or his or her estate. The partnership agreement will also normally specify under what conditions the partnership will dissolve, how much notice should be given when one partner wants to leave or retire, and what are the rights and obligations are of the partner who is leaving.

[8] *Partnership Act*, R.S.B.C. 1996, c. 348, s. 36.1.b.

[9] *Partnership Act*, R.S.O. 1990, c. P. 5, s. 33.1.

Case Summary 7.6 *Ernst & Young v. Stuart* [10]

Non-Competition Clause Unreasonable, but 12 Months Notice Requirement Is Okay

Mr. Stuart was a partner in the accounting firm of Ernst and Young and had worked for that firm (and its predecessor) for 14 years when he was persuaded to leave and join the rival accounting firm of Arthur Andersen and associates. The Ernst and Young partnership agreement provided that upon leaving a partner had to give 12 months notice and could not compete with the firm for a radius of 50 miles for a one-year period. Ernst and Young sued Mr. Stuart for breach of contract and Arthur Andersen for inducing breach of contract. At trial, the notice period and the non-competition clause were both found to be an unreasonable restraint of trade and unenforceable. The problem was that the non-competition clause prevented Stuart from acting in his practice within 50 miles of the financial heart of Vancouver. Because he was an insolvency specialist this effectively prevented him from practicing in the province of British Columbia. On appeal the court determined that while the non-competition clause was an unreasonable restraint of trade, the 12 months required notice upon leaving was a valid term of the contract and Mr. Stuart was in breach. Since his agreement

with Arthur Andersen clearly provided that he was to be compensated for any damages he had to pay for breaching his contract, it was clear that they had knowingly encouraged him to breach his partnership agreement with Ernst and Young.

The matter was sent back to trial to determine damages to be paid by Stuart and Arthur Andersen, but for our purposes the case illustrates that although a partnership can normally be dissolved upon giving notice to the other partners, that provision can be overridden by a partnership agreement, which will prevail. In this case because these two firms were "mega partnerships," minor partners like Stuart had very little say in what the terms of that partnership agreement would be. The court took this into consideration in determining that the non-competition clause was unreasonable, preventing him in effect from working in his profession. Partners have to be very careful as to what they include in such agreements. This is also a good example of the tort action of inducing breach of contract, which applies to inducing breach of partnership agreements as well as other forms of contracts.

The normal way for a partnership to dissolve is simply by one partner serving notice to that effect on the others. Of course, if the partnership was created for a specific period of time or for a particular project, the completion of the specified time or project will also cause the partnership to dissolve. It will also dissolve if the activity becomes illegal or a court orders it to be dissolved. This normally happens where there has been misconduct, breach of the partnership agreement, or where one partner becomes incapable of fulfilling his or her partnership obligations. Partnership agreements will often state that a certain amount of notice must be given or that dissolution will only take place with the agreement of all partners. When one disgruntled partner wants to leave with shorter notice or despite the fact there is no agreement, the only way to do is this is to obtain the consent of the other partners, or failing that have the court dissolve the partnership. However, the courts are reluctant to interfere with partnership agreements in the absence of some other wrongdoing or incapacity.

When the partnership is dissolved, all of the firm's resources must be devoted to paying the debts and liabilities of the partnership. If there are not enough funds, the individual partners will be required to use their own personal resources to meet those obligations. Where there are excess funds, they are first used to pay back expenses incurred by the partners. Then the partners will divide the capital, assets, and excess profits equally among them or according to the terms of the partnership agreement.

Partnership dissolves upon notice

Partnership dissolves upon court order

Assets first go to pay off liabilities and expenses

Assets are then divided equally or as per the agreement

---

[10] (1997), 144 D.L.R. (4th) 328, [1997] 5 W.W.R. 253, (B.C.C.A.).

Case Summary 7.7 *Kucher v. Moore*[11]

When Partners Lose Trust in One Another

Moore was a dentist who was suspended from practice when he became seriously depressed, overbilled his patients, and failed to keep proper records. He and his partner had acquired disability insurance with the understanding that any payments would go to the partnership. But Moore misled his partner, claiming the benefits received were only $19 000 per year, when in fact he was receiving $90 000 per year. Upon application to the court by his partner, the partnership was dissolved,

and Moore was ordered to pay over half of the proceeds from the disability insurance. Any property included on the partnership books was also to be divided between them. Although the partnership agreement did not allow for it to be dissolved upon notice, the court always has the power to dissolve a partnership when it is "just and equitable to do so." Here the fraud and deceit destroyed the trust required for a partnership to continue.

Limited Partners

An important similarity between a partnership and a corporation is that the partnership can sue or be sued in the name of the business, but unlike a corporation, each partner is individually responsible for the debt. It is this characteristic of unlimited liability that separates partnerships and sole proprietorships from corporations. Still there are two ways that limited liability can come about in a partnership arrangement.

Limited liability refers to an investor's risk of losing only the amount invested. Thus a shareholder in a corporation can lose what he or she has paid for shares, but is not responsible otherwise for the debts and liabilities of the corporation. This same protection is available to a limited partner. Limited partners are essentially investors in the partnership who don't actually take part in the partnership business. If they do participate in the management, they will lose their status as limited partners and risk the same unlimited liability as the other general partners.

The following requirements must be met for such a limited partnership to be created:

- there must be at least one general partner in the firm,
- the limited partnership must be registered as such with the appropriate government agency, and
- the name of the limited partner must not be listed as part of the name of the partnership business.

This allows individuals to invest in the partnership business without assuming any responsibility. But limited partners are in a precarious position and can easily lose their limited liability status by participating in the partnership or failing to meet one of the other qualifications. Often, through carelessness, the limited partnership will not be properly registered. Also, when the business gets into trouble there is a great temptation for the limited partner to get involved. By doing so the limited partner becomes a general partner with unlimited liability.

Typically limited partnerships will involve one general partner, often a corporation, and several limited partners, each holding shares (called units) in the business. When the business fails the general partner will be liable for all debts and obligation that are

Limited liability given to limited partners if:
- They don't take part in management
- There is one general partner
- The limited partnership is registered

The name of the limited partner is not included in the firm name

[11] (1991), 3 B.L.R. 50 (Ont. Gen. Div).

not satisfied by the assets of the partnership. If that general partner is a corporation that has been incorporated for that purpose there will normally not be any additional assets available beyond those already contributed by the partners. The obligation of the limited partner is limited to the unit share already paid (if it is still owing it must be paid to satisfy the creditors). The limited partner will have no further obligation unless they have assumed some additional obligation such as signing as a guarantor or signing a promissory note. For tax reasons these agreements often contain a provision subjecting the limited partner to the payment of further funds if required by the business. This defeats the limited liability objective of a limited partnership. The investor should exercise great care to read the contract carefully before investing, and then be careful to avoid the pitfalls that could change the status of a limited partner to a general partner.

Limited partner can become general partner with unlimited liability

A limited partnership can be a very effective method of carrying on business for even large projects. A few years ago PWA (the parent of Canadian Airlines), Air Canada, and Covia (an affiliate of United Airlines) entered into a partnership as limited partners with Gemini as general partner. Gemini was a corporation owned by the limited partners. This was set up to create an automated joint booking operation, which unfortunately was not successful, but does illustrate that even large operations can be constructed this way.

Case Summary 7.8 *Haughton Graphic Ltd. v. Zivot et al.*[12]

When Limited Partners Lose Their Protection

Zivot and another individual were limited partners in *Printcraft* (a new magazine) with Lifestyle Magazine Inc., which had been incorporated so that it could be the only general partner. Zivot was also the president of Lifestyle Magazine Inc. and as such played an active role in controlling the business of *Printcraft*. Houghton was an unpaid supplier and sought payment directly from Zivot. The court held that under the Alberta *Partnership Act*, Zivot lost his limited partnership status when he participated in the *Printcraft* business. It didn't matter that he was acting as an employee of Lifestyle or even if he had informed the suppliers that he was a limited partner. Because he was taking part in the control of the *Printcraft* business, he lost his status as a limited partner and was liable as a general partner. This case shows the nature of a limited partner and how easily that status can be lost.

Limited Liability Partnership

Because professionals face much broader and more extensive liability for their mistakes, they have brought pressure on government to pass legislation reducing the unlimited liability feature of partnerships. Since professionals are not allowed to obtain limited liability through incorporation, most provinces have passed legislation permitting the formation of limited liability partnerships. To create such a firm, the partners need only enter into an agreement designating the relationship as a limited liability partnership and stating that the Act relating to limited liability partnerships governs the agreement. Also, the name of the partnership must be registered and must end with the words "Limited Liability Partnership" (LLP). It must be stressed that only members of professional organizations governed by a separate statute such as Ontario's *Law Society Act* are eligible, and then only where the organization

Most provinces allow limited liability partnership

Must be registered and use LLP designation

Must be permitted by professional organization and have insurance

---

[12] Ont. S.C.J., as reported in *Lawyers Weekly Consolidated Digest*, Vol. 6 (May 1986).

permits its members to carry on business as limited liability partnerships. Those organizations must also require their members to maintain a minimum amount of liability insurance.

Carrying on business as a limited liability partnership protects a partner from liability for the negligent acts or omissions of the other partners. Where one partner, or a person supervised by him, acts negligently, that partner will still be personally liable to compensate the victim. Essentially, the partner acting negligently is in the same position as any partner in a normal partnership faced with unlimited liability to compensate. All of his personal assets are exposed to risk, but the other partners will not be responsible for that partner's negligence. In this sense their liability is limited to their own negligence, not that of their partners. Thus, if one accountant makes a mistake with respect to an audit and causes significant losses to investors, only that one partner, along with his insurers, will be required to compensate the victims. In this way the risk faced by professionals doing business in professional partnerships is considerably lessened. But some would argue that it defeats the whole principle of professional responsibility. Finally, it should be noted that in some provinces professionals have been given the right to incorporate, but these professional corporations do not grant the professional the limited liability that would be present in a standard corporation. They do, however, allow the professional all of the tax and other benefits associated with the incorporation process.

Negligent partner retains unlimited liability

But other partners are not liable

Where professional incorporations allowed, they don't give limited liability

CORPORATIONS

The essential thing to remember about corporations is that they are artificial creations of government, which have no existence in reality. It is merely a convenient legal fiction that is properly referred to as the corporate myth. A sole proprietor consists of one legal personality—the sole proprietor. Likewise, a partnership is not a legal person separate from the partners. But if there are 10 shareholders in a corporation there are 11 legal personalities—the 10 shareholders and the corporation itself. The corporation is considered a legal person, separate and apart from the shareholders that make it up. It is in that last legal personality—the corporation—that we find the corporate myth or the legal fiction. It is an artificial legal personality recognized by the courts and all other official bodies as well as the various elements of our business communities, but in reality it has no existence separate from its parts (see Figure 7.3).

The first business corporations were created by royal charter to deal with large trading expeditions that required many investors. Incorporation proved a popular and efficient way to do business, and eventually smaller corporations were formed and used in regular business activities. In fact, there are many such legal entities in our society, including cities, universities, and societies as well as banks, trust companies, and special act companies such as the Canadian Broadcasting Corporation (CBC) and the Canadian National Railroad (CNR). We will concentrate our discussion on closely-held and broadly-held corporations that ordinary business people can use to carry on their business. Still, much of what is said is applicable to all of these various legal entities.

A corporation is a legal fiction

But recognized by the courts as a separate legal person

Corporations have been created by royal charter

Corporations have been created by special act

Figure 7.3 Corporate Relationships

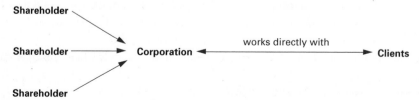

Creation

In Canada these corporations can be created either under the federal or various provincial and territorial statutes. There are three different methods used to incorporate. Nova Scotia still uses the registration method of incorporation where a **memorandum of association** and **articles of association** are submitted to the appropriate government agency, which in turn issues a certificate of registration recognizing the corporation. Quebec and Prince Edward Island are the only provinces still using the **letters patent** method of incorporation. Upon application by subscribers, letters patent are issued, thus granting a charter creating a corporation. Most provinces and the federal government have adopted the American approach where incorporation is accomplished by the filing of **articles of incorporation** and the issuance of a certificate of incorporation by the appropriate government agency.

These incorporating documents, in most provinces called articles of incorporation, are essentially the constitution of the company setting out such things as the name, the registered office, and the share structure, which includes different classes of shares, the number and power of directors, and any restriction on the types of business that can be engaged in. In addition, each corporation creates bylaws (unfortunately also called articles in British Columbia and Nova Scotia) setting out the normal operating rules of the company, such as the notice required and procedures for an annual shareholders' meeting, the responsibilities of directors and officers, and the management organization of the company. Note that it is at this initial stage of incorporation that shareholders will often enter into a shareholders' agreement. Such agreements can be extremely important and are described below.

No matter what method of incorporation is used, the outcome is essentially the same: the creation of a corporation that is a separate legal entity from the members that make it up. This has developed into an extremely efficient method of doing business, both on a large and on a small scale. In all jurisdictions the basic structures, including rights and responsibilities of directors, officers, and shareholders and the methods of financing, are the same. Although incorporation in one jurisdiction allows the corporation to carry on business in others, a registration fee must be paid to do so. For this reason incorporation should take place in the jurisdiction where the business will be carried out, or federally, which allows the corporation to carry on business in any province.

Structure

Business corporations can be either **broadly-held** or **closely-held**. Broadly-held corporations are also referred to as reporting, public, or offering corporations. A private or closely-held corporation is more like an incorporated partnership with only a few shareholders. Such a business is likely to be small. The directors, officers, shareholders, and managers are likely to be the same people, and the reporting and accounting requirements are much simpler and less stringent. It is in these smaller corporations where a shareholders' agreement becomes so important (much like a partnership agreement as discussed above). Closely-held corporations also have restrictions placed on the free transferability of shares. Usually the shareholder will have to sell the shares to current shareholders or get permission from the directors to sell them to someone else. These closely-held corporations may be small in size, but that doesn't not mean they are insignificant. All small business

Federal or provincial companies

Creation by registration

Creation through letters patent

Creation through articles of incorporation

Result is creation of separate legal person

A company incorporated in one province may register to do business in another

Closely-held corporations are smaller with fewer regulatory controls

Closely-held corporations have restrictions on transfer of shares

corporations come under this umbrella and even some very large concerns, including companies with household names, are often owned and controlled by holding companies that are closely held.

Broadly-held corporations are larger and more regulated

A broadly-held corporation has many more regulations and controls that must be met. The rules relating to the protection of shareholders' rights, the responsibilities of directors, the requirements for annual meetings, and the reporting requirements are much more stringent. These larger corporations are generally traded on the stock market, which imposes even more regulations.

Shareholders

Shareholders are separate from corporation

Shareholders control corporations through their votes

The membership of the corporation is made up of **shareholders**. While they are separate from the corporation itself, they have very significant rights with respect to control of the corporation. Shareholders have the right to vote in shareholder meetings, and their vote controls what happens in the corporation. The supervision of the management and operation of the corporation is controlled by the **directors**, who are chosen by a vote of the shareholders, usually at an annual general meeting. The shareholders have a vote based on the number of shares that they have. For example, one shareholder holding 200 shares would outvote 10 other shareholders holding 10 shares each. The majority shareholder in a corporation has ultimate control, and the minority shareholder has very little say in the operation of the corporation. This is sometimes referred to as the tyranny of the majority. In fact, in broadly held corporations the shareholders will likely not actually attend the shareholders' meeting but will give representatives their right to vote, which is called a **proxy**. The exercise of those proxies allows a few individuals who have gained the confidence of the shareholders the power to control the meeting and choose the directors and vote on the various proposals presented. In closely-held corporations, where the shareholders are also likely to be directors and officers and are continually in contact with each other, an actual shareholders' meeting does not have to take place. They just have to report that they did as they file their annual report. Still the majority shareholder is in control.

Majority rules

Common shareholders have the right to vote and to dividends, once declared

In a corporation different classes of shareholders can be created, giving different rights and restrictions with respect to the shares. These usually take the form of preferred and common shares. **Common shares** normally give the right to exercise control of the corporation through voting and to share in **dividends** when they are declared. Dividends are the method used to dispense the profits of the corporation to the shareholders. If the directors choose to pay out these profits rather than use them for other company purposes, they make a declaration to that effect, and the shareholders receive a payment based on the number of shares they hold. The shareholders also have the right to see certain documents, including financial statements and the company's annual report. It is also possible to create special shares with unique rights and restrictions. Holders of **preferred shares** usually are denied voting rights, but have a commitment from the company to receive a specific dividend payment each year. It should be noted that whether preferred or common shares are involved, there is no legal right to a dividend; the shareholder cannot sue if a dividend is not declared and paid. The best that the preferred shareholder can do is to demand to be paid the promised dividend before a dividend is paid to the common shareholders. If the promised dividend is not paid to the preferred shareholder that will typically trigger other rights such as giving the preferred shareholder a right to vote along with the common shareholders.

Preferred shareholders have no right to vote but are promised a regular dividend

Shareholders have no legal right to a dividend

But where no dividend is paid, other rights can be acquired by the preferred shareholder

Separate Legal Person

The key to appreciating the nature of a corporation is to understand the consequences of it having a separate legal personality. A corporation has the same powers of a natural person to carry on business. It can employ others, it can be an agent, and it can even be a partner. Since it is an artificial creation without a body, everything it does is done through agents. Because of this, and the limited liability principle discussed below, it is important that those dealing with it understand they are dealing with an incorporated entity and those behind it have limited liability. Any contracts or other dealings should include a clear indication that those contracting are dealing with the corporation and not the person representing it. The corporate name must be clearly indicated and must include the designation that it is a limited company (such as "ltd." or "corp." set out at the end of the company name). Failure to do so can lead to the loss of that limited liability as indicated in the following case.

A corporation is a separate legal person

A corporation has the same powers and capacity of a natural person

---

Case Summary 7.9 *Race-Way Construction & Management Ltd. v. Barker-Taylor*[13]
Limited Liability Can Be Easily Lost

Race-Way entered into a contract to renovate space in a mall with the "RBT Group of Companies." Payment was delayed and after some negotiation a different company, "345257 Ltd.," the lessee of the property where the work was done, issued a promissory note to them, which was also dishonoured. They were paid some funds from yet another company, but eventually they were still owed $27 441 when they sued Mr. Barker-Taylor and Mr. Shinyei personally for the amount owing. They were the principals (directors and shareholders) behind 345257 Ltd. and the parties Race-Way had dealt with. In fact RBT group didn't exist, either as an entity or as an incorporated company. It was just a convenient "handle" given to a group of companies that were carrying on business under that umbrella.

The court found that the provision of the B.C. *Company Act* required that whenever an incorporated business operated it had to do so in its own name indicating that it was a limited company. ". . . every company or extra-provincial company must display its name in legible characters . . . on all its contracts, business letters, and orders for goods, and on its invoices, statements of accounts, receipts and letters of credit." The act went on to impose personal liability on officers or directors who knowingly fail to do this. On the basis of this section the court determined that Mr. Barker-Taylor and Mr. Shinyei were personally liable for the amount still owing. The fact that Race-Way eventually accepted a promissory note from 345257 Ltd. didn't absolve them of that liability, since it took place after the original contract had been created and the work had been completed. Although this case dealt with the application of a section of the B.C. *Company Act*, the same result would have been likely in any jurisdiction since all require that, to obtain the protection of a limited liability corporation, it must be made clear to those being dealt with that they are dealing with the corporation and that there is limited liability.

Normally, there is no problem with a corporation having the capacity to contract since in all jurisdictions they now have been given all of the capacity of a natural person to contract. A word of caution, however: in the case of special act corporations (ones created by a special act of Parliament, such as the CBC or CN), it may be possible that they have restricted capacity. If you have dealings with such bodies and the transactions

Capacity may be limited with special act companies

---

[13] 2003 BCCA 163, 11 B.C.L.R. (4th) 304, 24 C.L.R. (3d) 76, 297 W.A.C. 113 (B.C.C.A.).

seem strange it would be wise to check the legislation and make sure it has the capacity to do what its representative has proposed. The same caution should be exercised with banks, trust companies, trade unions, insurance companies, as well as government agencies and departments. Of course, since all dealings with a corporation are through agents, people should always ensure the agent has been given the appropriate authority to act.

Agents acting for corporations may have limited power

Limited Liability

Shareholders are not liable for the debts and liabilities of the corporation

Perhaps the most important consequence of the separate legal entity status of the corporation is limited liability. Since the corporation is a separate legal personality, any debts, liabilities, or other obligations of the corporation are those of the corporation itself, not the shareholders. This was established by a famous case, *Salomon v. Salomon & Co.*[14] Mr. Salomon operated a shoe business, which he subsequently incorporated with himself holding all but a few shares. He then sold the assets of the business to the corporation and became a secured creditor for the debt. The business ran into financial difficulties and the creditors turned to Salomon for payment. The court held that the debts were those of the corporation, not Mr. Salomon, and that only the corporation was responsible for payment. Thus, Mr. Salomon had limited liability. To make matters worse for those creditors, Salomon as a separate person could also be a creditor, and as a secured creditor, he had first claim on the remaining assets of the corporation ahead of those other creditors.

Shareholders have limited liability

Court may lift corporate veil where there is crime or fraud

Limited liability then means that the debts, liabilities, and other obligations of the corporation remain with the corporation. In normal circumstances they will not be imposed on the shareholders, directors, or other participants in the corporate business. But it is always important to remember that the **separate legal person** aspect of the corporation is a myth or fiction created for the convenience of doing business. As a result, in rare circumstances, the courts are willing to look behind the corporate structure (lift the corporate veil) and impose liability on the shareholders directly. This approach is usually restricted to situations where the corporation is being used by the shareholder to commit a crime, fraud, or some other wrong including avoiding obligations of child support or division of assets in a matrimonial dispute. One important advantage of a corporation is that its separate legal personality makes it responsible to pay taxes on its earnings, while the shareholders only have to pay taxes on dividends when declared by the corporation. Because of the lower rates of taxation for smaller corporations, there is sometimes a temptation to create a number of smaller corporations that are taxed at a lower rate than one big one. But this is not permitted, and these corporations can be treated as one for taxation purposes. This is another example of the courts ignoring the separate legal entity status of different corporations when it is being used to accomplish some wrongful purpose. It should be noted that the position of the director is not always as protected as that of a shareholder. Because directors have a more direct involvement in decision-making, they have a significant duty of care to the corporation, and many statutes also hold them directly responsible for the decisions made. Directors' liability will be discussed below.

Several corporations may be treated as one for tax purposes

Directors do not have the same protection as shareholders

---

[14] [1897] A.C. 22 (H.L.).

But the Corporate Veil Can Be Lifted

Mr. Segal is a wealthy man and among other properties is the sole beneficial owner of two corporations that own substantial land in Ontario. He and his wife divorced and as part of the proceeds she obtained a judgment that she was unable to collect on because all of Mr. Segal's assets were offshore or otherwise protected and shielded through a series of holding companies and nominal owners. She located two properties in Ontario owned by corporations controlled by Mr. Segal. The court found that although Mr. Segal was not the actual shareholder of those corporations he was the beneficial owner through a chain of holdings and that the shares were held in trust for him. The court determined that this was an appropriate case to pierce the corporate veil and awarded the lands in question to Mrs. Segal to satisfy the judgment in her favour. The trial judge found that "the limited companies and

Mr. Segal are one and the same" and that "[Mr. Segal] is the beneficial owner of the property." He ordered that the lands be vested to Ms. Lynch (the former Mrs. Segal) in satisfaction of the monetary claims and costs.

The Court of Appeal agreed with the trial judge and in discussing the piercing of the corporate veil they quoted from another judgment.

> In the end, although a business person is entitled to create corporate structures and relationships for valid business, tax and other reasons, *the law must be vigilant to ensure that permissible corporate arrangements do not work an injustice in the realm of family law. In appropriate cases, piercing the corporate veil of one spouse's business enterprises may be an essential mechanism for ensuring that the other spouse and children of the marriage receive the financial support to which, by law, they are entitled.* The trial judge was correct to recognize that this was such a case.[16]

This is a good case to show how fragile the separate existence of a corporation can be where it is being used to accomplish an immoral or otherwise wrongful purpose.

Another consequence of the corporation being a separate legal person is that it doesn't die. Because the company is a fiction, it doesn't die of natural causes like a normal person, although it can be dissolved voluntarily or by court order. As a result, there are many corporations that have been in existence for hundreds of years and are still going strong. The Hudson's Bay Company (the Bay), established over 300 years ago, is an example, as is the Canadian National Railroad (CN). Also the corporation doesn't end when the shareholders die. The shares are merely assets held by the shareholders that are passed down to their heirs. The company carries on. Once issued, shares are assets that can be bought and sold without directly affecting the corporation. This has led to the creation of that venerable institution—the stock market. It is this characteristic of independence from the corporation that makes shares such an attractive tool for investment.

Another effect of the nature of a corporation as a separate legal person is the ability to have management that is separate from the owners or shareholders. In a partnership the partners are the management, but in a corporation a separate management group can be hired to manage the corporation. The management can even be from the shareholders themselves. They can be hired as employees, since unlike a sole proprietor or a partnership the shareholders are separate and independent from the corporation. This management team is answerable to the directors who are, in turn, answerable by election to the shareholders, who maintain ultimate control of the corporation but do not manage it. Note that "ownership" as it is used here is a little misleading. The shareholders don't

Corporation does not die

The corporation does not end with deaths of shareholders

Management and shareholders are separate

Managers are answerable to directors

---

[15] (2006), 277 D.L.R. (4th) 36; (2006), 26 B.L.R. (4th) 14; (2006), 33 R.F.L. (6th) 279; (2006), 219 O.A.C. 1 (ON C.A.).

[16] *Wildman v. Wildman*, [2006] O.J. No. 3966.

technically own the corporation or its assets. The shares only give the shareholder control of the corporation through voting. It is only upon dissolution of the corporation that the shareholder may have a claim to the assets of the company. Note, however, that there is a Supreme Court of Canada decision holding that the shareholder has a sufficient interest in the assets of a corporation to take out insurance and collect in the event of damage.[17]

Such separate management can have a downside as well. Often in large corporations the management side is separate and apart and develops different interests from the shareholders. As a result, it will sometimes act against the best interests of the shareholders to protect its own position. For example, frequently one corporation will attempt to take over another by offering a generous amount for outstanding shares. But the managers of the corporation to be taken over may see this as a threat to their jobs and do what they can to resist, even though the shareholders would be better off with the takeover.

Managers sometimes act against interests of shareholders

Another important result of the shareholders being separate from the company is that it allows the shareholders to carry on their own business activities without reference to the company. A partner has to be careful not to compete with the partnership and to always put the interests of the partnership ahead of his own, but a shareholder has no similar duty to the corporation. A shareholder is free to sell his or her shares, to compete, to hold shares in other similar or competing businesses, to withhold information, and to pursue other business or personal interests that may even be detrimental to the corporation. Only where the shareholder becomes a director, officer, or other employee of the corporation may fiduciary or other duties be imposed. Note also that where a shareholder holds enough shares to be classed as an insider in a publicly traded company, there are also important limitations placed on his or her ability to purchase and sell those shares because of the privileged information the shareholder is presumed to possess. It has been suggested that because shareholders have such extensive rights and benefits with respect to the corporation, they ought to have greater responsibilities as well. This is inconsistent with the historical position of a shareholder and the reasons for the creation of corporation in the first place. Certainly at the time of writing the responsibilities of a shareholder remain minimal.

Shareholders are not required to act in best interests of corporation

Insiders must not act on privileged information

Shareholders' Rights

Although there are very few duties imposed on the shareholder, there are several mechanisms built into the corporate structure designed to protect the interest of the shareholders and their investment. As discussed, shareholders have a right to vote at the annual shareholder meeting and a right to a dividend if one is declared. They also have a right to a share of the assets of the corporation if it is wound up (dissolved). Also they have the right to inspect certain financial and other records of the corporation that are kept at the company's registered office for that purpose. In addition to these rights, there are several mechanisms designed to protect them from abuse. Sometimes the elected directors will make decisions that negatively affect the shareholders (usually a minority shareholder in particular). If the decision involves a major change for the good of the corporation that will have a negative impact on minority shareholders, the minority shareholders may have a right to **dissent** and have their shares purchased by the corporation at a "fair value." Sometimes the directors representing the majority shareholders will make decisions that have a negative impact on both the corporation and the minority shareholders.

Shareholders have:
- *Right to vote*
- *Right to dividend*
- *Right to assets upon dissolution*
- *Right to inspect records*

- *Right to dissent*

---

[17] *Kosmopoulos v. Constitution Insurance Co. of Canada*, [1987] 1 S.C.R. 2 (S.C.C.).

Usually there has been a falling out and the majority shareholders are simply using their power to hurt the minority shareholders. Sometimes the majority shareholder through the directors may strip assets from the company for his own benefit or transfer, sell, or otherwise bestow a benefit onto a company he owns, all at the expense of the corporation and the oppression of minority shareholders. When this happens, the minority shareholder can apply to the court seeking protection from such **oppression**. If the court agrees, there is considerable latitude in what they can do. This includes stopping the offending conduct, compensating the victim, setting aside the offending contract or transaction, or altering its terms. It may also declare that new directors or a receiver be appointed, that terms in the articles or shareholders' agreement be changed, or that the corporation be wound up.[18] Note, as well, that the remedy of oppression is not limited to shareholders but can be brought by any "security holder, creditor, director or officer of the corporation."[19] In recent times the courts have shown more of a reluctance to allow oppression actions by shareholders and thus shareholders are turning more commonly to a representative or derivative action discussed below.

■ Right to be free of oppression

Case Summary 7.11 *Piller Sausages & Delicatessens Ltd. v. Cobb International Corp.*[20]

Actions of the Defendant Were Oppressive to Creditor

Piller Sausages had ordered and paid for a sterilizing machine from Cobb International, which was never delivered. Piller obtained a judgment against Cobb International for $70 299 and sought to recover it. Upon further investigation the principals of Piller learned that after the failure to deliver the machine, Kenneth Cobb of Cobb International had stripped the assets of the company by paying out substantial dividends, paying a sum of money to another company, and transferring assets to a third company all owned by him. A substantial management bonus was also paid to Mr. Cobb, leaving nothing left to satisfy the judgment. Piller brought this action against Cobb International and Kenneth Cobb for oppression.

The court found that oppression was established and held each of the defendants (Kenneth Cobb and the three companies he controlled) jointly and severally liable for the amount of the judgment. The plaintiffs proved oppression when they established that the actions of the defendant Kenneth Cobb in these circumstances amounted to unfair prejudicial conduct against the plaintiff, unfair disregard for the interests of the creditor Piller, and that the owner in control of the corporation had directed its affairs so as to divert the corporation's money to himself and render the corporation unable to pay a judgment debt. Although this case is unusual in that it is a creditor that is bringing the action for oppression, it is a good example of the kind of conduct that will qualify as actionable oppression.

Another way that the interests of a minority shareholder could be adversely affected is through the issuing of more shares. When incorporated, a company will be given authority to issue a large number of shares (authorized share capital) but, in fact, will actually issue only a portion of those shares. The company is free then to raise funds through the issue of more shares in the future. Issuing more shares can have an adverse effect on the position of the present shareholders if the shares are not offered to them first, especially if a closely-held corporation is involved. For example, suppose 10 000 shares have been

---

[18] *Business Corporations Act*, R.S.O. 1990, c. B.16, s. 248.

[19] *Ibid.* s. 207.

[20] 2003 CanLII 35795 (ON S.C.) (2003), 35 B.L.R. (3d) 193.

issued and a minority shareholder holds 4000 of them. If 5000 more shares were issued but not offered to that minority shareholder, his or her share of the company would drop from a 40 percent interest to a 27 percent interest. If there were a number of shareholders, none with a clear majority, the issuing of such shares could completely alter the control structure of the company, depending on to whom they were issued. To prevent this abuse, corporations are allowed to state in their incorporating documents whether or not a portion of any newly issued shares must be offered first to the present shareholders sufficient to maintain their percentage control of the corporation. These are called **preemptive rights**. In this example it would mean that the minority shareholder having 40 percent of the outstanding shares would have to be offered 2000 of the newly issued shares to maintain his or her position. In those jurisdictions where such preemptive rights are not included in the statute, they are often built into the incorporating documents or into a shareholders' agreement.

Perhaps the most important right of the minority shareholder is the right to bring a **representative action** (sometimes called a **derivative action**). The corporation may have the right to sue someone and the directors may choose not to do so. This may be the result of the majority shareholder obtaining some benefit from the decision as would be the case where the majority shareholder has an interest in the offending company or is seeking some other advantage from them. Or it may be the directors themselves who have failed in their duty to the corporation and, not surprisingly, refuse to sue themselves. Sometimes the victim company is a subsidiary, and it is the parent company that is the major shareholder and the wrongdoer. In these circumstances any shareholder has a right to bring an action on behalf of the corporation (a representative action) and pursue the claim. Note that it is still the company that is doing the suing. The shareholder must first have the action certified by the court and the shareholder then proceeds with the action on behalf of the corporation, much like a parent would bring an action on behalf of an injured child.

Shareholder may have preemptive rights

Shareholder has right to bring representative action

Case Summary 7.12 *Re Richardson Greenshields of Canada Ltd. and Kalmacoff et al.*[21]

Derivative Action Used to Thwart Directors

Security Home Mortgage Investment Corporation had both common shares held privately and preferred shares sold to the public. A management company involving some directors and the CEO of Security Home ran the company. Dissatisfaction arose with the arrangement. A vote was held among the shareholders, including the preferred shareholders; it was decided to terminate the services of the management company. The board complied, but then simply rehired all of the same people to manage Security Homes directly.

Richardson Greenshields, which had been involved in the public offering of the preferred shares and the successful vote, protested. They stated that rehiring the managers went against the stated wishes of the shareholders. When their protest was ignored, they bought several preferred shares of Security Home and brought this derivative (representative) action against the directors.

Was Richardson Greenshields an appropriate complainant with the right to bring such an action? The trial judge said they were not, since they had purchased the shares after the rehiring had taken place. But the Court of Appeal disagreed. They found that even though they had purchased shares after the action complained of had taken place, and with the express purpose of launching this derivative action, they were still entitled to do so and qualified as a proper complainant under the Act.

\>

[21] (1995), 123 D.L.R. (4th) 628 (Ont. C.A.).

This case dramatically shows that any shareholder can bring such a derivative (representative) action on behalf of the company with the court's permission as long as he or she was bringing the application in good faith, and there was a legitimate issue to be tried. Here the court held that it was in the best interests of the company to determine whether the rights given to the shareholders had been "improperly extinguished or rendered meaningless by the directors."

Directors

While shareholders owe no duty to the corporation, the same is not true of the directors. Directors approve all the important decisions with respect to the operation of the corporation. They are the ultimate decision-makers and essentially the alter ego of the corporation, and they are only answerable to the shareholders in the sense that they must face re-election. Directors must function at a high standard when performing their responsibilities. They are required to "exercise the care, diligence and skill that a reasonably prudent person would exercise in comparable circumstances."[22] In the past the standard of care expected was much lower, and when it was increased, it caused many to resign— especially token directors who were given the positions because of their name and reputation, but didn't really function as directors. It is important to note that this duty is owed to the corporation, not to the shareholders. Normally only the corporation can sue the directors when they cause a loss through their carelessness or wrongdoing. It is for this reason that the representative action discussed above is so important. Although the shareholder can't sue the director, they can bring an action on behalf of the corporation and bring the director to account by that means.

Directors must exercise skill of reasonably prudent person

Director's duty owed to corporation

Directors must also "act honestly and in good faith with a view to the best interests of the corporation."[23] Thus, the director has a fiduciary duty, which is owed to the corporation, rather than the shareholders. As was the case in the discussion of partnership above and agency in Chapter 6, a fiduciary duty imposes an obligation on the directors to act in the best interests of the corporation, even to the point of putting the corporation's interests ahead of their own. Any information or business opportunities that come to a director because of his or her position in the corporation belong to the corporation, not the director. All such information must be disclosed to the corporation (the other directors), and any such business opportunity must be passed on to the corporation. Only where the board of directors rejects the opportunity and gives permission to the director to pursue it should he or she take advantage of the deal. Secret profits, commissions, kickbacks from suppliers, or other under-the-table dealings are all violations of this fiduciary duty and may also constitute a criminal offence. If the director finds himself in a position where the corporation's interests conflict with his own, he must disclose that conflict and not participate in the discussion of the matter in question or influence the decision. For example, if the corporation of which he is a director is considering the purchase of land and he has an interest, is part owner, or would otherwise be benefited by the purchase of one of the properties being considered, he would have to disclose this conflict of interest and excuse himself, leaving the room as the other directors discussed and voted on which property to purchase. Where this fiduciary duty is breached the director is liable to the corporation for any losses suffered and must account for any profits received.

Directors owe duty of honesty and good faith

Director must act in best interest of corporation

Information must be passed on to corporation

Business opportunities must be passed on to corporation

Hidden payments violate fiduciary duty

Conflict of interest must be disclosed

Where violation director must pay over any profit

[22] *Business Corporations Act*, R.S.O. 1990, c. B.16, s. 134 (1)(a) & (b).

[23] *Ibid.* s. 134 (1)(a).

Case Summary 7.13 *UPM-Kymmene Corp. v. UPM-Kymmene Miramichi Inc. et al.*[24]

A Director Breaches His Fiduciary Duty

Mr. Berg arranged through a company that he controlled to acquire majority control of Repap Enterprises Inc. This included the change of a number of old directors and the appointment of new ones under his control. As part of the process he had himself appointed as a director and senior executive officer of Repap. He then arranged for Repap to pay him an exorbitant compensation package, including a huge salary, stock options, bonuses, pension provisions, and a generous termination allowance. Eventually the old shareholders regained control of the company, appointed new directors, terminated Mr. Berg's contract, and refused to pay the $27 million he claimed he was owed for those services. This action is brought by the new directors for a declaration that Mr. Berg had breached his fiduciary duty to the corporation. In fact, he had not disclosed all the pertinent information to the new board members who had approved the compensation contract. There should have been an independent evaluation, which was not done. The company couldn't afford such an exorbitant amount for his salary and benefits, and Mr. Berg should have known it. This was a breach of his fiduciary duty and also amounted to oppression. The court set the contract aside, and Berg was deprived of any claim against the company under it.

Directors liable to creditors for improper dividends

Directors must forward taxes and deductions

Directors are responsible for unpaid wages

Director responsible for pollution and other statutory offences

In addition to these obligations owed to the company, there are other important duties and liabilities imposed on the directors by statute for the wrongdoings of the business. First, directors will be liable to creditors if they declare dividends when the company is insolvent. The capital of the corporation must be preserved and dividends can only be declared out of profits. Also, the corporation has an obligation to collect and forward PST and GST taken from customers and the deductions from the wages of employees for income tax, employment insurance, and workers' compensation assessments. The directors have the responsibility to see that this is done. They are even responsible directly to the employees for several months' unpaid wages, the actual number varying with the jurisdiction. Directors can also be held liable for environmental damage caused by the corporation, for offences under the Competition Act, and other federal and provincial legislation as well as direct liability for fraud or criminal activity. It is because of this potential liability that we often see directors resign as a group from large corporations that have run into financial difficulty. Even the director's claims that he or she didn't participate in the questionable decision or that he or she missed the meeting will not provide a sufficient excuse. Only where the directors can show that they exercised due diligence might they avoid such responsibility. Due diligence has become a very important concept in law, especially when dealing with government regulation. Due diligence can be expressed as the requirement that an individual, usually a corporate officer, must exercise all reasonable care to ensure that some prohibited event or conduct does not take place, or that the legislation in question is complied with. Note that this is a defence, and so the company or the individual director or manager is usually facing a charge, such as an environmental offence resulting from the escape of pollutants. The individual who was in control at the time might be charged personally, or the corporation itself might be charged for the director or other employees' actions, where that individual can be said to be the directing mind of the corporation or acting within his or her assigned duties or authority, or with the knowledge of superiors when the offending conduct took place. The due

[24] (2002), 214 D.L.R. (4th) 496 (Ont. S.C.J.).

diligence defence requires the corporation or officers charged to show that they have taken reasonable steps to ensure the violation didn't take place or to comply with the regulations. This may require putting systems in place to ensure that the complained of event will not happen, for example, proper selection and training programs for employees and the establishing of policies and procedures that will avoid the problem. Failure to establish adequate training for workers in the area concerned will likely destroy any due diligence defence.

A classic example involves a shoe manufacturing company that failed to properly store liquid waste. It was stored in barrels, which began to leak. Three executives were charged with environmental offences, but only one was able to raise due diligence as a defence and avoid responsibility. The plant manager made inadequate inspection of the site, and the director charged knew of the problem and failed to correct it. Only the president of the company was able to successfully claim due diligence on the basis of establishing appropriate procedures to avoid the problem, and reasonably relying on the competence of those given the responsibility to implement those procedures.[25] Note that in addition to environmental legislation, due diligence defences have been raised in many situations. These include failing to forward taxes (GST) and other funds collected on behalf of government; violations of the *Competition Act*, privacy legislation, and safety legislation for workers; food and drug act violations; building code violations; and even parking ticket violations. Note, also, that under many of these statutes both the corporation and the directors themselves can be held responsible. Establishing due diligence on the part of the directors, who are the guiding minds of the corporation, or the manager or employee responsible for the area, will protect the corporation as well.

An important responsibility of the directors is to appoint the various officers of the corporation that make up the management team. These are typically the chair of the board of directors, the president, vice-president, secretary, treasurer, general manager, and any others so designated. Their responsibilities are determined by the bylaws, but they bear a similar duty to the corporation, as do directors—to perform their duties with the care, diligence, and skill of a reasonably prudent person, and to act honestly and in good faith in the best interests of the corporation. They also are usually included along with directors with respect to the liability imposed under the statutes discussed above. In a closely-held corporation it is common for these offices to be reduced to a minimum and held by the directors and shareholders.

Directors appoint and control managers

Managers have similar duties to directors

Case Summary 7.14 *Machula v. Her Majesty the Queen*[26]

Director Responsible for GST Payment

This case is a good example of a director's obligation of due diligence. Machula was a director in three separate corporations, all of which failed to properly remit the goods and services tax (GST) owed. He claimed that he had exercised due diligence in all three cases and so should not be held personally liable. But the court held that he had only exercised due diligence with respect to one of the three corporations. For the first company he signed all cheques and received all benefits and so should have known of the GST owing and that it was not being paid. For the second company he was involved in on-going litigation, and since he was thoroughly informed about its financial dealings, he should have known that the GST had not been paid. In the case of the third corporation

>

---

[25] *R. v. Bata Industries Ltd.* (1992), 9 O.R. (3d) 329 (Ont. Prov. Ct).

[26] [2003] T.C.J. No. 481 (T.C.C.).

there were 800 employees, an up-to-date accounting system with current computers, software, and supervision in place, and he received financial reports every month with no indication that the GST was not being paid. In the case of the first two corporations, he should have known that the GST was not being paid. He had failed to exercise due diligence to ensure that it was properly paid and, therefore, was personally liable for that failure. But for corporation number three he had ensured that there was a proper system in place, which he should have been able to rely on. He was not in a position to know of the failure to pay and so, because he had exercised due diligence, was not personally responsible for that corporation's failure to pay the GST.

Promoters have duty not to mislead

It should also be noted that when a corporation is first formed, those promoting it have the same responsibilities to it as subsequent directors and officers, but they also have an obligation not to misrepresent or conceal information from future shareholders and not to sell property they hold to the corporation at an inflated price.

Corporate Governance—Abuses and Responsibilities

Although this is an introductory text, a few words must be added about the responsibilities of those in control of these corporations, especially where broadly-held corporations traded on the stock exchange are involved. In recent years there have been many examples of ineptitude, abuses, and even outright fraud and theft. The recent financial debacle in the United States has created a worldwide crisis with the near collapse of the economy, including the failure of several banking and trading organizations and the failure of the mortgage giants of Federal Home Loan Mortgage Corporation (Freddie Mac) and Federal National Mortgage Association (Fannie Mae). These have led directly to huge downturns in the stock and housing markets and are directly responsible for the global recession we find ourselves in (at the time of writing). The Enron scandal, which led to the failure of that company and brought down the respected accounting partnership of Arthur Andersen was the direct result of the fraud of the principals of that corporation. WorldCom (another accounting fraud) and the prosecution of Conrad Black are more examples of criminality resulting in tremendous losses to ordinary people. At the time of writing the largest **Ponzi scheme** in history, involving billions of dollars, had just been uncovered. A Ponzi scheme is like a pyramid, where investors are persuaded to invest their money in a project and the money invested by later investors is used to pay off the early ones, making it look very successful when in fact there is no investment at all. This recent Ponzi scheme was run by Bernard Madoff, now facing criminal charges, and has resulted in at least one suicide of an individual who had lost billions of the money he invested in that scheme on behalf of his clients.

All of these failures and frauds have resulted in increased vigilance and tighter regulation, but no matter how tight these controls are there will always be clever people who can get around them The most we can do is ensure that ethical standards practised in our own business endeavours remain high and that we take great care in selecting the people who will control companies. To encourage ethics in multinational corporations, the United Nations has established the **Global Compact**, a network of public and private institutions designed to advance ethical behaviour and to encourage all institutions and corporations to align their operations and strategies with the following 10 principles, which constitute a basic ethical guide.[27]

---

[27] See an overview of the UN Global Compact at http://www.unglobalcompact.org.

Table 7.1 Ten Principles of the Global Compact

Human Rights	1. Businesses should support and respect the protection of internationally proclaimed human rights; and
	2. Make sure that they are not complicit in human rights abuses.
Labour Standards	3. Businesses should uphold freedom of association and the effective recognition of the right to collective bargaining
	4. The elimination of all forms of forced and compulsory labour;
	5. The effective abolition of child labour; and
	6. The elimination of discrimination in respect of employment and occupation.
Environment	7. Businesses should support a precautionary approach to environmental challenges
	8. Undertake initiatives to promote greater environmental responsibility; and
	9. Encourage the development and diffusion of environmentally friendly technologies.
Anti-Corruption	10. Businesses should work against all forms of corruption, including extortion and bribery.

Most of the scandals mentioned above have involved attempts to manipulate the stock market through accounting or other frauds. Section 397 of the *Criminal Code of Canada* states that anyone who "destroys,, mutilates alters, falsifies, makes a false entry in or omits forms in a valuable security, book or document with an intent to defraud is guilty of an offence and liable to imprisonment for up to five years."[28] There are also many other specialized sections dealing with serious internal and external embezzlement and fraud.

In fact, the instances of such fraud are increasing, partly due to corporate downsizing, which weakens internal controls and creates employee uncertainty. These, in turn, affect loyalty. And mergers often lead to problems with integrating people from different organizations into a new one. Additional risks have been created by the communications revolution and the global economy. The combination of these things results in fewer mechanisms of detection and control, and more opportunity to defraud a business from within and without. It shouldn't be surprising that long-term employees in positions of trust and control commit most internal fraud, since they have the opportunity to divert company funds or initiate actions that manipulate the market. Fraud increases when the ethical structure of a business weakens. Technology and globalization contribute to the risk due to increased opportunity. Opportunity is also increased by dealing with strangers and with people with a wide range of values and business ethics. Business practices that are illegal here are sometimes common in other cultures.

Another significant factor contributing to the increase in corporate crime is the increased role played by organized criminal organizations both in Canada and in other countries where Canadian corporations deal. These organizations are often involved in laundering funds from other criminal activities, counterfeiting, forgery, and various forms of computer and internet fraud.

Fraud and embezzlement can constitute criminal offence

---

[28] *Criminal Code* sec. 397.

A major objective of a business should be the prevention and detection of corporate fraud. Management must take responsibility and institute appropriate measures. Often the appointment of a specific loss-prevention team will focus efforts in this area, enabling managers to buy into the loss-prevention process, even though it is unpleasant. Management that assesses risk and develops proactive strategies for risk avoidance is vital. Having good ethical standards and a published and distributed statement of the company's policies and code of conduct, combined with appropriate training for employees and staff, may go some way to avoid internal fraud. It may also serve to establish a due diligence defence by showing that reasonable efforts were made on the part of a corporation to avoid illegal activity.

FINANCING

Raising Funds

Perhaps the major advantage to incorporation after limited liability is the flexibility that structure allows with respect to raising funds. The company can obtain such funds through **equity financing** where investors purchase shares, and through **debt financing**, where money is loaned to the corporation by creditors (see Figure 7.4). As already mentioned, a company is incorporated with an authorized share capital and then a portion of those authorized shares are issued to investors. In most jurisdictions no value is put on these shares when issued and the market determines their worth.

In a closely-held corporation, shares, whether common or preferred, are usually sold directly to the participants in the business who are often officers and directors as well as shareholders. The formalities of reporting and communication of other information are less onerous but the requirement of disclosure is still very stringent. As mentioned, common shares normally have all the rights associated with shares including voting rights and earning dividends. However, preferred shares have restrictions. They usually have a specific dividend promised but have no right to vote, except where the dividend is not paid. But it must be emphasized that there is no actual right to a dividend whether the shares are common or preferred. If the expected dividend is not paid there is no right to sue.

In a broadly-held corporation where shares are sold on a stock market, the controls imposed on the participants are much more stringent and formal. The idea is to keep the market at a level playing field by preventing any participant, including those associated with the corporation (called insiders), from having an advantage over those with less information. Thus when shares are initially issued the corporation must issue a **prospectus**, which includes carefully drafted and regulated information that discloses to

Corporations allow flexible financing

Equity financing involves the issuing of shares

Issued shares usually much less than authorized share capital

Common shares have no special rights or restrictions

Preferred shareholders are usually promised dividend but can't vote

Unpaid dividends accumulate

Figure 7.4 Corporate Funding

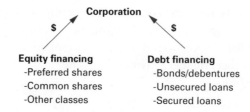

all potential investors the information that they need to decide to invest, and if important information is withheld or is misleading criminal charges may be imposed on those responsible.

Case Summary 7.15 *Kerr v. Danier Leather Inc.*[29]

Importance of Proper Disclosure in Prospectus

To support an issue of shares to the public, Danier issued a prospectus to that end. The information in it was correct at the day of issue, including a forecast of earnings, but because of an unexpected change in actual performance that forecast was misleading by the date the public offering closed. Section 57 (1) of the *Ontario Securities Act* required that the issuer of a prospectus disclose any "material changes" that take place after the prospectus is issued. No such disclosure was made and a class action was brought on behalf of investors who purchased shares relying on that prospectus, claiming the misrepresentation caused them a loss. The case hung on the definition of a material change. The Act states that a material change includes "a change in the business, operations or capital of the issuer that would reasonably be expected to have a significant effect on the market price or value of any of the securities of the issue." There was no such change here, rather what changed was a "material fact," that is,

the fluctuation of sales. Such facts have to be correct as stated in the prospectus at the time of issue, but not corrected as they change after that. On appeal to the Supreme Court of Canada, the class action failed.

The case illustrates how careful a corporation must be to ensure that any important information is disclosed and correct in a prospectus before selling shares and also illustrates the technical nature of the rules. It also illustrates the potential effectiveness of being able to bring a class action representing many shareholders. Although it failed here, such a class action can be a very effective method of enforcing shareholder rights. Also note that while this is a class action, the successful defendant Danier Leather was also entitled to its costs, which were very substantial. Those costs were awarded against the representative client who had to pay personally. That was within the discretion of the court and they exercised that discretion in this case.

Even the trading of shares is controlled. Often officers and directors as well as other people in the corporation will have information of events and situations that will affect the value of those shares before that information is disclosed to the public. If they act on that information before it is disclosed, by selling or purchasing shares, they have acted on **insider information** and may be subject to criminal charges. It is through the manipulation of the market, either by planting false or misleading information or by simply acting on legitimate information before it is disclosed to the public, that is at the heart of many of the abuses discussed above. This includes using clever but fraudulent accounting techniques to hide debts and mislead with respect to profits. These regulations apply not only to the actual insiders (those in the company aware of this confidential information) but also to the family and friends to whom the information is disclosed. As witnessed by recent events these controls cannot be said to have been very effective.

A corporation is a separate person in the eyes of the law, and, like anyone else, the corporation can borrow money. Thus, debt is another important method of financing the business. Often the shareholders will loan the corporation money to get it started. There is normally no advantage to purchase more shares, as that would only upset the control structure of the firm. The shareholder simply becomes a creditor for the amount of the loan and by taking a security against the assets of the business they can become a secured creditor.

Debt financing involves corporation borrowing money

Shareholders often loan funds to a corporation

---

[29] [2007] 3 S.C.R. 331; (2007), 286 D.L.R. (4th) 601.

Creditor usually takes security for loan

Or the company can borrow from some other creditor such as a bank. Creditors will usually require some security that will ensure the repayment of the money advanced if the business fails. This is often difficult for a new business, even where there are significant assets, and so the creditor will usually insist that the shareholders, directors, or some other financially stable person sign a personal guarantee, usually in addition to other forms of security, to repay the loan. If the corporation fails and cannot repay the debt, the individual guarantor is personally responsible for that debt (see Table 7.2). By this single stroke the major advantage of incorporation, limited liability, is defeated. And, in fact, most new businesses are in this position, much to the dismay of the entrepreneurs starting them.

Personal guarantee defeats limited liability

Where broadly-held corporations are involved they will often turn to another more unusual form of debt financing involving the creation of a large debt obligation, either secured or unsecured, which a trustee is then named to manage. Small portions of this debt (called **bonds** or **debentures**) are issued to the public and then traded on the market much like shares. No matter what form the debt financing takes, the creditor usually insists on a term in the contract giving them the right in the event of **default** to take over the business, replacing the directors with a **receiver**. This is referred to as a corporation going into **receivership**.

Note that this is not the bankruptcy process discussed in Chapter 6, although it may trigger that process. Rather, this is simply the creditor exercising a right included in the financing agreement. Of course, the creditor will have any other rights included in the agreement, such as the right to seek payment from a guarantor or to take possession and sell whatever has been used to secure the loan. Note that, as discussed in Chapter 6, one of the options under the *Bankruptcy and Insolvency Act* is to make a proposal to the creditors. When this is done, the rights of the creditors are frozen, giving the debtor a chance to reorganize his or her affairs and solve the financial difficulties. Such a proposal would also prevent a receiver from taking over the management of the business until the expiration of the protection period. An application by large companies to the court under the *Companies' Creditors Arrangement Act* would have a similar delaying effect. Creditors can also sue for oppression, as illustrated in the following case.

Proposals delay actions by creditors

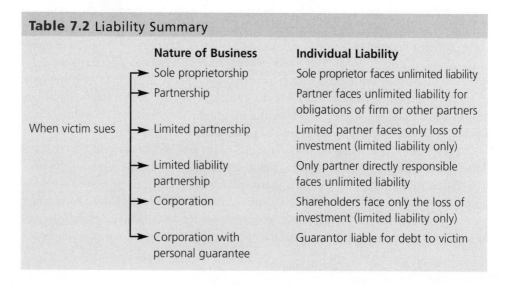

Table 7.2 Liability Summary

	Nature of Business	Individual Liability
	Sole proprietorship	Sole proprietor faces unlimited liability
	Partnership	Partner faces unlimited liability for obligations of firm or other partners
When victim sues	Limited partnership	Limited partner faces only loss of investment (limited liability only)
	Limited liability partnership	Only partner directly responsible faces unlimited liability
	Corporation	Shareholders face only the loss of investment (limited liability only)
	Corporation with personal guarantee	Guarantor liable for debt to victim

Case Summary 7.16 *Re S.C.I. Systems, Inc. and Gornitzki, Thompson & Little Co. et al.*[30]

Oppression Can Also Be Claimed by a Creditor

S.C.I. Systems was a creditor and held a promissory note against Gornitzki, Thompson & Little Co. Ltd. (G.T.L.). Instead of paying the note, the director and sole shareholder of G.T.L. had the company declare and pay dividends, pay down loans to themselves, and transfer funds to other related corporations so that there was no money left to pay S.C.I. As a result, S.C.I. sued the sole shareholder of G.T.L. for oppression against them as creditor. The court found that paying out dividends while insolvent was a violation of law, and that, combined with their other manipulations, was unfair and oppressive. The shareholder of G.T.L. was required to pay compensation to S.C.I. Both shareholders and creditors can sue for oppression when company affairs are manipulated in such an unfair way to their detriment.

The Shareholders' Agreement

Throughout this discussion several references have been made to shareholders' agreements. These usually are involved with smaller businesses where the corporation is closely held. Usually, there are only a few shareholders and they want to set out rights and responsibilities with respect to each other that are not included in the incorporating documents. For example, three shareholders may get together to set up a restaurant: They may divide the shares equally but that structure may not reflect how they want to divide their responsibilities in the business. Their rights and obligations can be specified in a shareholders' agreement. The contract might designate one as the investor, and the other two as full-time employees (one chef and one manager) specifying the terms of that employment. The shareholders' agreement is much like a partnership agreement and can set out any unique provisions with respect to their business relationship that they want. For example, it might include terms with respect to their obligations to purchase each other's shares if they decide to split up. Where the employment of one is terminated, the agreement might require the others to purchase that person's shares and the agreement would also likely include a method of valuation. Of course, there must be a consensus between them with respect to the contract and it must comply with any legislation in place.

Position of shareholders can be further refined through shareholders' agreement

Shareholders' agreement can protect minority shareholder

Shareholders' agreements can ensure employment and restrict control

Case Summary 7.17 *Philo Investments Ltd. v. Toronto Paramedical Management Inc.*[31]

Shareholder Agreements Can Cut Both Ways

Philo held 70 percent of Med-Chem Laboratories Ltd. shares, while Toronto Paramedical Management Company (T.P.M.C.) held the other 30 percent. There was a shareholders' agreement between them containing a "shotgun" clause. This provided that where one party offered to purchase the shares of the other at a specified price, the other shareholder could either sell at that price or turn the tables and purchase the offering shareholder's shares at that same stated price. Philo triggered this clause when they offered to purchase the shares held by T.P.M.C. for $3 million. To their surprise Toronto Paramedical opted to purchase the Philo shares instead of selling theirs. To accomplish this, T.P.M.C. attempted to arrange financing with its bank and another institution, but Philo did all they could to undermine that process. They informed the lenders that T.P.M.C. couldn't afford it. Several anonymous phone calls were made to

>

---

[30] (1997), 147 D.L.R. (4th) 300 (Ont. Gen. Div.).

[31] Ont. Gen. Div., as reported in *Lawyers Weekly*, Vol. 15 No. 45 (April 5, 1996).

both institutions telling them that T.P.M.C. was under police investigation; that an exposé on CBC was about to take place; and that their workforce was going on strike. Not surprisingly, T.P.M.C. was unable to arrange financing by the deadline, and this action was brought by Philo to force T.P.M.C. to sell them their shares, since they were not able to purchase those held by Philo. The court, however, agreed with T.P.M.C. that Philo had an obligation at least not to interfere with T.P.M.C. exercising their rights under the contract. "In any event, the applicants did everything they could to stop them and made their task almost impossible." Their request was refused and the court ordered that T.P.M.C. be given more time to arrange for financing the purchase and that Philo do nothing to interfere with the process. This case shows just how important a shareholders' agreement can be.

Flexibility

Companies can come together in a joint venture

Finally, it is important to point out that partnerships and corporations as set out above are the basic building blocks of modern business. There are many different combinations of these structural elements that can be arranged to satisfy the needs of various enterprises. For example, it is common for companies to engage in **joint ventures** with each other. These are contractual relationships where two or more businesses get together for some project, usually of limited duration. In fact, joint ventures can take many different forms. They can be no more than a contractual arrangement, but they can also involve partnership arrangements, corporations, corporations in partnership, holding companies, etc. For example, two different oil companies might cooperate to develop a pipeline or combine their resources to open a particular gas field. They might incorporate a separate company to take on the project, each making a financial contribution as a shareholder in that new corporation and each appointing directors to run it. There would likely be a shareholders' agreement and the money might well be put forward as a shareholders' loan. Or the two companies might enter into a partnership to carry on the project, again with particulars set out in a partnership agreement. Remember that although the partnership conveys unlimited liability, the partners themselves are corporations each with the advantage of limited liability for the shareholder.

Corporations and partnership can be used in combination

Holding companies ensure control

Another common way these organizations are combined is with a holding company. One individual might have 51 percent of the shares in a company that, in turn, has 51 percent of the shares in another company that, in turn, has 51 percent of the shares in a third company. That individual, with only a fraction of the actual equity ownership of the third company, still retains complete control of all of them.

Preferred shares, shareholders' loans, and shareholders' agreements can also be used in joint ventures and other business enterprises, giving the business person a very flexible canvas on which to create a structure to do business that is completely unique to his or her needs. As a result there is no specific form these business ventures can take, and the liability of the participants will be based on agency, partnership, and corporation principles, depending on the vehicle chosen.

FRANCHISE

Another common method of doing business today is through a **franchise**. A franchise is not a specific legal structure of carrying on business, but has become an important vehicle, especially for retail business in Canada. In a franchise arrangement one business enters into contract with another to sell its product exclusively with appropriate names, logos, and advertising exclusive to the chain. From the point of view of the franchisor it is a very effective way to expand their business with little risk, and from the point of view of the franchisee they become part of a successful business enterprise. It must be emphasized that the franchisee and the franchisor are two different corporations, and they are normally not considered to be in partnership with each other.

Typically the franchisor will sell the right to do business in a given area to a smaller corporation (the franchisee). The franchisor provides the product and other supplies and equipment; advertising; a licence to use the name, trademark, and logos; any secret formulas; as well as training and careful supervision, including management help. They sometimes even provide financing to the franchisee. Usually a standardized accounting system is supplied, likely more to protect the franchisor than to assist the franchisee. The franchisee must comply with rules, standards, and specifications with respect to the preparation of products, prices, advertising, and accounting so that there is a commonality among the various franchisees and different locations. Often the franchisor will actually own the land and build the facility.

In addition to an initial investment of capital, the franchisee is normally required to pay a substantial franchise fee as well as regular payments to the franchisor for supplies and services, and often a percentage of the profits. Common examples of franchises in Canada range from fast-food outlets like Tim Hortons, A & W, KFC, and Starbucks, to other forms of businesses, including Budget and other car rental agencies, computer stores, and the like. The franchisee, of course, gets exclusive access to the product, the advantage of the advertising, the right to use the trademarks, company logos, and other promotional materials, and to participate in promotions and other activities generated by the parent company.

One important drawback to these arrangements is the unequal bargaining position of the parties. Typically, the franchisor is a very large organization and the franchisee is a small entrepreneur who is not in a position to insist on favourable terms in any agreement. Standard form contracts are thus imposed on the franchisee, usually greatly favouring the parent franchisor with the inclusion of restrictive covenants and limited liability exemption clauses. Still, it is in the franchisor's interest to do all they can to ensure the success of the franchisee outlet, and so many of these arrangements have proved a very successful method of carrying on business. This structure is open to abuse and there are many examples of such abuse both by the franchisor and the franchisee. Because of this, several provinces (Ontario, Alberta, PEI, and New Brunswick at the time of writing) have statutes regulating the franchise business. The idea is to create a more level playing field between the parties much like consumer protection legislation. The main provisions of these acts are the obligation of fair dealing for both parties and the disclosure requirements imposed on the franchisor as well as the remedies imposed for violations. The following case is an example of what happens when those disclosure provisions are not followed.

Danger of unequal bargaining position of franchisee

Statutes passed to control abuses

Case Summary 7.18 *Machias v. Mr. Submarine Limited*[32]

An Example of Franchising Abuse

George Machias entered into a franchise agreement with Mr. Submarine Ltd. to operate a store at a Montreal location. The franchisor made several misleading representations with respect to the business, including a forecast indicating that the location would gross $300 000 annually, and that he would make approximately a 27 percent

>

[32] (2002) 24 B.L.R. (3d) 228, [2002] O.J. No. 1261 (Ont. S.C.J).

return on his investment. The costs were also underestimated. The business never came close to bringing in $300 000 annually, and even if it had the costs would have still caused the store to operate at a loss. In fact, over a two-year period the losses were over $50 000 each year. The franchisee finally brought this action to rescind the agreement and in the alternative a claim for damages for fraudulent misrepresentation. The original contract called for payment to the franchisor of $150 000 to be used to renovate the premises and any excess over the costs of renovation were to be returned to the franchisee. In fact the renovations were delayed and when eventually done the costs were inflated to bring it up to the $150 000 so that nothing was returned to the franchisee. The franchisee had stopped paying royalties and rent by this time, and the franchisor countered with an application to have the agreement terminated and the business returned without compensation on the basis of the franchisee's breach of the agreement. There were several exclusionary clauses, which the franchisee claimed prevented the franchisee from complaining about what had happened.

The court found that there had been serious misrepresentation before and after the execution of the contract with respect to the profitability of the business. In fact that location had never been profitable and the franchisor had an obligation to advise the franchisee of that history as well as advising of the fact that other franchises had failed in the Montreal area. The conduct of the franchisor amounted to fraudulent misrepresentation and the court ordered the rescission of the contract and the return of the purchase price. The franchisee was also entitled to the return of the overpayments made to the franchisor for the renovations and compensation for expenses and losses. The court ruled that the exclusionary clauses did not apply, on the basis of unconscionability. This is a typical example of the kind of abuse that franchisees are often subjected to, especially inexperienced franchisees. It also illustrates what the courts are willing to do about it. Note that although there was legislation in place[33] requiring disclosure and fair dealing between the parties, it did not apply in this case since it only applied to businesses carried on in Ontario and this franchise operation was in Montreal. Still, because of the fraudulent misrepresentation the result was the same even without the act.

Many variations accommodate business

There are many different variations of this kind of arrangement, and likely many more will be developed by creative business people. The point is that these various methods of doing business as described in this chapter are only the basic organizations. They can be combined and varied to such an extent that most business needs can be accommodated.

Key Terms

articles of association (p. 177)

articles of incorporation (p. 177)

bonds (p. 192)

broadly-held corporation (p. 177)

closely-held corporation (p. 177)

common shares (p. 178)

conflict of interest (p. 171)

debentures (p. 192)

debt financing (p. 190)

default (p. 192)

derivative action (p. 184)

directors (p. 178)

dissent (p. 182)

dividends (p. 178)

equity financing (p. 190)

franchise (p. 194)

Global Compact (p. 188)

insider information (p. 191)

joint ventures (p. 194)

letters patent (p. 177)

limited liability (p. 174)

limited liability partnerships (p. 170)

memorandum of association (p. 177)

oppression (p. 183)

partnership (p. 166)

partnership agreements (p. 171)

---

[33] *Arthur Wishart Act (Franchise Disclosure)*, 2000, S.O, c.3.

Ponzi scheme (p. 188)

preemptive rights (p. 184)

preferred shares (p. 178)

profit (p. 168)

prospectus (p. 190)

proxy (p. 178)

receiver (p. 192)

receivership (p. 192)

representative action (p. 184)

separate legal person (p. 180)

shareholders (p. 178)

sole proprietor (p. 164)

unlimited liability (p. 164)

Questions for Student Review

1. Why is it so important to take care in choosing the method used to carry on a business?

2. Explain the nature of a sole proprietorship and the liability of a sole proprietor. Why do professionals often do business in this way?

3. Describe the nature of a partnership, the purpose and effect of the *Partnership Act*, and the effect a partnership agreement can have on the relationship between the parties as set out in that statute.

4. What factors will indicate the existence of a partnership?

5. Explain the nature of the liability of partners and the effect of a partnership agreement on a partner's liability to outsiders. How will the retirement of a partner affect those obligations?

6. Explain how major decisions are made in a partnership and how partners get paid.

7. What is the nature of a partner's duty and to whom is that duty owed?

8. Explain what will bring a partnership to an end and how the assets of the partnership are to be distributed upon dissolution.

9. What is a limited partner? What is the extent of limited liability? What qualifications must be met for such a limited partnership to exist and how it can be lost? Distinguish such a limited partnership from a limited liability partnership.

10. What is the effect of incorporation and what is meant by the term "corporate myth"?

11. Distinguish between the registration system, the letters patent system, and the articles of incorporation system of incorporation.

12. Distinguish between broadly-held and closely-held corporations.

13. Explain the right of a shareholder with respect to control of the corporation, how that right is exercised, and what is meant by shareholders' limited liability.

14. Explain under what circumstances the courts may "lift the corporate veil," and the consequences of that happening.

15. Under what circumstances can a corporation be brought to an end, and what happens to a corporation when all of the shareholders die?

16. Describe the advantages and disadvantages of having the ownership and management of a corporation separate.

17. What is meant by a shareholder's right to dissent, to be free from oppression, and pre-emptive rights with respect to the corporation?

18. Explain what is meant by a representative action, when it arises, and who can bring such an action.

19. What are the duties of a director and to whom are those duties owed? What standard of care is required of that director? What constitutes a director's duty of good faith?

20. What are the various ways a director can breach his or her fiduciary duty? Explain the consequences of such a breach.

21. Explain a director's liability for improperly declared dividends, failure to collect deductions from employees, and the consequences of such a failure. How does due diligence affect those obligations?

22. Distinguish between authorized and issued share capital, and common and preferred shares. Explain the rights of a preferred shareholder when they are not paid the dividend promised.

23. Distinguish between equity and debt financing. Explain the nature of bonds and how they differ from shares.

24. Explain what is meant by a company going into receivership. How does receivership differ from bankruptcy? Explain how a proposal under the *Bankruptcy and Insolvency Act* may affect the position of a creditor.

25. Describe the kind of corporations where a shareholders' agreement would likely be found and the effect it will likely have on the position of a minority shareholder.

26. Explain what is meant by a joint venture, a holding company, and a franchise. Why are they attractive ways of doing business?

27. Describe effective strategies for a corporation to avoid being the victim of fraud and theft.

Questions for Further Discussion

1. One of the great advantages of a corporation over a partnership is the limited liability of the shareholder investors. If the business runs into trouble, the debts are the corporation's rather than the shareholders', who can only lose what they have invested. This is one of the most important characteristics of a corporation and one of the significant limitations of a partnership. Discuss whether such limited liability is appropriate from a business point of view. Is it fair to all parties? What about creditors or others who have claims against the business because of poor decisions that have been made? Who should be responsible? In your response consider the movement toward creating limited liability partnerships (LLPs) and whether this is a forward or a backward step. Also consider the creation of the corporate myth, which is the basis for the limited liability of shareholders.

2. It is possible to be in partnership with someone else without knowing it, simply by getting into some sort of cooperative business venture. The burdens associated with partnership, especially unlimited liability for a partner's actions, can be very onerous. Discuss whether people should ever have partnership imposed on them in this way or whether this relationship should be limited to those situations where there is a clear understanding between the parties to create such a partnership relationship.

3. A corporation is considered a legal entity, separate and apart from the shareholders who make it up. This is a myth or fiction and has no basis in reality. Most of the unique characteristics of corporations result from this separate legal entity status. Discuss whether this bit of make-believe in our legal system is justified, considering the result. In your answer consider the recent well-known events involving corporate crime, swindles, and other abuses such as Enron or WorldCom and the banking and subprime mortgage scandals. Do you think doing away with the corporate myth would make any difference?

4. While shareholders are isolated from liability for the careless actions of corporations, this protection is not always carried through to directors who may be held criminally and

civilly liable for the actions of the corporation, especially when they cause physical injury to others. Directors, like partners, also owe a fiduciary duty to the corporation and can be personally sued when they violate that duty. Discuss the relative obligations of directors and partners to each other, to the business, and to outsiders. Consider whether the imposition of such liability goes too far or not far enough from a business and ethical point of view. In your discussion consider the nature of fiduciary duty and whether such an overwhelming obligation has any place in the business world.

Cases for Discussion

1. *Redfern Farm Services Ltd. v. Wright*, 2006 MBQB 4 (CanLII) (2006), 200 Man. R. (2d) 12

    Michael and Kyle Wright and their father, William Wright, all carried on business as farmers in Manitoba. Each had separate farm property registered in their own names, but they carried on the business of farming indiscriminately as to who owned what. They fed and pastured the animals together and carried on other aspects of their business together. "The three operations were all quite intertwined." They did carry on the crop production aspects of their businesses separately, but that was only a small, unprofitable part of the overall operation. They also maintained separate herds of cattle and kept the profit for themselves when they were sold. Note that although the herds were separately identifiable they were fed, corralled, and nurtured as one common herd. In response to questioning by the plaintiff with respect to the grain operation the father said "I order the seed, I order the fertilizer, I order the spray, I order the day custom applicator, I talk to Darryl, I'm the one that does the crop rotations, I use everybody's fields as my own. I'm the one that pays the bills."

    The father bought the supplies used by all and owed $55,365.82 to Redfern, which was not paid. Redfern sued all three. What are the arguments that can be advanced for Redfern and for the brothers? What is the likely outcome of the case?

2. *Public Trustee v. Mortimer et al.* (1985), 16 D.L.R. (4th) 404 (Ont. H.C.J.).

    Mortimer was a partner in a law firm and acted as the executor for the estate of Mrs. Amy Cooper. When she died, he distributed the proceeds of the estate to a series of beneficiaries. He also stole over $200 000 of the estate, keeping it for himself. The problem here was whether the other partners were also liable for Mr. Mortimer's wrongful conduct. Discuss the arguments on both sides. What kind of information is needed to answer the question?

3. *Rochwerg et al. v. Truster et al.*, [2002] O.J. No. 1230 (C.A.).

    Mr. Rochwerg was a partner in an accounting firm, and while he paid over some of the remuneration he received from serving as a director on two associated companies, he failed to disclose the fact that he was also entitled to stock options. When the other partners discovered the existence of the stock options, they demanded an accounting. Explain whether Rochwerg is or is not obligated to turn over these shares to the partnership.

4. *Nedco Ltd. v. Clark et al.* (1973), 43 D.L.R. (3d) 714 (Sask. C.A.).

    Employees of Nedco were involved in a lawful strike when they extended their picket lines to Northern Electric, Nedco's parent company. The Alberta legislation permitted secondary picketing, but Northern Electric asked for an injunction to stop the picketing, arguing that although Nedco was a wholly owned subsidiary of Northern Electric they were separate companies, and as such, were legally independent of each other. Explain what arguments can be brought by the parties and the likely outcome.

5. *400280 Alberta Ltd. v. Franco's Heating & Air Conditioning (1992) Ltd.*, [1995] 4 W.W.R. 558 (Alta. Q.B.).

   Watts and Franco started up Franco's Heating and Air Conditioning Ltd. (a metal fabrication business) to support Watts' successful plumbing and mechanical contracting business. Because Franco generated some business directly, Watts held only 30 percent of the shares. Unknown to Watts, Franco incorporated another company (Franco 92 Inc.) where he owned all of the shares and diverted as much business as he could to it. When Watts discovered what had happened he sued. Explain the basis for his action and the likely outcome.

Chapter 8
Property

Learning Objectives

- Distinguish between real and personal property

- Identify the rights and responsibilities associated with possession of personal property, keeping in mind owners, finders, and bailees

- Recognize the rights of real property owners

- Outline the process for transferring title to land in various jurisdictions

- Describe the rights and responsibilities of landlords and tenants

- Discuss the implications and regulations of environmental protection for property owners

- Note the role of insurance in risk avoidance

One of the most important decisions that business people face relates to their investment in, acquisition, and use of property (see Table 8.1). The monetary amounts are significant, so that mistakes can have a very serious negative impact on a business. **Real property** consists of land and the things permanently affixed to it such as buildings, bridges, dams, and other structures. The other major category of property is called **personal property**, which consists of tangible and movable things called **chattels** or **goods**. Various forms of intangibles are referred to as a **chose in action**. Today we often hear reference to another type of property called **intellectual property**. In fact, intellectual property is another form of intangible personal property. In this information age, however, intellectual property has become extremely important for businesses, and will be dealt with as a separate topic in Chapter 9. In this chapter we will briefly look at personal property and then do a more thorough examination of real property including landlord–tenant relationships and *mortgages*. No matter what form of property is involved, it is always important to reduce risk by anticipating damage to or loss of that property. A brief discussion of insurance has been included in this chapter with reference to that risk management objective.

Real property consists of land and buildings

Personal property may be tangible or intangible

Table 8.1 Property	
Real property	Land
	Things affixed to the land
Personal property	Chattels (tangible goods or movables)
	Choses in action (intangible claims)
	Intellectual property (ideas and information)

PERSONAL PROPERTY

Property relates to your rights to something rather than the thing itself

The term *property* does not refer to the thing itself; rather, it refers to a person's rights in relation to that thing. For example, a person's property is not the house or car, but the property rights that person has in the land or in the car. This allows us to separate the thing from the title or right to it, so that you can loan your car or rent your house and still be the owner. This is a difficult but vital concept to keep in mind as we discuss all forms of property in this and the next chapter.

Tangible personal property is called chattels or goods

As mentioned, personal property includes both tangible and intangible personal items. Tangible personal property comprises movables called chattels or goods as opposed to real property or land, which by its nature is always fixed in one location. We have already dealt with tangible personal property when we discussed its transfer under the *Sale of Goods Act* and its use as security in Chapter 5. In Chapter 4 we talked about negotiable instruments as an example of intangible personal property. Cheques, drafts, and promissory notes have no intrinsic value but represent claims or rights. Below we will examine some other aspects of personal property.

Who Has the Right to the Goods?

Possession gives right to goods over all but someone with prior claim

Because chattels are movable, they often find their way into the hands of others, and the question arises as to who has the ultimate right to them. Basically, the person in possession of the goods has the right to them over anyone else, except someone with a prior title that has not been extinguished (see Table 8.2). A person's right to the chattel will largely depend on how it was acquired. If it was purchased or received as a gift, title has been conveyed from the prior owner to the new owner. But if the chattel was found, the basic principle is "finders keepers." This means that the finder of the goods will have a better claim to them than anyone, except the rightful owner who lost them. If you find a watch or camera in the public part of a shopping mall and take it to the lost and found, if the rightful owner doesn't claim it, you, as the finder, would have a better claim to it than the owners of the mall. If the per-

Rightful owner has title

son who lost it requested its return, however, that claim would override any claim you have to it. Note that if an employee of the mall found the watch, or you found the watch in an area where the public did not go (a private part of the mall), then the owner of the mall would have a prior claim over anyone else except the rightful owner. Of course, if it is established that the money came from an illegal drug transaction, or some other prohibited activity, those funds would go to the government. The following cases illustrate the principle.

Table 8.2 Rightful Owner Depends on Where Goods Are Found

Order of Priority	First Claim	Then
Goods found on public property	Rightful owner	Finder
Goods found on public part of employer's property by non-employee	Rightful owner	Finder
Goods found by employee doing job on employer's property	Rightful owner	Employer
Goods found on private part of employer's property by non-employee	Rightful owner	Employer

Case Summary 8.1 *Thomas v. Canada (Attorney General)*[1]

Are Finders Always Keepers?

Mr. Thomas found in his post box a package addressed to another person with a different post box number. The package contained $18 000 in cash. He turned it over to the police who investigated but could not determine who sent the package. The person to whom it was addressed claimed to have no knowledge of it and refused to acknowledge ownership. In this action both the Crown and Mr. Thompson claim the money. The court could not find any criminality associated with the funds and so applying the principal that a finder has a right to the funds over anyone except someone with a prior claim gave Mr. Thompson the money.

But compare this to *Her Majesty the Queen v. Curti and Ingleby*.[2] Mrs. Ingleby found several items in a garbage can near her work including a leather jacket, two shoeboxes, and a duffle bag containing a considerable amount of cash and documents. In this action the Crown claims the funds as the proceeds of crime. The documents found with the cash indicated that the items belonged to Mr. Curti, who rented a storage facility near where the items were found. A police dog found traces of drugs and Mr. Curti was an associate of the Hells Angels. The court found that on the basis of the evidence provided the police had established beyond a reasonable doubt that the funds were the proceeds of criminal activity and no one was entitled to them and so they went to the government.

Who the rightful owner is will depend on the history of the item in question. The rules with respect to transfer of title as set out in the *Sale of Goods Act* are discussed in Chapter 5. Any other contractual provisions that may affect who has claim to those goods, any other legislation that may affect those rights, such as the *Personal Property Security Act*, and whether the goods were stolen or wrongfully converted to another in the past, would all have an effect on who is ultimately entitled to them. The person who finds them also has an obligation to take care of those goods as a bailee.

Bailment

A **bailment** takes place when one person takes possession of and cares for the goods of another. The person delivering the goods is the **bailor** and the person taking care of them is the **bailee**. With such bailment the important question is the extent of the duty of the bailee to look after and care for those goods while they are in his or her possession. Historically, the nature of a bailee's obligation to care of the goods varied with the nature of the bailment. When the bailment was voluntary, the duty varied with whoever was benefited (see Table 8.3). If someone were to borrow your tools to work on her house, this is a **gratuitous bailment for the benefit of the bailee** and the duty imposed to look after those tools is quite high. On the other hand, if you agreed to store a friend's tools at your home because there was no room in his new apartment, this would be a **gratuitous bailment for the benefit of the bailor**, and the duty to look after the tools would be lower. Of course, the nature of the thing being stored also affects the obligation. The duty would be higher with respect to a valuable violin than with a rake or a shovel. When a person forgets a coat at a friend's home or even at a restaurant, this is an **involuntary bailment**, and the duty of care required of the bailee is only what would be expected of him with respect

Rightful owner has title

Bailment involves one person

holding goods of another

Duty higher where voluntary for

---

[1] [2007] 408 A.R. 207; [2006] 12 W.W.R. 742; (2006), 64 Alta. L.R. (4th) 1 (AB. Q.B.).

[2] 2006 BCPC 495 (CanLII).

Table 8.3 Bailment

Duty of Bailee	Low	High	Per Contract	Per Statute
Gratuitous bailment for bailor	X			
Gratuitous bailment for bailee		X		
Bailment for value		X	X	
Innkeepers/common carriers			X	X

Note that these standards vary with the nature of goods and application of the reasonable person test.

to caring for his own goods and then only if the bailee takes control of the item in some way such as putting it away. In practice, the judge will impose the reasonable person test and take into consideration which party benefits from the bailment.

If the bailment is of mutual benefit or pursuant to a contract, it is referred to as a **bailment for value**, and the duty of care imposed on the bailee, unless specified otherwise, is that of the reasonable person in the circumstances, which is usually determined by the normal standards expected in the particular industry involved. Leaving a fur coat with a storage company for the summer or a ring with a jeweller for repair are examples of such a bailment for value. In such commercial relationships the bailee will usually limit his or her obligations of care in the bailment contract, which often specifies a maximum responsibility for the loss, for example $50. As has been discussed, the court usually applies exculpatory clauses limiting the liability of one party at the expense of the other in favour of the person disadvantaged by the provision. Also, if the failure is substantial enough, a court may be persuaded that such an exculpatory clause, even though worded broadly enough, was never intended to cover such a fundamental breach. (Fundamental breach was discussed in Chapter 4.)

Common carriers and innkeepers have a particularly high standard imposed on them to care for the goods of their customers. A common carrier is a bus line, railroad, or trucking company in the business of taking goods from the general public and shipping them to other locations for a fee. Innkeepers provide transient accommodation (food and lodging) to travellers. Under the common law they are responsible for any damage to their customers or their property, even where there was no negligence involved. This liability would be imposed unless the problem was caused by some defect in the goods themselves or the fault of the bailor. Today, legislation now places limits on such liability, either by reducing the standard imposed, or by allowing the bailee to limit the maximum amount that can be claimed. In Ontario, for instance, the innkeeper's liability is limited to $40 unless the loss is caused by the negligence of the innkeeper or an employee or if the lost or damaged goods were actually left with the innkeeper for safekeeping.[3] When a bailee for value is not paid for the services rendered, the common law provides the right of a lien against the goods, even allowing their sale to recover the bailee's costs. Today specific statutes extend or enhance these common law liens in specific businesses such as storage warehouses or repair services. This allows them to hold onto the goods if they're not paid for their service. Note that it is a criminal offence for a bailee not to surrender property to a sheriff or other official who is properly seizing it under a valid agreement (*Personal Property Security Act*) or court order. The *Criminal Code* also makes it a crime to possess

Where bailment for value, duty is determined by contract or industry standards

Duty of common carriers and innkeepers now determined by statute

Bailee for value can hold goods when not paid

---

[3] *Innkeepers' Act*, R.S.O. 1990, c. I.7, s. 4.

stolen property and has created several offences relating to how personal property is used. These include firearms offences and possession of tools and paraphernalia for producing illegal drugs, forging credit cards, and breaking into houses.

Case Summary 8.2 *Bel-Pas Jewelers Ltd. v. 1365683 Ontario Inc.*[4]

Jewellery on Consignment Creates Bailment

Mr. Reppas was a jeweller operating a business in the city of Toronto. Mr. Mirkalami was an auctioneer in the same city. Mr. Reppas took items of jewellery that did not sell and gave them to Mirkalami to be sold at auction. If the items did not sell they would be returned and if they did sell the proceeds were to be paid over to Reppas. This arrangement worked well for a number of years until 2001 when Reppas claimed that he had given Mirkalami 41 items of jewellery but only 28 items were returned or paid for. That left 13 items valued at $40 000 unaccounted for. Mr. Mirkalami took the position that he never had the items in his possession and was not responsible for what happened to them. Reppas brought this action for their recovery.

The relationship between the two men was based on trust and a handshake. It was established that Reppas had carefully itemized, tagged, and consecutively numbered every item that had been sent to Mirkalami. The court characterized the relationship as a classic bailment and the transfer of the property to Mirkalami created an obligation on him as bailee to exercise reasonable care and diligence in their safekeeping. This he failed to do and was ordered to pay Rappas $39 990 plus costs. This is a good case to show the obligations imposed in a bailment for value or commercial bailment and the importance of written agreements and keeping good records.

REAL PROPERTY

The acquisition and use of real property can be one of the most important problems facing businesses. Real property consists of the land and things permanently attached to it. This usually involves buildings, but may also include other types of structures such as dams, aqueducts, bridges, and the like. It can also include heavy-duty machinery that has to be affixed to the land for it to operate. Prior claims on such items can cause problems since they are personal property (movable) until attached. Special rules have been developed with respect to such **fixtures**.

Another problem relates to just what the land includes. The old theory that it extends vertically out into space has been modified; now the land itself only extends as high as the owner can make use of it. Thus, you can't sue the owner of an airplane that flies over your property for trespass. Still, there is a right not to have some other structure permanently intrude onto the property. If your house is located next to a tall building and your neighbour puts up a sign that hangs over your property, it would constitute a trespass, and you could force your neighbour to remove it. The same applies to under-the-surface rights. A property owner only has a right to that part of the land beneath the property that can be used. Mines, caves, and other underground activities that don't interfere with the surface will not give rise to a complaint. When the right to land is acquired, normally the under-surface mineral rights, as well as oil and gas rights, are not conveyed with the title. The owner of the land will not have the right to minerals and other valuables found under the land. As a result, the owner may have to tolerate

Personal property can become part of real property when affixed to it

Real property above and below ground is limited to what the holder can reasonably use

Mineral rights usually withheld by Crown

[4] 2006 CanLII 3654 (ON S.C.).

Table 8.4 Limitations on Fee Simple Ownership
• Extends only to reasonably useable distance above the surface
• Extends only to reasonably useable subsurface
• Mineral rights usually withheld
• Restrictions (covenants, building schemes)
• Government powers (building permits, taxation, expropriation)

prospectors looking for minerals and even have to submit to some interruption on the surface to accommodate a mine or oil well. As well, the owner will get little compensation when such valuables are discovered.

Fee Simple Estates

The law of real property is based on rules developed in feudal times and still incorporates some aspects of that ancient law. For example, in those days all land belonged to the king. Others had a right to hold it and use it—called an **estate** in the land—which was based on various types of services given to the king. An estate, then, is different from the land itself. It is a right to the land or a right to use the land. In fact, there were many different types of estates in land, based on different forms of service to the king, but today the only type of estate remaining that is equivalent to ownership is the **fee simple estate**. We still don't "own" our homes or property; rather we have an estate or interest in the land called a fee simple, which gives us the same kinds of rights as ownership, including the right to develop, use, sell, and will it to others. The difference is more theoretical than practical (see Table 8.4). But we should always be aware of the overriding power of government to control and restrict how we use land through licensing and zoning, even to the point of forcing its sale through expropriation. Landowners also have an obligation to use their land in a way that does not interfere with their neighbours' enjoyment of their land. This is called a **private nuisance** and the neighbour can sue in tort as was discussed in Chapter 2.

In some circumstances the fee simple estate in land is split. A beneficiary in a will, such as a spouse, may be given a life estate in a particular property to ensure that person is cared for during his or her remaining life. The estate will go to other heirs when that person dies. During their lifetime the beneficiaries are said to have a **life estate** in the property and the other heirs have a **remainder** interest, or a **reversion**, if the interest goes back to the estate as opposed to a specified individual (see Figure 8.1). Note that there is a restriction on the holder of the life estate not to do anything to hurt the property that might decrease its value, for example, having a forested property logged.

Fee simple estate equivalent to ownership today

Governments have power to control or acquire land

Note obligation not to interfere with neighbours

Life estate lasts for life and then reverts

Figure 8.1 Life Estate

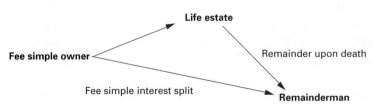

Leasehold Estate

Here the tenant is given exclusive possession and right to use the land for a specified period. Lease arrangements are common to both commercial and residential properties. Most last for just a few years, although 99-year leases are not uncommon. It is also common for a lease to be periodic in nature, meaning it is from month to month, or year to year. In effect, it is for only that one month but is renewed automatically, unless notice is given by either party to end it. The landlord–tenant relationship will be discussed in more detail below.

Leasehold estates are for specified time but may also be periodic

Lesser Interests in Land

It is sometimes necessary to allow a power line, water, or sewer line to permanently cross over or under one property to service another or to allow one building to permanently overhang another. When this is done, the legal arrangement made with the property owner is called an **easement**. When the intrusion is not permanent, but is simply the right for a vehicle or individual to cross over one property to get to another, it is called a **right of way**. Such easements are also an interest in the land, and the formalities associated with having an interest in land should be complied with.

Easement gives others the right to use the land

Right of way is a type of easement, giving someone the right to cross property

Another right often incorporated into land transactions is a **restrictive covenant** (see Figure 8.2). When land is sold, the seller might put some sort of restriction on what the land can be used for or what can be built on it. For example, where a person subdivides her lot she might be concerned that the portion separated not be used for commercial purposes, or she might want to preserve her view by restricting the size of any building that is erected on that property to no more than two stories or no larger than 4000 square feet. The thing to remember with such restrictive covenants is that they must be negative in nature to bind all future owners. If the contract of sale required the purchaser to build a house on the land within six months (a positive covenant) and the purchaser sold the property to someone else, this would not bind the subsequent owner because of the principle of privity of contract. The new owners cannot be affected by the original contract of sale, because they were not a party to it. Restrictive covenants that are negative in nature, like other interests in land, are said to "run with the land," binding all subsequent owners.

Restrictive covenants must be negative and restrict how property can be used

Restrictive covenants bind future owners

A **building scheme** is very similar. In this case all of the properties in a particular development have the same restrictions put on them: all houses must be no more than three stories; or no style can be erected except Tudor; or no other roof can be used except shake or tile. (Note that by wording the requirement negatively as a restriction, all builders are forced to build to certain specifications.) Restrictive covenants will have one property that benefits (the **dominant tenement)** and one property that is restricted (the **servient tenement**). But with a building scheme all properties are benefited, and all are restricted. A building scheme accomplishes similar outcomes as municipal zoning, except that it is done privately by the developer.

Building schemes are like restrictive covenants but bind whole subdivisions

Figure 8.2 Restrictive Covenants

Sometimes people are given the right to use or access property for some particular purpose. This is a **licence**, not an interest, in land. It is simply a contractual right to use the land for some limited purpose. Thus when you rent a hotel or motel room, you are not given the exclusive right to use it. Others will come in and clean it, and you can be required to move to another room if necessary. Another example would be leaving a car at a parking lot. It is a bailment if control is surrendered to a parking lot attendant, as with valet parking, or where the keys are given to the attendant. But where the car is simply parked in a given slot, locked, and a fee paid upon leaving, control has not been surrendered and the use of the property is by licence. A similar right called a *profit à prendre* gives a right to remove something such as gravel or trees from the land.

A licence does not convey an interest in land

Owning Property Together

When people wish to share the ownership of property, there are two main ways this can be accomplished. The **joint tenancy** arrangement is often used by family, especially spouses, to get around inheritance taxes and probate fees. Here, both tenants own the whole property, but neither can point to any portion of it as exclusively theirs. When one dies, the other still owns all of the property, only now he or she owns it exclusively. That person has taken complete title of the property by survivorship. The important point is that the property did not go through the estate. The survivor owned it all, together with the other joint tenant, and after death continued to own it all. Note that it is not only real property that can be owned in joint tenancy. Bank accounts, cars, boats, and other assets are often held jointly for the same reason.

Joint tenancy includes right of survivorship

The other way to own property together is by **tenancy in common**. Here both parties have an undivided interest in the property. Again, neither party can point to any part of the property as his or hers alone. They both own an interest in every part of it, equal to their designated portion. But in this case, if one dies, the other still only owns his or her part interest. Either party can sell his or her portion of the property, use it as security, or otherwise deal with it during his or her lifetime. Upon death, the deceased person's interest will go to his or her heirs. Note that if people own property as joint tenants, and they don't want to continue as joint tenants, that joint tenancy can be severed. When that is done, the result is a tenancy in common. When one party sells or attempts to sell his or her interest, that will sever the joint tenancy. Or an application can be made to the court to have the joint tenancy partitioned, accomplishing the same result.

Tenancy in common does not include the right of survivorship

A joint tenancy can be changed to a tenancy-in-common

It is important to understand that this severance cannot be accomplished in a will. The will takes effect after death, and the right of survivorship in a joint tenancy will take effect with death. Hence, there is no interest left to will to your heirs, as the right of survivorship has already operated to give the survivor the whole interest in the land. Note as well that shared claims to property have also been created by statute. **Dower rights** and **homestead rights** have traditionally protected a spouse in the event of marriage breakdown. Today, modifications of these statutes and other family relations statutes in various forms are in place in all provinces giving a spouse (whether formally married or not) a claim to family assets even where they are not registered on the title.[5]

---

[5] For example the *Homesteads Act, 1989*, S.S. 1989–90, c. H-5.1; *Family Relations Act* [R.S.B.C. 1996] c. 128; *Family Law Act*, R.S.O. 1990, c. F.3.

Case Summary 8.3 *Kish v. Tompkins; Tompkins Estate v. Tompkins*[6]

Negotiation of Severance Does Not Sever Joint Tenancy

Mr. and Mrs. Tompkins owned their home in joint tenancy, but they had separated and were negotiating the division of their property, including the severance of the joint tenancy, when he died. There were even letters between their lawyers with the understanding that the home was to be sold with each getting a share, but these were all headed "Without Prejudice." The question for the court was whether the joint tenancy gave Mrs. Tompkins full claim to the house as survivor or whether it had been severed before death, creating a tenancy in common. The court decided that although they had anticipated and talked about severing the joint tenancy, it had never actually taken place and that Mrs. Tompkins was entitled to the house. The case illustrates the difference between a joint tenancy and tenancy in common, and how important that difference can be.

Condominiums   The growth of high density housing in cities has led to a unique statutory development in common ownership called the **condominium**. These allow people to own property that is separated vertically as well as horizontally. Condominium owners have a fee simple interest in their individual unit and share an interest in the common elements of the development. The units can be sold, mortgaged, or otherwise dealt with as any fee simple property. The sale or mortgage of one unit doesn't affect the other units in any way.

> Statutes now allow fee simple to be separated vertically and horizontally: condominiums

The unique aspect of condominium ownership is the shared ownership attached to each unit with respect to common property such as hallways, foyers, and elevators as well as fitness and recreational facilities, pools, lawns and gardens, and parking lots. The owners of each unit must pay a maintenance fee for the operation and upkeep of these common areas, including insurance on the common areas and the building as a whole. Those fees, as well as other rules and restrictions applicable to the use of the property—even including what can take place within each unit—are set by the **condominium corporation** (sometimes called the *strata corporation*). Each unit owner has a vote and can participate in elections to a condominium council that sets the fees, makes the rules, and otherwise makes decisions with respect to the condominium as a whole. One of the dangers of such condominium ownership is that the owner of each unit is at the mercy of the others as far as fees and restrictions on what they can do. Normally, the fees set are reasonable, but when things go wrong, those fees can become excessive. Unlike normal ownership, condo owners are responsible to cover major expenses that occur with respect to the whole building or complex. Normal maintenance can be built into the regular fees and, if the condominium council shows wisdom, a contingency fee for unusual expenses. But there can be large unexpected expenses for such things as a leaky building, plumbing or electrical problems, a new roof, or the replacement of elevators. When such problems arise, a special levy will be ordered, and each individual owner may be required to pay thousands of dollars per unit for the unexpected expense. Owners can be forced to sell if their fees are unpaid or they have committed sufficient violations of the rules. These potential expenses and unwanted rules and restrictions often discourage some people from condominium ownership.

> Condominiums involve shared property and rules

> Special levy for unusual expenses

---

[6] (1993), 99 D.L.R. (4th) 193 (B.C.C.A.).

Older buildings are often converted to condominium ownership, and this poses another problem for potential owners. It may be a new unit to them, but if the building is 50 years old, it likely has a limited life expectancy. Certainly the maintenance and repair costs will be higher than with a new building, making them much less attractive investments. **Cooperatives** are similar in that the property is owned together but instead of each member owning a fee simple interest in a specific part, here the members own the whole property together and each share entitles them to occupy a specific apartment.

There are still other kinds of interests in land to consider. Sometimes when property is to be sold, an **option to purchase** the land will be arranged. As you will recall from the discussion of offer and acceptance in Chapter 3, an option is a subsidiary contract where, for a fee, the offeror commits to hold his offer open for a given period of time. Thus, the offeror is bound by its terms and can't revoke the offer during that period. But the purchaser has no obligation beyond paying the normally small option price. Developers will often use this arrangement when they are trying to assemble a block of properties from several different owners. They will acquire an option on each property, usually for a small fee. When they have options on all of the properties they need, they exercise the options and purchase the properties. If they can't persuade some key property owners to sell for a reasonable price, they can walk away from the transaction, losing only what they paid for the option agreements. Speculators will also purchase options and resell them as a method of flipping property, earning substantial returns for very little investment. Note that such options like other interests in land must be registered to protect their value.

The common method of financing the purchase of property is through a **mortgage**. Here the purchaser conveys the title to the creditor (usually a bank or other financial institution), and the bank holds onto the title as security until the final payment is made. The bank then conveys title to the debtor. While the debt is outstanding, the creditor has title as security. If there is a default, the creditor can take steps to reclaim the property, but mortgages must be registered to be effective against third parties. Mortgages will be discussed in more detail below.

Requirement of Registration

As indicated in the discussion above, it is important to register any of these interests in land for protection against outsiders who might deal with the property in question and otherwise defeat the unregistered interest. The problem is that any business people dealing in property might have their position weakened by other competing claims for the property of which they are unaware. The registration systems were developed to ensure that does not happen. There are two different systems of land registry in place in Canada. The traditional **land registry** involves the creation of a depository or registry to keep copies of documents that affect the title of land (see Figure 8.3). The purchaser or lender has the assurance that only those documents registered in the land registry will affect them, but they have to search the documents themselves to determine just who the rightful owner is and what claims there are against the property. If you purchase a house, for example, one of the first things your lawyer will do is to go through those documents, checking the chain of ownership to make sure that the seller has the right to sell the house and that there are no other undisclosed interests such as judgments, easements, or mortgages registered against the property. Hence the expression "searching the title." Most unregistered claims will have no effect on subsequent purchasers.

Option to purchase holds offer to sell open for specified time

Options often used by developers and speculators

Mortgages on property used to secure loan

Registration protects creditor's security against third party

Land registry depository of documents

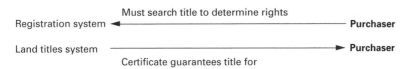

Figure 8.3 Land Registry

The other system of land registry used in Canada is the **land titles system,** first adopted in British Columbia and now used in most other provinces and districts. It has the singular advantage of guaranteeing title. When property is transferred, a form is filed with the land titles office, which generates a new "certificate of indefeasible title," certifying the purchaser as the registered owner of the property. The key to understanding the difference between the two systems is that the **certificate of indefeasible title** is guaranteed and is conclusive evidence of who has title to the property in any court. Note that any mortgages, **liens**, judgments, or other interest such as an easement or right of way are noted on the certificate form as *charges* against the title. No other claims can affect subsequent purchasers. Sometimes this can lead to problems when mistakes are made or titles are changed by fraud. Title fraud is becoming more common and places a considerable burden upon homeowners and other innocent parties as illustrated in the Lawrence case.

> In land titles jurisdictions title is guaranteed by certificate

---

Case Summary 8.4 *Lawrence v. Maple Trust Company*[7]
Owner Protected in Fraud Scheme

Susan Lawrence owned a home in Toronto. A person, posing as Ms. Lawrence, went to a lawyer with a forged agreement to purchase and had the property transferred to another person who called himself Thomas Wright. He obtained a mortgage for $291,924 from Maple Trust Company, which was duly registered against the property. An existing mortgage on the property in favour of the TD Bank was paid off and the imposters took the remainder. Maple Trust had no knowledge of the fraud and had in fact lived up to their due diligence requirements with respect to the transaction. Ms. Lawrence was also innocent, having no idea of what had happened. The problem is to determine who should bear the loss. The whole idea of a land titles system is that the certificate of title can be relied on as proof of ownership and this is what Maple Trust did. But to recognize their claim to the property would impose a terrible injustice and hardship on Ms. Lawrence.

At the trial level the decision was in favour of Maple Trust but this was overturned on appeal. The case is very complicated with involved reasoning interpreting the Ontario *Land Titles Act*, but essentially, the substance of the decision was that Maple Trust dealt directly with the imposter and had an opportunity to investigate the *bone fides* of the parties and detect the fraud, and therefore could not rely on the certificate of title to cure what was a void transaction. Note that if the imposter, Wright, had instead sold the property to another innocent buyer, who then obtained a mortgage from Maple Trust, that mortgage would have been enforceable because Maple Trust would have been relying on the certificate of title when dealing with an innocent registered owner. Had that happened Ms. Lawrence would have had the right to seek redress from an assurance fund set up for that purpose.

This case illustrates the importance of the certificate of title and also that there are limits to its effect. Note that the Ontario *Land Titles Act* has been amended to ensure that homeowners will be protected in similar cases. Note as well that because the legislation is different in other provinces the result might not be the same in those jurisdictions.

---

[7] 2007 ON C.A. 74 (CanLII) (2007), 84 O.R. (3d) 94; (2007), 278 D.L.R. (4th) 698; (2007), 220 O.A.C. 19.

Transferring Land

The traditional method of transferring land involves the use of a *grant*, often called a **deed of conveyance**. Initially, a contract in the form of an **agreement of purchase and sale** is concluded between the parties. This may contain conditions that have to be met before the deal is finalized. At the closing date a deed of conveyance under seal is executed, which accomplishes the actual transfer. Of course, the documents are then deposited in the registry to ensure protection against subsequent claimants. In a land titles jurisdiction a similar purchase and sale agreement is concluded, which establishes the rights of the parties, but the actual transfer is accomplished by completing and filing the appropriate transfer form with the land titles office. That office then generates a new certificate of indefeasible title. The importance of preserving the authenticity of these documents is emphasized in the *Criminal Code*, which makes it a criminal offence punishable by up to 10 years' imprisonment to destroy, cancel, conceal, or obliterate the title to goods or land (section 340a). And more specifically, in section 385 it is a criminal offence for someone in possession of documents that affect title, when asked to produce them, to conceal them, or to falsify the pedigree on which title depends (an indictable offence punishable up to two years). This is primarily designed for offences that take place in a land registry jurisdiction. Section 386, which makes it an indictable offence to make a false representation or suppress or conceal anything material to the registry, applies more to a land titles jurisdiction.

In the past, rights to property were sometimes acquired through use alone. Where a person occupied property openly without the actual owner taking steps to get rid of them for over 20 years, after that time it was too late and the "squatter" obtained a right to the land through **adverse possession**. Similarly, where people regularly cross over land and the owner does nothing to stop them, after 20 years they have acquired the right to continue to cross over by **prescription**. It is still possible to acquire an interest in land in this way in a land registry jurisdiction but not so in a land titles system where whatever is stated on the certificate of indefeasible title must prevail. Acquiring interests in land through use in these jurisdictions is specifically prohibited by statute.[8]

It should also be noted that a major advancement that has taken place in the field of registration of interests in land is the adaptation to technological change. Now most data storage and even the transfer of interests in land takes place electronically.

Mortgages

Most real property transactions involve financing, with the mortgage the most common form of security taken. In the following discussion, since the mortgage is a form of security given by the debtor, that debtor is called the **mortgagor**. The creditor or person in receipt of the security is called the **mortgagee**.

When land is used to secure debt, the title is transferred as security, but possession remains with the debtor. Since the title is returned upon repayment of the loan it is a dead transfer, or a *mortgage*. Originally, if there was a default, the transfer of title allowed the creditor to take possession of the property as well, but in addition the debt was still owed by the debtor. This was unfair to the debtor and the Courts of Chancery intervened. They

---

Transfer by deed in land registry jurisdiction

Form submitted to transfer title in land titles jurisdiction

Criminal offence to falsify or conceal title documents

Right to land may be obtained by adverse possession or prescription in land registry jurisdiction . . .

■ but not in a land titles jurisdiction

Mortgage involves transfer of title to creditor as security

---

[8] *Land Title Act*, R.S.B.C. 1996, c. 250, s. 24; and *Limitation Act*, R.S.B.C. 1996, c. 266, s. 12.

recognized that the transaction was primarily the loan of money and that the transfer of property was only incidental as security. The court recognized a right in the debtor to redeem his or her property from the creditor even after default by paying what was owed. This **equity of redemption**, as it has become known, has a distinct value and is of central importance in today's law of mortgages (see Figure 8.4). If property is worth $500 000 and the debt secured by the mortgage is $200 000, the value of the equity of redemption would be $300 000. This term has been shortened to **equity** and is used commonly in all our financial dealings to describe the value of the interest we have in a possession after the amount owing on it has been deducted.

Equity of redemption allows debtor to regain property even after default

This *right to redeem* was unfair to the creditor, who could face the possibility of the debtor redeeming the property even years after the default, and so the Courts of Chancery, at the request of the creditor, put a time limit on the exercise of that equity of redemption. After the expiration of that time limit, the debtor/mortgagor was forever foreclosed from exercising that equity of redemption. This describes the origin and the nature of the **foreclosure** process. The mortgage represents security by the transfer of title, and if the debt is paid, the title is retransferred. If there is a default, the foreclosure process takes place in two stages. First, the creditor/mortgagee asks the court to put a time limit on the exercise of the equity of redemption, for example, six months. After that period expires and payment is not made the creditor/mortgagee returns to the court and asks that the foreclosure be made absolute. During that redemption period efforts are usually made by the mortgagor to refinance or to sell the property.

Foreclosure puts a time limit on debtor's right to redeem

Final order ends equity of redemption

Since the equity of redemption has value, it too can be transferred to a creditor as security. This is known as a **second mortgage**, and because it is the right to redeem that is being transferred, there is more risk to the second mortgagee. If there is a default, the foreclosure process is aimed at stopping that right to redeem, and so the second mortgagee has to be prepared to pay off the first mortgage or lose the security (see Figure 8.5). Hence, a higher interest rate is charged because of the higher risk. It is also possible to have a third or fourth mortgage, but these are rare because of the even higher risk for these creditors.

Equity of redemption can be used to secure further debt

Second mortgagee must be prepared to pay out first

In the jurisdictions using the land registry system, the process takes place as described above with the title actually transferring to the creditor. The second and subsequent mortgages are then referred to as *equitable mortgages*, because it is the equity of redemption that is being used as security rather than the legal title to the property. In land titles jurisdictions the mortgagor remains the registered owner on the certificate of title and the first, second, and subsequent mortgages, and other claims are simply listed as charges on that title document, with the priority among them established by the order of registration. The rights existing among the parties are essentially the same in both systems.

Mortgage doesn't actually transfer title in land titles jurisdiction

Figure 8.4 Nature of Equity of Redemption

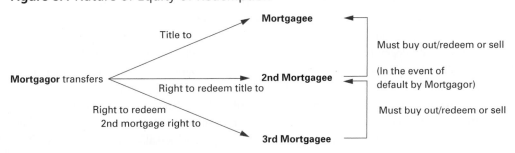

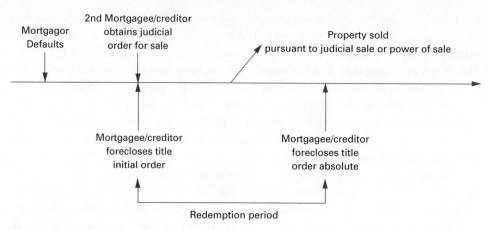

Figure 8.5 When Mortgagor Defaults

The possibility of foreclosure puts the second and subsequent mortgagees as well as any other creditors that might have a claim against the property at considerable risk. Consequently, during that redemption period the court gives these parties the right to try to sell the property. This is referred to as an order for judicial sale or an exercise of the power of sale, depending on the jurisdiction. In British Columbia, for instance, an application is brought before the court and the judge orders the property to be sold (a **judicial sale**). In Ontario the court simply endorses the exercise of the provision contained in the mortgage agreement to sell in the event of default (the **power of sale**), but the result is essentially the same. During that six-month period, referred to as the *redemption period*, these parties are given the right to find a buyer and sell the property. The process then is for the first mortgagee upon default to go to court and get an order of foreclosure setting the redemption period and for the second mortgagee and other claimants at that same hearing to apply for a court order (order of judicial sale or power of sale depending on jurisdiction) to sell the property immediately. The result is that the property might be sold in the next week even though the redemption period has several more months to run. The mortgagor/debtor often fails to understand this. They think they have six months to solve their problems, when in fact their home might be sold right away to satisfy the debt. The immediate sale of the property may seem harsh, but given the value and amounts owed, there is often very little likelihood that there would be anything left for the mortgagor. Because of interest and costs, every delay increases the amounts owed, reducing the likelihood of recovery for the mortgagor, the second mortgagee, or any other claimants. Note that the actual process of foreclosure may vary to some extent between jurisdictions. In some provinces there must be an attempt to sell the property first and in Nova Scotia the only remedy is the sale of the property (referred to as foreclosure and sale).

If the property is sold pursuant to a court order and there is not enough to pay off the second mortgage and other claimants completely, the debtor may still be required to pay the shortfall, depending on the jurisdiction. If a property sells for $160 000, a first mortgage claim of $125 000 might increase to $140 000 because of the added interest and legal costs. Similarly, a second mortgage of $30 000 might become $40 000 with the result that after the first mortgage claim is paid, there is only $20 000 left leaving a shortfall of $20 000 still owed to the second mortgage. This is not an uncommon scenario, especially when the economy declines, causing people to lose their jobs, which also often leads to a decline

The exercise of the power of sale/judicial sale shortens the redemption period

in the housing market. Typically, a mortgage agreement will also give the mortgagee the right to take possession of the property in the event of a default, but this is seldom pursued unless the property has been abandoned. The process is further complicated by family law considerations. Essentially each spouse has a half interest in the matrimonial home no matter in whose name the property is registered.

A less common remedy involves taking possession of the property

---

Case Summary 8.5 *Bank of Nova Scotia v. Dorval et al.*[9]

Obtaining Property Through Foreclosure Eliminates Right to Deficit upon Resale

The Dorvals borrowed money from the bank, giving a mortgage on their property as security. Upon default, the bank went through the foreclosure process—obtaining a final order, obtaining the title to the property through foreclosure, and then selling the property. The amount obtained from the sale was less than what was owed, and they sued the Dorvals for the shortfall. The court held that the nature of a foreclosure was that they had taken title to the house as their remedy and were not entitled to anything else. If they had obtained more than owed in the sale, the creditor would have been entitled to keep it and so they could not complain if they received less. Had the bank asked for a judicial sale supervised by the court before the final foreclosure order, their claim for the deficit would have been enforced. This case shows the difference between a judicial sale and a sale after foreclosure, and the importance of making the right choices.

Case Summary 8.5 *Bank of Nova Scotia v. Dorval et al.*

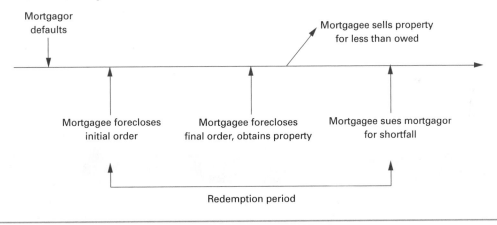

Leasehold Estates

A **leasehold estate** provides the tenant with a right to exclusive possession and use of the premises for a specified period of time. Such leases may be of short duration such as a month or for much longer periods, even 99 years. **Periodic leases** are also common where the lease is only for one month but then is automatically renewed every month until notice is given to terminate. Any period may be specified, but month-to-month is the most common, with week-to-week and year-to-year also used. This discussion must distinguish between commercial lease and residential lease arrangements. Both may be

A lease conveys possession of property for a specified period

Periodic leases involve automatic renewal until notice

---

[9] (1979), 104 D.L.R. (3d) 121 (Ont. C.A.).

governed by statute, but the commercial tenancy acts normally allow the parties much more scope to alter their rights and obligations by agreement in the lease itself. Residential tenancy acts (or their equivalent in place in all provinces) are more like a form of consumer protection legislation, imposing many obligations on the parties that cannot be modified by agreement. The following general discussion relates primarily to commercial tenancies. Remember, however, that the principles discussed here also apply to residential tenancies, except where they have been changed by statute. These statutory modifications for residential tenancies will be discussed separately below.

Commercial Tenancies

Statute of Frauds requires longer leases to be evidenced in writing

One of the requirements of the *Statute of Frauds* is that any interest in land, including a lease, must be evidenced in writing to be enforceable. Most jurisdictions modify this, so leases, whether residential or commercial for less than three years, are still enforceable even without writing. The doctrine of frustration does not apply to leases under common law. So if leased premises were to burn down through no fault of either party, the tenant would still have to pay rent unless, of course, the parties have specified otherwise in the lease agreement. In some jurisdictions, such as Ontario, the doctrine of frustration is made applicable to leases by statute, with the result that the tenant's obligation to pay rent would be ended if the premises were destroyed by fire that was not the tenant's fault.[10]

Frustration applies to leases in some jurisdictions by statute

Even where frustration has not been imposed by statute, if the lease relates to an office in a highrise and the building is destroyed, the obligation to pay rent would likely end, since you can't lease something that doesn't exist. Because a lease is an interest in land, even though it is created by contract, the leasehold interest will *run with the land*. Suppose Jones leased his home to Smith for five years and then sold that home to Green. Because the interest is attached to the land, if it was properly registered Green would be bound by the terms of that lease, even though he was not party to the contract that created it.

Leases are binding on a subsequent purchaser if registered

Case Summary 8.6 *Fitkid (York) Inc. v. 1277633 Ontario Ltd.*[11]

Accepting Rent Overrides Notice to Vacate

The commercial lease was to run to 2006, but in 1999 a disagreement arose between the landlord and the tenant, Fitkid, over the amount of rent to be paid and repairs to the roof. For several months Fitkid withheld rent and then paid after a default notice. When a rent increase came into effect, the tenant paid rent at the lower rate, not the increased one. Finally, in April 1999 after again accepting rent at the lower rate, the landlord changed the locks and evicted the tenant. Fitkid could not find other premises and went out of business. In this action Fitkid is seeking damages from the landlord for wrongful termination of the lease. The court held that the failure to pay the proper rent would have been grounds for evicting the tenant, but when the landlord took the lower payment in April before changing the locks, he reinstated the lease and lost the right to evict. Accepting the rent payment was inconsistent with the termination of the landlord and tenant relationship. As a result, Fitkid was awarded $198 201 in damages. Note that seizing the tenant's property before termination has the same effect, and landlords should seek legal advice before resorting to such action.

---

[10] *Tenant Protection Act*, 1997, S.O., c. 24; or *Frustrated Contracts Act* in various jurisdictions.

[11] 2002 CanLII 9520 (Ont. S.C.J.).

Although the lease agreements can modify these obligations between the parties, there are some basic obligations that are normally in place in all tenancies. For example, the landlord has an obligation to deliver **vacant possession** of the property. This means that he has to make sure that any prior tenants are gone before the scheduled time for the new tenants to occupy the premises. The landlord also has to provide **quiet enjoyment**, which means the tenant has to be able to use the premises for the purpose for which they were let. If there is blasting going on nearby that interferes with the tenant's work or sleep, or no stairs to the suite, or even a major leak so that the premises are no longer fit for human habitation, all of these things are breaches of the tenant's right to quiet enjoyment.

Agreement determines obligations in commercial lease

Landlord must deliver vacant possession and quiet enjoyment

The question of who has the obligation to make repairs is normally an obligation that is specified in a commercial agreement. Usually neither party has an obligation to make repairs where normal wear and tear is involved. The tenant takes the premises in the condition let and returns them in the same condition, except for normal wear and tear. If the tenant causes damage beyond normal wear and tear, either wilfully or through neglect, he or she will be responsible to repair it. Sometimes the tenant causes more damage than expected by using the premises in a way different from what was intended when it was originally let. For example, if the premises were let as an office but were used for heavy manufacturing, the tenant would be responsible for any excess damage caused by this non-approved use. As mentioned above, if there is unusual damage that causes the premises to be unusable such as a major leak or fire that interferes with the tenant's right to quiet enjoyment not caused by the tenant, the landlord has an obligation to make the repairs.

Responsibility for repairs is subject to agreement

Tenant must use premises as agreed

A problem often arises with respect to the termination of the tenancy. Of course, if the lease is for a set time, such as two years, the tenant will have to be out at the expiration of that term. Sometimes the tenant, either with or without the agreement of the landlord, stays after the expiration of the lease. If the landlord wants the tenant out, he can take steps to have the tenant removed and the landlord is entitled to compensation from the over-holding tenant. But if rent is paid and accepted, normally a month-to-month periodic tenancy is created. Where a periodic tenancy is involved, it can be terminated by either party giving one clear rental period notice. Thus, in a month-to-month tenancy where the tenant wants to move at the end of May, that tenant must give notice at the end of April to be effective at the end of May. If the rent is due on the first day of the month, the notice must be given the day before (April 30 in this case) to be effective the last day of the next month (May 31). Unsophisticated landlords and tenants often make the mistake of giving notice on the same day the rent is paid, expecting it to be effective at the end of that month. This is improper notice and will be ineffective, unless the other party agrees to accept it. The amount of notice required is usually one of the changes imposed in residential tenancy legislation.

Commercial lease terminated at end of specified lease period

Where a periodic lease is involved, one clear rental period notice is required

The obligations of the tenant consist of paying rent, using the property only as agreed, and otherwise living up to the terms of the lease agreement, which may include other obligations such as paying taxes, insurance, and utilities. If the tenant fails to pay rent, the landlord must make a choice. In a commercial tenancy he can terminate the tenancy by removing the tenant, or he can **distrain** for rent. Terminating the tenancy, even by simply changing the locks, is called **forfeiture** and no court order is needed. Note that an important right of the tenant in these circumstances is to ask the court to order **relief against forfeiture**, which will allow the tenant to reinstate the lease by paying the back rent due. Distraint involves seizing the tenant's goods for the rent owing. This is inconsistent with termination of the tenancy, since the rent is being paid by the seized property.

Tenant must comply with agreement and may be required to pay utilities and taxes

In the event of default, the landlord can evict tenant

In the event of default, landlord can seize tenant's goods

Since there is no longer a breach of the lease, the tenancy continues. Where the tenant abandons the premises before the lease period is up, the landlord can sue for the rent for the remaining term of the lease. The landlord is not required to find another tenant or otherwise mitigate his losses. But if he does take over the premises or leases them to someone else, the landlord has accepted the tenant's surrender of the premises, and the tenant's only obligation would to be to pay any arrears in rent. Other remedies such as monetary compensation (damages) for damage to the premises or an injunction to stop certain practices inconsistent with the lease terms may also be available. The tenant may also have an action for damages or obtain an injunction where the landlord has breached important terms of the lease.

Neither the landlord nor tenant will be required to repair normal wear and tear unless specified in the lease. Where major repairs are needed, the tenant must notify the landlord of the problem. If the landlord then fails to make appropriate repairs as required in the lease, the tenant can seek a court order whereby he will be allowed to pay less rent (**abatement**), using the excess to make the required repairs. Other terms often included in commercial leases are a right for the tenant to renew the lease and an option for the tenant to purchase the property at the expiration of the lease period. These terms must be specific and clearly state the amounts to be paid, or how the funds involved can be calculated in order to be binding on the parties. The tenant is also generally permitted to sublease the premises or to assign them to someone else, although in both situations they remain primarily responsible on the lease. This right is usually restricted in the lease agreement, which normally requires the landlord's consent before the assignment or sublease can take place. Note that the landlord cannot unreasonably withhold this consent.

Another problem regarding just what they can take with them often arises when tenants leave. A fixture is something that has been permanently attached to the property, such as a building or foundation, and it becomes part of the real property. But tenants often attach items onto the property to use in their business that they have no intention of leaving with the property. The general rule is that tenants can detach such items and take them with them, providing they do no serious harm to the property in the process. Tools in a workshop often have to be attached to the floors or walls in order to operate, and these would normally be tenant's fixtures that they could take with them at the end of the lease period.

Where legislation is in place with respect to commercial tenancies, the statutes only make minor changes to the common law. The parties are allowed to make whatever kind of arrangement they want by setting it out in the lease agreement. The same is not true for residential tenancies. Here important statutes are in place that impose obligations on both parties and make substantial changes to the common law.

Residential Tenancies

Under the common law there is very little distinction made between commercial and residential tenancies. But all jurisdictions have passed legislation that considerably modifies the common law and essentially creates a consumer protection scheme, designed primarily to protect tenants. There are considerable differences among jurisdictions, and so no comprehensive attempt will be made to cover the subject. In the discussion below we will look at the main areas where changes have been made by the various residential tenancy acts. These areas of change deal primarily with rent increases, security deposits, termination requirements, repairs, privacy, and services.

Margin notes:

If tenant defaults, landlord can sue for rent for remaining term

Landlord has no obligation to mitigate

Injured party can seek damages or injunction

Normally neither party is required to pay for normal wear and tear

Court may authorize tenant to pay less rent to pay for repairs

Lease also may provide right for tenant to renew, to sublease, or assign

Tenant's fixtures can be taken with them when they go, if they've caused no damage

Commercial tenancy statutes normally allow parties to determine lease obligations

Legislation creates protection for residential tenants

Several jurisdictions require the tenancy agreement creating the lease to follow a standard form, and all require a copy to be in writing and delivered to the tenant within a few weeks of its creation. Most permit some terms to be added if they are reasonable, but *acceleration clauses*, requiring all payments to become due if any default, are generally prohibited.

Consistent across jurisdictions is an obligation on the landlord to make general and emergency repairs to the premises and to maintain minimum health standards. That means that the premises must be reasonably fit for human habitation, satisfying the local municipal bylaws with respect to health and sanitation. There is a corresponding obligation placed on the tenant to maintain the premises to a minimum standard of cleanliness. The tenant is also responsible for any damage caused by his or her own wilful or negligent conduct or that of a guest. But the tenant is not responsible for the normal wear and tear that takes place on the premises, nor is the landlord, unless it expands into other damage that interferes with the tenant's use and enjoyment of the premises. Thus, if a leak developed in the roof and the landlord didn't bother to repair it, that leak could expand, eventually destroying that part of the roof and making the premises uninhabitable.

One consistent provision in all of these statutes is a restriction placed on the landlord from entering into the premises once rented. In general, the landlord has a right to inspect or to enter to make repairs, but only upon giving the tenant notice and only during the day. This right expands slightly once notice of termination has been given and it becomes necessary to show the premises to potential tenants. In the same vein, neither the landlord nor the tenant can change the locks or re-key them without the agreement of the other party. Tenants also generally have the right to sublet or assign the leased premises. This means they can find someone to replace them for a portion or the duration of the lease. But they have to obtain permission from the landlord to do this, and the statutes state that such permission shall not be unreasonably withheld.

In most jurisdictions the practice has developed of landlords taking a **security deposit** to cover any damage done or rent not paid. This practice is controlled in all provinces with most restricting the amount to one month or one-half of one month's rent. In most provinces the security deposit is to cover damages to the premises, but with the agreement of the tenant it can also be used to help cover the last month's rent. But Ontario allows one month's rent to be taken as security deposit, which can only be used against unpaid rent, not damage. In all cases the landlord is required to hold the funds in trust and to pay the tenant a specified rate of interest on those funds within a short time after termination.

- Standard form leases often required
- Landlord obligated to make general and emergency repairs
- Tenants are obligated to pay for damages they cause
- Neither party required to repair normal wear and tear
- Landlord restricted from entering premises
- Tenant can sublease or assign with landlord's permission
- Amount and purpose of security deposits restricted and must be returned with interest

Case Summary 8.7 *626114 & 626115 Ontario Ltd. v. Tirado*[12]
Tenancy Disputes Can Be Resolved by Tribunals

Mrs. Tirado lived at the premises in question for a period of six years when this application was brought for her eviction. As part of her tenancy agreement she had paid a last-month's rent security deposit. According to the Act she was entitled to six percent interest on that security deposit to be paid annually, but she had not been paid anything over the six-year period. In this action she is challenging the tribunal's decision to support her eviction and

>

[12] 2005 CanLII 36461 (ON S.C.D.C.) (2005), 203 O.A.C. 14.

that the landlord only had to pay interest on the security deposit for one year. The court determined that they would not interfere with the eviction decision of the tribunal since it was based on her failure to pay rent and the decision was not patently unreasonable. The court overturned the tribunal's decision to limit her interest claim to one year, which was an error of law, and concluded that Mrs. Tirado was entitled to 6 percent interest on the last-month's rent deposit for the entire 6-year period. The case illustrates the general role played by the tribunals that are charged with dealing with disputes that arise under residential tenancies statutes, but also illustrates the power of the courts to supervise that function and the right that a tenant has to interest on security deposits taken by a landlord.

Rent increases normally limited to one per year with substantial notice

Most jurisdictions limit how often the rent can be increased (usually once per year) and some limit the amount it can be increased or require the landlord to justify the increase. Notice of the increase must be given to the tenant several months in advance (at least 90 days in Ontario).

There are also special rules with respect to the termination of the tenancy. Notice must be given at least one clear month before termination of a month-to-month tenancy under common law, but most jurisdictions have expanded this with respect to notice to terminate by the landlord. In Ontario, 60 days' notice of termination must be given and this even applies where the lease is for a fixed term. Even more notice may be required where the premises are to be converted to ownership units or are to be used by the landlord's family. The tenant is only required to give one month's notice, and in several jurisdictions this is even shorter, to allow the tenant to give notice of termination on the same day he or she pays rent.

Notice period for landlord to terminate lease is extended

Tenant can give notice when rent is paid in some jurisdictions

In addition to these specific requirements, landlords are generally prohibited from making changes or charging more for the services provided. For example, where parking is included or laundry facilities are provided, withdrawing the service or charging a higher fee for them would be an indirect rent increase and so is prohibited.

Landlord must maintain services

Where the tenant breaches the lease, for example by not paying the rent or using the unit for an inappropriate purpose, the landlord may be able to give the tenant reduced notice to vacate. Usually the landlord will turn to a tribunal where disputes can be arbitrated or the officer can make an order requiring the breach to stop or even requiring the tenant to vacate the premises. If the order is not obeyed, there is normally provision for an application to the court to enforce the order. In most jurisdictions the remedy of distress, where the landlord seizes the tenant's property for failure to pay rent, has been abolished with respect to residential tenancies. Also, when the tenant abandons the premises, the landlord is now required to mitigate the damages by re-renting the premises to another tenant. The tenant can also bring complaints to the tribunal. The officers have considerable power to award remedies that will overcome the problem, ranging from ordering the landlord to stay out of the premises, to reducing the rent to pay for repairs or in recognition of reduced services, to even ordering the landlord to restore services that have been discontinued. It should also be noted that the doctrine of frustration does apply to residential tenancies.

Landlord may give reduced notice where tenant is in default

Landlord cannot seize tenant's property and must mitigate loses

Statutes establish tribunals to hear complaints

Frustration applies to residential tenancies

The statutes also usually contain special provision for dealing with unique situations such as mobile homes. In that case only the pad is rented, but it is extremely difficult for the tenant to vacate, which would involve moving the mobile home. Some acts, including Ontario's *Residential Tenancies Act*, contain provisions with respect to special care homes for disabled tenants.

Finally, it should be noted that under the *Criminal Code* several types of property use are prohibited and the landlord may be charged as well as the tenant. For example, using premises for unauthorized gambling or for prostitution and even for an immoral theatre production are prohibited.

Property owners and occupiers responsible for immoral acts on property

REGULATION OF THE ENVIRONMENT

A discussion of property law would not be complete without an examination of environmental regulation and the responsibilities imposed on landowners and businesses that use land in a way that encroaches on the environment. Environmental protection has become an increasingly important concern of the public and governments at all levels. There has always been the recognition of an individual's right to protect his or her immediate environment from pollution and degradation by others under the common law. The large-scale expansion of mining, forestry, coal, oil, hydro-electric, and nuclear generating plants as well as other undertakings including local activities such as the polluted ground left by a service station, has put an increasing strain on the environment. There has been a general recognition of the deterioration of the environment and the need for greater controls, not only to prevent further damage, but also to correct the damage that has already occurred. Statutory intervention at the federal, provincial, territorial, and municipal levels has become an important consideration in doing business, especially when a new venture is undertaken.

Increasing environmental regulation has become important concern of business

The Common Law

The main area where common law provides protection is with riparian rights, which give people living on a river or stream (except for normal domestic depletion) the right to have the water continue to flow to them with undiminished quantity or quality. This basic right continues but is often overridden by a government's statutory power when it issues water-use permits to industries and municipalities. Thus, if the government grants a permit to a pulp mill to dump pollutants into a river, the downstream users can't complain, as their riparian rights have been overridden by the exercise of a statutory power.

Riparian rights are the right to continued quality and quantity of water flow

Riparian rights are often overridden by statute

The tort of private nuisance can be used to seek a remedy when a neighbour interferes with a person's enjoyment of his or her property, through the escape of water, noise, smoke, odours, etc. The injured party can bring an action seeking damages or an injunction. Even negligence or the principle of strict liability as discussed in Chapter 2 can be relied on when dangerous things escape from one property, causing damage or injury to those on a neighbouring property. In rare circumstances, where there is actual physical interference with a property, the law of trespass can be used to obtain a remedy. But all of these common law provisions have one thing in common. They require an individual to go to the expense and take the time to sue. The polluting activity is treated as a private matter between the person injured and the offender. Someone who is not directly injured has no right to bring an action. There is no community right to action, and except in the most serious of cases, most individuals won't go to the trouble or expense to sue. These factors make the common law an ineffective tool to control pollution or protect the environment in any comprehensive way.

Nuisance can be used to stop pollution

Common law is not efficient in protecting the environment

Case Summary 8.8 *Scarborough Golf & Country Club v. Scarborough (City)*[13]

Golf Course Has Riparian Rights

As the City of Scarborough expanded, more and more rain runoff was diverted into a particular stream, eventually causing considerable damage to a golf course. The golf course sued the city, claiming nuisance and a violation of their riparian rights (the right to have water continue to flow in undiminished quantity and quality). The city had the right to natural drainage through the stream, but they had diverted water into it, causing the damage. The court determined that this infringed the riparian rights of the golf course and the city had to pay compensation. The court also based the award of damages on private nuisance.

Federal Legislation

Environmental regulation comes from all levels of government

This is an area where both the federal (including territorial) and provincial governments have the power to pass legislation. A business may find itself dealing with provincial or federal regulatory bodies, and sometimes both, depending on the nature of their business. The federal jurisdiction applies to all areas where a business is involved in a matter given specifically to the federal government under the *Constitution Act (1867)*. This includes such areas as navigable waters, fish-bearing waterways, inter-provincial or international undertakings, railways, ferry services, banks, broadcasting, and air transportation. Note that almost every stream and river is fish-bearing, giving the federal government power to regulate in almost all areas involving natural resources, or where there is some discharge of polluting material in a water course. Historically the federal *Fisheries Act*[14] has been the most effective environmental protection legislation, allowing criminal charges to be levelled at anyone discharging any effluent into a fish-bearing water course. Section 36 (3) states

> Subject to subsection 4, no person shall deposit or permit the deposit of a deleterious substance of any type in water frequented by fish or in any place under any conditions where the deleterious substance or any other deleterious substance that results from the deposit of the deleterious substance may enter any such water.

Federal environmental regulation may apply even to local projects

Beyond this, the federal regulations can also apply to all businesses providing services to the federal government, federal agencies, or federally supported activities, including all projects that receive federal funding. This creates considerable overlap and businesses often find themselves dealing with federal, provincial, territorial, and even municipal environmental regulations, especially on larger projects.

Statute authorizes government department

Canadian Environmental Protection Act The main federal statute in this area is the *Canadian Environmental Protection Act*.[15] This legislation provides for the establishment of a government department charged with preventing pollution and protecting the environment and human health while contributing to sustainable development. In brief, the Act provides for research—the gathering, compilation, storage, evaluation, and publication of information and data; the setting of standards, guidelines, and codes of conduct; monitoring and inspection; the identification of prohibited and controlled

[13] (1988), 54 D.L.R. (4th) 1 (Ont. C.A.).

[14] R.S.C. 1985, c. F-14.

[15] S.C. 1999, c. 33.

activities; and the enforcement, remediation, and imposition of penalties when offences and violations take place.

Under the Act, where environmentally sensitive activities are involved, an individual or business can be required to develop and implement pollution prevention plans. Lists of toxic substances are specified, and their importation, export, and use in Canada are prohibited or controlled. Individuals are required to report the escape of such materials, and employees who do so (whistle blowers) are protected from reprisals.[16]

There are also restrictions on the disposal of waste at sea without special permits and on the use of unregulated fuels in Canada.

Enforcement officers have significant power under the Act. They can enter and inspect premises, stop and inspect conveyances to take samples, detain vehicles and material to make tests, and examine records and computers. They can issue environmental compliance orders, which may involve, among other things, the requirement that a person refrain from or stop doing something in contravention of the Act. Finally, they can charge individuals with offences where violations do occur. Note that these orders can be appealed to review officers and then to the Federal Court, if necessary.

When an unauthorized release of toxic substances or pollution does take place, and the property owner fails to report the release and warn the public, the enforcement officer can take the necessary action to remedy the situation and charge the costs back to the violator. Directors, managers, and agents of corporations can be held directly responsible unless they can show that they acted with due diligence. Due diligence requires the officer to show that they have set up systems to ensure that the Act will be followed, including training employees and establishing policies to ensure compliance.

Note that the Act also provides for civil remedies allowing an injured individual to bring an application in court for an injunction to stop an offending activity, or for monetary compensation where damages have been sustained, or to have an activity prohibited by the statute to end.

This brief summary of the Act just touches the surface, and we haven't looked at the great volume of regulations authorized under the Act to accomplish its objectives.

Canadian Environmental Assessment Act Another important federal act is the *Canadian Environmental Assessment Act*.[17] This Act requires all projects that the federal government has control over (through granting permits, licences, and funding, etc.) to go though an environmental assessment process. This assessment process can take several different forms, depending on the potential risks involved and the size of the project. It should also be noted as a practical matter that these federal agencies often show considerable flexibility in their enforcement regime to encourage voluntary compliance and to foster economic development. All provinces have legislation similar to *Canadian Environmental Protection Act*.

Provincial Legislation

While the legislation in place varies considerably from province to province and the territories, all have acts similar to the *Canadian Environmental Protection Act* designed to create general standards and monitoring and enforcement mechanisms to deal with

---

[16] *Canadian Environmental Protection Act*, S.C. 1999, c. 33, s.16(4).

[17] S.C. 1992, c. 45.

Margin notes:

Controls imposed and whistle blowers protected

Enforcement officers given significant powers of inspection and enforcement

Spills must be reported and remedied

If a company fails to act, costs can be imposed on the violator

Significant penalties are imposed on company and its directors

In most cases due diligence is available as a defence

Limited civil remedies are provided

environmental concerns in the areas of provincial jurisdiction. With the federal statutes as the examples, no attempt will be made here to do any kind of comprehensive review, but a few points should be noted. These statutes regulate the transport and disposal of waste, the use and transportation of hazardous materials, the cleanup of contaminated sites, the treatment of sewage, motor vehicle emission discharges, and the disposal of by-products from manufacturing, mining, and other activities. The statutes also control what happens at specific locations by limiting industrial, commercial, and residential uses. Most provinces, like the federal government, have an environmental review process that must be complied with before environmentally sensitive projects can go forward.

Provinces also require environmental assessment process

Government departments have been created to implement these policies. They establish codes of conduct and regulations that must be adhered to. To keep degradation of the environment to a minimum, government departments grant permits with restrictions and requirements, and supervise the discharging and storing of waste. There is an enforcement arm that is charged with enforcing those standards through inspection, investigation, the holding of hearings, and the levying of fines and other penalties. In fact, most of the litigation involving environmental matters takes place at the provincial level and involves provincial legislation. Often alternative remedies are provided that allow for negotiation, mediation, and agreements that facilitate working with the business to help them obtain compliance.

Provincial departments enforce environmental protection provisions

It is important to understand that even municipalities have extensive powers to deal with the environment. A business will often have to comply with municipal by-laws with respect to where a business is to locate. Nuisance, noise, odours, vibration, illumination, and dust emanating from the business, the discharge of sewage, and what can be discharged into the municipal drain system are also municipal concerns. This illustrates the major problem of overlap and duplication of environmental regulation at the various levels of government, especially where the granting of permits is concerned. For example, a permit under the provincial regulations may be granted for a pollution-causing activity, and yet it may still be in violation of federal statutes and punishable. Several provinces have taken steps to reform their environmental regulatory regime to make them more business friendly and eliminate red tape. For example, Nova Scotia has amalgamated several enactments into one statute. But the problem of complying with these various regulatory requirements at all levels of government remains and presents a serious problem for business.

Municipalities also have power to impose controls on business

Overlap of regulation poses a serious problem for business

INSURANCE

The main principle involved with insurance is the spreading of risk. Each participant pays a relatively small sum called a **premium** to cover a specified type of risk such as fire damage or lost property, and since only a few will have to be compensated, the risk of loss is thus spread among the many premium payers. In fact, huge sums are involved and large companies provide the insurance service, covering most of the various types of risk that may be encountered personally or in business. These companies will then often turn to even larger companies to insure themselves against unusual losses caused by unexpected circumstances such as the ice storm in Ontario and Quebec or the forest fires in British Columbia. This practice is called **reinsurance**. Because of the potential for abuse

Insurance involves paying a premium to spread the risk

Insurance companies will often reinsure to cover their risk

these companies are highly regulated, as are the insurance agents who sell the insurance coverage to businesses and the general public. Note that sometimes this insurance is obtained through an insurance broker rather than through an agent. The difference is that the **broker** represents the insured and arranges insurance for him or her with the companies, whereas the **insurance agent** represents the insurance company itself, either as an employee or an independent agent (see Figure 8.6). Today, acquiring insurance to cover many of the variables in business has become a vital aspect of carrying on business.

Insurance agents represent the company whereas insurance brokers represent the insured

The contracts involved, called **insurance policies**, usually take the form of a standard form contract dictated by regulation, and often a **rider**, which provides added coverage related to the unique needs of the particular customer, will be attached. The policies may be renewed each year with the premium changing to reflect changes in the market, higher costs of meeting the risks, or changes to the circumstances of the insured. When modifications to an existing policy are needed, an **endorsement** outlining the specific change is added.

Insurance policies may include riders or endorsements that modify or add to the original terms

A major area of insurance coverage deals with damage or loss of property, both personal and real. It is traditional in the insurance field to acquire specific coverage for different types of risk. Losses through fire, flood, accident, and theft must be specified. It is vital, therefore, that you exercise great care in determining the extent of the insurance coverage obtained. What is covered in the policy will vary from company to company and what looks like a more reasonable rate may only be lower because the coverage is less. Note that more comprehensive, all-risk policies are now available covering all of these risks.

Take care to read the contract, especially the fine print

There is a great similarity between insurance and a wager. A fee is paid and, if certain events take place, a large sum of money is returned. What makes insurance different is that when the event takes place, the insured doesn't "win" but is simply compensated for the loss. No windfall is experienced. Thus, to obtain insurance, the insured must have an **insurable interest** in the thing covered. If my neighbours took out insurance on my house and it burned down, they would not be able to collect since they have no insurable interest in my house and have, therefore, lost nothing. But if I were to take out insurance on my house and it burned down, I would be compensated for my loss to the extent of my interest. In the past it was thought that because a corporation is a separate legal entity, the shareholders had no insurable interest in the assets of the corporation. When a company was newly incorporated and assets were transferred to the corporation, any insurance policies also had to be transferred to the corporation. But the Supreme Court of Canada has made it clear that shareholders do have a sufficient, although indirect, interest in the assets of a corporation to take out insurance on them and receive compensation if they are damaged or destroyed.[18]

An insured must have an insurable interest to recover for a loss

Shareholders now have an insurable interest in a company's assets

Figure 8.6 Insurance

Agent of company

Insured

Insurance company

Broker agent of insured

---

[18] *Kosmopoulos v. Constitution Insurance Co. of Canada Ltd.*, [1987] 1 S.C.R. 2 (S.C.C.).

Case Summary 8.9 *Assaad v. The Economical Mutual Group*[19]

No Insurable Interest in Stolen Car

Mr. Assaad had a client who owed him $10 000 for financial services he had provided. That client sold him his car, valued at $30 000, for a payment of only $16 000, plus the cancellation of the $10 000 debt. Assaad insured the vehicle and, when it was stolen, made a claim. The insurance company investigated and determined that the car had been previously stolen, with the result that Mr. Assaad was not the rightful owner. Since the car was stolen, the client didn't have title to it or any right to transfer it to Mr. Assaad. The insurance company refused to pay the claim on the basis that Assaad, not being the lawful owner, had no insurable interest in the vehicle. At the Court of Appeal level the court agreed with the insurance company. The court held that because of the prior theft, Assaad had no right to the vehicle. Further, because he had no insurable interest, he had no right to claim. He had lost nothing because he had no right to the car in the first place. His only recourse was against the client who sold him the car, but he had left the country. This result may seem harsh, but it dramatically illustrates the nature of the requirement of an insurable interest to insure such assets.

Note also that any claim is limited to the extent of the insurable interest in the property. It would do no good to take out $500 000 insurance on a house only worth $400 000. The insurance company will only pay for the actual loss suffered, in this case no more than $400 000. On the other hand, there may be a temptation to underinsure a house to pay lower premiums covering only $200 000. This is also a problem. If there is a total loss there will only be partial coverage ($200 000 of the $400 000 loss), but even where the loss is less, because of **co-insurance** clauses in most policies, the insurance company will only pay a percentage of the loss. These clauses usually require that 80 percent coverage be maintained, so in this example, if the actual loss was only $50 000 and premiums paid were for $200 000 coverage, instead of the $320 000 required (80 percent of $400 000), the insurance company would pay only 200/320 of $50 000 = $31 250. Thus, you can readily see how important it is to maintain insurance approximately equal to the value of the property insured. In addition, insurance policies covering loss or damage to property usually require the insured to pay a deductible. For example, if a claim is determined to be $20 000 and there is a $1000 deductible, the insured will only receive $19 000 from the insurance company. As the deductible amount increases, the premium required will usually decrease. These principles apply whether real property such as buildings or personal property in the form of chattels are involved. The insurance company usually maintains the right to either repair the damage or replace the property insured. In either case they also retain the right to **salvage** whatever value they can from the replaced parts. Similarly, the insurance company will be **subrogated** to the rights of the insured. This means that once they have paid, they take over the rights of the insured to sue whoever caused the loss in the first place.

One major problem with property insurance is that it doesn't provide any compensation for the lost business opportunities caused by the delays in sorting out the rights of the parties and rebuilding or repairing premises. It is now quite common and quite prudent as a risk avoidance strategy for business people to obtain **business interruption insurance**, which provides an income during this downtime.

Be careful not to overinsure

Be careful not to underinsure

Insurer has the right to salvage what he or she can from the loss

Once paid, insurer assumes insured's right to sue

Insurance is also available to cover business downtime

---

[19] (2002), 214 D.L.R. (4th) 655 (Ont. C.A.).

Another major area of coverage deals with personal liability to others. This is called **liability insurance** and covers such things as other people or their property being harmed by a business person's personal conduct or through the operation of the business. Examples of such injury would be people injured while on business premises or in accidents involving vehicles owned by the company or driven by employees, as well as the malpractice of professionals. Normally, such liability insurance will not only provide coverage for the loss, but also will provide legal representation when the insured is being sued. This is in the insurance company's best interest, since it will ultimately have to pay if the insured is found liable for the loss or damage claimed.

As a rule insurance will only cover negligence in these situations, not the wilful actions of the insured or their employees. **Bonding** is similar to insurance and involves the business purchasing a **fidelity bond** to cover wrongful conduct by employees. If an employee steals or cheats clients, the bonding company will provide compensation, but retains the right to go after the employee to recover what they have to pay out. Sometimes a construction company will be required to put up a bond to ensure they will perform as required in a contract. This is a **surety bond** and guarantees performance of a contract rather than compensation for wrongful conduct.

> Liability insurance covers injury or loss caused to others

> Bonding is available to cover wrongful acts of employees . . .

> Or failure to perform contractual obligations

Case Summary 8.10 *Andrusiw v. Aetna Life Insurance*[20]

False Disability Claim Costs Claimant over a Quarter Million Dollars

Mr. Andrusiw had been receiving disability payments for several years as the result of a stroke, when the insurance company discovered he was still going into work regularly and supervising the operation of his own business. They cut off his payments and he brought this action to have them reinstated. With testimony from employees that he came to work every day and was making all the important decisions, the court held that he had misrepresented his level of disability. He was not only cut off from further benefits but the court ordered that the benefits he had received in the past also had to be repaid. This amounted to $259 000. People are often tempted to make insurance claims that are not justified, but this case dramatically illustrates what can happen when such false claims are made.

There are many other types of insurance that are commonly available. **Life insurance**, for example, provides compensation to named beneficiaries when the insured dies. **Term insurance** involves a premium paid strictly to insure against the death of the insured. **Whole life insurance** involves a certain investment aspect as well as the insurance coverage, so that the insured will receive a return on that investment to assist in his or her retirement. There are many different combinations of these various schemes, some of which have important income tax implications. From a business point of view, partners will often take out life insurance on their partners to sustain the business if one dies. Larger businesses will also take out life insurance on key personnel for the same reasons. Today, businesses also often supply health and disability insurance for their employees, providing extended coverage for such things as dental care and drugs over and above the basic provincial coverage provided in all jurisdictions in Canada. **Disability insurance**

> Life insurance pays beneficiary when insured dies

> Businesses often obtain life insurance on key personnel

> Health and disability insurance are also common

[20] Alta. Q.B., Murray J., June 13, 2001, as reported in *Lawyers Weekly Consolidated Digest*, Vol. 21.

provides an income to the insured when, because of accident or sickness, they can no longer work. For those who are professionals, self-employed, or in a business where such extended coverage is not provided, it can be obtained by paying a separate premium, often at higher rates, to an insurer on an individual basis. To have a separate policy and pay a separate premium for each of these various types of risk is not only a nuisance but would very likely result in gaps in the coverage. Today it is common to obtain comprehensive policies that will provide coverage for all or most of these various forms of risk in one policy without the requirement that each type of risk covered be specified. The cost may be a little higher, but the advantages usually outweigh the disadvantages. In today's business world an important component of business strategy is to reduce the risks faced by that business as much as possible. As can be seen from this discussion, acquiring appropriate insurance coverage is a vital aspect of realizing that goal of risk reduction.

A comprehensive policy covering all or many risks may be the best solution

Insurance involves a **good-faith relationship** between the insured and the insurance provider. That means that there is an obligation on the part of the insured to provide full disclosure of any condition or circumstance that might affect the creation of the policy or the cost of the premium. For example, with real property there is an obligation to inform the insurer if the premises are to be left vacant for any extended period of time or to be used in a way that exposes them to extra risk, for instance, storing fireworks, or changing its use from an office to some other function such as furniture manufacturing. With life or disability insurance there is an obligation to inform the insurance company of any pre-existing condition or disease that would put the insured at greater risk. Where this kind of information is intentionally withheld from the insurance company, it constitutes misrepresentation and may void the policy. A good example of this is found in a Quebec case[21] where the beneficiary of a smoker was denied the benefits of a life insurance policy, even though he was killed in a car accident. He had lied on his insurance application claiming he no longer smoked, and as a result he obtained insurance coverage at a reduced premium. This was sufficient for the insurance company to avoid payment of the benefit, even though the cause of death had nothing to do with his smoking. It should also be noted that this duty of good faith works both ways as illustrated by the following case.

Case Summary 8.11 *Whiten v. Pilot Insurance Co.*[22]

Punitive Damages Upheld for Insurance Company Abuse

The Whitens experienced a total loss of their home to fire on a winter night in 1994. The husband, wife, and daughter had to take refuge outside in sub-zero cold.

Mr. Whiten suffered serious frostbite to his feet as a result. The insurance company initially made a payment of $5000 for living expenses, which only covered expenses for a few months. They then cut off payment, leaving the family in very difficult financial circumstances. The company refused to pay any more, claiming the family had set fire to their own home. This resulted in lengthy litigation and trial, with the insurance company dragging its feet and adopting a confrontational style through the whole process. Finally, at trial the lawyer for the insurance company, in face of strong evidence from the fire chief and

>

---

[21] *Ouellet v. L'Industrielle compagnie d'assurance sur la vie*, Que. C.A., 1993, as reported in *Lawyers Weekly*, Vol. 12 No. 44 (March 26, 1993).

[22] [2002] 1 S.C.R. 595, 2002 SCC 18 (S.C.C.).

even from their own expert witness, was compelled to admit there was no basis for the claim of arson and no basis for the refusal of payment of the benefits of the insurance policy. Madam Chief Justice McLachlin characterized this conduct as exceptionally reprehensible. It was planned and deliberate, taking place over a two-year period. It not only denied the Whitens compensation for their loss and the extra costs of finding new accommodation, but also imposed considerable unnecessary legal costs as well. An incensed jury not only awarded $345 000 for the insurance claim and $320 000 for legal costs in compensation but also $1 million in punitive damages. This was reduced on appeal but reinstated by the Supreme Court of Canada in this very important decision. This case illustrates the special relationship of trust between an insurance company and their clients. It also indicates the powerful impact of punitive damages as a method of controlling abuses of such good-faith relationships.

Key Terms

abatement (p. 218)

adverse possession (p. 212)

agreement of purchase and sale (p. 212)

bailee (p. 203)

bailment (p. 203)

bailment for value (p. 204)

bailor (p. 203)

bonding (p. 227)

broker (p. 225)

building scheme (p. 207)

business interruption insurance (p. 226)

certificate of indefeasible title (p. 211)

chattels (p. 201)

chose in action (p. 201)

co-insurance (p. 226)

condominium (p. 209)

condominium corporation (p. 209)

cooperatives (p. 210)

deed of conveyance (p. 212)

disability insurance (p. 227)

distrain (p. 217)

dominant tenement (p. 207)

dower rights (p. 208)

easement (p. 207)

endorsement (p. 225)

equity (p. 213)

equity of redemption (p. 213)

estate (p. 206)

fee simple estate (p. 206)

fidelity bond (p. 227)

fixture (p. 205)

foreclosure (p. 213)

forfeiture (p. 217)

good-faith relationship (p. 228)

goods (p. 201)

gratuitous bailment for the benefit of the bailee (p. 203)

gratuitous bailment for the benefit of the bailor (p. 203)

homestead rights (p. 208)

insurable interest (p. 225)

insurance agent (p. 225)

insurance policies (p. 225)

intellectual property (p. 201)

involuntary bailment (p. 203)

joint tenancy (p. 208)

judicial sale (p. 214)

land registry (p. 210)

land titles system (p. 211)

leasehold estate (p. 215)

liability insurance (p. 227)

licence (p. 208)

lien (p. 211)

life estate (p. 206)

life insurance (p. 227)

mortgage (p. 210)

mortgagee (p. 212)

mortgagor (p. 212)

option to purchase (p. 210)

periodic leases (p. 215)

personal property (p. 201)

power of sale (p. 214)

premium (p. 224)

prescription (p. 212)

private nuisance (p. 206)

profit à prendre (p. 208)

quiet enjoyment (p. 217)

real property (p. 201)

reinsurance (p. 224)

relief against forfeiture (p. 217)

remainder (p. 206)

restrictive covenant (p. 207)

reversion (p. 206)

rider (p. 225)

right of way (p. 207)

salvage (p. 226)

second mortgage (p. 213)

security deposit (p. 219)

servient tenement (p. 207)

subrogated (p. 226)

surety bond (p. 227)

tenancy in common (p. 208)

term insurance (p. 227)

vacant possession (p. 217)

whole life insurance (p. 227)

Questions for Student Review

1. Distinguish between real property, personal property, and intellectual property. Distinguish between a chattel and a chose in action. Explain how personal property can be used to secure a loan.

2. Explain how the expression "finders keepers" relates to property law. Explain who is entitled to goods found in the public part of a building. What if it is found by an employee of the owners of the building?

3. Explain bailment and the obligations of the bailee when it is a gratuitous bailment for the benefit of the bailee. What if it is for the benefit of the bailor? What if the bailee is an inn-keeper or common carrier?

4. Explain what is meant by a fee simple estate in land and any limitation on a person's right to that land. How can personal property become real property?

5. What is the nature of a life estate? Who is entitled to the reversion and what obligations are imposed on the holder?

6. Distinguish between a leasehold estate and other interests in land. Explain what is meant by a periodic tenancy.

7. Distinguish between an easement, a right of way, a restrictive covenant, and a building scheme.

8. Compare a joint tenancy and a tenancy in common, and explain severance and its effect on such tenancies.

9. Explain the nature of a mortgage and how it is used to secure a loan. Identify the parties to the mortgage.

10. Distinguish between the effects of registration in a land registry as opposed to a land titles jurisdiction, and explain why registration of interests in land is important. How does a mortgage affect the title in these jurisdictions?

11. Explain what is meant by adverse possession and prescription, and the role these principles play in land titles and land registry jurisdictions.

12. Describe an equity of redemption, foreclosure, and the redemption period. Why are they important to mortgage transactions?

13. Explain what is meant by a lease and distinguish the lease from other types of interests in land. What is meant by a periodic lease and how is it ended?

14. Summarize the landlord's and tenant's obligations with respect to commercial tenancies and the lease terms on those obligations. Indicate the amount of notice that must be given by the parties to terminate the tenancy or to increase the rent.

15. How do most residential tenancy statutes modify the obligations of the parties to make repairs to the premises? Explain how the rights of the landlord to enter residential premises have been restricted.

16. Explain the nature of a security deposit and any restrictions on how much can be taken and what it can be used for.

17. Explain the landlord's obligations with respect to services provided during the term of the tenancy. What can a landlord do when a tenant defaults in a residential tenancy?

18. Why does federal legislation with respect to the environment become important to landowners and business people?

19. Explain the role of the *Canadian Environmental Protection Act* and how its objectives are realized.

20. Explain the role of enforcement officers appointed under the *Canadian Environmental Protection Act* and how they can interact with business.

21. Who can be charged with an offence under the *Canadian Environmental Protection Act*?

22. Explain what is meant by an insurable interest, and distinguish between an insurance agent and a broker.

23. Explain the nature of the insurance policy, a rider, an endorsement, and reinsurance. Summarize the different types of insurance that are available to businesses.

24. Distinguish between liability, property, and life insurance. Explain the difference between whole life and term insurance, indicating why life insurance might be important for a business or for professionals to acquire.

25. Distinguish between bonding and insurance. Explain the difference between a fidelity bond and a surety bond.

Questions for Further Discussion

1. There is a considerable difference between the laws with respect to residential and commercial tenancies. Most of the statutory changes favour the tenant and have led to considerable complaints by landlords about the difficult position they find themselves in. Do you feel that the changes introduced by statute have unfairly interfered with what should be a relatively simple commercial relationship? Is this another instance of government imposing inappropriate regulation that unfairly restricts a landlord's right to manage his or her property? Consider this as a form of consumer protection legislation and ask what problem it was intended to solve, whether an adequate solution has been arrived at, and whether the solution creates more problems than it solves.

2. Bailment involves one person putting his or her personal property into the care of another. The responsibility to look after that property is often limited in the contract creating that relationship. Do you think that a party agreeing to be responsible to look after another's property, either in the process of repair, storage, or otherwise, ought to be able to contract out of their responsibilities with an exemption clause? This question really is much broader. This is because, whenever an exemption clause is included in any contract, one party is severely disadvantaged. Should the parties to contracts, especially where the

bailment of goods is involved, be able to contract out of such basic responsibilities? In your discussion consider the often unequal bargaining power of the parties, standard form contracts, and the concept of fundamental breach discussed in Chapters 4 and 5 and how it should be applied to these contracts.

3. Consider the laws that have been imposed on individuals and businesses to control pollution and reduce waste. Is this a reasonable demand? Consider how these policies might impact Canadian businesses that operate abroad, perhaps to evade these costly requirements.

4. A serious problem that often arises for an insured claiming on an insurance policy is the requirement that all information be accurate or that any changes in circumstances be communicated to the insurance company. Benefits have been denied when the loss takes place when the premises were left vacant, where the use of the premises has changed, or where the information on the application is accidentally or knowingly incorrect—even if the information has nothing to do with the event giving rise to the claim. Discuss whether such an approach is too harsh and gives too much advantage to the insurance companies and whether consumers are adequately protected from abuse.

Cases for Discussion

1. *Senecal v. The Queen* (1983), 3 D.L.R. (4th) 684 (F.C.T. D.).

   Mr. Senecal was an employee of Air Canada, working as a loading supervisor at Dorval airport, when he found a packet of money on the floor of the cafeteria and turned it over to the RCMP. It turned out to consist of US$10 000. He was told that if it were not claimed by the rightful owner within three months, it would be returned to him. After waiting the three months, Mr. Senecal asked that he be given the money but his request was refused. Instead, the regional administrator chose to give him only $2000 and gave the rest to charity. Mr. Senecal brought this action to recover the entire $10 000 to which he felt entitled as the finder. Discuss the rights of the parties in this situation. How would it affect your answer to learn that there was a regulation in place empowering the administrator to dispose of personal property by choosing one of the following courses of action: 1) by returning it to the finder if the finder was not an employee of the department; 2) by disposing of the property by private sale or auction; 3) by disposition to a charitable institution; or 4) by destruction? (See section 3 of the *Airport Personal Property Disposal Regulations*, C.R.C. 1978, c. 1563, made pursuant to the *Department of Transport Act*, R.S.C. 1970, c. T-5.)

2. *Heffron v. Imperial Parking Co. et al.* (1974), 46 D.L.R. (3d) 642 (Ont. C.A.).

   Mr. Heffron parked his car in a parking lot operated by Imperial Parking Company and left the keys in the ignition as instructed by the attendant. When he returned at about 1:00 a.m., he found the car missing. It was eventually found with considerable damage and several personal items missing. The lot in fact closed at midnight but the practice was for the attendant to take the keys of the cars remaining and give them to an attendant at a nearby parking garage, who would then return them to the owners when they claimed their cars. Discuss the obligation of the operators of the parking lot in these circumstances.

   How would it affect your answer if the ticket involved contained the words, "We are not responsible for theft or damage of car or contents, however caused." What if the driver had merely parked the car and taken the keys with him?

3. *Paramount Life Insurance Co. v. Hill et al.* (1986), 34 D.L.R. (4th) 150 (Alta. C.A.).

Mrs. Audrey Hill owned a house, and her husband, without her knowledge, forged her name on transfer documents to his business partner, Mr. Laidlaw. He then arranged for a mortgage on that property with Paramount in the name of the new owner, Laidlaw. Mr. Laidlaw then rented the premises back to Mr. Hill. No mortgage payments were made by Laidlaw, who thought the Hills were making them. Mr. Hill died and Mrs. Hill knew nothing about the mortgage. Paramount commenced foreclosure proceedings against the property. When Laidlaw learned what had happened, he retransferred the property to Mrs. Hill. She claimed in this action that the mortgage should be set aside because of the fraud and that full title to the home should be restored to her. There was no evidence that Mr. Laidlaw or Paramount knew anything about the forged documents or Mrs. Hill's claims. Discuss what would likely happen in a land titles jurisdiction and how this would be different in a normal land registry system. What other recourse might be available to Mrs. Hill in a land titles jurisdiction?

4. *R. v. Petro-Canada* (2002), 222 D.L.R. (4th) 601 (Ont. C.A.).

Petro-Canada was charged with "discharging a contaminant into the environment," an offence under the Ontario *Environmental Protection Act*. In fact, a pipe had failed and leaked gasoline, but Petro-Canada responded quickly. It was also established that there were a number of safety systems and procedures in place. Petro-Canada claimed due diligence as a defence. Explain what must be established to succeed in a due diligence defence and on which side the onus of proof resides. How would it affect your deliberations to know they had used piping "not up to industry standards?"

5. *Cleghorn v. Royal & Sunalliance Insurance Co.*, 2002 NBQB 399 (CanLII) (2002), 256 N.B.R. (2d) 153.

Ms. Cleghorn bought a car (a Volkswagen Fox) from Mr. Gaudet at a coffee shop for $150. She had a friend drive it home for her and on the way the car was involved in a collision. She had no insurance on the car and did not intend to drive it until her 21st birthday 10 days later. Ms. Cleghorn was under the impression that the insurance of Mr. Gaudet would remain on the car until the next day. In fact that insurance was cancelled by a phone call to the insurance agent with the cancellation effective officially the next day. The insurance company took the position that as soon as the car was sold and title transferred, which took place in the coffee shop, Mr. Gaudet's insurance no longer applied. Ms. Cleghorn sued claiming she was the insured under Mr. Gaudet's policy. Explain the arguments on both sides and the likely outcome of the action.

Chapter 9
Ideas and Information

Learning Objectives

■ Distinguish between intellectual property and other kinds of property

■ List and describe what is protected under copyright law

■ Explain what a patent protects, and how patent protection is obtained

■ Describe what is protected by the *Trade-marks Act*

■ Describe confidential information and the ways it can be protected

■ Consider the role of privacy acts and describe how they protect a business from disclosure of confidential information

Great changes caused by computers and internet

An information revolution has taken place over the past 30 years, fuelled primarily by the use of computers. This chapter discusses the intersection between law, business, and information technology. It includes an examination of intellectual property, including copyright, patents, and trademarks, as well as a review of the legal issues associated with securing information and protecting personal privacy. The following chapter is devoted to examining the legal issues associated with electronic commerce and international trade and includes a discussion of doing business over the internet. These issues have become extremely important in recent times with the general impact of technology on business. Not only is technology changing so fast it is difficult to keep up, but our understanding of the social impact of these changes and the development of laws to govern them are also lagging behind technological change. In this chapter we can do no more than outline the problems and the directions in which our lawmakers seem to be going.

INTELLECTUAL PROPERTY

We identified the forms of property in the last chapter, dividing personal property into chattels (tangible, movable goods), and choses in action (intangible personal property).

Intellectual property is intangible personal property

Intellectual property is a special type of intangible personal property. Copyright does not refer to a particular book, song, or painting, but to the right to control its reproduction. In the same sense patents, trademarks, and industrial designs do not refer to actual things produced, but to the protection of the idea, mark, or design associated with a product.

Intellectual property is a valuable business asset that can be stolen or damaged. Unauthorized exploitation may deprive the author of income from a copyright, or damage the goodwill associated with a trademark. Patented inventions can be misappropriated, and confidential information can be misused. Intellectual property is often underdeveloped, undervalued, and underprotected by business people. A business may be so focused on marketing that it fails to realize the potential of a production process or software that has been developed for its own purposes. If a business does sell or licence the process or software, there may be a failure to properly account for royalties.

Intellectual property law usually requires that active steps be taken to protect an asset. The federal government has enacted legislation dealing with intellectual property, including copyrights, patents, and trademarks. Thus, most disputes dealing with intellectual property matters are heard by the Federal Court, but this is one area where federal and provincial courts both have jurisdiction, and so these matters may be dealt with by provincial superior courts as well.

Copyright

The federal *Copyright Act*[1] protects books, photos, music, and other artistic works. Keep in mind that it is only the expression of the idea that is protected, not the idea itself. If someone photocopies the text that you are now reading, they will be in breach of the author's copyright, but if they simply write another book expressing the same ideas in a different way, they have a right to do that. **Copyright** protection is extended to authors and artists for 50 years after the death of the creator of the work. In effect, the owner of the copyright controls the reproduction of the work during that period, after which the work becomes part of the public domain and no longer subject to anyone's control. The idea is to give the creator of the intellectual property the exclusive right to profit from and otherwise control his or her creation for a specified period of time. This period is reduced to just 50 years when a corporation is involved, the author is not known, or the work involves such things as movies, photographs, or sound recordings.

It is common for a publishing company to produce and market the work and for the author, artist, or composer to receive royalties from the sales. **Royalties** consist of a percentage payment (for example, 10 percent), based on the net proceeds the publisher receives from each item sold. The copyright is then assigned to the publishing company. Of course, creators can publish their own material, retaining for themselves complete control over the copying, reproduction, or performance of their work.

Even where the copyright has been assigned to a publisher or some other party, the author retains some significant rights. **Moral rights** consist primarily of the author having the right to continue to have his or her name associated with the work as creator, and to have the integrity of the work preserved. This means that the work cannot be modified, distorted, or defaced without the author's permission, even after it has been sold. If an author assigned the copyright of a book to a publisher, who then decided to publish it using the name of a different author, that would violate the original author's moral rights. An example of the protection of moral rights involved a sculpture of Canadian geese in a shopping mall. A retailer decided to hang red ribbons on it for Christmas. The sculptor protested; the court agreed that the added decoration interfered with the artist's moral rights not to have his work degraded and ordered the mall to remove the ribbons.[2] It is not always the creator of the work who is entitled to copyright. Where an author is working as an employee, the work created will belong to the employer, unless the employment

Businesses often undervalue and fail to protect intellectual property

Federal and provincial courts often have concurrent jurisdiction with respect to intellectual property

Copyright protects the expression of the idea, not the idea itself

Copyright lasts for the life of author plus 50 years

Copyright can be assigned, but authors retain moral rights

Employers entitled to copyright unless agreement otherwise

---

[1] *Copyright Act*, R.S.C. 1985, c. C-42.

[2] *Snow v. Eaton Centre Ltd.* (1982), 70 C.P.R. (2d) 105 (Ont. H.C.J.).

contract states otherwise. Also, where consultants write an instruction manual for a software producer, for example, the contract may state that copyright will be held by the software company. It is vitally important that contractors specify not only what work is to be created, but also which party will acquire copyright.

Case Summary 9.1 *Parker v. Key Porter Books Ltd.*[3]

Punitive Damages Awarded for Copyright Infringement

Tonya Maracle was a Mohawk artist who produced several small, unique wood pieces called dream catchers (a striking circular piece constructed of interwoven twigs and other material.) A representative of Key Porter Books Limited approached Ms. Maracle and expressed an interest in publishing photographs of them and to that end she gave her permission so long as they would be used only in a children's book and that Soaring Eagle, the business she owned with her sister, would get the credit. This was agreed and several of the dream catchers were taken and she heard nothing more for several weeks. Finally, she received a letter returning them but with no explanation. She simply assumed that Key Porter had changed their minds. But her sister discovered a book published by Key Porter Books, *Dreamcatchers: Myths and History*, which contained 21 photographs of Ms. Maracle's dream catchers, including a picture on the cover. A total of 9550 copies of the book had been published. This action was brought against Key Porter Books

for breach of copyright. The judge found that the book distorted the history of dream catchers and was further inaccurate in portraying the pictures of Ms. Maracle's work as Ojibwe art when it was in fact Mohawk. Damages were awarded representing the profits that Key Porter Books had made on the sales, for the goodwill that had been generated in favour of Key Porter by its infringement, and for failing to credit Soaring Eagle as required. It is interesting that the judge ordered $25 000 be paid because of the damage done to the business of Soaring Eagle. Their business of selling dream catchers had substantially fallen off as soon as the book was published. Note that the books contained detailed instructions on how to make dream catchers. The plaintiff also asked for punitive damages, but although the court found the conduct of Key Porter disgraceful, it was not an appropriate case to award punitive damages. The total award of damages was for $40 000 for infringement on copyright.

Computer software is now protected by copyright

In addition to the creative products mentioned above, there are several less obvious areas that are covered by the *Copyright Act*. Copyright can extend to "every original literary, dramatic, musical and artistic work" produced in Canada as well as a "performer's performance, sound recording, and communication signals." Past confusion about whether computer programs and software were better protected under patent or copyright legislation resulted in amendments to the *Copyright Act* to protect computer programs as literary work. Table 9.1 lists examples of what is included in these various categories. Note that there can be considerable overlap among them.

Copyright protection in Canada can give protection in other jurisdictions

Other nations have similar laws, and there are treaties between nations giving copyright protection in one nation to works created in another. So long as the originator is a citizen or resident of Canada, or of a country that is a signatory to the Universal Copyright Convention, the Bern Convention, the Rome Convention, or is a member of the World Trade Organization, that work has copyright protection in Canada and those other countries.

---

[3] (2005), 40 C.P.R. (4th) 80 (ON S.C.).

Table 9.1 The Scope of Copyright

Category	Examples
Literary works	Books, manuals, computer programs, and translations
Dramatic work	Plays, recitations, mime, movies (including the scenery)
Musical work	Musical compositions and arrangements
Artistic work	Paintings, drawings, maps, charts, plans, photographs, engravings, and sculptures
Performances	Dancing, singing, instrumentals, acrobatics, and acting
Sound recording	Tape recordings, records, computer memory, compact disks, memory cards, and DVDs
Communication signals	Radio, television, cable, and internet broadcasts

It is also important to note that no special steps need be taken in Canada to create copyright. Registration is not required, since the mere production of the work creates the copyright. Still, registration is permitted under our Act[4] and this is often done to establish when the work was created or to ensure that the work has copyright protection in other nations that require such registration. Copyright is indicated by the symbol © accompanied by the year of publication and the name of the copyright holder.

Copyright protection is automatic in Canada but registration provides additional benefits

Case Summary 9.2 *Boudreau v. Lin et al.*[5]

Students Own Copyright in Papers Written for Professors

Boudreau was an MBA student attending university under the supervision of the defendant Lin. As part of the requirements, he prepared a paper and submitted it to Lin. Lin later published it along with another professor as contributor with only minor revisions and without acknowledging the role Boudreau played in its preparation. The paper was later included in a casebook, which was used in other classes at the university. When Boudreau discovered his paper in the casebook, he brought this action against both the university and Profession Lin. The court found that Professor Lin "was neither the originator nor the developer of any substantive ideas or concepts. His contributions consisted of general comments that were directed to polishing the paper and were those which one expects from a professor who is editing and discussing a paper written by a student. None of the changes he proposed affected the substance of the paper." He could not even be called a co-author. The court found that Professor Lin and the university as his employer were liable for breaching Mr. Boudreau's copyright with respect to the paper in question. Note as well that the court determined that Mr. Boudreau's moral rights in the paper had also been breached by the changes made, which affected the integrity of the work, and by the removal of his name as author. The judge characterized this as an example of plagiarism and academic dishonesty, which "most certainly should not be tolerated from the professors who should be sterling examples of intellectual rigour and honesty." The actual award of $7500 in general damage didn't reflect his loss which was difficult to calculate, rather the amount was in recognition of his indignation and the wrong committed against him. The court also issued an injunction to refrain the defendants from interfering with Mr. Boudreau's copyright in the paper.

---

[4] *Copyright Act*, R.S.C. 1985, c. C-42, s. 54.

[5] (1997), 150 D.L.R. (4th) 324 (Ont. Gen. Div.); *Aubry v. Duclos et al.*; *Canadian Broadcasting Corp.*, *Intervener* (1997), 157 D.L.R. (4th) 577 (S.C.C.).

To qualify for copyright protection, the work must be original. This doesn't mean it has to satisfy some critical standard, but it must originate with the author. Facts, numbers, images, or material copied from other sources are not protected by copyright, only the part that originates with the author or artist is protected. The protected work must also be fixed in some permanent form as in the recording of a song in digital format or capturing of an image on film. It could also include a written choreography, a stage play, or a manuscript stored on computer.

It is only when substantial portions of the work are copied that there is an infringement of the copyright. Photocopying a few pages of a textbook for personal use might not violate copyright but copying several chapters or even a few lines of a vital portion clearly would. Use of small portions of a work for research or for private study is permitted, and there is no infringement when portions of a work are reproduced for review, criticism, or news reporting. Educational institutions, as well as libraries, museums, and archives have additional rights to use portions of such works for educational and research purposes. Special exceptions are made for reproductions that are done to facilitate someone who is blind or deaf. But just because an item is available in a library or archive doesn't mean it can be freely copied without consequence.

The solution is to get a licence from Access Copyright, which is the non-profit body set up to represent authors in these matters. Access Copyright collects a fee and distributes it to the author, legitimizing a reasonable amount of photocopying. SOCAN provides the same service for musicians and composers of recorded music. The Copyright Board, a government regulatory body established under the *Copyright Act,* sets the royalty fees charged by these bodies and other matters, including the arbitration of some disputes with respect to copyright.

Canadian intellectual property law is now under attack as being outmoded and not providing appropriate protection for artists, authors, and producers. Primarily this is based on a failure to impose sufficient restrictions on the uploading and downloading of music, video, and other material on the internet and for a failure to effectively prevent the illegal copying of movies and their export. Twenty-five percent of the global pirating of movies takes place in Canada. In the United States, for example, downloading of music over the internet is considered a violation of copyright and effective measures have been introduced to stop it. A jury recently awarded the Recording Industry Association of America a $220 000 judgment against Jamie Thomas, a young Minnesota woman trading music in a peer-to-peer internet process.[6] In Canada, at least at the time of writing, her conduct would not be actionable.

The United States Trade Representative has placed Canada on a watch list for its lack of intellectual property protection measures. There is tremendous pressure for Canada to ratify a series of treaties developed by the World Intellectual Property Organization (WIPO), which would incorporate these protective measures, and while there is dispute here as to whether the adoption of such a restrictive approach is a good idea, it is likely that Canada will not be able to resist the pressure. In fact, at the time of writing there is legislation being advanced to amend the *Copyright Act* by adopting the much more stringent American approach to downloading from the internet.

For copyright protection work must be original and fixed in a permanent form

Limited copying is permitted

Licences to copy can be obtained for a fee

---

[6] "RIAA Wins $220,000 Judgment in First Lawsuit Over Music Downloads," *Lawsuits & Judgments*, October 5, 2007, http://lawsuitsandjudgments.com/riaa-wins-220000judgment-in-first-lawsuit-over-music-downloads-35.html.

Patents

A **patent** is a form of monopoly that gives an inventor the exclusive right to produce and profit from his or her invention for a period of 20 years. A government regulatory body created for that purpose deals with applications. The inventor must disclose in the form of drawings, plans, and text material enough information so that someone else could reproduce the invention. Inventors are encouraged to share their invention with others who will then benefit by the knowledge and be inspired to further innovation and invention. There is no obligation to disclose this information by getting a patent, but when it is kept secret, there is the danger that someone else will independently produce the same item. In such a case the first inventor will have no protection. If the second inventor is granted a patent, the original inventor will be prohibited from using his or her own invention. The source of these rights in Canada is the federal *Patent Act.*[7]

> Patent protection continues for 20 years but requires disclosure

Unlike copyright, it is the idea that is protected in a patent, not the expression of the idea. Thus, if someone produces another product that is quite dissimilar to a patented invention, but incorporates the same principles or ideas, it would still be an infringement of the patent associated with that invention. The Act defines an **invention** as ". . . any new and useful art, process, machine, manufacture or composition of matter, or any new and useful improvement in any art, process, machine, manufacture or composition of matter."[8] To be patentable the invention must be useful in the sense that it is functional or can do what it claims and contributes in some way to improving our society by making some aspect of production more efficient or our lives more enjoyable. It also must be new. A patent will not be granted to someone who simply finds some process or machine that is in use but has not been patented. A patent will be denied if the invention has been the subject of prior publication more than a year before the application. It will also not succeed if the invention is embodied in some product that has been sold prior to the application or if the nature of the invention can be discovered by examination of the product, known as **reverse engineering**.

> Patent protects the idea, not the work itself

> Invention must be new and useful

Case Summary 9.3 *Canwell Enviro-Industries Ltd. v. Baker Petrolite Corp.*[9]

Patent Protection a Business Concern

Baker Petrolite developed a product to remove the offensive odour from sour gas. But its patent was challenged on the grounds that it had been disclosed to the public more than a year before the patent had been applied for. In fact, Petrolite had started to sell the product more than a year before applying for patent protection in either the United States or Canada, and the court held that this amounted to such disclosure and refused the patent. Although they didn't actually disclose how the product could be made, it was a simple matter of reverse engineering for an expert in the field to take the product, analyze it, and reproduce the effect. The patent was invalid. Note the dilemma of the manufacturer, who is often pressured to get the product to market as fast as possible but also to delay long enough to get patent protection.

---

[7] R.S.C. 1985, c. P-4.

[8] *Patent Act*, R.S.C. 1985, c. P-4 s. 1.

[9] (2002), 23 C.P.R. (4th) 346 (F.C.C.A.).

Nor will a patent be granted for some improvement to an existing machine or process that would have been obvious to someone with similar knowledge and training. The Act also makes it clear that, "No patent shall be granted for any mere scientific principle or abstract theorem."[10] Thus Einstein's famous formula $E = MC^2$ could not be the subject of a patent.

No patent is granted for obvious improvement, scientific principle, or higher life form

Also, higher life forms such as modified animals are not patentable in Canada.[11] But the Supreme Court has made it clear that a modified gene can be patented. To protect that gene, the court will also protect the animal or plant produced by that modified gene, thus arguably accomplishing the patenting of modified animals indirectly.[12]

It has become common practice in the United States to patent unique methods of carrying on business, but such **business patents** were thought not to be available in Canada. In recent years, however, this has changed and business patents have been granted in Canada, albeit not on the same scale as in the United States. It has also been thought that computer software was not patentable in Canada but this has also changed, especially where some physical component or technological device is associated with the software program.

Special provisions are in place with respect to the production of patent medicines in Canada. These are designed to consider the interests of consumers and protect them from excessive pricing, while providing sufficient protection and income to the patent holder. Historically, Canada forced international companies to grant licences at low cost to Canadian companies so that they could produce cheaper generic drugs for this country. That was changed in 1993. Drug manufacturers gained greater patent protection with the cost of patented drugs going up as a result. This has been balanced by introducing the requirement that the prices at which patent-protected drugs are sold must be justified before a Patented Medicine Prices Review Board (PMPRB). The result has been a significant increase in the price of patent-protected drugs in this country. To make matters worse, practices such as "**evergreening**" have been introduced to further increase the length of patent protection. This involves developing some small change in the already successful drug so that it can be treated as a new drug with another 20-year span of patent protection.

Note that the problem is much worse for third-world countries that simply cannot afford the costs of modern drugs. The World Trade Organization (WTO) now permits the creation of generic drugs, under licence, for export to third-world countries, and this has gone some distance toward responding to the battle against AIDS, especially in Africa. Historically, this had to be left to the generosity of the drug producers, the patent holders, to supply such drugs for such third-world requirements. Now that licences are granted to other producers, cheaper drugs are available, but there is also a growing problem with the cheaper drugs getting back into Western countries at the lower costs.

Patent must be applied for and fee paid

Unlike copyright, patent protection does not come automatically, but must be applied for. The process of applying for a patent is complex and expensive, and is best left to the experts who are registered patent agents. They, typically, will make a search of the patent registries of Canada and other countries to see if a similar patent has been granted. Then they will submit an application in which they set out full disclosure with respect to the invention. The documentation must also describe what is new and innovative about the

---

[10] *Patent Act*, R.S.C. 1985, C. P-4 s.27(8).

[11] *Harvard College v. Canada (Commissioner of Patents)*, [2002] 4 S.C.R. 45 (S.C.C.).

[12] *Monsanto Canada Inc. v. Schmeiser*, [2004] 1 S.C.R. 902 (S.C.C.).

invention. The application must be provided in a specified form, along with accompanying documents and a fee to the patent office. The documents are examined to determine if the invention qualifies as something new. If it is indeed new, and the requisite fees are paid, the commissioner for patents grants approval for the patent. The payment of an annual maintenance fee is also required to maintain the patent protection over its 20-year life.

Once a patent has been obtained, the invention must be used. Inventors can't simply sit on their invention, using their patent rights to prevent others from using them. Upon application to the patent board, an individual can require a patent holder to grant a licence to use the invention, thus ensuring that the public benefits from it.

Where patent not used, the patent holder can be forced to grant a licence

Although a patent granted in Canada only provides patent protection in this country, once a patent has been granted here, protection can be obtained in other countries that are signatories to applicable treaties. The general rule is that the first to apply is the one entitled to the patent. But under these treaties this priority is established with the original application in Canada, not the later date of application in another country. The reverse is also true, of course, giving patents obtained in other countries priority in Canada as well. Foreign patents are vitally important for Canadian businesses involved in significant international trade.

Canadian patent establishes right to patent in other jurisdictions

As was the case with copyright, it is important to include provisions that clearly state who is entitled to any patent arising from work done under the contract or pursuant to the employment in contracts with consultants, employees, and independent contractors. Note that when an employee creates copyrightable material, there is an assumption that the copyright vests in the employer, but the same is not true with a patent. In that case, without a contract stating otherwise, the employee inventor is entitled to the patent even if created during working hours unless inventing was the purpose of his employment.[13] As was the case with copyright, patents can be assigned to third parties and can be used as security for a corporation's financing arrangements.

Employee has right to patent unless agreement otherwise

Decisions to grant or not grant a patent or patent infringements may be challenged in the Federal Court, which has the ultimate jurisdiction with respect to the validity of such patents and the rights associated with them. Where an infringement has taken place, the *Patent Act* gives both the federal and provincial courts concurrent jurisdiction to deal with that infringement and to provide appropriate remedies.

Federal and provincial courts can hear patent infringement case

Two other acts providing similar protection are the *Industrial Design Act* and the *Integrated Circuit Topography Act*. These federal statutes are relatively unknown but can provide significant protection in the right circumstance. The *Industrial Design Act*[14] protects distinctive designs, shapes, or patterns associated with a product that have no useful function, but simply add to the appeal. The distinctive shapes of a utensil, a chair, or even the unique icons found on computer screens are examples. Protection of such designs is acquired by registration lasting for 10 years with the payment of the appropriate fees. The *Integrated Circuit Topography Act*[15] is legislation intended to protect the unique design of the integrated circuits that are the heart of the modern computer revolution. The various components that make radios, televisions, computers, automobiles, watches, and most other modern products work are now miniaturized onto semi-conductor material. They form the *integrated circuits* protected by this Act. To obtain this protection the design must be registered, and the protection also continues for a 10-year period.

Industrial Design Act protects distinctive shapes

Integrated Circuit Topography Act protects printed circuit design

---

[13] *Comstock Canada v. Electec Ltd.*, 38 C.P.R. (3d) 29, 45 F.T.R. 241 (FCTD).

[14] R.S.C. 1985, c. I-9.

[15] S.C. 1990, c. 37.

Trademarks

Trademarks are names, symbols, logos, or other distinctive marks that are associated with a business. A valuable business asset is its good relationships with customers, suppliers, and the public. This is referred to as goodwill and is often associated with the business name or some distinctive mark such as McDonald's golden arches or the shell symbol appearing on all of Shell's service stations and other operations. The federal *Trade-marks Act*[16] provides a mechanism for trademarks to become registered and protected in a formal way. This protection gives the owner of the trademark the exclusive right to use it throughout Canada with respect to the particular type of business, or similar products or services as indicated on the application. This protection lasts for a period of 15 years and is renewable, but it must be used during that time or it will be considered abandoned. A trademark registered in Canada will provide proof of ownership for registration in another country. The converse is also true; registration in another country will provide proof of ownership in Canada.

Trade-marks Act protects distinctive names and logos

Trademark protection is obtained by registration and lasts for 15 years

If another business uses a similar symbol so as to cause confusion, making its customers think they are dealing with the actual owner of the trademark, an infringement has taken place. Intentional copying of a registered trademark is not the only way an infringement can take place. Any use of a similar mark that devalues the goodwill or reputation of the business can qualify as an infringement, whether intentional or not.

Infringement involves others using the mark to confuse the public or devalue the business

---

Case Summary 9.4 *Mattel, Inc. v. 3894207 Canada Inc.*[17]

What's in a Name?

A numbered Ontario company was doing business as "Barbie's" Restaurants in several locations in Montreal. When it attempted to register a trademark to that effect, it was opposed by the Mattel company, claiming that it infringed on their registered trademark for their "Barbie" doll, a very successful toy doll marketed by that company. The restaurant chain countered that the use of the name was with reference to the term Bar-B-Q as in "Throw some ribs on the barbie" and that it was so different that it would not cause confusion among the public. The Trademarks Opposition Board of Canada agreed, allowing registration of the "Barbie" trademark for the Montreal restaurant chain. This was appealed by the Mattel organization all the way to the Supreme Court of Canada, with each court agreeing with the board and allowing registration of the restaurant's "Barbie" name. The Court upheld the original decision finding that there was little likelihood of confusing the "Barbie" doll with the restaurant chain. "Barbie's" fame was tied to dolls, not restaurants, and so there was no confusion created.

A similar result took place when Toyota challenged a food company for using the name "Lexus foods"[18] and when the producers of Cliquot Champagne tried to prevent a chain of small women's clothing stores from using the "Cliquot" name for their stores.[19] These cases show that similar trademarks can sometimes exist side by side if they are for different products and don't cause confusion in the market place.

---

[16] R.S.C. 1985, c. T-13.

[17] [2006] 1 S.C.R. 772; (2006), 268 D.L.R. (4th) 424; (2006), 53 Admin. L.R. (4th) 1; (2006), 49 C.P.R. (4th) 321.

[18] *Toyota Jidosha Kabushiki Kaisha v. Lexus Foods Inc.*, [2001] 2 F.C. 15; (2000), 194 D.L.R. (4th) 491; (2000), 9 C.P.R. (4th) 297; (2000), 189 F.T.R. 319 (F.C.A.).

[19] *Veuve Cliquot Ponsardin v. Boutiques Cliquot Ltée*, [2006] 1 S.C.R. 824; (2006), 270 D.L.R. (4th) 1; (2006), 49 C.P.R. (4th) 401 (SCC).

When an infringement takes place, the owner of the trademark may seek a remedy in either the Federal Court or the superior courts of the provinces. The advantage of going to the Federal Court is that the judgment can be enforced throughout Canada.

Trademarks can consist of words, expressions, trade names, symbols, logos, designs, or combinations of them. The apple logo associated with the word "Apple" on Macintosh computers is an example of such a combination. Trademarks include the specialized marks associated with quality or standards such as the CSA (Canadian Standards Association) approval found on electrical appliances. These are called **certification marks** and have the same protection in Canada as other forms of trademarks. Organizations associated with the government such as Canada Post and the Red Cross can also register "**official marks.**" These are actually stronger than trademarks since they don't have to prove that there is no other pre-existing mark that they will be confused with. Good examples of this are the official marks that have been registered with respect to the 2010 Olympics. The organization responsible for the Olympics has registered many names and symbols associated with the games, including symbols such as the name Olympics, the interlocking rings, and even the term "Gold medal" as official marks. It is also possible to register the distinctive shape of a product or its container such as the unique Coca-Cola bottle shape. This is called a **distinguishing guise** and registration also provides trademark protection. But if that unique shape is functional in the sense that it is part of what makes the object do what it is supposed to do, it will not constitute a trademark. Recently Lego argued that their unique system of eight knobs on the top of their blocks constitutes such a mark but the Supreme Court of Canada refused to recognize this because those knobs were functional in that they were an essential aspect of the design that caused the blocks to join together.[20]

Under the *Trade-marks Act* an application can also be made for a **proposed trademark**, where the mark has not yet been used and is not known to the public but will be used in the future.

The process of applying for and registering trademarks in Canada is a complex one, usually requiring the services of experts called *trademark agents*. Searches of indexes and registries must be made in Canada and usually in other countries—especially the United States—to determine if the mark has already been granted or is in use here or elsewhere. Then the agent makes the application to the Registrar of Trademarks, setting out a description of the mark, the wares or services it is to be used with, and the names and addresses of the agent and owner of the trademark along with the appropriate fee.

There are several restrictions on what can be used as a trademark. For example, anything associated with royalty, national flags, institutions such as the Red Cross or R.C.M.P., or provincial or national coats of arms cannot be used without permission. Of course, anything obscene or illicit is also prohibited. Normally, a simple surname of a living or recently deceased individual will not be accepted. But there are exceptions if the name has already become associated with the product or business. Also, a term that is simply descriptive of the product, the nature of the service, the location, or one that is misleading in any way will be rejected. And of course, no trademark can be used that can be confused with the registered or unregistered mark of another similar business or one selling similar products or services. Also, the trademark in a name or symbol can be lost when it is no longer unique in that it no longer identifies a particular business, but is used generally to describe any number of similar products. For example, the terms nylon and escalator have lost their trademark value

Trademarks can be words, symbols, or both in combination

Certification marks, proposed trademarks, and distinctive shapes are also covered by the Trade-marks Act

Trademark protection requires registration and the payment of a fee

Trademark must be distinctive, socially acceptable, and not associated with prohibited institutions

---

[20] *Kirkbi AG v. Ritvik Holdings Inc.*, [2005] 3 S.C.R. 302; (2005), 259 D.L.R. (4th) 577; (2005), 43 C.P.R. (4th) 385 (SCC).

for the companies that originated the term due to their common use. Google, the internet search provider, has recently sent off notifications to media and other users to stop using their name as a verb to prevent the same consequence taking place for that term.

Disputes with respect to the registration of trademarks are handled by the Registrar of Trademarks, with appeals going to the Federal Court. It is appropriate, although not required, to indicate the presence of a trademark by the symbols ® where the trademark is registered or ™ when unregistered. Trademarks can be challenged up to five years after registration. It should also be noted that such trademarks as well as the licences associated with them can be assigned to other companies.

Trademarks can now be licensed for use by others

Passing-off   The *Trade-marks Act* provides statutory protection for registered trademarks, but even unregistered marks and names are protected under the common law tort of passing-off. Any people or businesses that advertise their service or product in such as way as to lead others to believe they are being supplied by or associated with another business, when they are not, is liable to be sued for the tort of passing-off. Counterfeit Rolex watches and Hermes handbags are examples.

A business that passes itself off as another may be liable

Sometimes a business will use a similar name, which might lead customers to believe they are associated with another business when they are not. This too may qualify as passing-off. For example, the B.C. Supreme Court issued an injunction restraining a newly formed real estate company from using the name Greystone Properties Ltd. on the basis that it caused the public and the customers of the already established Greystone Capital Management Inc. to be confused. Their use of the name devalued the goodwill of that company, even though the plaintiff company was based in Saskatchewan. It had no office in British Columbia, but did some business with the real estate and pension fund investment community in that province. The court found that: 1) the plaintiff had a reputation of goodwill in British Columbia that could be injured; 2) the businesses were similar enough to cause confusion by the action complained of; and 3) the value of the goodwill or reputation was injured. These are the necessary elements to establish a passing-off action.[21] In effect, the ability to bring a passing-off action prevents other businesses from trading on the reputation and goodwill of another business through intentional or accidental misrepresentation and in the process injuring the value of that reputation and goodwill. A passing-off action will be available to an injured party whether or not their trademark is registered under the *Trade-marks Act*. Table 9.2 provides a summary of the legislation protecting intellectual property in Canada.

A registered trademark not required for a passing-off action

Case Summary 9.5 *Walt Disney Productions v. Triple Five Corp.*[22]
The Danger of Using Similar Names

When in 1983 the Edmonton Mall used the name "Fantasy Land" for their new amusement park, the Walt Disney Corporation, which had used that name in association with their amusement park for decades, sued them for passing-off. The court agreed that the use of the similar name would cause confusion in the minds of the public and issued an injunction against the Alberta corporation that prevented the continued use of the name. Even though Walt Disney Corporation didn't carry on business in Alberta, they did advertise there, and the goodwill developed by that promotion had been damaged. The fact that there was no intention to mislead did not take away from the damage caused, and an injunction was the appropriate remedy.

---

[21] *Greystone Capital Management Inc. v. Greystone Properties Ltd.* (1999), 82 C.P.R. (3d) 501 (B.C.S.C.).

[22] (1994), 113 D.L.R. (4th) 229 (Alta. C.A.).

Table 9.2 Intellectual Property Legislation

Statute	What Is Protected	Requirements	Protection Period
Copyright Act	Original books, photos, music, and other artistic works (the expression)	Mere production	Death of author of work plus 50 years or in some cases only 50 years
Patent Act	Original invention or innovation (the idea)	Application and registration	20 years from filing
Industrial Design Act	A product's distinctive design, shape, or pattern	Registration	10 years from registration
Integrated Circuit Topography Act	Design of integrated circuits	Registration	10 years from filing or use
Trade-marks Act	Trade names, symbols, and logos associated with a business	Registration*	15 years renewable

*Note that some trademarks receive unregistered protection through passing-off action.

Remedies

The remedies available to the court when intellectual property rights are infringed are similar in all cases (see Table 9.3). Damages are available, but only at trial and after a lengthy delay. The needs of the parties in intellectual property disputes are usually urgent, requiring a more immediate remedy to prevent further losses. Often when an infringement is discovered, the offended party will make an immediate application to the

Table 9.3 Remedies for Interference with Intellectual Property

Remedy	Nature of Order	When Available
Damages	Statutory damages	Awarded at the discretion of judge under copyright act
	Monetary damages	Common law remedy awarded at discretion of the judge where available at trial
Injunction	Order to stop offending conduct	Interim injunction available before trial Permanent injunction available at trial
Anton Piller order	Order to seize documents or other material before it can be destroyed or moved	Before trial and without notice to the other party
Accounting	Disclosure and payment to the plaintiff of improper profits made from offending conduct	At trial
Criminal	Imposition of fine and/or Imprisonment	At trial

Interim injunction requires the balance of convenience to favour the applicant

Interim injunction common where need for remedy is urgent in intellectual property disputes

Anton Piller order provides for seizing of offending documents or products without notice

court for an injunction to stop the offending practice until the court can deal with the matter at trial. An **interim injunction** will only be granted when the applicant can show a strong case, indicating a likelihood of success at trial and also that the **balance of convenience** is in the applicant's favour. This means that the court has to be convinced that more damage will be suffered by the applicant if the injunction is not granted than would be suffered by the offending party if the injunction were issued. Another effective interim order is an **Anton Piller order**. Here the court orders that offending products or records be seized before they can be destroyed or removed. To be effective this must be done without notice to the offending party. Such an order will only be granted where the applicant can demonstrate: 1) there is a strong *prima facie* case; 2) there is danger of considerable further damage to the applicant; and 3) it is clear that the offending party has the documents or products in its possession and is likely to destroy or otherwise dispose of them before any hearing or trial. Anton Piller orders are sometimes abused where they are used to support a fishing expedition or as a tactic to interfere with a competitor's business. Because of this courts are reluctant to grant such remedies except in the most extreme cases.

Any other remedy must wait until trial, but often, given the fast pace of intellectual property disputes, once an interim injunction is or is not granted, there is no sense in taking the matter further. If the dispute does go to trial, the object is usually to make the injunction permanent or to obtain damages. But the actual value of intellectual property involved and the damages suffered are often difficult to determine. Often, it is more appropriate to seek an order for an accounting. As explained in Chapter 1, with this remedy the court determines any improper profits made by the defendants through their offending conduct and orders these profits to be paid to the plaintiff, or a reasonable royalty (in the case of patents) is calculated based on those profits and that royalty must then be paid over to the victim of the infringement. Of course, if there are no profits, damages are a more appropriate remedy. The court may also order that the offending product or documents be surrendered to the plaintiff and can then be destroyed, but an award of damages or an injunction are still the primary remedies when intellectual property rights are infringed.

Accounting requires improper profits to be paid to victim

Because of the difficulty often encountered in assessing the actual losses to be compensated, there is an increasing tendency to award punitive damages in these cases. Because of these problems the *Copyright Act* allows the victim of an infringement to elect an award of **statutory damages** without the necessity of actually proving the actual loss. The election for statutory damages can be made anywhere in the process and the award will be between $500 and $20 000 at the discretion of the judge.

In addition to the civil remedies available for copyright and patent infringement, both of these acts contain specific provisions that make some forms of infringement a criminal offence. Under the *Copyright Act* the penalties when the prosecution is by indictment can be as high as five years in jail and a million dollar fine. The penalties for a *Patent Act* infringement are considerably less, even when treated as an indictable offence. The maximum penalty for pricing offences with respect to patented medicines can be as high as $5000 ($100 000 for a corporation) and six months in jail. Note, however, that with some specific forms of infringement, each day the infringement continues can be treated as a separate offence with the penalties accumulating. When patent infringements with respect to other forms of inventions are involved, the penalties are much less.

Criminal penalties in *Copyright Act*, *Patent Act*, and *Criminal Code*

Case Summary 9.6 *Lari v. Canadian Copyright Licensing Agency*[23]

And When We Don't Listen?

Riaz Lari carried on businesses as U Computer Copy Shop in Montreal and persisted in photocopying textbooks for students at the local university. Actions had been brought against him in the past with the award of a permanent injunction to stop the practice. He ignored the injunction and continued to photocopy the texts. He had been fined in the past, and in a civil action was ordered to pay $500 000 damages and a further $100 000 as punitive damages. This didn't stop him. Access Copyright (The Canadian Copyright Licensing Agency)—formerly known as CanCopy, an organization representing authors—learned he was again photocopying and successfully obtained an Anton Piller order forcing the surrender of the offending copies as well as another injunction. He had been found in contempt in the past and on this occasion the court imposed a six-month jail term for his continued contempt. The jail term was suspended but there was also an order that he perform 400 hours of community service and an order that if he violated the injunction again the plaintiff could apply *ex parte* for a committal order. This was appealed to the Federal Court of Appeal, which upheld the lower court decision. This is a very serious case, which indicates that the courts take such infringement seriously and are willing to enforce their orders when necessary.

The *Trade-marks Act* itself contains no criminal penalties, but there are specific offences found in the *Criminal Code* relating to trademark infringement. In addition, other general remedies associated with fraud and theft—sections 406 to 412—make it an indictable offence to forge, alter, deface, conceal, or remove a trademark or even to refill a bottle with someone else's trademark to deceive or defraud. Also, passing-off as well as the practice of reselling goods without disclosing them to be used or reconditioned are also indictable offences. The potential punishment is two years in jail if treated as an indictable offence.

Undervaluing and failure to keep track of intellectual property resources and to account for licensing fees and royalties is a major problem when dealing with this type of asset. Where circumstances permit, businesses and individuals should take steps to keep track of and protect these resources. And when such an infringement is detected, usually speedy intervention is required to prevent significant damage.

PRIVACY, SECURITY, AND CONFIDENTIAL INFORMATION

Almost all businesses have some sort of confidential information that they want to keep away from competitors, customers, shareholders, or the public. This might be in the form of trade secrets, customer lists, or negative information about the company, the executives, or other key employees. Much of the intellectual property of a company is stored in databases that summarize such information as its customers and their buying habits, future production plans, or even secret strategies, processes, or techniques. The common thread is that the information is not generally known, and its disclosure will cause harm to the business. When secret processes, recipes, or formulas are involved, they are known as trade secrets and are often not protected by patent, copyright, or trademark. While not property in the strict sense, so long as it remains confidential, such information constitutes a valuable asset of the business and must be safeguarded.

---

[23] 2007 FCA 127 (CanLII) (2007), 56 C.P.R. (4th) 177.

There are no federal or provincial statutes designed to protect such **confidential information,** but as a rule, employees, suppliers, and contractors have a common law obligation not to disclose this information to others. This may be based on a fiduciary relationship of trust or simply as part of the contractual obligations between the parties. A fiduciary duty arises where one party places trust in another and is vulnerable to harm if that trust is abused. Examples of such fiduciaries are partners, senior employees, and agents. This duty can best be described as an obligation to act in the best interest of the party to whom the fiduciary duty is owed. An important aspect of that duty is the obligation to keep confidences. Even without a fiduciary duty, there can be a legal obligation not to disclose such information or to use it for your own purposes where the information was given in confidence.

Such an obligation can also be imposed by contract, either expressed or implied. When businesses work together, or when a consultant or contractor does work for a business, it is good practice to include a non-disclosure provision in the contract. An employer will often include a restrictive covenant in the initial employment contract, requiring an employee not to work in the same industry or for a competitor while employed and for a specified period after that employment ends. This protects the employer, not only from having customers follow the terminated employee, but it also prevents that employee from disclosing customer lists, production plans, and even manufacturing methods to a competitor. Even without such a contract, the courts have no hesitation in finding that employees have breached an important obligation when they solicit clients in the last few days of their employment with the idea of taking them with them when they leave. But even an honest employee can be guilty of disclosing confidential information, if he or she doesn't know that it is confidential. It is, therefore, vital to make sure employees understand what is confidential and what is not.

The most common remedies associated with abuse of confidential information are the award of damages, injunction, and in some cases where improper profits have been made, an accounting. Damages, as well as an accounting, are only obtained after the loss has been suffered. Often the most effective weapon to keep the confidential information from being disclosed is to obtain an interim injunction where the employee, contractor, etc. is ordered not to work for the competitor or not to disclose the information. Sometimes a competing employer will attempt to hire away a key employee, primarily to get access to this kind of confidential information or better access to the competitor's customers. Where the competitor has encouraged the employee to leave and to breach his or her duty of confidentiality or contract of employment, it may be possible to seek redress from that competitor in the form of damages for **inducing a breach of contract.** This would also be an appropriate situation for the remedy of an accounting, which requires the competitor to disclose any profits earned by his or her abuse and to surrender them to the injured employer.

Margin notes:
Common law requires confidential information not to be disclosed or used by the confidant

It is a good policy to include non-disclosure provisions in employment and consulting contracts

Important to inform employees of what is confidential

Injunction is often more effective as a remedy than damages or accounting

Inducing breach of contract can sometimes be claimed when an employee moves to a competitor

Case Summary 9.7 *Polyresins Ltd. v. Stein-Hall, Ltd. et al.*[24]
Obligations That Last Beyond Termination

Three employees who were aware of the secret formulas used by Polyresins Ltd. to develop acrylic thickeners quit that company and were hired by a competitor, which shortly thereafter began to develop similar products. This interlocutory application was brought by Polyresins for an injunction to prevent those former employees from

>

[24] (1972), 25 D.L.R. (3d) 152, [1972] 2 O.R. 188 (Ont. H.C.J.).

disclosing the secrets and to prevent the production and sale of the products developed from such improper disclosures. Because this was an interim order, Polyresins only had to establish a strong *prima facie* case. The judge found that without the injunction Polyresins would suffer irreparable harm, so that the balance of convenience favoured Polyresins. The injunction was granted. The court decided the obligation not to disclose secrets followed the employees to their new employment, and since Polyresins would be more harmed if the injunction were not granted than the new employer would be if it was, the interim order was made.

Privacy

Closely related to confidential information is the topic of privacy. There is no separate privacy protection under common law. In most provinces it is only where the conduct constitutes some other tort, such as defamation or trespass, or where a contract or fiduciary duty has been breached that it will be actionable under common law. Several provinces have statutes making breaches of privacy actionable torts.[25] These acts leave it to the court to determine what constitutes a violation of privacy, but they also state that privacy may be violated by eavesdropping, surveillance, or by the unauthorized use of a name or portrait. The technological advances in data compilation and email communications have led to a number of statutes, both at the federal and provincial levels, being enacted to protect personal information. The federal government, in response to international pressure and the threat of lost business, enacted two statutes. The *Privacy Act*[26] protects personal information in the hands of federal government institutions, limits its collection, and provides for limited access where appropriate. It also establishes the office of the Privacy Commissioner. It is the second Act that is more important for business. This Act, referred to as the *Personal Information Protection and Electronic Documents Act* (*PIPEDA*),[27] is unique in that it is declared to be the law in areas of federal jurisdiction and in all provinces unless a province enacts a "substantially similar" act. Several provinces including Quebec, Ontario, and British Columbia have enacted their own legislation, but it is yet to be seen whether all of these statutes qualify as "substantially similar."

> Several provinces have made breach of privacy an actionable tort

> Federal *Privacy Act* protects personal information in federal government institutions

> Federal *PIPEDA* applies in all provinces that don't have substantially similar statute

Other provinces have simply adopted the federal act by not passing a similar statute. These acts are meant to control the collection, use, disclosure, and disposal of personal information. The federal act came into force in three stages, but as of January 1, 2004, it applies to all organizations in Canada involved in the collection, use, and disclosure of personal information in connection with a commercial activity. The only exceptions are companies already subject to "substantially similar" provincial legislation. Note that this applies to both health and non-health information such as medical conditions, prescriptions and other medical services, customer lists, consumer purchasing habits, credit and entertainment information, information gathered from websites, as well as subscriptions to magazines and internet services by an individual, or any other personal information that a company has in its possession that relates to identifiable individuals. It applies not only to the personal information of customers and clients but also to anyone about whom the business compiles personal information, including—to a limited extent—their employees. The provincial acts impose much more stringent standards with respect to an

> These acts impose restrictions and obligations on all companies that have personal information in their control

---

[25] For example, *Privacy Act*, R.S.B.C. 1996, c. 373; and *Privacy Act*, R.S.N.L. 1990, c. P-22.

[26] R.S.C. 1985, c. P-21.

[27] S.C. 2000, c. 5.

employer's compilation, use, and disclosure of personal information, especially the health information of employees.

The federal act requires the business or organization to develop a privacy policy that will protect such private information from being disclosed to others. A model policy is included in Schedule 1 of the *PIPEDA* (adopted from a prior model policy developed by the Canadian Standards Association when voluntary compliance was hoped for). Each organization is required to develop and implement policies and procedures to protect personal information, to handle complaints and inquiries, and to train staff about the policies developed. Each business must develop its own policies and procedures, but they must satisfy the following:

Businesses must develop policies and procedures:

■ To make business accountable for information

■ To place limits on information use, retention, and disclosure

■ To ensure accuracy and safeguard information

■ To provide access and a process for challenging the information's accuracy

■   The organization must be accountable for the information collected.

■   Consent must be obtained from those whose information is used (although in some circumstances this can be implied).

■   Reasonable limits must be placed on the collection, use, retention, and disclosure of the information.

■   Provisions must be in place for maintaining the accuracy and safeguarding of personal information, including safeguarding from abuses by the employees of that organization.

■   Individuals must have access to the collected information to determine its accuracy and challenge the information collected where appropriate.

An individual in the organization should be identified who will be responsible for implementing these policies and for the organization's compliance, even when that information is conveyed to third parties.

The obligations associated with a company's collection and use of such personal information have become a significant aspect of doing business; something as commonplace as selling a customer or subscription list can run afoul of these statutes. While current enforcement of these provisions may be somewhat haphazard, the intense concern about the misuse of personal information compiled in various databases associated with the internet and the ease of accessing that information make it likely that this will be an area of intense regulation in the future. All businesses must develop policies and procedures to protect the private and personal information in their possession in compliance with protection of privacy statutes.

All businesses must develop policies and procedures to protect private information

The *PIPEDA* also contains serious penalties for infractions. Failure to provide requested information, obstructing the process or an employer, or dismissing or otherwise disciplining an employee for acting as required under the Act constitutes an indictable offence, punishable by fine up to $100 000.

There is also a prohibition against "invasion of privacy" that can be effective in curtailing interference with the internet and other forms of electronic data communication and storage. Section 184 makes it an indictable offence to wilfully intercept a private communication using electronic or other means. Section 184 of the *Criminal Code* makes it punishable by up to five years' imprisonment with the unusual additional remedy of up to $5000 in punitive damages, which can be awarded to the victim.

Security

Whether a business is concerned with protecting the private information of others or their own confidential information, keeping such information secure has become a great concern. The problems associated with security relate to preserving information, protecting

Keeping information secure requires action by business

it from corruption, and preventing its interception and disclosure to others. These are not areas where government regulation will likely be of much help.

When information was stored on paper, filing vast quantities of it posed a considerable problem. Today, whole libraries can be stored on one small disc or memory card, and while this eliminates one problem, it raises another. Discs are easily lost, stolen, or destroyed. The decision to dispose of information may be made consciously, but when it is erased unintentionally, the results can be disastrous. For example, a large amount of valuable raw data collected by Statistics Canada was deleted from a permanent collection because of unclear guidelines.[28] Even the crash of a hard drive or the loss or destruction of a CD or DVD can cause the loss of volumes of irreplaceable information.

Digital storage makes information subject to easy loss, whether intentional or inadvertent

The solution, of course, is to make regular backups of all important information and to store them in a different location. But it is surprising how many individuals and businesses fail to follow such a fundamental requirement. It is certain that the days of great paper archives of information and libraries full of books and collections of periodicals and government publications are ending. Paper archives are being replaced by digital storage, but mechanisms must be in place to preserve the information so that it is accessible even by different technologies in the future. We must protect such information from inadvertent or intentional destruction.

Importance of backups stored in different locations can't be overemphasized

An equally important problem for business is to protect confidential information from interception or accidental disclosure. Email communication is not secure; it's more like a postcard than a sealed letter. It is now common for email communications to be systematically scanned by hackers or even government agencies that use sophisticated programs to look for key words and phrases. But the information can also be misdirected inadvertently simply by typing in the wrong email address or by returning a message to a group rather than an individual. The best way to ensure the privacy of electronic communications is through **encryption**. Email has been judicially recognized as not secure and a business may soon be required to use encryption of email communication and other stored personal information to meet their obligations under the federal *PIPEDA* or equivalent provincial privacy legislation discussed above.

Encryption is important to keep information secure, especially for electronic communications

Passwords go some way to protect information, but many of us either don't change our passwords often enough, or we make them too simple to provide protection. Encryption is a much better way of ensuring that sensitive information won't be intercepted. There are software programs available that provide different levels of encryption. As the name suggests, encryption basically puts the information needing protection into code. The more complex the code, the more difficult it is to intercept the information. But no level of encryption is perfect. Someone with adequate resources, determination, and access will likely be able to intercept all but the most sophisticated encrypted information. Still, for most purposes, a high level of encryption, combined with restricted access to the data storage devices, will provide the greatest protection possible for most businesses. Information that is no longer needed, but still sensitive, should be removed from the system. However, simply deleting email messages or the files from a computer's hard drive will not erase them. This process only allows the computer to write over the confidential data. It is relatively easy to recover most deleted information. Emails are also

Even encrypted communications are not completely secure

Simply deleting computer files does not remove them

---

[28] Claridge, Thomas, "Disappearing digital info a hot topic at CALL," *Lawyers Weekly*, Vol. 22 No. 4 (May 24, 2002).

easily recovered. Further steps have to be taken to ensure removal. Again, encryption should help.

The threat to a business's computer system is not always associated with the internet or the direct accessing of a company's computers on their premises. When a business uses a wireless network, communications can be accessed by computers outside or in another part of the building. There are security programs available to protect businesses from this kind of violation.

Security concerns of individuals and businesses must extend much further than their computer resources. For example, electronic banking abuses such as credit and debit card fraud are now commonplace. The signature requirement on credit card transactions is a limited safeguard against misuse. When a card has been stolen or the number copied and misused, banks will usually not charge the rightful owner for the loss unless there has been some negligence involved. But the problem is more difficult with debit cards. The key is to guard the personal identification number (PIN) at all costs. There are schemes ranging from false fronts on automatic banking machines to double striking debit cards to get access to your accounts. But in all cases the culprit must obtain your PIN as well. Sometimes there is a false security camera or someone may be looking over your shoulder, but in all cases there must be someone watching the victim enter his or her PIN to get access to it. One incident at a bank ATM involved the use of an almost invisible pinhole camera.

Any business allowing payment by debit card must take great care to protect their customers' privacy. Rather than the retailer swiping the card, the customer should do it, and a handheld unit on a cord should be provided. And, of course, the units themselves, and the employees operating them, should be regularly monitored to make sure they are not part of a fraudulent scheme.

Identity theft is becoming even more of a problem. Here, by accessing some basic information, a new driver's licence and other identifying documents are obtained. With them bank accounts are opened and new credit cards and debit cards are issued in the name of the victim. Huge debts can be compiled and only with great difficulty will the whole mess be resolved.

Dishonest or careless employees can pose a greater threat to a business than dishonest customers. Aside from theft, fraud, and other forms of white-collar crime, employees may cause harm through inadvertent conduct. They may disclose confidential information unwittingly or cause damage and loss though misuse of the business computer and communication system. Beyond simple waste of resources, where the computers are used for personal purposes such as playing games or using the internet for personal entertainment, employees may expose the company to embarrassment and liability when they use company equipment or company email accounts for illegal or otherwise inappropriate purposes. This may include accessing a customer or client's private information; downloading inappropriate material such as child pornography; gambling; or distributing defamatory, sexually explicit, harassing, or hateful material. The remedy is for the company to have mechanisms in place to monitor the employees' use of the computers and other company resources. If this is done surreptitiously, however, it may violate the employees' right to privacy and subject the business to fines or other punishment. The best option is to inform employees at the outset that their phone calls, computer use, and other employment-related activities are subject to monitoring. This not only avoids the problem of being accused of violating employees'

Marginal notes:

Wireless networks can be easily compromised

Credit card and debit card fraud becoming a big problem

Steps must be taken to ensure that PINs are protected

Employees and the machines should be regularly monitored to ensure that there is no misuse

Employers may be liable for employees' abuses

Solution is to monitor employees' use of computers and other resources

Important to inform employees of surveillance

privacy, it also informs them of what they can and cannot do with respect to company resources.

Of course, there is always the danger of an employee being persuaded by a competitor to convey confidential information or trade secrets such as the company's new line of products to a competitor. It is difficult to prevent this problem other than by being extremely careful when hiring. But the risk may be contained to some extent by making sure that this kind of confidential information is only given to those that require it as part of their jobs. Passwords to computers should only be given to those that need them. Different levels of password protection can be arranged so that even on the same computer, information is only given out according to the level of the password used. Blocking software can also be used to prevent employees from accessing inappropriate websites. In all cases the best protection against improper conduct of employees is the development and communication in writing of clear policies and procedures with respect to the use of company resources; careful hiring practices, including criminal and credit record checks; thorough training; and appropriate accountability, including surveillance and monitoring.

Confidential information should be contained, and employees should be told what information is confidential

As can be seen from this discussion, while there has been some attempt to regulate privacy and confidential information, effective protection falls largely on the shoulders of the individual or corporation. In addition to the general provisions relating to fraud, gambling, obscene material, and the like, the *Criminal Code* contains specific provisions relating to computer and internet offences. Section 184 makes it an indictable offence to intercept private communications and is punishable with up to five years in prison. Section 342.1 specifically prohibits the fraudulent obtaining of computer and internet services, whether directly or indirectly, including the possession of passwords and various forms of equipment to accomplish that purpose. This is an indictable offence, punishable with up to 10 years in prison. Section 430 prohibits the commission of mischief and includes a special section prohibiting the destruction of or interference with computer data or with someone's authorized use of that data. This would cover hackers as well as computer viruses that wreak havoc on computer information and operations. Mischief, with respect to data, can also be treated as an indictable offence, punishable with up to five years in prison.

Careful hiring practices are the best safeguard

Computer viruses and the conduct of hackers in all forms have become known as cyber-crimes and the effect can be devastating. The above sections of the *Criminal Code* can be effective, but often hackers and virus creators are underage and are subject to the less rigorous penalties included in the *Youth Criminal Justice Act*. For example, the infamous "Mafia Boy" from Montreal who interfered with eBay, Amazon.com, and CNN was only 15 years old at the time of the offence. It is generally accepted that only the amateurs get caught. Most sophisticated hackers are also effective in covering their tracks. Hackers often consider themselves to be crusaders fighting big business domination of the internet and computers generally, and some claim to be advocates of reforming computer services. Many, however, are simply mercenaries profiting from the information they manage to steal or the destruction they cause. Whatever the motivation, the effects are extremely costly to business.

The only sure way for businesses to protect themselves is to take their own defensive measures. Like the ongoing battle between the creators of viruses and virus protection programs, a business must take steps to protect itself from the threats posed by the internet and quickly changing computer technology.

Key Terms

Anton Piller order (p. 246)

balance of convenience (p. 246)

business patents (p. 240)

certification marks (p. 243)

confidential information (p. 248)

copyright (p. 235)

distinguishing guise (p. 243)

encryption (p. 251)

evergreening (p. 240)

identity theft (p. 252)

inducing a breach of contract (p. 248)

interim injunction (p. 246)

invention (p. 239)

moral rights (p. 235)

official marks (p. 243)

patent (p. 239)

proposed trademark (p. 243)

reverse engineering (p. 239)

royalties (p. 235)

statutory damages (p. 246)

trademarks (p. 242)

Questions for Student Review

1. Distinguish between intellectual property and other kinds of property, and explain which courts have jurisdiction with respect to intellectual property disputes.

2. What is protected under copyright law? How is that protection obtained and how long does it last?

3. Who is entitled to patent and copyright protection when an employee or consultant develops the material?

4. What federal statute protects computer software?

5. What qualifications must be met for a work to qualify for copyright protection?

6. Explain what a patent protects, how patent protection is obtained, and how long that patent protection lasts.

7. What qualifications must an invention meet to qualify for patent protection? What will not qualify?

8. What do the *Industrial Design Act* and the *Integrated Circuit Topography Act* protect?

9. Distinguish between a certification mark, a trademark, and a distinguishing guise.

10. Explain the distinction between a trademark infringement action and a passing-off action, and indicate when one would be chosen over the other.

11. Explain what the *Trade-marks Act* protects; how that protection is obtained, and how long it lasts.

12. What harm does a trademark infringement cause a business?

13. What will cause an application for trademark to be refused?

14. Distinguish between an injunction, an Anton Piller order, damages, and an accounting. Explain where one would be preferred over the others.

15. Explain the common law obligations with respect to people who are given confidential information.

16. What steps should be taken by a business to ensure their employees don't divulge confidential information?

17. Explain the importance of provincial privacy acts, the federal *Privacy Act* and the federal *Personal Information Protection and Electronic Documents Act* and how they interrelate.

18. Explain why the *Personal Information Protection and Electronic Documents Act* is in force in some provinces and not in others.

19. What must be included when a business develops policies and procedures under the *Personal Information Protection and Electronic Documents Act*?

20. Explain why digitally stored information is particularly vulnerable to loss or disclosure. How can that information best be secured from intentional or inadvertent loss?

21. How can a business best protect their communicated information from inadvertent disclosure or intentional interception?

22. Explain how a business can ensure that their employees are not involved in any illegal or other inappropriate activity with respect to computers, the internet, and voice mail.

23. What steps should be taken to ensure that the employees don't become involved in such inappropriate activities in the first place?

Questions for Further Discussion

1. There are two ways of looking at the problems associated with intellectual property. As with any form of property law, the rules restrict and protect that property for the use of one individual or group and exclude others. But intellectual property is the vehicle for commercial and economic progress and is not restricted by international boundaries. Also, because it is intangible, the use by one group does not deny it to others as would be the case with a stolen car, for example. Third World countries, even emerging economic giants like China and India, often look at such intellectual property laws as a way to restrict their advancement and further the profits of Western capitalistic nations and corporations at their expense. The same kind of debate happens at home between those who copy music over the internet and those large record companies and artists that feel that such activities are akin to theft. Consider these positions and discuss the relative merits of both sides. Is there any way to accommodate these conflicting interests?

2. The AIDS epidemic is just one of the catastrophic health problems that illustrate the disparity between medical advances and the costs that make them inaccessible to those who need them. Today, steps are being taken to provide low-cost drugs to Third World countries, but the general problem remains, and it surrounds the patent protection provided to the companies that develop the drugs. Consider the balance now struck between guaranteeing profits of pharmaceutical giants that developed these drugs and the need for inexpensive variants in those countries and ours to preserve life. Discuss the negative impact of our patent protection policies in these areas and consider what can be done to overcome the problem.

3. Consider the recent introduction of privacy laws at both the federal and provincial levels and the restrictions and controls this imposes on business. Does this place an unreasonable burden on business? How would you suggest that these provisions be expanded, reduced, or otherwise altered?

Cases for Discussion

1. *CCH Canadian Ltd. v. The Law Society of Upper Canada,* [2004] 1 S.C.R. 339 (S.C.C.).

   CCH Canadian Ltd. published compilations consisting of court judgments and sold them to lawyers and others for a fee. The Law Society provided a library service to their members. They made single copies of these cases, which they sent out by fax. They also allowed members to make their own copies by using the Law Society's photocopier. There is a sign above the photocopier summarizing the copyright law. CCH sued, claiming the Law Society was infringing copyright. Indicate what arguments each side could raise and the likely outcome.

2. *Wolda v. Techform Products Ltd. et al.* (2001), 206 D.L.R. (4th) 171 (Ont. C.A).

Wolda had been employed by Techform for a number of years when he retired and was given a contract to consult on special projects. The contract was for one year, was renewable, and could be terminated on 60 days' notice; there was no provision with respect to patents or ownership of intellectual property. During this period of consultancy, he designed a special hinge, and the employer presented him with an Employee Technology Agreement (ETA) to sign, which surrendered all claims to this and other inventions that he might develop while employed by the company. He signed reluctantly, fearing he would be terminated if he did not. He also put a question mark beside the word employee, showing that he doubted that it applied to him as a consultant. Subsequently, he designed another unique hinge and applied for the patent. Note that company employees assisted him in the development and a company patent attorney assisted in preparing the application. He tried to charge a fee for the design and for assigning it to the company. As a result he was terminated, and he brought this action for a declaration that he was entitled to the patents for these special hinges. The company brought a similar application. Explain the arguments that Wolda and the company could use to support their positions, and indicate the likely outcome of the action.

3. *Hermes Canada Inc. v. Henry High Class Kelly Retail Store*, 2004 BCSC 1694 (CanLII) (2004), 37 C.P.R. (4th) 244.

The defendants operated a store in the Vancouver area that carried a line of handbags and other products all of which were copies of the famous Hermes brand. The term Hermes didn't appear on any of the products and on very close inspection "HENRY HIGH CLASS KELLY" (the name of the store) was imprinted on the handbags and other products in question. Hermes brought this action to stop the sales of these products. On what basis should Hermes base their complaint and what remedy would be appropriate? Would it affect your answer to know that there is no registered trademark or other protection in the design of the bags themselves, just the Hermes name?

4. *International Corona Resources Ltd. v. LAC Minerals Ltd.* (1989), 61 D.L.R. (4th) 14 (S.C.C.).

Corona owned certain valuable mining claims in Ontario and was looking for a partner to help develop them. LAC Minerals was invited to participate, and their representative came out and visited the site. While there, they were informed that Corona didn't own the claims surrounding this property, but were hoping to acquire them. The partnership deal did not materialize, but LAC Minerals, without informing Corona, managed to acquire the surrounding claims and the two companies developed the adjoining properties. Corona brought this action, claiming that LAC Minerals had violated their obligations to Corona when they acquired these properties. Explain what obligations were violated and what defences LAC Minerals could raise. What is the likely outcome?

5. *Athans v. Adventure Camps Ltd. et al.* (1977), 80 D.L.R. (3d) 583 (Ont. H.C.J.).

The waterskier, Athans, had a promotional photograph taken that was well known, as it had been used on various brochures and for other commercial purposes. The public relations firm associated with Canadian Adventure Camps (a summer camp program for children) took that photograph, made a line drawing of it, and used it on the camp's promotional material. It is clear that they didn't intend any harm but just wanted to have a waterskiing photo on their brochure. Athans sued. Explain the nature of his complaint and his likelihood of success.

Chapter 10

Electronic Commerce and International Trade

Learning Objectives

- Describe the nature of electronic commerce and its impact on business relationships

- Outline the jurisdictional issues that complicate online transactions

- List kinds of online communications that can lead to disputes

- Recognize specific kinds of tortious conduct that are pervasive on the internet

- Compare standard contract formation and online contracts

- Discuss the trends toward criminal activity on the internet

- Describe the concerns electronic and global business transactions have in common

- Outline the legislation in place to regulate online activity

- Explain difficulties in engaging in international contracts

- Describe how contractual problems are best resolved in the global environment

- Justify the use of arbitration in international transaction disputes

- Outline how international commerce is regulated

- Discuss jurisdictional issues and enforcement of judicial decisions

For most of us the internet has changed the way we do business. We can order everything from groceries to cars online. We may never deal with a salesman, an agent, or a manufacturer. We can order a product and have it shipped from anywhere in the world without leaving our home or office. Whether we are functioning as an individual consumer, a small business, or a large corporation, it's inevitable that a considerable portion of what we do will be done over the internet and probably across borders. While international trade has always been an important source of business relationships, the internet has facilitated the trading process in ways that could not have been imagined two decades ago. It is necessary to look at the laws affecting these two areas and consider how they are applied in both electronic and global commerce, as well as the need for and the impact of government regulation in both these areas. They share some commonalities which will be discussed in this chapter, including contractual processes, jurisdictional issues, and the resolution of disputes.

BUSINESS AND THE INTERNET

The enormous expansion of the internet has brought about another round of significant and basic changes to our economy and society. Communication of information has never been so easy and so seamless. The internet is much broader than just a business tool. It also provides education, entertainment, and social interaction. It has, to a large extent through electronic mail services, supplanted paper correspondence. It also facilitates socially irresponsible conduct, including pornography, gambling, and other illegal activities.

Internet facilitates business and education

From a business point of view, electronic commerce consists of not only the purchase and sale of goods and services at the retail level that we are so familiar with, but also those same interchanges between businesses of all sizes. Another even more significant aspect of ecommerce deals with communications between businesses where even the most complicated forms of business transactions are now largely completed over the internet or involve other forms of electronic communication including fax and telephone communications. It is also important to remember that all of these transactions normally involve third parties that facilitate the deals. In retail sales, service providers such as eBay and PayPal advertise the products and facilitate payment and collection. Less obvious are the services supplied by the internet service provider itself (the ISP), which makes ecommerce possible.

Normal civil and criminal remedies apply to internet

The development of the internet and electronic commerce has moved forward at an astounding rate and has created a free and open Wild West–style online environment, which is still relatively free of government regulation and legal restrictions. It is important to note that the various forms of law, including civil remedies for fraud, breach of contract, and tort, as well as most forms of criminal law and federal and provincial regulation, apply to transactions and activities conducted online. The difficulties consist primarily in determining the laws of what jurisdiction should apply and enforcement. The laws that are in place are often not readily adaptable to this new form of communication, and the courts, legislators, and regulators have been slow to respond. The lack of effective regulation may explain why some business people are still reluctant to make a move into the world of ecommerce while others are reluctant simply because they feel overwhelmed by the new technology.

Laws are outdated and regulation is lacking with respect to the internet

One of the greatest fears of the proponents of the internet and other forms of digital communication is government control that would inhibit the freedom that has been the basis of the tremendous growth and flexibility that has characterized the medium thus far. Governments, realizing that too much regulation would destroy the very nature and value of the internet, have also been reluctant to introduce regulation and control too quickly. But that is gradually changing.

Jurisdiction

An important feature of the internet is that it is not restricted to one country or state. It does not recognize borders, which gives rise to some serious problems for internet users. For example, what is legal in a jurisdiction such as Nevada, where gambling and sexually explicit material are common, might well be prohibited in another state or province, and yet material on the internet is generally available to everyone. Valid laws may apply, but from which province or state—where the product originates or where it is used? The difficulty posed by trying to make every advertisement or service conform to the local laws of each nation, state, or province is overwhelming and would completely destroy the freedom of internet communication. Similar problems have arisen with gambling as well as with obscene, racist, subversive, and seditious material.

A major problem is to determine what laws apply to internet and internet transactions

Another difficulty is that it is often not clear whom to sue, or where to bring the legal action. One advantage of the internet is that a company or individual can work anywhere in the world, and the place of origin of the material will not be apparent to the users. Kazaa, for example, is a popular music downloading service on the internet. The program was developed for a company in the Netherlands, which then sold it to another company operating from a small Pacific island, whose executives and principals work out of Australia. Which jurisdiction is appropriate for an action to be brought against them? Could they bring an action in the Netherlands or Australia, or are they limited to suing in that small Pacific nation where the laws likely neglect to mention such offences? Online gambling leads to a similar result. U.S. law[1] prohibits taking bets over a network, such as the internet, and this has led several significant internet gambling businesses to set up offshore, particularly in Caribbean countries, which encourage this activity. It is impossible for U.S. authorities to intercept these gambling operations, which have created a billion-dollar industry with most of its customers in the United States. Some regulatory steps have been taken to overcome these difficulties, but each has the potential effect of limiting freedom of expression, movement, or association—rights the courts are bound to protect.

Another major problem is determining where an action should be brought

Regulations can compromise freedom of expression

A huge online retail business has developed as well. This has caused a considerable problem for local jurisdictions with respect to taxation. A store physically located in a province or state is required to collect sales tax from its customers, but that is easily avoided where the purchase is made over the internet. Laws have been passed in some areas requiring online retail businesses to pay local sales taxes or to levy taxes on the internet service provider, but enforcement is a continuing challenge.

The general rule is that a particular location can exercise jurisdiction if the person being sued is resident in that jurisdiction or if that is where the complained of action took place. The problem is that most offensive content does not target a particular victim in a particular state, but is directed at anyone with a computer. Many jurisdictions have passed **long-arm statutes** allowing them to take jurisdiction even when no resident is directly involved, with the result that business people providing an internet service from one area where the activity is completely legal will find themselves being sued or prosecuted in jurisdictions they were not aware of, and where they had no idea they were breaking the local law. A better approach is to allow a judicial action only where there is a close connection between the jurisdiction and the act complained of. Thus, if an internet site offers pornographic materials or gambling services, and an internet user in a particular state or province subscribes or places a bet, that would establish the jurisdiction and an action could be brought there. But even this goes too far for many.

Internet providers may be subject to different laws in many jurisdictions

Case Summary 10.1 *Dow Jones v. Gutnick*[2]
Unsettled Questions of Jurisdiction

In this case an article by an American company published on the internet defamed an Australian resident. The Australian court found that the harm done was in Australia, thus creating a sufficient connection between the defamation and that country for the case to be heard in an Australian court. The American company, Dow Jones, pointed out that this would require them to know and comply with the laws of every country, "from

>

---

[1] *Federal Interstate Wire Act*, 18 U.S.C. § 1084.

[2] [2002] H.C.A. 56 (Aust.).

Afghanistan to Zimbabwe." In a similar case brought in Ontario[3] an article published on the website of the *Washington Post* stated that the United Nations, after several investigations, failed to renew Mr. Bangoura's contract because of "misconduct and mismanagement." In fact Mr. Bangoura was not an Ontario resident at the time of the conduct complained of, but only moved there later and initiated the action in that province. The *Washington Post* brought an application to have the action dismissed, claiming that the most convenient jurisdiction was the District of Columbia. Note that the libel laws in the United States are much friendlier to media than in Canada, and require proof of actual malice when public figures are defamed. At the trial court level the judge dismissed the application, but on appeal the Ontario Court held that since the plaintiff did not reside in the province at the time of the alleged liable, and there was little other connection between Ontario and the libel action (there were only eight subscribers to the *Washington Post* in the province at the time), the application of the *Washington Post* to stay the Ontario action was granted. In the Australian case the plaintiff lived in Australia and the harm done was in that country. In the Canadian case there was little connection to that province and the courts refused to hear the matter. These cases illustrate the general approach used when determining whether a court has jurisdiction to hear a case or not.

Canada requires a real and close connection for action to be brought

Canadian courts are willing to find jurisdiction where there is a real and substantial connection between the act complained of and the province. But even then jurisdiction will be declined if the court can be convinced that it would be more reasonable for some other jurisdiction to deal with the matter. It is evident that there is a great potential for people doing business online to find themselves embroiled in disputes in various jurisdictions all over the world. Only if the business can demonstrate that the internet message was passive in the sense that there was no interaction in that jurisdiction, that no bets were taken, and no orders or subscriptions were sent, then there is little likelihood that an action could be brought against that business in the courts of that state or province. But it is often difficult to selectively do business in that way. It may help to state within the contract of service or goods that the law of a particular jurisdiction, such as Ontario or British Columbia, will govern the transaction. It could also be stated in the website or internet pop-up advertisement that the offer is not extended to specific provinces or states where the activity is prohibited. But even these steps are no guarantee that such a business won't find itself sued or prosecuted in another jurisdiction.

Passive internet messages are more likely to be exempt

Internet offer or service should state limitations of availability

For example, the Ontario *Consumer Protection Act*[4] specifically provides that the rights set out in it apply to all consumer transactions where the consumer or the other party is located in that province at the time of the transaction[5] and that the rights set out in the Act apply despite any agreement to the contrary.[6] The Act even has a provision stating that any clause requiring arbitration in a consumer contract is invalid where it attempts to limit the consumer's right to bring an action in the Ontario Superior Court.[7]

Of course, when a foreign judgment is obtained against a business or individual, there is always the problem of enforcement. But that protection is often an illusion. If the business has assets in the foreign jurisdiction or there are treaties in place to allow

---

[3] *Bangoura v. Washington Post*, 2005 CanLII 32906 (ON C.A.) (2005), 258 D.L.R. (4th) 341; (2005), 202 O.A.C. 76.

[4] S.O. 2002, c. 30, Sch. A.

[5] Ibid., s. 2.

[6] Ibid., s. 7.1.

[7] Ibid., s. 7.2.

for enforcement, a substantial threat does exist. It can be very dangerous to ignore such actions, even when commenced in some remote province or state. Also note that where criminal conduct or regulatory offences are involved, it can be difficult, if not impossible, to extradite and prosecute the accused who resides in another country.

Dangerous to ignore foreign actions since judgments can be enforced in other jurisdictions

Business Transactions over the Internet

Many businesses did not appreciate the potential significance of the internet and failed to take the steps necessary to protect these valuable assets by registering their business and brand names. When they eventually tried to do so, they often discovered someone else had appropriated their name or phrase by registering it first. It is not surprising, therefore, that conflicts have arisen over **domain names**.

Initially, business often failed to register domain names

Such conflicts may arise legitimately because of the global nature of the internet, where two similar businesses in different locations try to register the same name, or two dissimilar businesses have similar names. Registering a trademark or a copyright, even when done in more than one jurisdiction, will not normally be sufficient to give that registrant a sure claim to a corresponding domain name. The problem is that each domain address is unique and not limited to the geographical location where the business is active. Only one of them can have that domain name. Conflicts also arise when less well-intentioned individuals register the names first and then, in effect, hold the names for ransom. Sometimes similar names are registered so that visitors making slight but expected mistakes are intercepted and redirected to a competing business. This is called **cybersquatting**, and even when there are methods for dealing with such practices, it is often cheaper for a business to simply purchase the address, name, or phrase from the cybersquatter who has managed to register it first.

Each domain name is a unique address, giving rise to considerable conflict

Cybersquatters capture domain names that rightfully should go to others

Arbitration and litigation is possible, but it is often cheaper just to buy the name

---

Case Summary 10.2 *Black v. Molson Canada*[8]
Who Owns a Domain Name

Mr. Black, a resident of Ontario, went through an auction process and obtained and registered the internet domain name "Canadian.Biz." Molson's, a producer of beer in Ontario and elsewhere in Canada, produced a product called "Canadian" and they took the position that Black's registration of the domain name "Canadian Biz" infringed their trademark and demanded that the registration be transferred to them. Black refused. Molson brought an application to the National Arbitration Forum (NAF), the body authorized to hear disputes in such matters and they decided in favour of Molson's, ordering Black to transfer the domain name registration to Molson Canada. Black again refused and brought this action to the Ontario court to over-turn the decision. The problem is that the term "Canadian" is generic and can refer to many different businesses and situations. To decide in Molson's favour the NAF had to find that not only was the name used identical to their trademark but also that Black had no legitimate use or intended use for the name and that it had been registered or used in bad faith. As far as legitimate interest, Black had intended to start an internet business using the name but was reluctant to do so until these proceedings were concluded. The judge found that Black did have a *bona fide* business purpose in mind when he registered the name nor had they established bad faith, and so Black was entitled to the domain name "Canadian.Biz."

---

[8] 2002 CanLII 49493 (ON S.C.) (2002), 60 O.R. (3d) 457.

Arbitration processes have been established to deal with disputes over the entitlement to domain names, reducing the problem to a significant extent. The bodies responsible for the registration of domain names, for example the Canadian Internet Registration Authority (CIRA), have established a policy for the arbitration of bad-faith domain name registration disputes, which gives preference to the businesses with the more legitimate claim. In Canada, for *.ca* designation domain names, bodies such as the British Columbia International Commercial Arbitration Centre (BCICAC) and Resolution Canada Inc. have been authorized to provide arbitration services in such disputes. The largest organization providing domain name dispute arbitration services is the World Intellectual Property Organization (WIPO). Disputes involving legitimate conflicting interests can be handled through traditional trademark or passing-off litigation.

It is important to take steps to avoid name infringement problems

---

Case Summary 10.3 *Bell Express Vu Limited Partnership v. Tedmonds & Co.*[9]

Freedom of Expression on the Internet

Bell, the operator of a properly licensed satellite TV service under the registered trademark of "Express Vu," brought this action for trademark infringement against the defendant company, which operated a rival but unlicensed satellite TV service, when they registered an internet website using the domain name of "expressvu.org." The opening page made it clear that this website was not associated with Bell, but was set up to criticize Bell's service. Bell sued for trademark infringement, but the judge considered this a non-commercial use, which was protected by the freedom of expression provisions of the Charter, and so he refused to grant an injunction. This was only an application for summary judgment, but it does illustrate how proprietary rights might conflict with freedom of expression.

Compare this to *Itravel2000.com Inc. (c.o.b. Itravel) v. Fagan,*[10] where a travel company had been using the name "ITravel" for several years before they tried to register it as a domain name. They discovered that another company had registered the name a month earlier, and then offered to sell it to the travel company for $75 000. There was no internet name registration dispute mechanism in place at that time, and so this action was brought. The plaintiff applied to stop the second company from using or selling the name, claiming it was a trademark violation. Neither company had registered the name as a trademark, but it was clear that the travel company had been using the name under various circumstances in Ontario for years. The defendant had not used the name and had no connection to the travel industry, and so an injunction was granted. The difference in the two cases is that in the second the registration of the name was simply being used as a method of extracting funds from someone who had a superior claim.

Torts

The most common type of tort on the internet is defamation, but the approach will likely be the same where passing-off, fraud, or other forms of tort are involved. Widespread distribution and uncertain jurisdiction are the factors that make internet cases unique. As with written communications, online defamation can take many different forms, ranging from a remark made in a private email message, to chat room conversations, Facebook, and blogs, or to an article posted on a business' website that says disparaging things about a competitor. Even newspapers and magazines run into problems when they place their material on the internet.

Internet defamation is a particular problem because of ease of widespread distribution

---

[9] [2001] O.J. No. 1558 (Ont. S.C.J.).

[10] [2001] O.J. No. 943 (Ont. S.C.J.).

Case Summary 10.4 *Stanley Young v. New Haven Advocate et al.*[11]

Defamation on the Internet

In this case offensive material defaming a prison guard in Virginia was published in Connecticut and distributed over the internet. The Connecticut article was prompted because that state was considering sending some of their prisoners to serve time in Virginia. Young brought his action in Virginia, but the court held they didn't have jurisdiction, as the published article was only intended for local consumption.

Contrast this to the *Dow Jones v. Gutnick*[12] case, where the Australian court did have jurisdiction and the *Bangoura v. Washington Post* case where a Canadian court did not (see Case Summary 10.1). Whichever approach prevails, it is clear that the wide availability of remarks made on the internet poses an ever-increasing vulnerability.

As demonstrated in the cases discussed above, there are conflicting cases with respect to jurisdiction for defamation, which should emphasize the danger for businesses that are not careful about their internet and email communications. Note that not only will the person making the defamatory statement be liable, but the business that employs him or her may be liable as well, especially if company email services or websites are used to publish the offending statements. When a business provides access to their website for chat rooms or for discussion forums, there is also the danger it too could be held responsible for any defamatory or otherwise offensive statements that are made. It is unlikely that the actual ISP (the internet service provider) will be liable, unless it fails to remove or block the offending messages once required to do so by a court. It is likely that those businesses or individuals providing access to the internet will also be responsible where criminal law or other government regulations are infringed, depending on the degree of control they had or should have exercised over the offending communications.

> Note the danger of liability extending to employer or business providing bulletin board or chat room service

Online Contracts

Whether a company is involved in direct retailing of products, software, or service to consumers over the internet or is simply contracting with other companies through email or a website, they are transacting business and creating new legal relationships. The common thread with respect to all of these internet transactions is that their legal status is determined by contract law.

> Electronic commerce is becoming a significant method of doing business

Written evidence of a contract, while not generally required, is a sensible thing to have. It is a permanent record that can be referred to later and constitutes evidence if any disagreement arises. In some cases, under the *Statute of Frauds* or equivalent legislation, such writing and signatures are required for the transaction to be legally enforceable. But when transacting business electronically, there are no signatures or written documents. It is true that written copies can be produced, but they are unreliable due to the ease with which they can be altered.

> Traditional contract rules apply to internet transactions

Consensus   Under the auspices of the federal government, a working group following international recommendations produced the *Uniform Electronic Commerce Act*

---

[11] 315 F. 3d 256 (4th Cir. 2002).

[12] *Dow Jones v. Gutnick*, [2002] H.C.A. 56 (Aust.).

Provinces are adopting federal *Uniform Electronic Commerce Act* guidelines

Statutes recognize electronic equivalent of written documents and signatures

The parties can declare in the contract which jurisdiction's law will apply

Clicking a button will bind party to terms

Post-box rule will not apply to internet transactions

(UECA).[13] This document has no legal standing, but it serves as a model for the design of provincial legislation so that similar statutes will be in place throughout Canada. Every province has enacted such a statute, although they vary considerably between jurisdictions.[14] The object is to make electronic documents and signatures as binding on the parties as are written ones. In general, the UECA and provincial acts do not change the law with respect to the requirement of written documents and signatures. Rather, they recognize electronic or digitally stored documents and signatures, or their equivalent, as satisfying those requirements. A signature equivalent might be a password or some other form of encryption, which is controlled by the author of the document (and possibly verified by a trusted third party). The password or encryption would authenticate the document and give it the same status as one that was written and signed. Note that this doesn't apply in all cases and some types of documents, such as wills, still have to be in writing and signed to be valid. Note, as well, that there are important variations between provinces and that some provinces now allow many forms of government documents, including court registry filings and land registry transactions, to take place electronically. Many jurisdictions also allow the use of electronic documents relating to proxies, prospectuses, and other documentation related to the purchase and sale of securities.

Another problem that arises with respect to the formation of contracts is to determine when and where the contract was created. This can determine whether an offer was accepted within time, what law applied to the transaction, and whether a particular court had jurisdiction to hear a dispute. It might also determine whether the individuals involved were minors or adults at the time, whether transactions involving such things as pyramid selling schemes, gambling, or pornography are legal, and what consumer protection statutes apply to the transaction, all of which varies with the jurisdiction. A business will often state that the law of a particular jurisdiction will apply to the transaction, and, while this is helpful, it does not always end the dispute.

In online commercial transactions the concerns over consensus are addressed by the understanding that hitting an "I accept" button on a website is the equivalent of removing the shrink-wrap on a package or downloading software. It entitles the purchaser to limited use of the product. The seller is the person making the offer. The "I accept" button indicates to the seller that the buyer has read and agreed to the terms of the contract. It achieves the consensus element of a binding contract. The seller then confirms that the order has been received. It is now generally accepted that where such instantaneous methods of communication are involved, the post-box rule should not apply. Thus, an offer will be accepted and a contract formed only when and where the offeror learns of the acceptance. This is consistent with the recommendations of the UECA with respect to contracts formed over the internet discussed above. Also, although internet communication involves intermediaries located in other jurisdictions, the UECA recommendations make the location of these intermediaries irrelevant in determining the validity of the contract and the legal obligations between the parties. Whether a contract or another form of internet communication, these provisions determine that a message is sent as soon as it is committed to the system (hitting send), and it is received as soon as it arrives on the recipient's computer, even if it is

---

[13] http://www.chlc.ca/en/us.

[14] http://mccarthy.ca/pubs/ht-netlaw_2002_binding_contracts/sld022.htm.

never read. As you will recall, an offer ends when a revocation is received and, where implemented, these *UECA* recommendations determine when that takes place and can have a direct impact on that pre-contract negotiation process.

In an Ontario case, *Kanitz v. Rogers Cable*,[15] the court was asked to determine whether unilateral changes to the terms of a contract were valid when they were merely posted on the offeror's website. It was decided that as long as that possibility was stipulated on the website, it was sufficient notification that the terms of the contract were being altered. It is important that both sellers and purchasers be aware of such a condition in the electronic contract. As with contracts generally, when exemption clauses are included, these must be brought to the attention of the person accepting. This is effectively done in most cases by forcing the consumer to indicate they have read and accepted all of the terms before they can click the acceptance button completing the contract. Of course local legislation will protect consumers where standard form contracts include disadvantageous terms, but the problem remains to determine the law of what jurisdiction will apply to the transaction. Typically, the agreement will also include a term stating the law of what jurisdiction will apply and where any action or arbitration must be brought.

Capacity   It is difficult to determine in an online transaction whether the parties actually have the capacity to enter into a contract. A person's age, mental capacity, or even whether a business has or has not been incorporated are difficult to verify online. Parties should take care to find out as much as they can about the company or individual, relying on more than the webpage to gain that information. The question of authenticating someone's identity may also present a challenge, as trust is a diminishing quantity in the online environment. **Electronic signatures** are most effective in identifying people if used in conjunction with trusted third parties who provide a digital certificate that authenticates the identity of a party to the contract. The federal government has provided guidelines for the development, implementation, and use of authentication products and services in Canada.[16]

> It is difficult to be sure with whom you are dealing over the internet

Legality   The legality of the activity that is at the heart of the contract is also a concern and it is important to note that illegal activity is rife on the internet. The potential to remain anonymous and avoid regulation and policing of one's activities have provided an opportunity for every sort of criminal activity in the real world to move into the virtual world. For example, internet gambling is a $5 billion industry, accounting for 4.3 percent of ecommerce.[17] Other investigators conclude that financial incentives and consumer demand for this kind of activity makes legal prohibitions ineffective.[18] The United States has attempted to make online gambling illegal but has only succeeded in moving the operations offshore, ensuring that the "business activity, employment, and tax benefits will accrue overseas. Further, the more that established and legitimate companies are threatened for engaging in any activity connected with internet gambling, the more

> Illegal activities are rampant on the internet

---

[15] 2002 CanLII 49415 (ON S.C.).

[16] Industry Canada, *Principles for Electronic Authentication*, May 2004, http://www.ic.gc.ca/epic/site/ecic-ceac.nsf/en/h_gv00240e.html.

[17] *Crimes of the Internet*, ed. Frank Schmalleger and Michael Pittaro (Pearson, Upper Saddle River, New Jersey, 2009), p. 145–146.

[18] Ibid.

opportunity it provides for marginal and perhaps unethical companies to enter the field and reap tremendous profits."[19]

While the sales of goods acts and consumer protection legislation theoretically apply to online transactions, it is extremely important that buyers be careful as fraudulent scams are commonplace in this medium. The law cannot keep up with the creative schemes of people who take advantage of the opportunities to disguise their intentions in online communications. One means of avoiding the rules in a given jurisdiction is to simply move the illegal operation outside of the countries where the activity is deemed illegal, thus avoiding liability when dealing with their clients. Victims of such scams usually find it extremely difficult to seek redress when the perpetrator is in another country or on another continent.

Payment Online   Even when the goods are being legitimately bought and sold, payment for products purchased also becomes a problem. Many services have been created, such as PayPal, to insure the customer gets what he has paid for or provide a remedy if a dispute arises. The problem is that, as sure as these methods seem foolproof, there is a constant presence of scam artists developing ways to overcome them and separate people from their money. A third party holding the funds is an effective way for significant transactions between large businesses to be conducted. Usually a bank or other financial institution is chosen to hold the funds and advance them to the manufacturer or other contracting party only upon them satisfying some aspect of the contract and a release from the payer. Historically, this has been accomplished even before the advent of ecommerce by issuing a bill or exchange or draft drawn on a bank usually chosen by the payee so they can be assured the funds are there before delivering the product.

Online payment difficult to secure

Jurisdiction   Determining where the contract was formed is an important factor in determining the laws of what jurisdiction will apply to the transaction and whether dispute can be brought in a local court. This can determine whether the individuals involved were minors or adults at the time, whether transactions involving such things as pyramid selling schemes, gambling, or pornography are legal, and what consumer protection statutes apply to the transaction, all of which varies with the jurisdiction. In determining jurisdiction a court will normally ask whether the matter is closely linked to the place in which the plaintiff wants to sue. Because a website is universally accessible, to convince the court that it has jurisdiction the plaintiff must establish that the defendant was targeting the location in which he resides. From the point of view of the business offering the service there is the danger of running afoul of the law of a jurisdiction that prohibits such transactions. It is important to remember and stipulate where necessary which jurisdiction's laws will apply to an online transaction, although this is not always effective (see the provisions of Ontario *Consumer Protection Act* noted above). Even with legitimate transactions it may be difficult to enforce the terms of a contract if something goes wrong. If an item is purchased from a company in Texas, it is important to note whether the company will only deal with the Texas courts if there is a dispute. In some cases a company in one jurisdiction will use a website server in another and stipulate that that jurisdiction's rules will apply. It may be that the reason for this is to avoid regulations altogether and there may be no recourse, if the contract is challenged. It may not be

Legality varies with jurisdiction

Close connection and other factors determine jurisdiction

---

[19] David Giacopassi and Wayne J. Pitts, "Internet Gambling: The Birth of a Victimless Crime?" in *Crimes of the Internet*, ed. Frank Schmalleger and Michael Pittaro (Pearson, Upper Saddle River, New Jersey, 2009), p. 430.

possible to appeal to the courts in the jurisdiction in which you reside because the courts may determine that the matter is not closely enough connected to that jurisdiction for them to handle it.

Case Summary 10.5 *Disney Enterprises Inc. v. Click Enterprises Inc.*[20]

Canadian Courts Can Enforce Foreign Judgments

Phillip Evans, through Click Enterprises, operated a software and internet business in Ontario to facilitate the illegal copying and downloading of movies. Disney Enterprises Ltd., a movie producer, brought an action against Click in New York State. After being personally served, Mr. Evans and Click did not defend the action and in a default judgment were found to be acting illegally and ordered to pay damages of US$468 442.17. It is this judgment that the Ontario court is being asked to enforce against Click and Mr. Evans personally. As a matter of policy the Ontario court will enforce a New York judgment if that court had the jurisdiction to hear the matter in the first place. That question of jurisdiction is determined on the basis of whether there was a real and substantial connection between the conduct complained of and the state. In this case the services were provided to residents in New York State and payments were made to the defendants. In this case Click's involvement in the United States was not passive, but consisted of tendering their products and selling directly to residents in that state, making a profit and being paid for their services in the United States. This created sufficient connection with that state and the Ontario court ordered the enforcement of the New York judgment. The growth of international commerce and especially the internet and the flow of wealth and services across borders require modification of the law of jurisdiction.

To avoid these problems, contracting parties should include product warranties or disclaimers on their websites such as "only available in Canada" or "Alberta laws and regulations will apply." Stating that the service or product is only available in a specific jurisdiction such as Canada or the United States, or stating that it is only available in those jurisdictions where it is legal, will go some way to protect the provider from prosecution.

Parties should declare what law applies and what court has jurisdiction

Alternate Dispute Resolution

When large amounts of money are involved it is important for the Canadian seller or purchaser to know how a dispute will be resolved and if an arbitrator has been selected to deal with the matter. In fact, seeking an arbitrated settlement either online or through a professional arbitration service may be the best way to seek for a resolution, since the courts must first deal with the jurisdiction question and will be reluctant to pursue cases outside of their own jurisdiction. Provisions to provide for such arbitration ought to be included in not only consumer transactions but also transactions between businesses of any size. Note, however, that there may well be consumer protection legislation in place making any term that provides for mandatory arbitration rather than recourse to the courts invalid. (See the Ontario *Consumer Protection Act* discussed above.)

Problems can be avoided by including arbitration clause

Online dispute resolution services are now available for electronic transactions. These services are considerably less costly and less time consuming than traditional court

---

[20] 2006 CanLII 10213 (ON S.C.) (2006), 267 D.L.R. (4th) 291.

Many organizations facilitate arbitration of disputes

processes. The National Arbitration Forum has been very effective in handling internet domain-name disputes.[21] Other provincially based arbitration companies in British Columbia, Ontario, and other provinces may also extend their services to ecommerce disputes. Negotiation and mediation services such as eResolution or Cybersettle.com also offer their services. Arbitration has proved to be a valuable tool for ecommerce disputes but arbitration can also have its downside, as illustrated by the Dell case discussed on page 272.

It has always been hoped that users of the internet would self-regulate, but that seems not to be the case. It will be left to national governments enforcing international treaties and even international organizations to regulate on a global scale.

Regulating the Internet

Little effective regulation of the internet

Governments have been alert to the development of online business, and while there is considerable reluctance to introduce legislation and regulations in the attempt to control illegal activity that would require enormous effort and expense to enforce, they are somewhat more anxious to regulate the collection of taxes. This entails its own difficulties since Canadian goods can be sold from other countries and it is another challenge to discover and tax goods and services that can be downloaded on private computers. Some companies seek to avoid the imposition of taxes on their products by selling their products from other jurisdictions. Attempts to insure that tax laws are properly enforced have had mixed results. One angle where control has been attempted is by holding the Internet Service Providers (ISP) responsible to control illegal online activity, but this also has had limited success. In a federal Court of Appeal case the court refused to order internet service providers to disclose identity of customers.[22]

An illustration of the general reluctance of governments to try to regulate online activity is the fact that at the time of writing there is no anti-spam legislation in spite of the recommendations of a 2005 task force, which argued that Canada should prohibit such offenses as address harvesting or at least create a registry of spammers and require ISPs to refuse to permit them to operate.

The Canadian government was recently successful in forcing the Canadian components of eBay to disclose their financial records on certain "power sellers" to Revenue Canada, even though records of such transactions are kept at their San Jose California facilities. This was done to ensure that these parties pay the required income tax on their successful business activities.[23] One significant problem that arises is the threat to our privacy. If the Canadian government or any arm of it can force these businesses to disclose such information, there is nothing to protect this and other information from similar access to government and government institutions, whether our own or foreign.

---

[21] National Arbitration Forum, "Cybersquatters Infringed Anheuser-Busch and Patrick Dempsey Trademarks, We The People LLC Denied Domain Name Rights," October 14, 2008, http://www.globeinvestor.com/servlet/story/PRNEWS.20081014.AQTU519/GIStory.

[22] *BMG Canada Inc. v. Doe*, [2005] 4 C.F. 81; (2005), 252 D.L.R. (4th) 342 (FCA).

[23] *eBay Canada Ltd. v. Canada (National Revenue)*, 2008 FCA 348 (CanLII).

INTERNATIONAL BUSINESS TRANSACTIONS

Because of the borderless nature of the internet, much of what has been covered in the first part of this chapter applies to the international aspects of business law as well. What follows are issues and information relating specifically to doing business in other jurisdictions. At the outset it should be noted that there is no international court that deals with private disputes between businesses doing business between jurisdictions. Rather, the parties must look to local courts in either jurisdiction to resolve their problems. In fact there are international dispute resolution mechanisms such as the International Court of Justice, the World Trade Organization (WTO), and guidelines such as the General Agreement on Tariffs and Trade (GATT), but they only deal with disputes between sovereign nations applying public international law. An important recent development has been the implementation of the panel system of the World Trade Organization, which sometimes enables governments to appeal adverse decisions of foreign domestic tribunals, thus sidestepping national courts. But they do not deal with private matters between individuals or businesses.

No international court to litigate private matters

In addition to internet activities, Canadian businesses can become involved in business in a different country in many different ways. Perhaps the most common involves the import and export of products, but Canadian businesses can also be involved in dealings with intellectual property including copyrights, patents, and trademarks. This usually involves licensing agreements of intellectual property, particularly patented processes and inventions and the use of copyrighted or trademarked material. Disputes often arise where such intellectual property interests are not recognized and patents or copyrighted material is wrongfully reproduced without respect for the rights of their creator. This can involve direct copying, but also can include the practice of selling **grey market** materials, which involves importing materials from another jurisdiction in violation of a local distributors exclusive right to distribute the product. Brand name electronic goods, watches, and fashion accessories brought in from another jurisdiction where they sell for less are examples. Often the laws in place in that foreign jurisdiction are different from ours and they either don't recognize our intellectual property interests or don't provide adequate enforcement measures.

Import and export of goods most common

Protection of intellectual property serious problem

In addition to the selling and licensing of physical and intellectual products in other countries, Canadian businesses will often become involved in providing or acquiring services from other jurisdictions. This may involve call centres for banking, credit card, telephone, and other services but also may include warehouse distribution centres, which are increasingly being located offshore They will also become involved in activities in those other countries such as mining and resource exploration development and management. This can involve joint ventures with a business in that foreign country or setting up branch plants, local offices, or distribution facilities. Whatever forms those international business activities take, there are some common legal considerations that must be kept in mind. Properly drawn contracts, controlling as many variables as possible that might arise when dealings between jurisdictions are involved, are a vital aspect of doing business abroad. Secondly, the parties must carefully comply with government regulations both in Canada and in the foreign jurisdiction. And finally, all possible steps must be taken to ensure that when disputes do arise they are resolved favourably with as little time delay as possible and minimal expense.

Contract governs all international transactions

Contracts

Before even contemplating the terms of a contract, the importance of knowing who you are dealing with can't be overemphasized. No amount of precision in the language in a contract can replace careful research into the reliability and reputation of the people you are dealing with whether in Canada or in a different jurisdiction. Disputes can still arise, but at least you can be somewhat assured that you are dealing with honourable and reputable people.

Important to know who you are dealing with

Just as with any business contract, the parties must be careful to set out all the obligations and expectations of both parties. Any assumptions that these obligations are based on should be set out as well, eliminating all ambiguous language. At the outset it must be emphasized that any contract to be applied in a foreign jurisdiction must take into consideration the specialized rules or practices in that jurisdiction. For example, when dealing with a civil law jurisdiction or even some other common law jurisdictions, and especially when dealing with less sophisticated countries, the very terminology used may have different meaning. The only way to safely deal with this kind of problem is to acquire the services of a professional specializing in the law of that jurisdiction.

Expert help needed to draw up agreements

It is particularly important to include provisions in the contract setting out what will happen if things go wrong. A dispute mechanism other than the courts is usually vital and can avoid much hardship, as can clauses setting out the law of what jurisdiction is to govern the transaction and be applied in the event of a dispute. Note that the declared law does not have to be the local law of either party but may be that of some third jurisdiction, usually chosen because it better deals with the types of transactions involved. Using the phrase "the agreement will be interpreted under the laws of Ontario," will normally determine what law will govern the transaction, but it will not determine which court will have exclusive jurisdiction. For example, if such a phrase were used in a transaction between parties in Ontario and Arizona, the Arizona court might well be able to hear the dispute, but the rights of the parties should be determined using Ontario law. This would be established by producing a witness who is an expert in Ontario law. In most cases the Arizona judge would respect the choice and apply Ontario law, but that judge would not be bound to do so and could choose to follow Arizona law if the situation required it. A better approach would be to make it clear in the contract that not only would Ontario law apply to the transactions but also that Ontario courts would have exclusive jurisdiction to hear any dispute arising from it. Even then that choice may be overridden by local rules or circumstances. For example, the designated court may determine that they are not the appropriate court to deal with the matter because of where parties live, where the witnesses reside, where the contract was negotiated, or where the alleged breach took place and will acquiesce to the jurisdiction of a different court in another jurisdiction. And there may be legislation in place in that other jurisdiction that simply prevents the ousting of the jurisdiction of the local court. For example, the new Ontario *Consumer Protection Act* makes any attempt to limit the jurisdiction of the Ontario court in such transactions "invalid."

Important to declare what law applies

And what court has jurisdiction

It is important to be aware of the differences between local law and the rules in place in the foreign jurisdiction where you are doing business. For example, it would be a significant mistake to include a restriction limiting the territory where the product could be sold or the price it could be sold at in that jurisdiction if that were to run afoul of any anti-competition provisions in place there. Similarly, government requirements may make it impossible to comply with non-disclosure provisions in the agreement.

Know what you can and can't do in that foreign jurisdiction

Financial Reporting   Another important provision to include in such contracts is a method to account for profits or royalties (depending on the nature of the transaction). This usually includes specifying what records must be kept by that foreign partner or customer and providing access to them by your accounting department or by a specified accounting firm mutually agreed on by the parties.

Foreign Ownership   Where the business activity contemplated involves actually setting up a branch operation in that foreign country, this will likely require incorporation. Often these countries have legislation in place restricting foreign ownership of land as well as shares or directorships in such corporations. This will likely require contractual relationships to be established with local residents who will own the land and the majority of shares, and function as directors, causing more complication and risk. Of course, operating a branch business in a foreign country subjects the Canadian business to all of the laws in place in that jurisdiction and all must be complied with whether they govern the workforce, prices charged and paid, marketing practices, or environmental restrictions.

Specialty Contracts   Note that depending on the nature of the transactions, additional specialized contracts may also be involved, such as a bill of lading establishing the rights and obligations of the parties and the carrier when goods are shipped through a third party carrier; a letter of credit or other financing instrument, where a third party is used to ensure that the selling party is paid when the purchasing party is satisfied; and insurance to cover the risks of the transaction. Note also that whenever common documents such as these are involved there are standard form contracts in place using tested terminology that are generally accepted by all parties and used exclusively. In addition the governments of both parties often require customs declarations and invoices and other information relating to the transaction.

> Supplementary standard form contracts:
> - Bills of lading
> - Letters of credit
> - Insurance

Dispute Resolution

Because of the great costs of litigation and because of the uncertainty of the outcome there is a growing practice to include an arbitration clause in such contracts. The clause requires that all such disputes be determined by arbitration and sets out how the arbitrator is to be chosen, as well as the powers and procedures to be used. But even these can be overridden where the local rules or circumstances require.

> Arbitration clause can avoid litigation

Alternate dispute resolution was discussed in Chapter 1 but it is reviewed here because of its profound value in international transactions. All of its advantages over litigation especially apply to international transactions because of the lack of any court of international jurisdiction to deal with private disputes, and because of the uncertainty and risks associated with submitting to a court in a foreign jurisdiction. Alternate dispute resolution can consist of negotiation, mediation, and arbitration. Negotiation and mediation are, of course, just as valuable in international dealings as in domestic relationships, but it is arbitration that is particularly appropriate when dealing with international disputes. The risks and potential expense and delay associated with the litigation process are amplified significantly when dealing with foreign courts. The idea, of course, is for the parties to include a provision in their contract to submit any dispute arising from the transaction to an arbitrator chosen by them, and also setting out any limits on what that arbitrator can decide and what kind of decisions and remedies can be imposed. In effect the parties create a private court designating the judge and power of the court to resolve disputes arising between them and local courts will usually honour such contract provision. The parties then exert some control and reduce the uncertainties, costs, and delays associated with the litigation process. When the parties include an arbitration clause in their contract they can determine who shall arbitrate any disputes between them. This normally makes both parties more satisfied with the outcome, no matter which side it favours. Also, they can specify an arbitrator with particular expertise in the industry or business that the transaction involves, thus having more confidence in a proper outcome and with the assurance that the decision will be made in a more expeditious and efficient manner. Any delays can be kept to a minimum and the dispute can be less confrontational and remain confidential, which is especially valuable where the relationship will continue. The main advantages of arbitration are the reduction of risk, respecting mutual obligations and rights, and the minimal costs.

Parties can control who arbitrates and arbitration process

Case Summary 10.6 *Dell Computer Corp v. Union des consommaterus*[24]

Arbitration Clauses Can Be Used Against Consumers

Dell computers had a head office in Toronto and a facility in Montreal. On April 4, 2003, an error was made on their internet ordering site that stated the price of two models of handheld computers substantially lower than they should have been. When the error was discovered Dell blocked orders on the site, issued a correction, and announced that they would not process any orders at the lower prices. When Olivier Dumoulin learned of the low price he found the site blocked and used a "deep link" to get around the block and place an order. When Dell refused to honour that order he, along with a Quebec consumer group, brought this application to commence a class action against Dell. Dell opposed the application and submitted that the parties be directed to use an arbitration process as required in the order of sale contract. Despite a provision in the Quebec Civil Code stating that in consumer transactions the Quebec courts will have jurisdiction to hear a dispute despite an arbitration clause to the contrary, the Supreme Court of Canada held that the arbitration clause

prevailed, the class action application should be dismissed, and the matter should be referred to arbitration. This was done despite the inconvenience of the American process of arbitration specified in the contract. The court held that the contract did not require the dispute to be submitted to a foreign authority, but that the arbitration clause was a private agreement between the parties and the private aspect of the contract was being enforced. Note that a similar case for class action proceedings against Dell in Ontario was successful using different legislation, and so it is not clear whether Dell will be able to hide behind this arbitration clause in their standard contract in the future.[25] Dell's preference for its arbitration clause is easily understood when you realize that Dell is much better off if they can stop any class action suits against them and force individuals to submit their complaint to arbitration, because it is unlikely that any such actions will proceed given the minimal amount of money involved and the difficulty of dealing with a U.S. jurisdiction.

The main disadvantage to arbitration used to be a difficulty in enforcing the award. This is less the case today, with Canadian courts showing considerable deference to the awards of an arbitrator, whether domestic or international. An example of an ADR initiative is a joint venture between the University of Windsor and the University of Detroit

---

[24] 2007 SCC 34 (CanLII), (2007), 284 D.L.R. (4th) 577.

[25] *Griffin v. Dell Canada Inc.*, 2009 CanLII 3557 (ON S.C.).

to provide an international commercial dispute resolution process to corporations in NAFTA's three signatory nations: Canada, the United States, and Mexico.[26]

Additionally, provincial and federal legislation provide for the enforcement of such international arbitration awards pursuant to international treaties and conventions signed by Canada and many other nations. Pursuant to these agreements, arbitration awards can be submitted to the courts and will be enforced as a term of the contract using the court's enforcement facilities. It is interesting to note that in fact such international arbitration awards are now more likely to be enforceable in our courts than are the foreign judgments as discussed below. It is important to recognize, as well, that an "international ADR culture (particularly arbitration and mediation) is taking root as the use of ADR to resolve international disputes accelerates."[27]

Of course, many problems can be avoided altogether by simply arranging for adequate insurance coverage to support the transactions. Payment services such as PayPal essentially provide this service, ensuring that the customer gets what he has transacted for and providing a remedy and a resolution process when disputes do arise. When purchases are made through a credit card, an insurance service is also provided.

Arbitration awards enforceable in courts

Litigation and Jurisdiction

What Court?   As noted above, there is no international court that has jurisdiction over private disputes between individuals or businesses. When the matter disputed involves interests in more than one country, the problem arises as to where to launch a lawsuit. Typically, the plaintiff will bring an action in her jurisdiction and an application will then be brought by the defendant to have that court declare that they will not deal with it. This is referred to as an application for an order of *forum non conveniens* but a court is often reluctant to surrender jurisdiction in such matters. Note that the stated choice of law or jurisdiction is most likely to be overruled where it is clear that one party was stronger than the other and the choice of law imposed benefits the one at the expense of the other. Such abuse is most often found in consumer transactions. The following table lists the questions the court will consider before determining whether it has jurisdiction.

Right of a court to hear action may be challenged

Table 10.1 Factors Determining Jurisdiction

1. Where was contract formed?
2. Where was it to be performed?
3. Where do the parties (and witnesses) reside?
4. Where did the problem occur?
5. Where are the goods or property located?
6. Does the choice by either party benefit the stronger?
7. Which jurisdiction is most closely connected?

---

[26] J. Furlong, " U.S.-Canada joint venture seeks to promote international trade and commerce through ADR," *Lawyers Weekly* 15, no. 35, January 1996.

[27] *Lawyers Weekly*, February 2007.

Many jurisdictions are tackling these problems through statutory enactment. For instance, British Columbia recently passed legislation stating how the jurisdiction of B.C. courts is to be determined.[28] Basically, the legislation follows a Supreme Court of Canada decision and recommendations by the Uniform Law Conference of Canada simplifying the process of determining when the local courts have jurisdiction.[29] The test is **"territorial competence,"** the term replacing more involved and vague terminology found in the common law. Essentially B.C. courts will have territorial competence or jurisdiction where there is a close connection between the province and the facts giving rise to the case or where 1) a party being sued has agreed that the court will have jurisdiction, 2) they have attorned (submitted) to that jurisdiction, or 3) they are ordinarily resident in British Columbia. Ordinary residence for a corporation may include having an office or other place of business in British Columbia or managing their business from a location in that province. Note that the court will have territorial competence if one of these factors is present regardless of what the parties have agreed. In a tort action the B.C. court has jurisdiction where the tort was committed in British Columbia or where the defendant resides in that province. Several other provinces, including Saskatchewan and Nova Scotia, have passed similar legislation. Given the Supreme Court of Canada decision referred to above, this indicates the most likely future direction for all provinces. An important feature of the act allows the court to transfer an action started in British Columbia to a court in another jurisdiction where it is convenient to do so, thus eliminating the problem of the plaintiff having to start all over again.

Legislation replaces common law in determining jurisdiction of court

Legislation allows transfer of the action

Case Summary 10.7 *Noble v. Carnival Corporation*[30]

Where to Sue?

Robin Noble was a resident of Ontario working on a cruise ship as a tour manager. As part of her job she was inspecting sites in Russia when she was involved in a serious automobile accident. Ms. Nobel was only temporarily assigned to this ship and so she claimed an employment relationship with several different cruise lines and tour providers, all of which she is suing in Ontario for breach of their employment obligations to her. None of these defendants had offices or assets in Canada. (Two had head offices in the United States and one in Hong Kong.) The question was whether the Ontario court had jurisdiction to hear the case. Her contract of employment had a provision that any disputes arising under it would be dealt with in English courts (the place of the ship's registration). She sued in Ontario. The court held it had jurisdiction. It was held that there was no closer place than Ontario and that it was less inconvenient for the defendant to defend in Ontario than anywhere else. The dispute forum clause was ambiguous and the plaintiff was in an unfavourable bargaining position with respect to it. Also her employer would have known that if she were injured she would have to return to Ontario.

Enforcement   Once the judgment has been obtained there remains the problem of enforcing it. That is not a serious difficulty where the losing party has assets in the jurisdiction where the judgment was rendered. The judgment can be enforced against those assets like any other judgment. The problem arises when the party obtaining the judgment

Difficult to enforce a court order in another jurisdiction

---

[28] *Court Jurisdiction and Proceedings Transfer Act,* S.B.C. 2003, c. 28.

[29] *Morguard Investments Ltd. v. De Savoye,* [1990] 3 S.C.R. 1077.

[30] [2006] O.J. No. 143.

from a court in one jurisdiction wants to enforce it in another where the losing party does have assets. At the outset a court in one jurisdiction simply does not have the power to make an order enforceable in another. The result is that such an order will only be effective in that other jurisdiction if a court in that jurisdiction adopts it. This is true even between provinces and a receivership order from an Ontario Court, for example, will have no effect in Alberta. To seize assets in Alberta, the Alberta court must adopt the Ontario order. While this is commonly done in common law jurisdictions, it is often a serious problem when dealing with foreign jurisdictions, especially developing countries. Again there are conventions between nations, provinces, and states to solve this problem and most provinces and many states in the United States and countries such as Australia have reciprocating enforcement statutes allowing the judgment or order of one jurisdiction to be enforced in another as if it were an order of that court. If there is no such reciprocating enforcement agreement in place the person wanting to enforce the order in another jurisdiction will have to start all over, suing on the judgment in that other state to get at the assets of the debtor.

Foreign courts will enforce a judgment if reciprocal enforcement agreement in place

Most foreign jurisdictions will recognize the validity of a judgment of a Canadian court, but the process of suing on that judgment is more involved, with many more pitfalls and greater expense than simply registering that judgment and enforcing it as is done in a reciprocating state. Proof that the debtor has actually been properly served in such an action is often a problem and it is common practice for an absconding debtor who is trying to escape his obligations to move to a jurisdiction where there is no reciprocating enforcement agreement and then avoid being served. Such tactics can be overcome, but the process is delayed and made more expensive and often is just not worth the trouble.

Defences   When suing on a foreign judgment there are many defences that can be raised to prevent its enforcement. A problem with process, such as improper service or where a party was not allowed to give evidence, may be fatal to the action. When laws are different in the foreign jurisdiction where you wish to enforce the judgment, it can also pose an insurmountable difficulty. That country will not enforce a judgment based on a legal principle that they do not recognize. For instance, if a judgment is based on the breach of a non-competition clause in a contract for the sale of a business, and that country does not allow such as restriction on competition, they are not likely to enforce the judgment or order. Finally, it should also be noted that the awards of internationally recognized arbitrators can also be enforced by filing them with a local court in the same way as a foreign judgment. In fact they are often easier to enforce because there are more comprehensive agreements and conventions between nations in place allowing for such enforcement.

Judgment will not be enforced where laws are different

Courts more likely to enforce arbitration award

Case Summary 10.8 *Bad Ass Coffee Company of Hawaii Inc. v. Bad Ass Enterprises Inc.*[31]

Arbitration Provision in Contract Binding

An Alberta company entered into a franchise agreement with Bad Ass Coffee Company of Hawaii Inc. to operate a franchise operation in Alberta. They entered into a contract to open the first store in February 2000 and a second agreement to open another store in December 2000. These contracts were personally guaranteed by Mr. Ronald Plucer. The franchisee and franchisor worked together and royalties were paid until April 2004. At that time the

>

---

[31] 2008 AB Q.B. 404 (CanLII) (2007): [2008] 427 A.R. 241; (2007), [2008] 1 W.W.R. 738; (2007), 81 Alta. L.R. (4th) 31.

Alberta company stopped paying royalties and in fact opened a third store using the same name without further reference to the Hawaiian franchisor. In all the contracts there was an arbitration clause requiring that any disputes arising between the parties be arbitrated pursuant to a specified process and that the laws of the State of Utah would govern the transaction. The Hawaii franchisor brought the matter to arbitration, but the Alberta company refused to submit to or recognize the jurisdiction of the arbitrator and did not attend. The arbitrator proceeded in their absence and found against them, awarding substantial damages. The arbitration award was filed with the courts of Utah and this is an application to enforce that Utah judgment in Alberta.

There is an Alberta statute that states that, "Any provision in a franchise agreement restricting the application of the law of Alberta or restricting jurisdiction or venue to any forum outside Alberta is void with respect to a claim otherwise enforceable under this *Act* in Alberta." and "Any waiver or release by a franchisee of a right given by this *Act* or the Regulations or of a Requirement of this *Act* or the Regulations is void." The court found that the judgment for damages for breach of contract didn't fall under the *Franchise Act* and the contract requiring the arbitration of any disputes be in Utah was valid and could be enforced in Alberta. There was also a provision in *The Guarantees Acknowledgment Act* of Alberta that all guarantees must be notarized and the guarantees of Mr. Plucer were not. But since the law of Utah applied, which had no such requirement, the judgment against the guarantor was also enforceable in Alberta.

GOVERNMENT REGULATIONS AND TREATIES
International Treaties

From the above discussion and from prior chapters it should be clear that there are a number of international treaties and conventions that Canada is party to that either directly or indirectly affect the transactions carried on between business people in different countries. For example, as noted in Chapter 9, Canada has adopted the Bern and Rome conventions with respect to copyright, with the result that rights of copyright holders in other countries that are signatories to those conventions are recognized here and in turn Canadian copyright holders have rights to protection in those countries as well. Canada also has accepted the United Nations convention and created an international sale of goods act.[32] This requires that each province pass their own version of the international sale of goods act; and, like the regular sale of goods Acts discussed in Chapter 5, this Act supplies missing terms into contracts between businesses for the sale of goods across borders. Like the normal sale of goods Acts, where the parties include terms in their agreements that are inconsistent with the terms of the *International Sale of Goods Act*, the contract terms will override the provisions of the Act. Of course when the terms of the *International Sale of Goods Act* are applied to a contract, it is generally an indication of a failure on the part of the parties to create a comprehensive and complete contract covering the transaction.

Provinces have enacted versions of international sale of goods act

Perhaps the most important consequence of international treaties signed by Canada is the encouragement of free trade between certain nations. These agreements reduce or eliminate tariffs and duties that are usually imposed by a nation to protect their own industries. Canada was an early signatory to GATT (General Agreement on Tariffs and Trade). GATT was an agreement or treaty rather than an organization, and it developed from a failed attempt to create a international trade organization after World War II. Over

---

[32] United Nations, "United Nations Convention on Contracts for the International Sale of Goods (1980)"; *International Sale of Goods Contracts Convention Act*, S.C. 1991, c. 13.

the years the members of GATT met regularly and negotiated to reduce trade barriers in the form of tariffs and trade between the member nations. The process is very difficult, involving an attempt to fairly balance rules in place in all nations to support and subsidize local industries, while at the same time preventing **dumping** of lower priced goods in that nation that would drive their own industries out of business. The idea is to promote fair trade, encourage balanced competition, and prohibit or control abusive practices. GATT required that a member grant all other members the same tariff advantage as the lowest tariff they charged on similar goods from any nations. This was called "**most favoured nation status**." The agreement also required that goods that were imported into the country from a member state had to be treated the same as domestic goods, with no special requirements or restrictions.

GATT has since been incorporated into the WTO (World Trade Organization), whose object is the same, to reduce trade barriers, thus encouraging international trade, cooperation, and generally contributing to the process of globalization. The WTO goes further than GATT in that it is an organization of countries rather than just an agreement between them. It adds a dispute resolution process, and while GATT was limited to the trade of goods, the WTO covers subjects beyond goods, including financial and other services and intellectual property. GATT started as a negotiated agreement between 23 contracting parties, but the WTO is an organization now consisting of 153 member countries (at the time of writing).

Continental Treaties   In addition to these world organizations, Canada is also a participant in more localized trade treaties in the form of NAFTA (North American Free Trade Agreement). NAFTA is an agreement between Canada, the United States, and Mexico, and is designed to promote easier trade relations between the three countries, eliminating trade barriers in the form of tariffs and duties as much as possible and promoting free trade between the three countries. The agreement in essence expands on the WTO agreement between these three countries and most duties and tariffs have been or are being removed on goods and services traded between them. But this free trade is extended to allowing professionals free access to the other nations as well, allowing them to move freely and practice their profession in any of the three countries. There are also environmental protection provisions and labour standards included in the agreement. NAFTA also provides for a dispute resolution mechanism. Note that there is a movement to admit other countries into NAFTA and so we are likely to see something like a North and South American free trade agreement in the not-too-distant future. Note as well that these agreements are very complex and this discussion only indicates the basic features, but in no way is it an attempt at a comprehensive summary or critical analysis. When dealing with NAFTA, the WTO, or any other of the many treaties and conventions that may affect your business transaction, there is no substitute for specific advice from a professional.

Canadian Regulations

World trade negotiations generally deal with such concerns as free trade between countries, eliminating trade barriers, prohibiting dumping of goods, protection of third world economies, allowing for sustainable use of natural resources, and protection of the environment. When Canada subscribes to such international agreements, they commit to the regulations imposed by trading partners and expect that other countries will do the same.

GATT reduces trade barriers

WTO expands on GATT

NAFTA creates free trade zone between Canada, U.S.A., and Mexico

NAFTA includes dispute resolution mechanism

The Government of Canada has imposed a considerable body of regulations that must be adhered to when doing business between countries. In this final section of the text we will look at a few of the statutes in place in this country designed to regulate businesses carrying on their business across borders.

Canada imposes few restrictions on exports

Export   There are only a few federal statutes that affect the export of Canadian products to other countries. There are controls in place that are mainly concerned with security and anti-terrorism measures, the laundering of money, and the avoidance of taxes. In addition, the *Export and Import Permits Act*[33] empowers the federal government to restrict certain exports to specific countries. The government department involved (International Trade Canada) manages several lists that set out certain countries to which some exports are restricted. If the specified goods are to be exported to one of these designated countries a permit must be obtained from that body. There are also a number of statutes regulating specific goods or practices such as the *Softwood Lumber Products Export Charge Act* (2006),[34] the *Export and Import of Rough Diamonds Act*,[35] the *Cultural Property Export and Import Act*,[36] and the *Corruption of Foreign Public Officials Act*.[37] There are also restrictions on the export of certain strategic materials such as weapons and sophisticated computer technology as well as the trade of exotic and threatened species. But these are relatively insignificant restrictions on exports.

The main problem for Canadian businesses involved in exporting is to overcome the restrictions imposed on them including significant tariffs and duties by the importing nation. Canada is essentially an exporting nation, which is why international trade conventions and organizations like NAFTA and the WTO are so important to us. They go a long way in removing the roadblocks that have historically restricted the import of our goods into other countries. Also, one of the main functions of the various government

Canadian government agencies assist export process

agencies operating at home and abroad is to support Canadian businesses, helping them to develop markets, expand their businesses, and otherwise smooth the road for companies doing business in foreign countries. This involves everything from trade missions by government officials and business leaders to the ironing out of individual problems by direct intervention with foreign officials. Note that the Export Development Corporation also assists and encourages foreign trade by offering a wide range of protective services to reduce many of the risks associated with foreign business transactions.

Imports   The regulation of imports coming into Canada is another matter. Import of goods is regulated in Canada primarily by the *Customs Act*[38] that empowers customs officials (the Canadian Border Services Agency, CBSA) to enforce various regulations restricting what can be imported or imposing duties of varying amounts on those goods. CBSA officials have significant enforcement powers that may lead to confiscated goods and imposition of

CBSA officials have extensive powers

penalties for failure to properly comply with the declaration permit and duty regulations. Canada, the United States, and other developed countries all have statutes in place

---

[33] R.S.C. 1985, c. E-19.

[34] S.C. 2006, c. 13.

[35] S.C. 2002, c. 25.

[36] R.S.C. 1985, c. C-51.

[37] S.C. 1998 c. 34.

[38] R.S.C. 1985, c. 1 (2nd Supp).

preventing the sale of products manufactured in other countries that unfairly compete with products manufactured in their own, either because of subsidies, unusually low wages, or simply because of the foreign manufacturer selling below cost to get rid of excess production. This is called dumping, and in Canada extra duties are imposed under the *Special Import Measures Act*[39] to overcome the unfair advantage. Also the *Excise Act*[40] creates special procedures requiring licensing, permits, and duties for the import of beer, wine, and spirits.

Practice of dumping controlled

As mentioned above, the WTO and NAFTA give goods imported from nations associated with these treaties special status, with generally lower or no tariffs imposed, but the application of the regulations to actual imports can be very complex. These agreements have force in Canada under the *North American Free Trade Agreement Implementation Act*[41] and the *World Trade Organization Agreement Implementation Act*.[42] In addition there are a number of special bilateral agreements that Canada has implemented giving certain developing nations, such as Costa Rica, favoured trading status. As mentioned above, under the *Export and Import Permits Act*,[43] certain countries are put on a list to which exports are restricted. This act also restricts imports coming from these listed countries. Of course, there are also restrictions on the import of hazardous products and those posing a health risk, as well as products that are generally prohibited, such as certain types of weapons, or exotic and threatened animals, animal products, and other threatened species such as exotic plants and wood products. The point is that there is a veritable forest of regulations potentially affecting any business that imports products or services into this country, and a business doing so must determine ahead of time just what duties and permits are necessary given the foreign country involved and the product to be imported.

NAFTA and free trade reduces regulation of imports

Restrictions on the import of dangerous, hazardous, and environmentally sensitive goods

Extraterritorial Reach

Finally, it should also be mentioned that some counties, particularly the United States, have enacted laws that attempt to work extraterritorially. A recent example of American legislation that has an effect extraterritorially is the *PatriotAct*,[44] passed in reaction to the 9/11 tragedy. An earlier example is the legislation passed by the United States that was designed to punish individuals and businesses in Canada and other countries that did business with Cuba after the Cuban revolution. Canada passed legislation attempting to protect its sovereignty by shielding its citizens from the operation of such laws. *The Foreign Extraterritorial Measures Act*[45] is designed to thwart the operation of U.S. laws that attempt to punish Canadian businesses dealing with countries such as Cuba. Other examples of retaliatory legislation have been passed in Canada, but these are generally ineffective because Canada is primarily an exporting nation and these retaliatory measures generally have to be imposed on imports. Unfortunately, retaliatory measures often simply encourage more restrictions on our exports in turn.

Some foreign governments attempt to apply their regulations beyond their borders

---

[39] R.S.C. 1985, c. S-15.

[40] S.C. 2002, c. 22.

[41] S.C. 1993, c. 44.

[42] S.C. 1994, c. 47.

[43] R.S.C. 1985 c. E-19.

[44] *Uniting and Strengthening America by Providing Appropriate Tools Required to Intercept and Obstruct Terrorism Act, 2001* (USA PATRIOT Act) Public Law 107-56, U.S. Congress.

[45] R.S.C. 1985, c. F-29.

Key Terms

cybersquatting (p. 261)

domain names (p. 261)

dumping (p. 277)

electronic signatures (p. 265)

grey market (p. 269)

long-arm statutes (p. 259)

most favoured nation status (p. 277)

territorial competence (p. 274)

Questions for Student Review

1. How has the internet changed the nature of doing business?

2. Explain the problems with jurisdiction that arise in internet business transactions.

3. What must be demonstrated for a Canadian court to hear an action in a dispute involving an online transaction?

4. What is the danger of ignoring an action brought in a foreign jurisdiction?

5. Explain why internet defamation has become a greater potential problem compared to ordinary written or spoken defamation. What other torts can be committed on the internet?

6. What sorts of opportunities does the internet provide for losing control over personal information?

7. Explain the unique problems associated with the formation of contracts over the internet and what federal and provincial governments have done to respond to these issues.

8. Explain the role played by the federal *Uniform Electronic Commerce Act* and how it relates to provincial legislation.

9. What is cybersquatting and what attempts have been made to control it?

10. What is the most appropriate means of resolving disputes over online transactions?

11. What are the common law obligations with respect to people who are given confidential obligation?

12. What steps should a business take to insure that employees don't misuse confidential information or engage in other inappropriate online activities while in the workplace?

13. Explain the reluctance of governments to regulate the internet's business or even criminal activities.

14. Describe some of the overlapping concerns of electronic and global commercial transactions.

15. What are some of things a business person who is contracting with a foreign person should consider?

16. Outline the terms that should be included in a cross-border contract.

17. What provisions should be made for dispute resolution?

18. What is the likelihood of successfully pursuing a judicial action in a foreign jurisdiction?

19. What international organizations are set up to assist in the resolution of disputes?

20. What questions will a court ask to determine whether or not to hear a matter related to an international contract dispute?

21. Explain the problems associated with enforcing a judgment in a foreign country.

22. How effective are international treaties in place to assist contracting parties?

23. Explain what statutes are in place in Canada to support international trade.

Questions for Further Discussion

1. One of the great advantages of the internet, and one of the reasons for its tremendous growth in recent years, has been its freedom from controls and regulation. It has been a little like the Wild West, with entrepreneurs, artists, and anyone with a desire to communicate free to do so, and only limited by his or her imagination. This has led to invention and creativity, but also to abuses. The debate today relates to control and regulation of the internet and the question for discussion is whether you think that this beast should be tamed. Consider the arguments pro and con, and discuss the various ways that such controls could be imposed. Look at the jurisdictional problems, but consider also how to maintain the freewheeling nature of the internet that has contributed to so much creativity.

2. A business person who is focused on the bottom line may overlook the social impact his business activities have on people, particularly if they occur in a foreign country. When financial interests are put ahead of public good, the results can be devastating. What concerns should an ethical business manager have in mind when contracting with or opening a plant in a developing country? Keep in mind economic, ecological, and social impacts. How can ignorance or dismissal of these factors negatively affect the business climate in Canada? Consider some examples from recent times where highly industrialized countries have exploited the people and resources of developing countries.

3. The U.S. administration is re-examining NAFTA with an eye to protecting their own interests, such as by insulating local industries from outside competition. What are the implications for Canada? How will it affect our trading relationships? Think about the problem of dumping. Should Canada make more of an effort to protect our manufacturing and commodities interests?

4. Can we depend on international treaties to regulate and control electronic and global commerce? What role should world trade organizations play in encouraging and regulating international transactions? Is this a forum in which the United Nations can play a positive role? How can economic powers be balanced between trading partners? Who should be responsible for protecting lesser powers?

5. Try drafting your own standard form contract for a business selling a product over the internet. Think about the elements that must be present for such a contract to be binding, including how the process of offer and acceptance will be accomplished. What kind of exemption clauses would you like to include? How would you solve the jurisdiction problem? How do you think a customer might react to these provisions?

Cases for Discussion

1. *R. v. Benlolo*, 2006 CanLII 19284 (ON C.A.) (2006), 81 O.R. (3d) 440.

   Alan and Elliot Benlolo sent thousands of invoices to various businesses for the renewal of their listing on an internet "Yellow pages business directory." The invoices looked very similar to those issued by Bell Canada. In fact the recipients had never been subscribers to such a service and were misled into thinking they were renewing a service they had been party to. Even after being warned by the Competition Bureau, the Benlolos continued further mailings and eventually were convicted for misleading advertising under the *Competition Act*. At the same time they were involved in this activity they were engaged in an international telemarketing stock swap scheme, which involved fraudulently getting people to pay for stocks at inflated prices and leading them to believe they were dealing with a legitimate stock brokerage. Note that millions of dollars were taken from their victims. What do you think might be an appropriate sentence or penalty in these circumstances?

2. *Easthaven v. Nutrisystem* (2002), 55 O.R. (3d) 334, 202 D.L.R. (4th) 560 (Ont. S.C.J.).

Easthaven Ltd. was a company registered in Barbados with a head office in that country. It registered the domain name of "sweetsuccess.com" to further an internet sports-related business. The domain name was registered with Tucows Inc., a company incorporated in Delaware but with a head office in Toronto. Nutrisystem.com Inc. was incorporated in Pennsylvania with a head office in that state as a weight loss business with products and trademarks based on the name "Sweet Success." When they approached Easthaven about the domain name, Easthaven offered to sell it to them for US$146 250. They brought a successful action in Pennsylvania asking that court to order that the domain name "sweetsuccess" be transferred to them. The Pennsylvania court sent an order to Tucows to transfer the name to Nutrisystem. In the meantime Easthaven brought this action in the Ontario court for damages against Nutrisystem and an order against Tucows to prevent the transfer of the domain name to Nutrisystem. Do you think the Ontario court should become involved? How could the matter best be handled? How would your answer be affected by the added information that before the action went to trial in Ontario, Tucows reversed their decision to transfer the domain name to Nutrisystem and put it on "Registrar Hold," meaning it could not be used by either party. In response to this Eastahaven withdrew their action against Tucows. This left Nutrisystem the only defendant in the Ontario action.

3. *Kanitz v. Rogers Cable Inc.*, 2002 CanLII 49415 (ON S.C.).

Rogers Cable Inc. provided cable and internet services to customers in Ontario and other areas of Canada. The plaintiffs were customers who brought this class action against Rogers claiming that they had breached their contract by providing interrupted, intermittent, and slow service over a specific period of time. The original contract that Rogers had subscribers sign when they first obtained the service had a provision allowing them to make changes to it. The subscribers' continued use of the service after notification of the change constituted acceptance. If they chose not to accept they were to cease the service immediately and notify Rogers. In fact in November 2000 such a modification was made by the inclusion of an arbitration clause in the contract so that all disputes had to be arbitrated following a specific process rather than litigated. What do you think? Should this provision be part of the contract? Does the Ontario court have the right to hear the class action brought by the plaintiffs? Would your answer be affected by the information that Rogers and Shaw cable had made a swap of customers and facilities in British Columbia and Ontario with the result that some of the customers were originally with Shaw and were not original contracting parties with Rogers? What other information would you need to know?

Appendix A

The *Constitution Act, 1867* (formerly the *British North America Act*)

SECTIONS 91 AND 92
VI. DISTRIBUTION OF LEGISLATIVE POWERS

Powers of the Parliament

91. It shall be lawful for the Queen, by and with the Advice and Consent of the Senate and House of Commons, to make Laws for the Peace, Order, and Good Government of Canada, in relation to all Matters not coming within the Classes of Subjects by this Act assigned exclusively to the Legislatures of the Provinces; and for greater Certainty, but not so as to restrict the Generality of the foregoing Terms of this Section, it is hereby declared that (notwithstanding anything in this Act) the exclusive Legislative Authority of the Parliament of Canada extends to all Matters coming within the Classes of Subjects next herein-after enumerated; that is to say,

Legislative authority of Parliament of Canada

1. (Repealed)
1A. The Public Debt and Property
2. The Regulation of Trade and Commerce
2A. Unemployment insurance
3. The raising of Money by any Mode or System of Taxation
4. The borrowing of Money on the Public Credit
5. Postal Service
6. The Census and Statistics
7. Militia, Military and Naval Service, and Defence
8. The fixing of and providing for the Salaries and Allowances of Civil and other Officers of the Government of Canada
9. Beacons, Buoys, Lighthouses, and Sable Island
10. Navigation and Shipping
11. Quarantine and the Establishment and Maintenance of Marine Hospitals
12. Sea Coast and Inland Fisheries
13. Ferries between a Province and any British or Foreign Country or between Two Provinces
14. Currency and Coinage
15. Banking, Incorporation of Banks, and the Issue of Paper Money

16. Savings Banks

17. Weights and Measures

18. Bills of Exchange and Promissory Notes

19. Interest

20. Legal Tender

21. Bankruptcy and Insolvency

22. Patents of Invention and Discovery

23. Copyrights

24. Indians, and Lands reserved for the Indians

25. Naturalization and Aliens

26. Marriage and Divorce

27. The Criminal Law, except the Constitution of Courts of Criminal Jurisdiction, but including the Procedure in Criminal Matters

28. The Establishment, Maintenance, and Management of Penitentiaries

29. Such Classes of Subjects as are expressly excepted in the Enumeration of the Classes of Subjects by this Act assigned exclusively to the Legislatures of the Provinces

And any Matter coming within any of the Classes of Subjects enumerated in this Section shall not be deemed to come within the Class of Matters of a local or private Nature comprised in the Enumeration of the Classes of Subjects by this Act assigned exclusively to the Legislatures of the Provinces.

Exclusive Powers of Provincial Legislatures

92. In each Province, the Legislature may exclusively make Laws in relation to Matters coming within the Classes of Subject next herein-after enumerated; that is to say,

1. (Repealed)

Subjects of exclusive provincial legislation

2. Direct Taxation within the Province in order to the raising of a Revenue for Provincial Purposes

3. The borrowing of Money on the sole Credit of the Province

4. The Establishment and Tenure of Provincial Offices and the Appointment and Payment of Provincial Officers

5. The Management and Sale of the Public Lands belonging to the Province and of the Timber and Wood thereon

6. The Establishment, Maintenance, and Management of Public and Reformatory Prisons in and for the Province

7. The Establishment, Maintenance, and Management of Hospitals, Asylums, Charities, and Eleemosynary Institutions in and for the Province, other than Marine Hospitals

8. Municipal Institutions in the Province

9. Shop, Saloon, Tavern, Auctioneer, and other Licences in order to the raising of a Revenue for Provincial, Local, or Municipal Purposes

10. Local Works and Undertakings other than such as are of the following Classes:

    (a) Lines of Steam or other Ships, Railways, Canals, Telegraphs, and other Works and Undertakings connecting the Province with any other or others of the Provinces, or extending beyond the Limits of the Province;

    (b) Lines of Steam Ships between the Province and any British or Foreign Country;

    (c) Such Works as, although wholly situated within the Province, are before or after their Execution declared by the Parliament of Canada to be for the general Advantage of Canada or for the Advantage of Two or more of the Provinces.

11. The Incorporation of Companies with Provincial Objects

12. The Solemnization of Marriage in the Province

13. Property and Civil Rights in the Province

14. The Administration of Justice in the Province, including the Constitution, Maintenance, and Organization of Provincial Courts, both of Civil and of Criminal Jurisdiction, and including Procedure in Civil Matters in those Courts

15. The Imposition of Punishment by Fine, Penalty, or Imprisonment for enforcing any Law of the Province made in relation to any Matter coming within any of the Classes of Subjects enumerated in this Section

16. Generally all Matters of a merely local or private Nature in the Province

Appendix B

The *Constitution Act, 1982*

CHARTER OF RIGHTS AND FREEDOMS
SCHEDULE B
CONSTITUTION ACT, 1982

PART I: CANADIAN CHARTER OF RIGHTS AND FREEDOMS

Rights and freedoms in Canada

Whereas Canada is founded upon principles that recognize the supremacy of God and the rule of law:

Guarantee of Rights and Freedoms

Fundamental freedoms

1. The *Canadian Charter of Rights and Freedoms* guarantees the rights and freedoms set out in it subject only to such reasonable limits prescribed by law as can be demonstrably justified in a free and democratic society.

Fundamental Freedoms

2. Everyone has the following fundamental freedoms:
   (a) freedom of conscience and religion;
   (b) freedom of thought, belief, opinion and expression, including freedom of the press and other media of communications;
   (c) freedom of peaceful assembly; and
   (d) freedom of association.

Democratic Rights

Democratic rights of citizens

3. Every citizen of Canada has the right to vote in an election of members of the House of Commons or of a legislative assembly and to be qualified for membership therein.

Maximum duration of legislative bodies

4. (1) No House of Commons and no legislative assembly shall continue for longer than five years from the date fixed for the return of the writs at a general election of its members.

Continuation in special circumstances

   (2) In time of real or apprehended war, invasion or insurrection, a House of Commons may be continued by Parliament and a legislative assembly may be continued by the legislature beyond five years if such continuation is not opposed by the votes of more than one-third of the members of the House of Commons or the legislative assembly, as the case may be.

5. There shall be a sitting of Parliament and of each legislature at least once every 12 months.   Annual sitting of legislative bodies

Mobility Rights

6. (1) Every citizen of Canada has the right to enter, remain in, and leave Canada.   Mobility of citizens

   (2) Every citizen of Canada and every person who has the status of a permanent resident of Canada has the right   Rights to move and gain livelihood

      (a) to move to and take up residence in any province; and

      (b) to pursue the gaining of a livelihood in any province.

   (3) The rights specified in subsection (2) are subject to   Limitation

      (a) any laws or practices of general application in force in a province other than those that discriminate among persons primarily on the basis of province of present or previous residence; and

      (b) any laws providing for reasonable residency requirements as a qualification for the receipt of publicly provided social services.

   (4) Subsections (2) and (3) do not preclude any law, program, or activity that has as its object the amelioration in a province of conditions of individuals in that province who are socially or economically disadvantaged if the rate of employment in that province is below the rate of employment in Canada.   Affirmative action programs

Legal Rights

7. Everyone has the right to life, liberty, and security of the person and the right not to be deprived thereof except in accordance with the principles of fundamental justice.   Life, liberty, and security of person

8. Everyone has the right to be secure against unreasonable search or seizure.   Search and seizure

9. Everyone has the right not to be arbitrarily detained or imprisoned.   Detention or imprisonment

10. Everyone has the right on arrest or detention   Arrest or detention

      (a) to be informed promptly of the reasons therefor;

      (b) to retain and instruct counsel without delay and to be informed of that right; and

      (c) to have the validity of the detention determined by way of *habeas corpus* and to be released if the detention is not lawful.

11. Any person charged with an offence has the right   Proceedings in criminal and penal matters

      (a) to be informed without unreasonable delay of the specific offence;

      (b) to be tried within a reasonable time;

      (c) not to be compelled to be a witness in proceedings against that person in respect of the offence;

      (d) to be presumed innocent until proven guilty according to law in a fair and public hearing by an independent and impartial tribunal;

      (e) not to be denied reasonable bail without just cause;

      (f) except in the case of an offence under military law tried before a military tribunal, to the benefit of trial by jury where the maximum punishment for the offence is imprisonment for five years or a more severe punishment;

(g) not to be found guilty on account of any act or omission unless, at the time of the act or omission, it constituted an offence under Canadian or international law or was criminal according to the general principles or law recognized by the community of nations;

(h) if finally acquitted of the offence, not to be tried for it again and, if finally found guilty and punished for the offence, not to be tried or punished for it again; and

(i) if found guilty of the offence and if the punishment for the offence has been varied between the time of commission and the time of sentencing, to the benefit of the lesser punishment.

Treatment or punishment

12. Everyone has the right not to be subjected to any cruel and unusual treatment or punishment.

Self-incrimination

13. A witness who testifies in any proceedings has the right not to have any incriminating evidence so given used to incriminate that witness in any other proceedings, except in a prosecution for perjury or for the giving of contradictory evidence.

Interpreter

14. A party or witness in any proceedings who does not understand or speak the language in which the proceedings are conducted or who is deaf has the right to the assistance of an interpreter.

Equality Rights

Equality before and under law and equal protection and benefit of law

15. (1) Every individual is equal before and under the law and has the right to the equal protection and equal benefit of the law without discrimination and, in particular, without discrimination based on race, national, or ethnic origin, colour, religion, sex, age or mental or physical disability.

Affirmative action programs

(2) Subsection (1) does not preclude any law, program, or activity that has as its object the amelioration of conditions of disadvantaged individuals or groups including those that are disadvantaged because of race, national, or ethnic origin, colour, religion, sex, age or mental or physical disability.

Official Languages of Canada

Official languages of Canada

16. (1) English and French are the official languages of Canada and have equality of status and equal rights and privileges as to their use in all institutions of the Parliament and government of Canada.

Official languages of New Brunswick

(2) English and French are the official languages of New Brunswick and have equality of status and equal rights and privileges as to their use in all institutions of the legislature and government of New Brunswick.

Advancement of status and use

(3) Nothing in this Charter limits the authority of Parliament or a legislature to advance the equality of status or use of English and French.

English and French linguistic communities in New Brunswick

16.1(1) The English linguistic community and the French linguistic community in New Brunswick have equality of status and equal rights and privileges, including the right to distinct educational institutions and such distinct cultural institutions as are necessary for the preservation and promotion of those communities.

Role of legislature and government in New Brunswick

(2) The role of the legislature and government of New Brunswick to preserve and promote the status, rights and privileges referred to in subsection (1) is affirmed.

17. (1) Everyone has the right to use English or French in any debates and other proceedings of Parliament.

(2) Everyone has the right to use English and French in any debates and other proceedings of the legislature of New Brunswick.

18. (1) The statutes, records and journals of Parliament shall be printed and published in English and French and both language versions are equally authoritative.

(2) The statutes, records and journals of the legislature of New Brunswick shall be printed and published in English and French and both language versions are equally authoritative.

19. (1) Either English or French may be used by any person in, or in any pleading in or process issuing from, any court established by Parliament.

(2) Either English or French may be used by any person in, or in any pleading in or process issuing from, any court in New Brunswick.

20. (1) Any member of the public in Canada has the right to communicate with, and to receive available services from, any head or central office of an institution of the Parliament or government of Canada in English or French, and has the same right with respect to any such institution where

(a) there is a significant demand for communications with and services from that office in such language; or

(b) due to the nature of the office, it is reasonable that communications with services from that office be available in both English and French.

(2) Any member of the public in New Brunswick has the right to communicate with, and to receive available services from, any office of an institution of the legislature or government of New Brunswick in English or French.

21. Nothing in sections 16 to 20 abrogates or derogates from any right, privilege or obligation with respect to the English and French languages, or either of them, that exists or is continued by virtue of any other provision of the Constitution of Canada.

22. Nothing in sections 16 to 20 abrogates or derogates from any legal or customary right or privilege acquired or enjoyed either before or after the coming into force of this Charter with respect to any language that is not French or English.

Minority Language Educational Rights

23. (1) Citizens of Canada

(a) whose first language learned and still understood is that of the English and French linguistic minority population of the province in which they reside, or

(b) who have received their primary school instruction in Canada in English or French and reside in a province where the language in which they received that instruction is the language of the English or French linguistic minority population of the province, have the right to have their children receive primary and secondary school instruction in that language in that province.

Continuity of language instruction

(2) Citizens of Canada of whom any child has received or is receiving primary or secondary school instruction in English or French in Canada, have the right to have all their children receive primary and secondary school instruction in the same language.

Application where numbers warrant

(3) The right of citizens of Canada under subsections (1) and (2) to have their children receive primary and secondary school instruction in the language of the English or French linguistic minority population of a province

(a) applies wherever in the province the number of children of citizens who have such a right is sufficient to warrant the provision to them out of public funds of minority language instruction; and

(b) includes, where the number of those children so warrants, the right to have them receive that instruction in minority language educational facilities provided out of public funds.

Enforcement

Enforcement of guaranteed rights and freedoms

24. (1) Anyone whose right or freedoms, as guaranteed by this Charter, have been infringed or denied may apply to a court of competent jurisdiction to obtain such remedy as the court considers appropriate and just in the circumstances.

Exclusion of evidence bringing administration of justice into disrepute

(2) Where, in proceedings under subsection (1), a court concludes that evidence was obtained in a manner that infringed or denied any rights or freedoms guaranteed by this Charter, the evidence shall be excluded if it is established that, having regard to all the circumstances, the admission of it in the proceedings would bring the administration of justice into disrepute.

General

Aboriginal rights and freedoms not affected by *Charter*

25. The guarantee in this Charter of certain rights and freedoms shall not be construed so as to abrogate or derogate from any aboriginal, treaty or other rights and freedoms that pertain to the aboriginal peoples of Canada including

(a) any rights or freedoms that have been recognized by the Royal Proclamation of October 7, 1763; and

(b) any rights or freedoms that may be acquired by the aboriginal peoples of Canada by way of land claims settlement.

Other rights and freedoms not affected by Charter

26. The guarantee in this Charter of certain rights and freedoms shall not be construed as denying the existence of any other rights or freedoms that exist in Canada.

Multicultural heritage

27. This Charter shall be interpreted in a manner consistent with the preservation and enhancement of the multicultural heritage of Canadians.

Rights guaranteed equally to both sexes

28. Notwithstanding anything in this Charter, the rights and freedoms referred to in it are guaranteed equally to male and female persons.

Rights respecting certain schools preserved

29. Nothing in this Charter abrogates or derogates from any rights or privileges guaranteed by or under the Constitution of Canada in respect of denominational, separate, or dissentient schools.

30. A reference in this Charter to a province or to the legislative assembly or legislature of a province shall be deemed to include a reference to the Yukon Territory and Northwest Territories, or to the appropriate legislative authority thereof, as the case may be.

Applications to territories and territorial authorities

31. Nothing in this Charter extends the legislative powers of any body or authority.

Legislative powers not extended

Application of Charter

32. (1) This Charter applies

Application of Charter

    (a) to the Parliament and government of Canada in respect of all matters within the authority of Parliament including all matters relating to the Yukon Territory and Northwest Territories; and

    (b) to the legislature and government of each province in respect of all matters within the authority of the legislature of each province.

(2) Notwithstanding subsection (1), section 15 shall not have effect until three years after this section comes into force.

Exception

33. (1) Parliament or the legislature of a province may expressly declare in an Act of Parliament or of the legislature, as the case may be, that the Act or a provision thereof shall operate notwithstanding a provision included in section 2 or sections 7 to 15 of this Charter.

Exception where express declaration

(2) An Act or a provision of an Act in respect of which a declaration made under this section is in effect shall have such operation as it would have but for the provision of this Charter referred to in the declaration.

Operation of exception

(3) A declaration made under subsection (1) shall cease to have effect five years after it comes into force or on such earlier date as may be specified in the declaration.

Five-year limitation

(4) Parliament or the legislature of a province may re-enact a declaration made under subsection (1).

Re-enactment

(5) Subsection (3) applies in respect of a re-enactment made under subsection (4).

Five-year limitation

Citation

34. This Part may be cited as the *Canadian Charter of Rights and Freedoms*.

Citation

PART VII: GENERAL

52. (1) The Constitution of Canada is the supreme law of Canada, and any law that is inconsistent with the provisions of the Constitution is, to the extent of the inconsistency, of no force or effect.

Primacy of Constitution of Canada

Glossary

A

abatement a court order to reduce the rent to be paid to compensate for breach of lease by landlord

aboriginal rights the rights of First Nations people to special status despite the *Charter of Rights and Freedoms*

absolute privilege exemption from liability for defamatory statements made in some settings (such as legislatures and courts), without reference to the speaker's motives or the truth of the statement

accounting court-ordered remedy where any profits made from wrongdoing must be paid over to victim. Also, where court orders agent to pay to the principal any money or property collected on behalf of that principal

act parliamentary enactments (federal or provincial) having the status of law, *see* **statute** and **legislation**

actual authority authority given to agent expressly or by implication

adverse possession a right to actual possession can be acquired by non-contested use of the land over a long period of time

affidavits written documents containing statements of witnesses made under oath

agency the service an agent performs on behalf of a principal

agreement of purchase and sale a contract between parties for the purchase of real property

anticipatory breach repudiation of contract before performance is due

Anton Piller order court order to seize offending material before trial

apparent authority conduct of principal suggests to third party that agent has authority to act on his behalf

appearance document filed by the defendant indicating that the action will be disputed

appellant the party to an action that initiates an appeal to a higher court

arbitration where the parties to a dispute employ the services of a third party to reach a binding decision resolving the dispute

arrest warrant document issued by judicial official authorizing police to arrest offender

articles of association sets out the procedures for governing a corporation in Nova Scotia and must be filed along with memorandum of association

articles of incorporation the constitution of a corporation that must be filed as part of the process of incorporation in most jurisdictions in Canada

assault an action that makes a person think he or she is about to be struck

assignment in bankruptcy a voluntary transfer of assets to a trustee in bankruptcy

assignment of book accounts merchants temporarily transfer to a creditor the right to collect money owed to the merchant by customers as security for a loan

assignment where one person transfers their rights under a contract to a third party

attachment under the *Personal Property Security Act* where value has been given pursuant to contract and the creditor now has a claim against assets used as security

B

bailee person acquiring possession of a chattel in a bailment

bailment for value where possession of a chattel is temporarily transferred to another with the exchange of some consideration

bailment when one person takes temporary possession of chattels owned by another

bailor the owner giving up possession of the chattel in a bailment

bait and switch where a product is advertised at a low price and the purchaser is persuaded to purchase a higher priced product when the lower priced one is not available

balance of convenience the test used by the court in an injunction application to determine which party will be most harmed by the issuance of the injunction

bankruptcy offence punishable wrongdoing associated with bankruptcy such as withholding information or wrongfully transferring assets

bankruptcy process by which an insolvent person voluntarily or involuntarily transfers assets to a trustee for distribution to creditors

battery unwanted physical contact

bid rigging where competitors biding on a project coordinate to determine the winning bid

bill of exchange negotiable instrument where drawer directs the drawee to payout money to a payee; drawee need not be a bank, and the instrument may be made payable in the future

bill proposed enactment submitted to the legislature, which once approved becomes a statute

bills of lading a receipt for goods in the care of the shipper

bonding a fee is paid for a bonding company to pay compensation to a third party harmed by the wrongful conduct of an employee or the failure of the company to properly perform some contractual obligation

bonds a share interest in the indebtedness of a corporation

breach of contract failure to properly perform the obligations agreed to in a contract

broadly-held corporation a corporation that has many shareholders and is usually publicly traded on the stock market; also called a distributing corporation in some jurisdictions

broker agent retained by the insured to ascertain their insurance needs and secure the necessary coverage

building scheme restrictions placed on all the properties in a large development

business interruption insurance a form of insurance to protect the insured if business is interrupted

business patent a new process or method of carrying on business unique enough to be considered an invention and to be patented

C

capacity Necessary ingredient for a contract. The legal standing to enter into a contract which is sometimes limited due to insanity infancy etc.

causation that the injury suffered was the direct result of the conduct complained of

cause of action the legally recognized wrong that forms the basis for the right to sue

certificate of indefeasible title a certificate generated by government agency that is conclusive evidence in any court as to who owns the property as well as other interests in it

certification government authorization of a union to bargain collectively with an employer

certification mark a special mark protected under the *Trade-marks Act*; used by official agencies to indicate the quality and standard of the certified product

charge or encumbrance an interest in property giving a creditor a prior claim to that property, often called a lien

chattel mortgages where title to a chattel is transferred to a creditor as security for a debt

chattel tangible moveable personal property or goods

check-off provision employees agree to have employer deduct union dues from payroll

cheque a negotiable instrument; a special form of bill of exchange drawn on a bank, payable on demand

chose in action the thing or benefit that is transferred in an assignment; intangible personal property, such as a claim or the right to sue

CIF a contract term placing the responsibility for arranging and paying for the insurance and freight for goods being transported from seller to purchaser

Civil Code the legal system used in most of Europe based on a central code, which is a list of rules stated as broad principles of law that judges apply to the cases that come before them

civil law the rules that govern our personal, social, and business relations, which are enforced by one person suing another in a private or civil action. Civil law is also used to refer to the legal systems based on the civil code used in France and other countries.

class action suit a court certifies that one action can be brought on behalf of a number of different parties who have all suffered essentially the same kind of loss arising from the same complaint

closed shop only workers who are already members of the union can be hired

closely-held corporation a corporation in which there are relatively few shareholders with restrictions on the transferability of their shares; referred to as "non-distributing corporations" in some jurisdictions

COD a contractual term where goods that are sold are paid for upon receipt

co-insurance an arrangement where the insured pays for only partial insurance coverage, and thus is only partially compensated for any loss that takes place

common law the legal system developed in Great Britain based on the practice of judges following precedent embodied in prior judicial decisions

common shares shares in a company to which no special rights or privileges attach

conciliation more commonly referred to as mediation, the process where a third

party acts as a go-between by making non-binding recommendations to help the parties resolve a dispute

condition precedent conditions under which the contractual obligations will begin; also called "subject to" clauses

condition subsequent conditions under which the contractual obligations will end

conditional discharge a bankrupt is discharged but still required to pay a specified amount to creditors, as opposed to an absolute discharge where no such conditions are imposed.

conditional sales the seller provides credit to the purchaser, holding title until the goods are paid for

conditions major terms of a contract

condominium an arrangement for owning real property separated vertically, as with an apartment in a high rise development

condominium corporation a vehicle for operating a condominium development, to charge fees and administer common areas controlled by individual condominium owners

confidential information secret information and data with restricted access, the disclosure of which can cause harm to the business

conflict of interest where a decision that would benefit the individual is not in the best interests of the organization as a whole

consensus necessary ingredient for a contract. The terms must be clear and both parties should have a shared understanding of them. Note that the test is objective.

consent where the person being assaulted has previously agreed to that treatment as with surgery

consideration Necessary ingredient for a contract. The exchange of commitments between parties to a contract often stated as the price one is willing to pay for the promise of another.

conspiracy where two or more individuals act together to accomplish an illegal purpose

consumer an individual purchasing goods or services not for resale or to be used in a business

consumer protection legislation designed to ensure that consumers are treated fairly in the marketplace

contempt of court where a person has disobeyed the rules of the court or a court order, the judge can impose punishment in the form of a fine or imprisonment

contributory negligence a claim that the plaintiff to an action has also been negligent and contributed to his own loss

control test employment relationship determined by employer's power to give instructions to employee of how to do the job

conversion a tort where a person takes property belonging to another and uses it as his/her own (corresponds to theft in criminal law)

cooperative a system of property ownership where the "owners" have a shared claim in the whole building but no specific estate interest to the suite they occupy

copyright an author's right to control the reproduction and use of his creation

counterclaim a statement of claim by the defendant alleging that the plaintiff is responsible for the losses suffered and claiming for those losses

counter-offer a response made by an offeree making a new offer with different terms from the original offer with the effect of ending that offer

Courts of Chancery the separate court that developed the law of equity

cross-examination the practice of one party putting questions to a witness produced by the other party to a litigation. Generally more latitude is allowed in such questioning compared to direct examination.

cybersquatting the practice of quickly registering a domain name so that it can be sold later to a more legitimate claimant

D

damages an amount of money that the court orders one party to pay the other in civil litigation paid by the defendant;

damages usually compensate the injured party but may be punitive as well

debentures a share interest in the indebtedness of a corporation similar to bonds

debt financing raising funds through the borrowing of money by selling bonds or debentures or though direct loans

deceit intentional misrepresentation where one party gains an advantage over another

deed of conveyance document transferring an interest in property

defamation a published false statement to a person's detriment

default the failure to pay a financial obligation when it comes due

defendant the party being sued by the plaintiff

democratic rights rights set out in sections 3–5 of the *Charter of Rights and Freedoms* protecting rights to vote, hold elections, and run in those elections

deposit money prepaid with the provision that the funds are to be forfeited in the event of a breach

derivative action *see* **representative action**

description where goods are purchased on the basis of a description set out in an advertisement or on packaged materials, including all manufactured goods

direct examination the practice of a party to litigation putting questions to a witness they have produced. Generally less latitude is allowed in such questioning compared to cross-examination

directors officers voted in by shareholders to control a corporation

disability insurance insurance arrangement whereby an insurer, for a premium, provides compensation when an insured through sickness or accident is no longer able to work and earn an income

discharge by agreement agreement by parties to end or modify a contract

discharge by performance where a party is relieved of further obligations by properly performing their contractual obligations

discharge where the bankrupt is relieved of his debts, and his assets are no longer under the control of the trustee

dissent the right of a shareholder in some jurisdictions to have their shares purchased where decisions are made that negatively affect their position

distinguishing cases the process judges use to decide which case is the binding precedent

distinguishing guise the unique shape of a product, which can also be registered under the *Trade-marks Act*

distrain a landlord's right to seize the property of tenant for failure to pay rent

dividends payments to shareholders out of company profits

Division One proposal an alternative to bankruptcy under the *Bankruptcy and Insolvency Act* giving corporations and debtors with significant debt the right to make a proposal to creditors, which if accepted and performed, will avoid bankruptcy

Division Two proposal an alternative to bankruptcy under the *Bankruptcy and Insolvency Act* giving individual debtors involving lesser indebtedness the right to make a proposal to creditors, which if accepted and performed will avoid bankruptcy

domain name the registered name of a website used to access that address over the internet

dominant tenement the property enjoying the benefit of the restrictive covenant imposed on another property

double ticketing this involves the practice of placing two prices on an item and the merchant charging the higher of the two

dower rights statutory protection of a spouse's interest in property

down payment an initial payment under a contract that must be returned to the purchaser in the event of a breach

due diligence doing everything reasonable to avoid the problem leading to legal liability

dumping the practice of selling goods produced in one country in another, below the cost of producing them

duress force or threat to enter into a contract

duty of care an obligation to take steps to avoid foreseeable harm; an essential element for establishing liability in the tort of negligence

duty of good faith a fiduciary duty where an agent has a duty to act in the best interests of a principal

E

easement the right of a person other than the owner to use a portion of private property

electronic signature any online mechanism that indicates that the person adopts or is committed to the contents of the electronic message being responded to

employee a person working for another who is told what to do and how to do it

employment insurance a government-sponsored program designed to provide a limited number of payments to an individual after his or her employment has ended

Employment Standards Act legislation in place in most jurisdictions setting out a number of standards and obligations that employers must provide for their employees

encryption technological mechanisms designed to protect data and information, usually involving some form of encoding so the use of a key is necessary to retrieve it

endorsement the signature on the back of a cheque of the person assuming the obligation to pay if the drawee or maker defaults; a term added to an insurance policy at some later date modifying some aspect of that policy

equality rights among the basic rights provisions in the *Canadian Charter of Rights and Freedoms*; include the right not to be discriminated against on the grounds of gender, age, religion, race, or colour, and the guarantee of equality before the law

equitable remedies remedies developed by the Courts of Chancery, including the right to an accounting, injunction and specific performance

equity financing raising funds through the issue of additional shares

equity mortgagor retains an interest in land even after default

equity of redemption mortgagor retains an interest in land even after default

equity value left in an asset after subtracting what the owner owes

estate a person's right to exclusive possession of land

estoppel when a person leads another to believe a certain fact is true, for example that "A" is my agent, he cannot later deny the truthfulness of that fact

evergreening the practice of changing some component or other aspect of a patented product so that a new patent can be applied for, thus extending the protection period

executory contracts when an agreement has been made, but before there has been any performance

exemption clause a term of a contract where one party tries to limit or eliminate obligations that would otherwise be present

expressed authority the authority that the agent has been given that has been directly communicated to him by the principal

F

fair comment defence available when defamatory statements are made about public figures or work put before the public

fair hearing a person to be affected by a decision is given an opportunity to present their side in a process where all of the rules of procedural fairness are followed including adequate notice, an opportunity to be heard, and no bias on the part of the decision maker

false imprisonment holding people against their will and without lawful authority

fee simple estate the highest interest in land that a person can have; equivalent to ownership

fidelity bond insurance against an employee's wrongful conduct

fiduciary duty a duty to act in the best interests of others such as partners, principals, and in some circumstances employers

fitness and quality a requirement of the *Sale of Goods Act* imposing an obligation on the seller to ensure a certain standard of fitness and quality on the goods they sell

fixture something attached or affixed to the land or building becoming part of the real property

FOB (free on board) a term designating the point that title and responsibility for goods sold transfers to the purchaser

foreclosure court process ending the mortgagor's right to redeem

forfeiture when lease is breached the landlord may terminate the lease and require the tenant to vacate the property

franchise arrangements based on contracts where a smaller party (usually a corporation) exclusively agrees to provide goods or services supplied by a larger corporation to consumers

fraud intentional misrepresentation where one party gains an advantage over another

fraudulent misrepresentation where the person making the misleading statement does not believe it to be true

frustration some outside, unforeseen event makes the performance of the contract impossible or fundamentally different

fundamental breach a breach that that goes to the very foundation of the contract and that is not covered by an exemption clause

fundamental freedoms the basic rights in the *Canadian Charter of Rights and Freedoms* including freedom of conscience and religion, of thought and belief, of opinion and expression, and of assembly and association

G

general damages an amount of money ordered by the court to compensate for losses that are not capable of direct calculation, such as pain and suffering or loss of future earnings

Global Compact a United Nations–sponsored group of private and public organizations committed to the advancement of global ethical behaviour

good title an obligation on the seller under the *Sale of Goods Act* to convey ownership in the goods being sold.

good-faith relationship the obligation to act honestly in the best interests of the other party with full disclosure of all relevant information

goods tangible, movable personal property that can be measured and weighed; also known as chattels

gratuitous bailment for the benefit of the bailee an individual (the bailee) borrows another's property for their own use without giving consideration

gratuitous bailment for the benefit of the bailor an individual (the bailee) voluntarily looks after another's goods

gratuitous promise a one sided promise given without any reciprocating promise in return and is not binding on the promisor

grey market goods imported from other countries to circumvent exclusive marketing and distribution agreements between the manufacturer and a Canadian distributor

guarantee a written commitment whereby a guarantor agrees to pay a debt if the debtor doesn't

H

holdback person owing funds under a construction contract must retain a specified percentage to be paid at a later time

holder in due course an innocent third party entitled to collect on a negotiable instrument in spite of any claims of the original parties

homestead rights statutory protection of a spouse's interest in property

human rights legislation provincial and federal statutes designed to protect people from racism, sexism, and similar wrongs committed by others

I

identity theft where others acquire a person's private information including name, address, social insurance number, and the like to obtain access to current or additional credit (new bank accounts and credit cards) and other assets

implied authority the authority of the agent that has not been directly communicated by the principal but that can be implied from the principal's conduct or statements

independent contractor a person working for himself who contracts to provide specific services to another

indictable offence serious criminal offence with a more involved procedure and more serious penalties as compared to summary conviction offences

inducing breach of contract encouraging someone to break his or her contract with another

injunction court order to stop offending conduct

injurious falsehood defamation with respect to another's product or business; also known as product defamation and trade slander

innocent misrepresentation where the person making the misleading statement believes it to be true and is not negligent in that belief

innuendo an implied statement that is detrimental to another

insider information information that can affect the value of the shares of that company that is known to directors, shareholders, and others but not generally known to the public

insolvent where a person is unable to pay his or her debts as they become due

insurable interest a real and substantial interest in specific property

insurance agents the agents for insurance companies who sell policies to customers

insurance policies contracts with insurers to provide compensation for covered losses

intellectual property intangible personal property in the form of ideas and creative work

intention Necessary ingredient for a contract. The parties should be serious and expect that legal consequences should flow from their agreement. Note that this is an objective test.

interest dispute disagreement about the terms to be included in a new collective agreement

interim injunction temporary injunction obtained before the actual trial

invention a new and unique machine, process, or composition of matter that is useful and can be reproduced

invitation to treat invitations (often advertisement) to engage in the bargaining process leading to a contract

involuntary bailment where someone acquires possession of the property of another unintentionally as where it is left on their property or is found

J

joint tenancy shared ownership with right of survivorship

joint ventures two or more corporations joining together to accomplish a major project

judgment creditor the winner of an award of damages in a civil action

judgment debtor the loser in a civil action who has been ordered to pay an award of damages

judicial sale court ordered and supervised sale of real property, usually resulting from default

jurisdictional dispute a disagreement over who has authority; in the labour context, a dispute between two unions over which one should represent a group of employees, or over which union members ought to do a particular job

just cause valid reason to dismiss an employee without notice

justification defamation defence that the statement is substantially true

L

land registry a system requiring all documents affecting the title of real property be kept in a land registry office available for the inspection of interested parties

land titles system registration system that guarantees title to real property

law of equity legal principles developed in Courts of Chancery to relieve the harshness of the common law

law the definition of law used in this text is the rules enforceable in court or by other government agencies

leasehold estate an interest in land giving the tenant the right to exclusive possession for a limited specified time

legal rights among the basic rights provisions in the *Canadian Charter of Rights and Freedoms* (sections 7–14); includes rights such as the right to life, liberty, and security of the person and security against unreasonable search and seizure and arbitrary imprisonment and detention

legality Necessary ingredient for a contract. Both the consideration and the object of the contract should not be prohibited by law and not be against public policy.

legislation parliamentary enactments (federal or provincial) having the status of law, *see* **statute** and **act**

letters patent method of incorporating granted by government when company is set up in some jurisdictions in Canada

liability insurance provides coverage for wrongs committed by self or employees

liability where one party to an action bears an obligation to provide some remedy to another

libel the written form of a defamatory statement

licence a non-exclusive right to use property; permission to use another's land that can be revoked

lien an interest in property giving a creditor a prior claim to that property, often called a charge

life estate an interest in land ending at death

life insurance coverage providing compensation upon the death of the insured party

limited liability where a person is liable to lose only what he has invested in the business and is not responsible for other debts or obligations of the business

limited liability partnership a new and unique form of partnership where each individual "limited liability partner" faces unlimited liability only for his own wrongful acts and not for the wrongful acts of his partners

liquidated damages a contractual provision requiring party responsible for a breach to pay a stated amount

lockout employer prevents employees from working

long-arm statutes where a jurisdiction has passed legislation giving them the right to take action against offending conduct taking place outside of that state or province

M

manufacturer's warranty a term of the sales contract limiting a seller's or manufacturer's obligations with respect to a product beyond what they would otherwise be under the Sale of Goods Act

mediation sometimes referred to as conciliation, the process where a third party acts as a go-between by making non-binding recommendations to help the parties resolve a dispute

memorandum of association constitution of a corporation in a registration jurisdiction which is filed as part of the incorporation process; now only used in Nova Scotia

minority language education rights the right to have English or French, as the case may be, taught in the schools or made available to speakers of those languages set out in the *Charter of Rights and Freedoms*

mistake a misunderstanding about the nature or subject matter of an agreement that destroys consensus

misunderstanding when two parties to a contract have a different understanding as to the meaning of a specific provision.

mitigation victims of a breach must make an effort to lessen the loss

mobility rights the right of all citizens of Canada to reside in or work in all parts of Canada as guaranteed by section 6 of the *Charter of Rights and Freedoms*

moral rights author's right to prohibit the copyright owner from changing or degrading the original work

mortgage means of securing loans; title of property is held by the money-lender as security in some jurisdictions; in other jurisdictions, a mortgage is simply a charge against title

mortgagee the creditor who takes the title to the property as security

mortgagor the debtor who grants the mortgage on his property as security for a loan

most favoured nation status the practice of treating goods imported from such a designated country in a no-less favourable way than the most advantaged trading partner

N

negligence inadvertent conduct falling below the reasonable person standard and causing injury or damage to another

negligent misrepresentation where the person making the misleading statement believes it to be true but has been careless in that belief

negotiable instruments substitutes for money or instruments of credit that bestow unique benefits; vehicles for conveniently transferring funds or advancing credit

negotiation the parties to the dispute directly or indirectly communicating with the object of settling that dispute

non est factum "It is not my act." Where a party is not bound by terms of a document because he didn't understand the nature of the document signed.

notice of action the document used in some provinces (such as Ontario) to commence a civil action

notice the requirement that a union give a required period of advance warning to the employer of an impending strike

novation when a new contract is created by substituting a new party for one of the original parties to the original contract

O

offer a tentative promise to do something if another party fulfills what the first party requests

offer and acceptance the party receiving an offer agrees to be bound by the terms set out in the offer

official mark a special mark protected under the *Trade-marks Act* to indicate an official organization has special status

one-sided mistake where only one of the parties makes a mistake with respect to the nature or effect of a contract; without misrepresentation, the contract will normally continue to be binding

oppression action brought against the directors or shareholders who have offended the rights of creditors or other shareholders

option agreement a subsidiary contract where some additional consideration is given to hold an offer open for later acceptance

option to purchase a subsidiary contract where some additional consideration is given to hold an offer open for later acceptance

organization test determines whether employment exists on the basis of the extent of a person's involvement in the employer's organization

P

paramountcy when a matter is covered by both federal and provincial legislation and there is a conflict, the federal legislation takes precedence

parliamentary supremacy the primary law-making body is Parliament or the provincial legislatures in their respective jurisdictions, and statutes take priority over the common law

partnership two or more people carrying on business together with a view toward profit and without incorporation

partnership agreement a contract between partners setting out specific obligations and benefits between them, usually modifying certain provisions of the Partnership Act

passing-off a tort action available to prevent someone from misleading the public into thinking it is dealing with some other business or product when it is not

past consideration some benefit conveyed before an agreement is made; it is not valid consideration

patent government-granted protection giving an inventor exclusive right to profit from that invention for a specified period of time

payment into court the defendant estimates the true value of the claim and deposits it with the court; if the decision is for less than the deposit the plaintiff will be penalized through payment of additional costs

perfection registering a security or taking possession of the collateral used to secure a debt under the *Personal Property Security Act*

performance of the obligations when each party has completed its obligations under the terms of a contract

periodic leases automatically renewing tenancy; usually monthly with no specific termination date

personal property also known as personalty, chattels (tangible, movable things), and intangible rights called choses in action

picketing job action during a legal strike when employees circulate at the periphery of the jobsite to persuade people not to deal with that employer

plaintiff the party who initiates a civil action

plea-bargaining the process whereby the accused and prosecutor negotiate, usually resulting in a lesser charge being imposed in exchange for a guilty plea avoiding a trial

pleadings the exchange of documents (statement of claim, statement of defence, counterclaim) between plaintiff and defendant at the early stage of a civil action

Ponzi scheme a fraudulent investment scheme where funds invested by later investors are used to pay off earlier investors, creating a false sense of success

post-box rule the rule that an acceptance is effective when posted when that method of response is appropriate

power of attorney written authority by a principal giving an agent power to act on his behalf

power of sale a normal term in a mortgage agreement giving the creditor/mortgagee the power to have the property sold in the event of a default

precedent a prior decision made by a court of higher jurisdiction that a lower court must follow in our common law system.

predatory pricing where a product is sold below cost to drive a competitor out of the market

preemptive rights a right given to a shareholder ensuring that in the event of a new offering of shares that shareholder will be given first refusal on enough of those shares to maintain his portion of control of the corporation

preferred creditors creditors that are secured so that they have a priority with respect to their claims against the debtor

preferred shares special shares structured to give the preferred shareholder a claim to a specified dividend each year. Normally they cannot vote unless that dividend is not paid.

premium an amount paid by the insured to secure insurance coverage

prescription a right to access property acquired by non-contested use of the land over a long period of time

presumption a condition or set of facts assumed to be true in the absence of any evidence to the contrary

price fixing where competitors agree on a fixed price for selling their services or merchandise thus keeping prices high and defeating competition

private law the rules that govern our personal, social, and business relations, which are enforced by one person suing another in a private or civil action

private nuisance a tort action protecting against the use of property in such a way that it interferes with a neighbour's enjoyment of theirs

privative clause terms in a statute that attempt to restrict the right of judicial review

privity of contract contract terms apply only to the actual parties to the contract

procedural law determines how the substantive laws will be enforced; the rules governing arrest and criminal investigation, pre-trial and court processes in both criminal and civil cases are examples; law can also be distinguished by its public or private function

product defamation false statement with respect to another's product or business; also known as injurious falsehood and trade slander

professional liability a person who puts himself forward as an expert must live up to the standard expected of a reasonable expert

profit the net proceeds of the business after expenses have been deducted

profit à prendre contracts to take resources off the land

progressive discipline the process using escalating measures to record failings and encourage, help, reprimand, and discipline that employee, eventually leading to rehabilitation or termination

promissory estoppel when a gratuitous promise to do something in the future causes a person to incur an expense, the promissor may be prevented from acting in a way inconsistent with that promise; also known as equitable estoppel

promissory note a type of negotiable instrument where a maker promises to pay the amount stated on the instrument to a payee

proposed trademark The *Trade-marks Act* permits an application to register a trademark that has not been used yet but will be in the future

prosecute when a criminal charge is laid against an accused and the government official (prosecutor) proceeds with a criminal process against him

prospectus a document issued by a corporation disclosing information to the public with respect to its financial position and prospects

proxy where one shareholder gives authority to someone else to vote that share on their behalf

public law rules with respect to government (constitutional law) and our relations with government, including criminal law, human rights, and regulation

punitive damages monetary payment ordered by the court designed to punish the wrongdoer rather than compensate the victim; also known as exemplary damages

Q

qualified privilege exemption from liability for defamatory statements made pursuant to a duty or special interest, so long as the statement was made honestly, without malice, and circulated only to those having a right to know

quantum meruit (as much as is deserved) reasonable price paid for requested services where there is no actual contractual obligation; sometimes called a quasi-contract

quasi-criminal offences offences under provincial legislation or federal regulatory statutes that impose penalties but do not qualify as criminal law

questions of fact just what happened, including events, injuries, damage, and consequences

questions of law what legal rules are applied to the situation

quiet enjoyment landlord must ensure that nothing interferes with tenant's normal use of the property

quiet possession goods must be usable by the purchaser in the way normally intended

R

Rand Formula option in collective agreement enabling employees to retain the right not to join the union, but they are still required to pay union dues

ratification majority agrees with terms of collective bargain; principal confirms a contract entered into by his agent

real property land, buildings, and fixtures attached to land or buildings

reasonable foreseeability test what a prudent and careful person would be expected to anticipate in the same circumstances as the defendant

reasonable notice the amount of notice that must be given in terminating an employment contract, taking into consideration the position of the employee and time served

reasonable person test the standard of conduct that would be expected of a careful and prudent person in the same circumstances as the defendant in a negligence action

receiver a person or organization appointed to take over the management of a corporation defaulting on its obligations to a creditor

receivership proceeding in which a receiver is appointed for a corporation that has defaulted on its obligations to a creditor to protect its assets for the creditors

receiving order court ordering the transfer of debtor's assets to a trustee as part of the bankruptcy process

recognition dispute dispute arising between unions and employers while union is being organized

rectify court corrects the written wording of a shared mistake in the contract

references direct application to the Supreme Court of Canada by government to answer some legal question

registration a legislated requirement for incorporating a company in some jurisdictions in Canada; also the process of filing a form to perfect a security under the *Personal Property Security Act*

regulations supplementary rules passed under the authority of a statute and having the status of law

reinsurance where an insurance company takes out insurance with another company to cover the risk they face if they are called upon to payout on the insurance coverage they have issued.

relief against forfeiture when a landlord retakes a property for failure to pay rent prior to the end of the lease term, the tenant can pay the arrears and apply in the court to have the lease reinstated

remainder third party with the right to the title of real property (fee simple) after the death of a life tenant

remote where the damages are too far removed from the original negligent act; in contract, where the damages could not have been reasonably foreseen by the breaching party when the agreement was made.

representative action the right of shareholders to sue the directors on behalf of an injured corporation; sometimes called a derivative action

repudiation one party indicates to the other that they will not perform their contractual obligations

rescission returning the parties to the position they were in before the contract

respondent the party who responds to the appeal launched by the appellant

restrictive covenant seller imposes restrictions on what the purchaser can use the land for; in employment law, it is a commitment not to work in a certain industry or geographical area for a designated period of time

reverse engineering the process of analyzing a completed product and from that determining the process by which it was created

reversion upon death of life tenant, the title to real property reverts to original owner

revocation withdrawal of an offer before acceptance (must be communicated to the offeree)

rider a term added to a standard form insurance contract usually arranging for extra or specialized coverage

right of way type of easement that allows the crossing of another's land

rights dispute disagreement about the meaning of a term or the enforcement of a collective agreement

royalties the payment publishers pay authors for the use and sale of their creations

rule of law the requirement that everyone in Canada is subject to the law and must obey it; government officials must be able to point to some law authorizing them to make the decision they have made affecting the rights of others

S

salvage that portion of goods or property which has been saved or remains after a casualty such as fire or other loss

sample a chattel used to indicate to a purchaser the nature of similar goods usually to be delivered in the future; those goods must match the sample

seal formal mark on a document (usually an impression or wafer), which eliminates the need for consideration in contract law

second mortgage where the equity of redemption retained after title is transferred to the first mortgagee is also used as security for a loan from a second mortgagee

secured creditors creditors who have taken steps to ensure that they will be paid, usually by acquiring first claim to some property that ensures payment over other creditors

secured transactions collateral right to debt giving the creditor the right to take back the goods or intercept the debt owing used as security in the event of a default

security deposit an amount of money taken by the landlord at the outset of a tenancy to cover damages or failure to pay rent

self-defence a person can respond to an assault with as much force as is reasonable in the circumstances

separate legal person the term used to describe a corporate entity that has a legally recognized existence separate and apart from those that make it up

servient tenement the property upon which the restrictive covenant is imposed

shared mistake both parties make the same mistake, sometimes called common mistake

shareholder the investment interest or equity of a corporation is divided into units referred to as shares which are held by shareholders

slander spoken defamation

sole proprietor one person carrying on business alone, without incorporation

special damages an amount of money ordered by the court to compensate for expenses capable of actual calculation

specific performance court orders a breaching party to live up to the terms of the agreement

standard of care the test used to determine whether a person has exercised sufficient care in dealings with others to avoid being liable for the tort of negligence. The degree of care required is usually that of a reasonable person in the circumstances

standard-form contract where one party uses a form of contract that is the same

for each transaction and not subject to negotiation

stare decisis a principle by which judges are required to follow the decision made in a similar case in a higher court

statement of claim the document setting out the nature of the complaint and alleged facts, which form the basis of the action served on the defendant at the beginning of the litigation process

statement of defence response to a statement of claim by the defendant setting out the alleged facts by the plaintiff and the contrary facts alleged by the defendant

Statute of Frauds Old English statute, a version of which is in place in most common law jurisdictions setting out the types of agreements that must be evidenced in writing to be enforceable

statute parliamentary enactments (federal or provincial) having the status of law, see **legislation** and **act**

statutory assignment an assignment of contractual rights and benefits that meets certain specified qualifications; assignee can enforce a claim directly without involving the assignor

statutory damages a special monetary award authorized in the *Copyright Act* to compensate the victim of copyright infringement

stoppage in *transitu* seller retains the right to stop the shipment in event of default

strict liability offences regulatory offences at the provincial or federal level where the accused can be found liable even though no fault is demonstrated; where liability is imposed without any demonstration of fault (intention or falling below a standard of care)

strike unionized employees withdrawing their services from the employer

subrogated the right of insurer, upon payment, to take over the rights of the insured in relation to whoever caused the injury

substantial performance the parties have performed all but a minor aspect of the contract

substantive law establishes both the rights individuals have in society and also the limits on their conduct

summary conviction offence minor criminal offence involving a simplified procedure with less significant penalties imposed as compared to indictable offences

summons to appear a document served on a person accused of a criminal offence requiring them to appear before a judge at a specific time and place

surety bond a commitment by a third party, such as an insurance company, to pay compensation if the company or individual on whose behalf the bond is issued fails to properly perform their contractual obligations

T

tenancy in common shared ownership but without the right of survivorship

tender of performance one of parties attempts to perform their contractual obligations, and where they are prevented by the other party, they are considered to have properly performed

term insurance life insurance that provides coverage for only a specific period of time and has no investment component

territorial competence the test used by the B.C. courts to determine whether they have the jurisdiction to deal with a matter brought before them that may also involve issues in another province or state

trademark a name, mark, or symbol associated with a business or product which helps to distinguish it from other businesses or products

trespass to chattels direct intentional interference causing damage to the goods of another

trespass to land entering upon another's land without permission or authority

trustee in bankruptcy licensed professionals who, for a fee, assist the debtor and creditors in the bankruptcy process, holding and otherwise dealing with that bankrupt's property for the benefit of the creditors

U

unconscionability when one of the parties to a transaction is under extreme disadvantage; merchants take advantage of disadvantaged customers

undisclosed agency where an agent fails to disclose he is representing someone else or the identity of that principal

undue influence a special relationship that induces a person to enter a contract to his disadvantage

unenforceable a binding contract or other obligation that the courts will not enforce, such as a contract that does not satisfy the *Statute of Frauds*

unfair labour practices practices by management or by employees in the collective bargaining process that are prohibited, such as intimidation or firing employees for their union activity

unilateral contract where an offer is made in such a way that to accept, the offeree must actually perform the act required as consideration

union shop new employees must join the union

unlimited liability where a person is liable for all of the debts and obligations of a business even to the extent of losing all personal assets

unsecured creditors (or general creditors); there is only a contract requiring a debt to be repaid, but no collateral contract giving that creditor priority with respect to some property in the event of default

V

vacant possession owner has obligation to provide premises that are empty and ready for occupancy

vicarious liability employer is liable for the injuries caused by employees during the course of their employment

void not a legally binding agreement because an essential ingredient is missing; there is no contract

voidable there is a contract but one of the parties has the option to end it

voluntary assumption of risk the defence to a negligence action where the plaintiff has voluntarily put himself in harms way

W

warranties minor terms of a contract

whole life insurance life insurance that provides ongoing coverage and includes a significant investment component

workers' compensation a government system set up to provide monetary compensation for someone who becomes sick or injured because of their employment

World Intellectual Property Organization (WIPO) an international organization set up to arbitrate disputes over the use of domain names on the internet

Table of Statutes

Note: The page numbers given in parentheses at the end of each entry refer to pages in this book.

Table of Cases

Index

Note: Key Terms and their page numbers appear in bold face.

insurance (*Continued*)
    disability insurance, 227–228
    employment insurance, 152
    endorsement, 225
    errors and omissions insurance, 49
    false disability claim, 227
    good-faith relationship,
        228–229
    insurable interest, 225, 226
    insurance agent, 225
    insurance policies, 225
    liability insurance,
        49, 227
    life insurance, 227–228
    negligence, 227
    premium, 224
    property, 224–229
    reinsurance, 224
    rider, 225
    subrogated, 226
    term insurance, 227
    and wager, 225
    whole life insurance, 227
insurance agent, 225
insurance policies, 225
intangible property, 201
    see also intellectual property
integrated circuit topography, 241
intellectual property, 201
    copyright, 235–238, 237*t*
    criminal offences, 246–247
    generally, 234–235
    legislation, 245*t*
    passing-off, 244
    patents, 239–241
    remedies, 245–247, 245*t*
    trademarks, 242–244
intention, 71–72
intentional torts
    assault and battery, 30–31
    false imprisonment, 31–32
    generally, 30
    nuisance, 33–36
    table of intentional torts, 37*t*
    trespass, 32–33
interest dispute, 150
interim injunction, 246
international business transactions
    alternate dispute resolution,
        271–273
    Canadian regulations,
        277–279
    contracts, 270–271
    defences, 275

dispute resolution, 269
dumping, 277
enforcement of judgments,
    274–275
export, 278
extraterritorial reach, 279
financial reporting, 271
foreign ownership, 271
generally, 269
grey market, 269
imports, 278–279
international treaties,
    276–277
jurisdiction, 273–276, 273*t*
litigation, 273–276
most favoured nation status,
    277
services, 269
specialty contracts, 271
territorial competence, 274
International Court of Justice, 269
international dispute resolution
    mechanisms, 269
International Sale of Goods Act, 276
international treaties,
    276–277
internet
    alternate dispute resolution,
        267–268
    and business, 258–268
    business transactions,
        261–263
    criminal offences, 253
    cybercrimes, 253
    cybersquatting, 261
    defamation, 262, 263
    domain names, 261–262
    electronic signatures, 265
    freedom of expression, 262
    gambling, 265
    jurisdiction, 258–260,
        266–267
    long-arm statutes, 259
    online contracts, 263–266
    regulation of, 268
    scams, 266
    torts, 262–263
intoxication, 68–69
invasion of privacy, 250
invention, 239, 241
    see also patents
invitations to treat, 57
involuntary bailment, 203
issues, 4

J
jewellery on consignment, 205
job action, 150–151
joint tenancy, 208, 209
joint venture, 194
judgment
    enforcement, 17*f*
    generally, 16–18
judgment creditor, 17
judgment debtor, 17
judicial sale, 214
jurisdictional dispute, 148
jurisdictional issues (international trade),
    273–276, 273*t*
jurisdictional issues (internet),
    258–261, 266
just cause, 141–142
justification, 34

L
labour law. *See* collective bargaining
land. *See* real property
land registry, 210–211
land titles system, 211
law, 1–2
    administrative law, 20–22
    in Canada, 5–7
    civil law, 2
    common law, 3, 221–222
    criminal law, 22–25
    importance, in business, 2
    law of equity, 4–5
    meaning of, 1–2
    vs. morality, 2
    private law, 2
    procedural law, 2
    public law, 2
    sources of law, 2–5, 5*f*
    statutes, 5
    substantive law, 2
law of equity, 4–5
leasehold estate, 215
    commercial tenancies,
        216–218
    generally, 207, 215–216
    periodic leases, 215
    residential tenancies,
        218–220
    security deposit, 219
leases with option to purchase, 119
legal rights, 9
legality, 70–71, 265–266
legislation, 7